THE SOUTH AFRICAN QUAGMIRE

Ballinger Series in

BUSINESS IN A GLOBAL ENVIRONMENT

S. Prakash Sethi, Series Editor
Baruch College, City University of New York

THE SOUTH AFRICAN QUAGMIRE

In Search of a Peaceful Path to Democratic Pluralism

Edited by
S. Prakash Sethi

BALLINGER PUBLISHING COMPANY
Cambridge, Massachusetts
A Subsidiary of Harper & Row, Publishers, Inc.

International Standard Book Number: 0-88730-191-6

Library of Congress Catalog Card Number: 86-28754

Printed in the United States of America

88-2961

Library of Congress Cataloging-in-Publication Data

The South African quagmire.

   (Ballinger series in business in a global environment)
   Bibliography; p.
   Includes index.
   1. Economic sanctions, American—South Africa.
2. Economic sanctions—South Africa. 3. Investments, American—South Africa. 4. Investments, Foreign—South Africa.
5. Apartheid—South Africa. I. Sethi, S. Prakash. II. Series.
HF1613.4.Z4U67   1987   320.5'6   86-28754
ISBN 0-88730-191-6

To

Alan Paton

author of *Cry, the Beloved Country*

who has spent his life fighting the
inhumanity and tyranny of apartheid

this book is affectionately dedicated.

Contents

PART IV THE SOCIAL PERSPECTIVE INSIDE SOUTH AFRICA

PART V U.S. PRESSURES FOR SANCTIONS

South Africa as a nation, and as a society, is an active volcano — never dormant — and particularly volatile now. It will erupt. There doesn't seem to be much doubt about it. The problem lies in our inability to predict the magnitude and direction of this eruption. The hope, if there is any, rests in our ability to contain the damage and prepare for the rebuilding effort that must ensue.

There is also a tornado swirling outside and no one knows when and where it will strike. This is creating further instability in the environment. There is no calm before the storm. Viewed from one perspective, these external forces are mobilizing internal groups and resources urging them to act now and prepare to deal with what might be a potentially highly violent sociopolitical turbulence. However, viewed from another perspective, these same forces are diverting internal resources from the slow but necessary process of rebuilding bridges of trust and viable structures for eventual political accommodations. By dictating predetermined approaches, they may be exacerbating the problem and thereby making solutions difficult to reach and far more expensive — in terms of human and physical costs — to implement.

There is a belief widely held among experts that 1986 will be the most critical year yet for South Africa. The window of opportunity has become extremely narrow, and if not utilized, may not be available in the future. Moreover, this view is held by almost all of the players regardless of their political persuasion, ideological orientation, or preference for a particular solution.

The debate on South Africa is also laden with contradictions. There is universal agreement that apartheid must go and that the South African nonwhites must have their legitimate share of political power and a say in sharing economic wealth. The unresolved questions are how long the transition period should be and what should be the political and social structure of postapartheid South Africa. Almost everyone asserts, both as a matter of principle and practical necessity, that any solution to the South African problem must come from the

South Africans themselves. However, having said that, most proceed with an outline of a solution that to them is at once clearly obvious, eminently fair, and morally justifiable.

Unfortunately, the discussion of the South African issue is continuously obfuscated by different advocates in euphemistic terms that are both positive and value neutral, and yet they cleverly disguise the determination of those in power to hold on to it by all possible means. At the same time, those seeking to dislodge the prevailing white minority often couch their aruguments primarily in terms of morality, justice, equity, and fairness. And yet, they may also disguise a hidden agenda that may be just as repressive as the current regime because it ignores the many deep, and often irreconcilable, differences among those who are bound together not so much by a common end as by a common enemy. The multiplicity of groups and viewpoints has become, like the Tower of Babel, full of noise but little comprehension.

My research and teaching interests for a long time have been dominated with concerns about the influence of large economic institutions in determining political agenda, and the many ways in which economic institutions of free societies create and distribute wealth, and through it, expand the assertion of individual political and economic rights and their enjoyment. I am strongly persuaded that a viable private economic system must be one of the foundations for the maintenance of a healthy democracy. Sharing of worldly goods and political power is always easier in periods of economic prosperity than in periods of economic hardship. And yet, economic institutions, notably large corporations, do not always act in the best interests of either the society or the free enterprise system. It is, therefore, perfectly legitimate and highly desirable that we must constantly examine and evaluate the role played by large economic institutions in influencing and shaping political choices. Economic freedom is incompatible with totalitarianism, a fact that is not always obvious to people in totalitarian and authoritarian societies that also have the semblance of private ownership and enterprise. However, to the extent that any prosperity exists in those countries, it is because of the degrees of freedom allowed private enterprise and despite the inefficiencies of the authoritarian regimes.

My interest in South Africa has both emotional and intellectual origins. As an Indian by birth, and growing up in India, I personally experienced the partition of that country and shared in the agony and loss of loved ones that resulted from the ensuing communal riots and civil strife. I have also witnessed the prejudices and cruelties inflicted by those in privileged positions because of religion, wealth, or political power, on their fellow human beings who were less fortunate by being born in the wrong caste or otherwise poorly placed in the social hierarchies of India. As a citizen of my adopted country, the United States, I also experienced the prejudice of color and race, as well as the determined effort of many to overcome it and obliterate it from influencing our sociopolitical order. These experiences have convinced me that while democracies do not always ensure social justice, it is impossible to even aspire to it in nondemocratic societies.

I have been involved in studying the South African situation and the role of U.S. multinational corporations in that country for over a decade. The apartheid issue in South Africa has become an obsession with me both for its similarities to my experiences in India and my fear of the potential blood bath that lurks just around the corner. At the same time, it has demonstrated a very unusual role for the business community in general and that of American business in particular. In most other international situations, we have constantly implored the multinational corporations not to interfere in the internal affairs of their host countries. However, in the case of South Africa, the American multinationals have argued in favor of staying in South Africa in the belief that by their presence they can exert influence on the South African government to make changes in that country's apartheid policies. They also claim that their presence contributes to the economic welfare of the black majority in that country. The corporate critics, on the other hand, have argued that these corporations are not putting enough pressure on the South African government. Alternatively, it is suggested that their presence helps the oppressive South African regime, and therefore, the only moral course for them is to get out of South Africa.

This book was conceived with the idea of bringing together, for the first time, and in one place, the authoritative views of the spokespersons from major interest groups and political and public opinion. Our hope is that it will set the stage to further the dialogue on the South African problem in directions that are more constructive and conducive to a peaceful solution. In this way, we would have made a small contribution in averting what might be one of the most tragic situations in the history of civilization.

Many of the chapters originally appeared as articles in the Spring 1986 and Summer 1986 issues of *Business and Society Review*. The present book contains all the articles from the *BSR* collection. Some of the articles have been revised and expanded while a number of new articles have been added to create a more comprehensive and systematic treatment of the subject matter and also to include a historical perspective on the issue of apartheid.

I also made every effort to seek the views of African National Congress (ANC), the newly organized black labor unions in South Africa, such as The Congress of South African Trade Unions (COSATU); representatives of the black press in South Africa and the network television in the United States. Unfortunately, these efforts were not successful becaue of limitations of time and the inability or unwillingness of the participants to prepare the necessary material. Notwithstanding, I believe that with these few exceptions we have been successful in this effort. The collection of articles and the authors is unprecedented. Although all the authors claim to speak only for themselves, they nevertheless represent the governments of South Africa and United States and also the elected leadership of the two nations. In addition, we have the views of the leadership of the religious, business, and academic communities in South Africa, the United States, and other parts of the world.

Putting together this book, as well as the two issues of *Business and Society Review*, has been a labor of love and lovingly labored. It has taken an intense period of eighteen hour days stretching over four months. Notwithstanding, this book would not have been possible without the willingness of all those authors who took the risk of expressing thier opinions at my urging while fearing being cast into the roles of villains, ideologues, or demagogues. I cherish their trust and hope that the treatment of their writings in the *Review* would justify their belief and encourage them to take additional steps to communicate with each other and create other forums to work out possible modus vivendi.

I am very grateful to Mr. Theodore Cross, *BSR*'s editor and a pioneer in the field of corporate social responsibility, for his support and encouragement for a venture which had a high probability of coming up stillborn. Managing Editor Bruce Slater provided logistical support and access to various sources of information, contributed to ideas for various articles, and in general made sure that the final product met the high standards we all set for *BSR*.

I also wish to acknowledge an immense debt of gratitude to four people who took substantial professional risks in using their personal contacts to vouch for me in seeking the cooperation of different authors and in persuading them to write candidly of their views and perspectives on the South African problem. Dr. James Armstrong, a professor at the Iliff School of Theology, Denver, Colorado, and an executive vice-president of Pagan International, a public affairs firm in Washington, D.C., helped me with the religious leadership involved in the South African debate. Dr. Armstrong is a former president of the National Council of Churches and for fifteen years was a bishop of the United Methodist Church. He generously expended his goodwill with the religious leaders and other prominent public figures, in encouraging them to write for this issue of *BSR*.

Mr. Sal G. Marzullo, chairman of the U.S. Industry Group of the Sullivan Principles Signatory Companies, and an executive of Mobil Oil Corporation, used his large network of friends and associates in the business community in the United States and South Africa to enlist their support for the *Review*, despite the fact that *BSR* often appears to the business community as somewhat unsympathetic to their viewpoint. Notwithstanding, with Mr. Marzullo's help I was able to secure articles from most of the business leaders whom I approached. I was impressed by the high regard held for by large number of black leaders in South Africa who were willing to accede to his urgings on my behalf.

Dr. Gerrit Olivier, a professor of political science at the Rand Afrikaans University, and a distinguished scholar, was generous with his time and effort in supplementing my academic network. He helped me secure the cooperation of some of the most well known scholars in South Africa to provide their insights on different aspects of the South African problem — among them education, economic development, regional mobility, legal aspects of apartheid, effect of international boycotts and sanctions, and political models of power sharing in deeply divided societies, to name a few.

Finally, I wish to thank Mr. Dany Fourie, Deputy Consul-General of South Africa in New York, for his assistance in identifying various senior South African government officials and in my gaining access to them. His assistance is reflected in the articles from two South African government ministers who are also heirs apparent to the present South African president Mr. P.W. Botha, both of whom would play an important role in any future restructuring and power-sharing arrangements in South Africa.

This book was prepared in cooperation with *Business and Society Review*. I also gratefully acknowledge the support and cooperation of the Research Program in Business and Public Policy, Center for Management Development and Organization Research, Baruch College, City University of New York. The Research Program receives partial financial support (with no strings attached) from the business community to conduct studies on different aspects of business and public policy. The Center's resources made available my time as well as other logistical support. Mr. Eric Neubacher, Head of Access Services, Baruch College Library, carried out the time-consuming task of maintaining the heavy flow of telex traffic between New York and South Africa. My research assistants, Mr. Steve Deshler and Mr. Joseph Mancheno, carried out the necessary library research for various documents and data sources. The secretarial tasks were performed variously by my wife, Donna, and son, Amit, and at the office by Mrs. Frances Krull and Ms. Michele Edwards. Their support in this effort is gratefully acknowledged.

Great Neck, New York
July 1986.

THE SOUTH AFRICAN QUAGMIRE

South Africa Beyond Apartheid Reformation of Institutions and Instruments of Change

S. PRAKASH SETHI

South Africa is facing a crisis of unprecedented magnitude. Its moral and ethical basis, on which all societies must ultimately be built, have severely eroded if not been totally disrupted. The political and legal basis of its governance, the consent of the governed, has lost its legitimacy. There is domestic turmoil, civil strife, and increasing violence, which continues to expand and engulf ever larger areas of the nation despite successively more repressive measures instituted by the government. Over 80 percent of the nation's population does not accept the legitimacy of the government in power because it had no role in the selection of those who exercise political and legal authority in the nation and possess men and materiel with which to subjugate the majorities against their will. And suppression breeds more rebellion, which in turn requires more suppression.

South Africa is surrounded by countries that are hostile to its aims. Although militarily weak, they are nevertheless a threat to its security. The rest of the Third World also finds its system of government abhorrent. The current South African regime, notwithstanding its trappings of a parliamentary democracy, has many of the attributes of governance and political control similar to other authoritative regimes both on the right and the left of the political spectrum. However, it cannot count even on their support because these regimes are not about to associate themselves with South Africa for fear of exacerbating their own problems. The white minority government of South Africa is also losing its support among the Western nations of the free world, with whom it shares a common heritage of values, social ordering, and legal and political frameworks.

And yet, crises do not yield to long-term solutions. Those who are under attack develop a siege mentality and display atavistic survival instincts. The attackers, smelling blood, seek vengeance and move for the annihilation or at least the subjugation of their adversaries. The movement once started is hard to control and seldom contained. If history is any guide, the process invariably destroys not only what was evil but also what was good. The insitutions that emerge from the rubble and ashes are not always what the victims had longed for or the crusaders had hoped for. The operation may be successful but the patient, more often than not, dies in the recovery room.

South Africa is fast approaching the crisis point from where any retreat to a peaceful and constructive resolution of its political and economic problems may be unreachable. If this situation were to come to pass, it would be a human tragedy of immense proportions. It would have implications not only for the South African people but also for the international community that are too severe to contemplate.

Among the African nations, South Africa stands as a land of tremendous economic and human resources. It has a stable political and social infrastructure. Its institutions are capable of developing and harnessing its vast resources. The country's economic and social progress has been held back for reasons that are almost totally of its own making. Given a stable sociopolitical environment, it has the potential for providing unprecedented economic growth and prosperity not only for all of its own people but also for the rest of Africa. It can and should become the dominant and stabilizing force for development in the African continent.

It is therefore, important to make every effort to help South Africa transform itself from the current authoritarian and suppressive regime into a democratic society where the rights of all its people are protected. This transformation will not come about if those who advocate change use only measures of threat and reprisal with which to extract concessions and impose reforms. If history is any guide, such repression is extremely costly and can be counterproductive. At the minimum such measures inflict, at least during the transition phase, untold harm on those very people whose interests the reformers are supposed to protect and advance. Furthermore, there is no guarantee, and indeed it is quite likely, that the victims may not be any better off in the postrevolutionary society. The independence movement since the end of the Second World War has created scores of new nations that are a living testimony to the inequities and atrocities inflicted by the homegrown rulers on their own people that are far worse than those imposed by their former colonial powers.

The objectives of this chapter are threefold. First, the chapter presents a systematic analysis of the activities and rationale of various groups both inside and outside South Africa who must play an important role in any outcome that would be acceptable to a large majority of the South African people. Second, it evaluates the role that governments of the free world might play in bringing about a peaceful transition to a democratic society in South Africa. Third, it suggests some guidelines by which the process of transition to a postapartheid South Africa might be approached.

I also contend that most nations and groups outside South Africa have resorted to threats and sanctions to push South Africa toward dismantling its system of apartheid. However, as I shall demonstrate, threats and sanctions are generally crude and not always successful in bringing about lasting social change. By inflicting heavy costs on those currently in power, and, therefore, those who stand to lose the most from such changes, they have the effect of increasing their resistance to the changes. Instead, I believe that any negative measures should also be accompanied by a set of more positive inducements for change that will not only reduce the level of sacrifices that the groups currently holding power will be called upon to make, but will also accelerate the rate of benefits accruing to the victims of the current state of political order. Such a process will create greater inducements for all concerned to participate more actively in reaching mutually acceptable solutions to a postapartheid South Africa.

I start by making three basic assumptions:

1. The abolition of apartheid as a system of governance is not negotiable both as to form and timing. It must be dismantled immediately, without any substantive caveats or qualifications. The question is not when and how apartheid should be dismantled. Instead the focus of our inquiry is on how, and in what form, an acceptable postapartheid South African society should be brought about.

2. All citizens of South Africa must have equal political and legal

rights regardless of race or color of skin. However, the process by which these rights are to be defined, codified, protected, and exercised, must be determined by the South Africans themselves through institutions and negotiations that have evolved through genuine participation of all significant groups in South Africa. In other words, any solution to the South African problem must come from within South Africa and must not be imposed from outside.

3. The goverments of the free world, and other groups — notably business and financial community, churches, and other critics of conscience, institutions of higher learning, and other public interest groups — must play an active role in facilitating the processes of negotiations among various South African groups and in shouldering the economic and social burden of helping South Africa meet the aspiration of its people in a postapartheid state. It is important to remember, however, that this facilitating role must be determined by the South Africans themselves and not arrived at through some preconceived notion of what we might consider to be the best thing for South Africa.

THE POLITICAL SITUATION IN SOUTH AFRICA — REFORMS AND NONREFORMS

In his opening statement to the South African Parliament in January 1986, President P.W. Botha declared:

In a world where freedom is becoming rare, our country today is a symbol of the expansion of freedom, of the upholding of freedom of religion and free enterprise, sustained by equal rights before an independent judiciary.

We accept unequivocally that the Republic of South Africa is part of the international community. We have no wish to isolate ourselves from the world, particularly not from Africa of which we form an integral part.

President Botha also outlined the measures that would be part of the current legislative agenda. Among these were the following:

Restoring South African citizenship to black persons who permanently reside in the Republic of South Africa, but who forfeited their citizenship as a result of the conditions of independence of Transkei, Bophuthatswana, Venda, and Ciskei.

Extension of the powers of the self-governing states; the involvement of Black communities in decision making; freehold property rights for members of black communities; and a uniform identity document for all population groups.

The amendment of the immigration selection policy by repealing discriminatory preference provisions; the restructuring of the system of provincial government to involve all communities; and legislation authorizing the lifting, suspending or amending of unnecessary restrictions on free entrepreneurship, particularly with regard to the informal section.

The drafting of legislation to remove existing influx control measures which apply to South African citizens in the Republic of South Africa. The present system is too costly and has become obsolete; the government is in favor of measures which will facilitate *orderly urbanisation* [emphasis added].

Botha went on to outline his notion of the concepts that would underlie the constitutional development to broaden the democracy in South Africa. These would include:

An undivided Republic of South Africa where all regions and communities within its boundaries form part of the South African state, with the right to participate in institutions to be negotiated collectively;
We accept one citizenship for all South Africans, implying equal treatment and opportunities;
All South Africans must be placed in a position where they can participate in Government through their elected representatives.

However, having so stated his objectives he went on to say:

The peoples of the Republic of South Africa form one nation. But one nation is a nation of minorities. Given the multicultural nature of South African society, this of necessity implies participation by all communities, the sharing of power between these communities, but also the devolution of power as far as possible and the protection of minority rights, without one group dominating another.

I now wish to announce that I intend to negotiate the establishment of a National Statutory Council, which will meet under my chairmanship.

I propose that this Council should consist of representatives of the South African Government, representatives of the governments of the self-governing national states, as well as leaders of other black communities and interest groups.

One is encouraged by the broad sweep of the statement and its intent to encompass most of the concerns that beset the black population of South Africa, and of the world community. If rhetoric is a precursor to action, one might view these statements as signs of hope. Unfortunately, the surfeit of promises is only exceeded by the glacial pace of reforms. Statements of purpose are encased in caveats that make their implementation on any other terms than those acceptable to the white minority that controls the South African government, all but impossible. If history is any guide, and the actions of the South African government to date support it, the gap between statement of intentions, commitment to action, and dedication to implementation would remain unacceptably wide and intolerably deep.

The South African government declares its purpose to abolish apartheid and to grant all the people equal rights. And yet it is trapped in its own mindset; too obsessed with its past to think boldly of the future; too mindful of preserving the uinjust gains of those who have them rather than making whole the rights of those who were denied them.

Even the most timid reform efforts have been riddled with backsliding. Every step forward is followed by two steps backward, thereby constantly raising the level of frustration and anger among the black people while giving further encouragement to the radical right that they can delay forever any efforts toward granting black South Africans' political or economic rights.

The government announces its intention to scrap pass laws and Influx Control laws thereby allowing blacks to move in any part of the country where jobs might be available to them. And yet the pass laws would be substituted by other uniform identity cards that would nevertheless record the racial identity of the cardholder. While all South Africans would be able to live in any area of their choice, *provided they can find an approved house or site*, the Group Areas Act through which black and white residential areas are segregated is to be retained. Since there is a great shortage of approved housing and even sites for blacks in urban areas, the real impact of changes in the Influx Control and pass laws on black mobility is likely to be minimal. Thus government's desire for an "orderly urbanisation" program when accompanied with an even tougher antisquatting law may turn out to be the same old influx control disguised in new clothes.

The government declares its intent to create a common department of education for all South African children and yet insists on keeping separate black and white schools. The governments' intent to maintain this separation of black and white children is confirmed by the new scheme it has devised to provide subsidy to private schools. This subsidy is based on a regressive scale based on the proportion of black students in a predominantly white school: the higher the proportion of black students the lower the per capital subsidy. The subsidy for each black pupil ranges from 45 percent (almost R700 per pupil) if the proportion of blacks were less than 10 percent, the subsidy would be reduced to 15 percent if the black student population constituted less than 20 percent, with no subsidy being given to schools where black student population exceeded 30 percent. This approach penalizes those schools (primarily Catholic schools and the nonracial private schools) which are trying to create an integrated educational system by placing an exorbitant financial burden on them.

The government proclaims its intent to be part of the international community of democratic nations and yet every effort by that community to seek peaceful resolution to the South African problem is thwarted. The recent raids by the South African military into neighboring countries, under the guise of destroying the terrorist bases, were roundly condemned by the world community including South Africa's most sympathetic friends, Great Britain and the United States. Furthermore, after some encouraging signs, the Commonwealth Group of Eminent Persons has ended its efforts to seek the freedom of Nelson Mandela and to create an atmosphere for negtiations between the South African government and the black leaders including the African National Congress.

The problem lies both in reasons for reform and the control of power in South Africa. President Botha's desire for changes in the apartheid laws is most likely born out of necessity rather than a vision of future based on a sense of equity, fairness, and justice. The necessity of black anger and violence, accompanied by international pressure, demands that he yield to some reforms. The economic costs of maintaining status quo are already quite high and are becoming increasingly so. And yet the necessity of maintaining political control constantly pulls him toward satisfying the extreme right wing of the white minority, which wants to maintain status quo at all costs. Thus he is being pulled in two directions.

Having declared his intent to form a democratic South Africa with equal rights and protection for all, President Botha states: "Committed as we are to these norms and values, we will have to defend the South African society against the forces of anarchy which seek to seize a monopoly of power and ultimately rule this nation, through the use of force, by an exclusive political clique. That will make a mockery of liberty."

Unfortunately, this is not the condition against which South Africa needs to protect itself. This is indeed the prevailing condition. Those who are decrying the potential use of force and violence on the part of black groups are indeed the ones who have made a mockery of liberty.

Moreover, President Botha has ascribed to himself to create the conditions under which the black leaders acceptable to him would meet to develop ideas for constitutional reform in a manner that would protect the rights of minorities in that nation.

Both of these conditions are unacceptable. Why should the offender have all the right of defining the terms of settlement and the victim all the obligations to live by it? Apartheid will not be dismantled if we waited for the pleasure of those who benefit from it.

The development of any political system acceptable to all South Africans must not be dictated by the South African government or for that matter any single group whether inside or outside South Africa. The South African government cannot deny representation to African National Congress under the pretext that it is communist dominated or that it advocates violence. By one measure, the current South African government's right to govern is also suspect because its parliamentary system is designed to share the spoils of power and is not based on the consent of the governed. Nor can it ask others to disavow violence when it makes extensive use of violence to protect the privileged position of a minority of the population and that of the entrenched oligarchy. A longer lasting and enforceable system of power-sharing and governance must come through the voluntary and willing participation of groups that speak for significant segments of the South African population.

Catering to the past means protecting the privileges of the few against the rights of the many. What South Africa needs is not more brutality and oppression, but greater compassion and understanding. South Africa must escape its history if it is to move toward an economically healthy and democratic future. The windows of opportunity are becoming increasingly narrow. South Africa is now beyond the politics of protest and reconciliation. It is engaged in the politics of confrontation, and if nothing is done soon, it will have to deal with the politics of revolution. At every stage the cost of maintaining order and stability grows higher. Despite increasing repression and police activity the government is barely able to maintain law and order. The violence constantly escalates. The government's state of emergency in 1985 was imposed to quell violence and bloodshed in the townships, and yet the result has been quite the contrary. Since September 1984 more than 1,600 blacks have been killed in the townships largely by police firing and as a result of fighting between rival factions. Many black areas have become ungovernable; there white authority is exercised only sporadically and then with excessive use of force.

Moreover, power not shared peacefully must be seized and maintained through the barrel of a gun. And victory achieved through the barrel of a gun, is not voluntarily yielded to the democratic process. By insisting on dismantling apartheid on its own terms and creating a democratic system of its own choosing, the South African whites are likely to lose their own democracy which cannot be maintained under conditions of extreme political instability. They will also doom any chances of democracy ever establishing on a sound footing in a postapartheid South Africa.

PROPOSALS FOR REFORM

South Africa needs visionary leaders who are willing to dare the present in order to shape the future. The movement toward a postapartheid democratic South Africa will progress only if we were willing to put more emphasis on the rights of those who have been denied them rather than the privileges of those who stand to lose some of them. Such a process will call several changes.

1. The immediate repeal of all apartheid laws, thereby giving all citizens the right to move, live, and work wherever their circumstances permit it, to express their thoughts freely, and to advocate lawful change, in a system of government they want to live in.

It has been argued that an immediate repeal would swamp the system of physical infrastructure of urban communities by bringing in hordes of people unequipped to deal with the urban work environment. While there is some danger of short-term dislocations, I believe anarchy and chaos their longterm impact is not likely to be substantial. Freedom of movement nevertheless carries with it certain economic costs. Movement is likely to take place more along economic lines rather than racial lines. And that should indeed be the case. The present scenario is deliberately being painted in economic terms to disguise its essentially racial and ethnic character.

Even if there are short-run dislocations, they reflect the heavy burden that has been hitherto imposed on the blacks of South Africa by the white minorities. Rather than curb freedom of movement, efforts should be made to ameliorate the situation through additional economic aid to the affected areas.

2. To expedite the process of freedom of choice in all walks of life, the government should prod the process through affirmative action subsidies. Municipalities, school systems, hospitals, recreation centers, and other social institutions should be required to show a sustained effort in gradually increasing the proportion of employees at all levels of activity. These institutions should be helped in this effort through "affirmative action programs" whose per capita value would increase to higher levels with every increase in the level of integration over the legally required minimum standards.

The cost of raising the socioeconomic status of South African blacks is likely to be very high despite recent efforts by the South African government and private sector to narrow the gap. In a country of over 23 million blacks, there are less than 500 black doctors, 17 dentists, and no veterinarians or paramedics. Among the 6,000 lawyers, there are only 300 blacks. Almost 80 percent of black teachers do not have even the equivalent of a high school education. The black conditions in terms of housing and employment are equally abysmal.

This is perhaps one of the most daunting fears of the white minority and perhaps is one of the important considerations in their reluctance to share power with blacks in South Africa. One of the difficulties in the peaceful transition to a democratic postapartheid South Africa is the immense economic costs that would have to be incurred to improve the physical and social infrastructure in South Africa if the blacks are to have any hope of even minimally enhancing their economic condition. Clearly the short-run costs would have to be borne by the productive sector of the South African economy: the private sector and the white population. But such a course of action would impose a terrible burden on that sector and inhibit growth and recovery. It would also inflict a severe loss of income and standard of living on the white population of such magnitude that it would be tantamount to committing economic suicide. It would have the effect of raising the resistance of the white population, thereby creating the potential for further bloodshed.

This is one of the most important areas where the United States and other Western nations can provide help to smooth the process of transition and also make its costs bearable for the whites of South Africa.

3. The government should move toward greater decentralization of power at the provincial and local level. This should allow for greater flexibility in seeking local solutions to the problem of power-sharing

and also provide greater experience to black leaders in participating in the democratic processes and in governance. Decentralization, however, should not be used as a ruse for maintaining white hegemony.

4. Any system of power-sharing must be based on the notion of universal franchise which includes the notion of one man one vote. However, the ultimate system of governance and of power sharing must take into account the special needs of the South African society where the rights of different minorities must be protected.

South Africa has strong ethnic communities similar to those found in most traditional societies and developing countries. One of the reasons that political restructuring failed in many countries that became independent after World War II was the fact that such restructuring was based on political lines that were arbitrarily drawn by the departing colonial powers. Political systems were imposed without regard to the ethnic character of those nations. For example, since its independence in 1947, India has had to resort to numerous realignments of its internal borders creating new states, thereby recognizing the need for creating political boundaries that were culturally cohesive. However, this has not taken away any of the democratic underpinnings of that society, but instead has strengthened them.

The United States offers another example of a highly multi-ethnic society where the rights of smaller states have been protected in the Constitution through the creation of two electoral houses at the federal level wherein the Senate two electoral seats were allocated to each state without regard to its population. Many countries in Europe have also fashioned different federal systems to allocate power between various groups and to protect the rights of minorities.

It would, however, be wrong if the notion of protecting minority rights is used to protect the white minority's hegemony and its right to dictate terms under which different groups among the black people would share power in the government. The best approach might be some form of proportional representation in the parliament based on the percent of votes received by a political party in an election. It is quite conceivable that in the initial phases different political parties would have a predominance of one or two ethnic groups. However, in the long run such a political configuration would provide avenues for different ethnic groups to join parties based on thier political preferences rather than be confined to a particular group based on accidents of birth. Should the South African government insist on separating the black population into various ethnic groups, in the interests of consistency it must also do the same for the whites and not treat all of them as if they were one ethnic group.

THE U.S. GOVERNMENT: POLICIES AND NONPOLICIES

The U.S. policy in South Africa is more rooted in inaction than action. Partly it is the result of a realization that United States has, at best, limited options. As I shall demonstrate later in this chapter, the option of imposing economic sanctions is rather a crude instrument and cannot be counted upon to deliver its intended objective even under the most optimal circumstances. However, at least a part of the inability of the United States to influence changes in South Africa arises from a lack of a coherent set of objectives and unwillingness to commit resources to achieve those objectives.

According to Ambassador Douglas Holladay, director of the South Africa Working Group in the State Department, the U.S. influence in South Africa "is principally moral, political and diplomatic. But our greatest leverage is perhaps psychological. The United States is a nation that has derived strength from its diversity to become a democracy of unrivaled global power. This fact stands as a reproach to the exclusionary policies of South Africa." More recently, Secretary of State George Shultz called apartheid unacceptable on moral, economic, and political grounds and said it must be dismantled expeditiously.

Thus the U.S. government has condemned apartheid and sought its removal throught the process of "constructive engagement." This has implied a qualified support of President Botha's efforts at "reforms" while at the same time a restrained level of support for the black groups who are agitating for a speedier rate and more substantive activity toward dismantling of apartheid and giving the blacks their citizenship rights and a say in the governance of their country. This ambivalence has led both sides to not quite believe or trust the U.S. commitment.

The U.S. policiy appears neither constructive nor engaging. Its dialogue is more soothing to those in power than comfort to those who are deprived of it. Its actions are superficial and lack evidence of serious commitment to help the disenfranchised black population of South Africa. Even the President Reagan's Executive Order of September 1985 imposing limited sanctions is seen as an attempt to forestall the more sweeping restrictions that were likely to be imposed by the Congress rather than as a part of well-thought-out strategy. the actions of the U.S. government seem to run counter to its political principles, and even its national security interests.

POLICY OPTIONS FOR THE UNITED STATES:
THE CARROT AND THE STICK APPROACH

Two main options are available to the United States: economic sanctions and financial aid. The first is negative in character and induces desired behavior on the basis of fear of penalties that will be inflicted on the country that is the object of sanctions. The second option provides rewards to the recipient of engaging in desired behavior and positive in character.

The success of any strategy, either of sanctions or of rewards, depends on three factors. The first is the ability of the country imposing sanctions to enforce those sanctions and channel their impact in desired directions. The second condition is the ability of the country against whom the sanctions are being imposed to adjust its economy to do without the products or services that it received from the country imposing the sanctions, to find substitutes for them, or to find alternative sources of supplies. And the third condition is the willingness of other countries that provide alternative sources of funds and goods, to cooperate with the sanctioning or the sanctioned country.

ECONOMIC SANCTIONS

History shows that economic boycotts have been less than successful even where enormous amounts of resources, including military, were used. Thus Cuba has survived a sustained boycott from the United States, and Rhodesia lived for a long time with world boycott while successfully selling its products and importing its necessities in a variety of ways.

The chances of any economic sanctions unilaterally applied by the United States, no matter how harsh and sweeping, being successful against South Africa are negligible unless they are joined by other major powers of the West with significant investments in South Africa. The United States' direct investment in South Africa is less than $2.0 billion, representing 10 percent of all direct foreign investment in South Africa but also accounting for less than 1 percent of the total U.S. overseas investments. In contrast, Great Britain has almost $17.0 billion in direct investments in South Africa and accounts for almost 50 percent of all direct foreign investments in that country. Almost 10 percent of British direct overseas investments are in South Africa.

Will countries like Great Britain, West Germany, and Holland go along with the United States to impose sanctions on South Africa? It is highly unlikely. One reason is that there is genuine doubt that a policy of sanctions is likely to be reasonably effective without at the same time imposing intolerable costs on the economies of the countries involved. It is not only South Africa that is dependent on foreign capital and trade, foreign countries are also dependent on their trade with South Africa and income from their investments in that country. For example, in the case of England, it is estimated that between 70,000 and 250,000 jobs will be lost in England as a result of partial or total trade and investment boycott against South Africa.

South Africa ranks twenty-first among the world's trading partners. The two-way flow of goods and services accounts for between 55 and 65 percent of the country's gross domestic product, one of the highest proportions in the Western world. The eight principal trading partners in order of the size of their total trade (exports and imports) are the United States, Japan, West Germany, Britain, Switzerland, Italy, France, and Netherlands. Together they account for almost 70 percent of South Africa's overseas trade. Trade and investments are substitutable for each other to a significant degree. Things that cannot be imported have to be manufactured at home and vice versa. Therefore, any sanctions to be effective will not only have to include countries that invest in South Africa but also countries that trade with South Africa.

Japan is a good example of this phenomenon. Japanese law does not permit investments in South Africa by Japanese companies. And yet Japan is South Africa's second most important trading partner accounting for almost 17 percent of South Africa's foreign trade. In 1984, Japan's exports to South Africa were valued at R1.96 billion and imports from South Africa amounted to R2.8 billion. It is the second largest seller of automobiles in South Africa and ranks first or second in a variety of other merchandise categories. Even if companies like General Motors and IBM were restricted from manufacturing or exporting to South Africa their places would be easily taken up by Toyota, Mitsubishi, and Matsushita or some other West German, British, Dutch, or Swiss companies. Nor can we seriously hope to impact South Africa's economy by restricting imports of such products as oil through putting restrictions on the activities of the U.S. based oil companies doing business in South Africa. Eighty-five percent of South Africa's energy needs are met through domestically mined coal. It also has a small domestic oil capacity. Its strategic oil reserves will meet the country's needs for at least three years and can be stretched much longer through conservation measures and curtailment of nonessential uses. Furthermore, the world is suffering from oil glut. Some of the developing countries with oil as their major source of foreign exchange are in desperate need of foreign income. Anyone with money can buy all the oil they need in the spot market and neither the buyers nor the sellers are interested in asking too many questions. It would be a sheer flight of fantasy to imagine that the United States, or for that matter any other country, could effectively blockade all essential imports to South Africa or refrain from purchasing essential goods from South Africa.

Those who advocate boycott must take cognizance of this simple fact of intertwined nature of international trade and investment, otherwise they would end up hurting the United States and its companies without having much effect in bringing about desired changes in South Africa. In fact, it can be argued that it would have a negative effect because the United States would have lost whatever little leverage it might have exercised by its presence in that country.

And what about the effect of boycott on the South African economy? Clearly, the South African economy is quite strong, industrially advanced, and capable of sustaining a viable industrial base and productive capacity even in the face of rather significant sanctions. The country is self-sufficient in food production and produces many of its own essential raw materials, but since it is a growing economy its need for capital exceeds its domestic savings. It must depend on foreign capital and technology to grow at an optimal rate. Therefore, any curtailment of foreign capital would adversely affect its economic growth, income, and prosperity. This will happen in two ways. First, some of the projects would not be undertaken for want of capital. Second, to the extent that certain products and services related to national security and other essential purposes cannot be imported or financed from abroad and must be financed from domestic resources only, they will divert resources from other purposes deemed nonessential, and being an economically inefficient use of resources, they would be more expensive and thereby adversely affect economic growth.

Therefore, when applied at a massive scale, sanctions will hurt the South African economy. The internal costs of even these sanctions will be unevenly distributed. It is quite likely that in South Africa the white business establishment would suffer, but the black population would certainly suffer a great deal more since its capacity to absorb such costs is infinitesimally smaller than that of the white minority. However, the important question to ask here is how will this hurt translate into persuading the South Africans to follow the wishes of the countries imposing those sanctions. While the short-run effect of economic sanctions may be dramatic indeed (witness the case of nonrescheduling of foreign loans) the long-term effect is likely to be much less dramatic. The South African economy has become highly diversified and the country can shift resources from one sector of the economy to another in order to offset the effect of trade sanctions.

Trade sanctions and shortage of foreign capital, however, will have the effect of slowing down economic activity. Clearly, the first casualties of such slowdown would be the poor blacks whose interests we are trying to protect. And that effect is not likely to be negligible. In addition to its own black population, South Africa provides employment to almost 2.0 million blacks from the neighboring countries. And if the price of lifting sanctions is to give up all the benefits of apartheid, why should South African whites accede to those demands? They are likely to percieve the price of not acceding to those demands as less onerous to their way of life and position of power.

The benefits currently enjoyed by the white minority are so massive that even a substantial loss of those benefits under external (U.S.) pressures for divestment would leave them in far better shape than if they were to accede to sharing political power with the black majority. This is especially so when they can point to the horrendously miserable experience of other black-dominated dictatorships and one-party governments in the rest of Africa. Thus it stands to reason that the South African government would use all possible repressive measures to maintain its stranglehold on power. Therefore, coercive and threatening measures for seeking a redistribution of power, without simultaneously somehow reassuring the white minority of the safety of their legitimate interests, would most likely lead to bloodshed and a tremendous loss inflicted on the South African blacks. One does not surrender easily if the price of surrender is certain execution while the price of fighting has at least the advantage of a glorious death and the knowledge of inflicting a heavy cost on one's enemy.

U.S. FOREIGN AID TO SOUTH AFRICA

Just as the United States has been ambivalent about its objectives in the use of economic sanctions, including the types of sanctions to be imposed on South Africa, it has been equally unclear about the goals of its foreign aid to South Africa, both as to the strategic importance of that country in remaining stable and democratic, and also the role foreign assistance can play in implementing U.S. policy in South Africa.

In 1985, South Africa received a puny $20.0 million in foreign aid, which amounts to less than $0.80 per black person in that country. The Agency for International Development (AID) budget request for fiscal year 1987 for South Africa is $25.0 million. In comparison, the approximately 200 U.S. companies who are operating in South Africa and are the signatories of the Sullivan Principles have provided, between 1977 and 1985, over $158 million to the South African blacks in the areas of health, education, community development, and other related activities. In contrast, in 1986 Israel and Egypt received over $6.1 billion in U.S. foreign aid representing over 48 percent of approximately $12.3 billion in U.S. foreign aid. The other big recipients of foreign aid were Turkey $739.0 million; Pakistan $628.5 million; El Salvador $435.7 million; Greece $431.9 million; Spain $396.7 million, and Philippines $240.9 million. If South Africa is important to the American national security interests, and as a bulwark of economic stability in the Southern African region, we certainly don't seem to take it seriously. If this is an indication of our commitment to help the poor blacks of South Africa, the magnitude of our largesse is exceeded only by our proclamations of good intentions. Even as guilt money, its puniness is embarrassing if not deplorable.

ACTIONS THAT U.S. GOVERNMENT CAN TAKE

The U.S. government has an opportunity to demonstrate its commitment to helping South African blacks and also stabilizing that country during the transition period. One difficulty in the peaceful transition to a democratic postapartheid in South Africa is the immense economic costs that would have to be incurred to improve the physical and social infrastructure in South Africa if the blacks are to have any hope of even minimally enhancing their economic well-being. Clearly the short-run costs would have to be borne by the productive sector of the South African economy: the private sector and the white population. Such a course of aciton would impose a terrible burden on that sector and thereby retard if not demolish any chances of growth and recovery. It would also inflict a severe loss of income and, therefore, standard of living on the white population of such magnitude that it would be tantamount to committing economic suicide. It would have the effect of raising the resistance of the white population thereby creating the potential for further bloodshed.

1. As a start, the U.S. government should make an initial commitment of $200 million dollars in foreign aid to South Africa. This amount is eminently reasonable and should be feasible through cuts in arms and other aid that we provide to many of the less deserving countries. This aid should be allocated primarily for the well-being of the South African blacks and should be directed toward housing, education, and economic development. It should be managed without the involvement of the South African government. Instead it should combine elements of private enterprise in the United States, and initiative and sweat equity on the part of the blakcs in South Africa.

2. The U.S. government should also make a declaration of its intent to increase the level of this aid in predetermined amounts in response to specific actions to be taken by the South African government in negotiations toward reaching a political solution of the South African problem and also in helping the black population toward improving its economic and social conditions.

3. At the same time, economic sanctions should be used in conjunction with the granting of foreign aid.

a. The sanctions should be specific in magnitude and very narrowly focused toward the removal of some clearly defined undesirable activity on the part of the South African government within a specific period of time. Blanket sanctions, seeking broad changes in sociopolitical structure and without any specific time table, are generally ineffective. Those attempting to comply with the sanctions do not know how far they must go in order to satisfy the conditions of compliance. There is also the fear of such conditions becoming open-ended, so that once a particular level is reached the demands would be further escalated. They diffuse their negative impact on a very large segment of the population and have the effect of coalescing otherwise diverse groups against a common external threat.

b. Sanctions should be aimed, at least initially, toward targets that are particularly odious and hard to defend in terms of public opinion and ultimate cost to the total economy.

c. Sanctions should also be directed toward forcing the South African government to implement expeditiously and effectively those reforms that it has promised on paper or through changes in its laws. Thus sanctions should be used to force South Africa to deliver on its promises and thereby overcome the reluctance of the civil service, which has been known for its reluctance to implement antiapartheid related reforms.

d. Above, all, sanctions should be sequentially imposed and built on gains made through earlier measures. They should be part of a well-thought-out agenda and have a realistic timetable.

e. Sanctions must be developed in consultation with the other countries that have a significant stake in South Africa.

f. Sanctions should take into account their potential impact on the nonwhite population of South Africa and should be developed in consultation with all the leaders of the black community and not only those who are vocal in their support for imposing sanctions regardless of their economic and social costs on various impacted groups.

ACTIVITIES OF U.S. AND OTHER FOREIGN MULTINATIONALS IN SOUTH AFRICA

There is no question that foreign capital and technology have played a major role in the industrialization and economic growth of South Africa. It also goes without saying that foreign multinationals, and through them the citizens of those countries, have also benefited from these investments. Foreign capital went to South Africa, and is primarily there, for economic reasons, and that is as it should be. No one should expect private enterprise to engage in economic activities that can be justified *only* on the basis of someone's idea of social good. To do so would negate the very purpose of private enterprise. It would subject it to arbitrary criteria of external legitimacy and political control which has consistently shown to be highly inefficient, corruptible, and manipulative. If it were not so, Russia would be truly a worker's paradise and we would all be taking guided tours of model factories and state-owned enterprises that have sprouted in many developing countries and have provided a constant stream of benefits to their benevolent leaders. These activities are the proper domain of governments where social choices are made, benefits are distributed, and costs are incurred based on commonly agreed principles.

Therefore I do not take seriously the protestations of many corporations that claim that their primary reason for sticking it out in South Africa, even under these adverse circumstances, is to be an instrument of social good. This simply is not sustainable. However, having said that, it should also be pointed out that the very reason private enterprise succeeds and strives is that, on balance, it creates far more social good than social harm when compared with any other form of organized economic activity. And where at the margin, the side effects of some private activity are creating more harm than good, it is the proper role of society's institutions — both government and nongovernment — to bring pressure to bear on the private enterprise to change its behavior, and when it is not forthcoming, to impose restrictions on its operations.

The question, in the case of foreign companies operating in South Africa, is therefore to examine the social costs and benefits of their being in South Africa, and also of their being withdrawn from South Africa. This question should also be addressed in a broader context: What should be the proper mode of behavior or private enterprise, especially foreign enterprise, in countries governed by authoritarian and repressive regimes?

Historically, influential public opinion in industrially advanced countries has insisted that multinational companies should not meddle in the internal political affairs of the host country. It has been argued that foreign multinationals are so large and powerful, when compared with the economies and political infrastructure of many poor and developing countries, that they can undermine domestic political processes for their own selfish purposes. However, in the case of South Africa, we are asking not only that foreign multinationals intervene in the domestic political process in that country, but that they do so forcefully, and if they do not succeed in achieving this noneconomic objective, they should be forced to withdraw from operating in that country.

The extreme argument in support of such a position would hold that apartheid is such an inherent evil that no civilized and moral society should in any way contribute to its sustenance, and, that the rewards for economic activity in South Africa are based, to a large extent, on the exploitation of black labor and are morally reprehensible. A more tempered line of reasoning would suggest that we must use all our institutions, including economic institutions, to create social good. All social institutions, and corporations are no exception, must meet society's expectations of ethical behavior and norms of social good. Corporations have no inherent right to exist or make a profit. They have a right not to operate in a country if the operating conditions are not acceptable to them. However, it must be understood that profits are not the price of doing business, but the reward for doing business in a manner that meet society's criteria of acceptable social behavior.

In the case of South Africa, we must evaluate whether, on balance, multinational corporations are likely to do more good than harm for the blacks of South Africa by staying there. Clearly, foreign multinationals cannot bring about political and social change in South Africa acting alone. Therefore, their performance must be measured in terms of the internal environment in South Africa, and the external environment, world opinion as well as the legal demands and sociopolitical expectations of the governments and people in their own countries.

AMERICAN COMPANIES IN SOUTH AFRICA

American companies, like most foreign enterprises in South Africa, have responded to pressures for change by making changes in their operating procedures to ensure a more equitable treatment of their black employees in a manner that goes beyond what the law requires in South Africa, and in many cases, in direct violation of South African law.

However, it should be mentioned here that this change in behavior has not come voluntarily but in response to pressure from outside forces, primarily in the United States, but also in South Africa. The response has been reactive rather than anticipatory or proactive. While American companies can complain about the pressures being exerted on them by outside groups, primarily the religious and other public interest groups, they cannot deny that this pressure has indeed resulted in a great deal of positive change affecting their black employees. The issues before us are as follows:

1. To what extent can the claims of the American companies be sustained in terms of their performance in South Africa as it impacts the black community in general, and their black employees in particular?

2. Have the American companies gone as far as they can be expected to go in making changes in their South African operations? A demand for further changes, without more tangible support from companies from other industrialized nations as well as the governments of those nations, will be extremely difficult, if not impossible, to attain.

3. Under what sociopolitical conditions in South Africa should we insist that American companies must totally withdraw from operating in that country, and who is to make such a decision?

4. What additional measure, if any, should we ask the American companies to take to further the interest of their black employees and also to contribute to the dismantling of the apartheid system?

American corporations, like most foreign corporations insist on their right to stay in South Africa, claiming that in the process they do more good than harm. They are a force for positive change and help bring about improved social and economic conditions for the black South African workers both by their actions, and also by setting an example for others to follow. As evidence of their good faith effort, they point to their compliance with the Sullivan Principles that call for elimination of all discriminatory practices at the place of employment. They also require signatory companies to help their workers in the communities where they live and also take positive action to pressure the South African government to dismantle the system of apartheid.

More than 200 of the approximately 275 companies presently operating in South Africa subscribe to the Sullivan Principles. They represent over 80 percent of all workers employed by the American companies in South Africa. The signatory companies keep detailed data of their performance, which is checked and reported by Arthur D. Little, Inc., an independent management consulting company, which rates companies into various categories. For a company to have a rating of I or II has become the litmus test to avoid pressure from the activists in the United States.

By one measure the American companies have indeed demonstrated their commitment to nondiscrimination and black equality by institutionalizing most of the actions demanded by the Sullivan principles. Although, there are a number of other codes, including one by the South African code, and the European Economic Community code, they are much weaker than the Sullivan Principles in terms of performance requirements, expectations of compliance, and reporting systems that are voluntary, nonuniform, and not subject to independent evaluation. Thus by adhering to a stricter set of criteria, the U.S. based companies not only have a higher level of performance in terms of black equality but create a higher standard of behavior which the non-American companies are then pressured to follow for competitive reasons. Similarly, American companies have spent approximately $158 million during the last nine years in support of their community-related activities under the Sullivan Principles.

There are, however, two major shortcomings with the evaluation of the U.S. companies' performance under the Sullivan Principles.

First, the reporting of the data is done by the companies themselves. The data are prepared by the companies' outside accountants. The evaluation process devised by Arthur D. Little contains highly qualitative and subjective elements which are assessed and scored by ADL's own judges. It is largely aggregated providing equal weight to different measures regardless of their differing importance in the overall scheme of things. Thus serious shortcomings in one area may be easily overlooked because of better performance on another dimension. According to Karen Paul, who has done an in-depth analysis of the Sullivan Principles reporting system, the system is so flawed that one cannot state with a high degree of certainty that the data indeed purport to show what actually is occurring in those companies, or that another judge looking at the same data would not come to somewhat different conclusions.

The second problem with the reporting system pertains to its paper chase character. The reporting system appears primarily to be designed to satisfy American critics of U.S. corporations. It focuses on numbers and elaborate bookkeeping and very little input from those it purports to impact—the companies' black workers or the communities involved. Thus the people for whose benefit the system is designed had no say in determining whether the criteria selected are indeed the criteria on which they would want the U.S. companies to be judged, and whether the reported performance does indeed meet with their perception of reality or what the companies are actually doing.

This leads to the next and perhaps the most important issue in this debate. To the extent that the U.S. companies have improved their performance in compliance with the Sullivan Principles, they have indeed instituted a commendable level of change in their corporations. The future problem, however, may not be with what the Sullivan Principles do but what they do not do. To wit, Sullivan Principles may not be an adequate mechanism to guide the corporations to the next phase of the black struggle in South Africa—that is, devising ways to speed the process of dismantling the apartheid system and help the black majority seek its rights in sharing power of governance in South Africa. It is therefore not surprising that a significant segment of even moderate black leadership considers compliance with the Sullivan Principles as no longer a relevant issue. Clearly it is regarded a necessary minimum condition, but not a sufficient condition with which to judge the performance of thr U.S. companies in South Africa.

An even more fundamental question has to do with the future of private enterprise in any postapartheid South Africa. In South Africa, as in many of the other poor countries that are often controlled by authoritarian regimes, private enterprise is invariably associated with dictatorships and corrupt regimes. It is no wonder that private enterprise and capitalism have come to be viewed as the tools of oppression in many of these countries becasue the poor have not seen private enterprise as playing the role of providing the underpinnings of a democratic society and protecting individual freedoms.

ACTION PROPOSALS FOR U.S. COMPANIES

The immediate question facing the American companies, and for that matter all business institutions whether South African and foreign, is not what they have already done, but what they must do to identify their interests with those of the black majorities who must eventually play an increasingly larger role in the governance of that country. Time is running out for the business community to become more active in contributing to conditions leading to a peaceful transition in South Africa. Thier capacity to do so is indeed quite limited. However, it must be exercised to the fullest possible extent if private enterprise, as we know it, is to have any future in a postapartheid South Africa. The question that will be asked of them is not what they have done, but what they should be doing in terms of their capacity for action and whether they are doing all that is possible.

As a minimum condition of operation companies must meet the performance criteria set forth in the Sullivan Principles. Moreover, the performance measures should not become overly slavish to bookkeeping standards, but instead be subjected to evaluation by independent outsiders, including those who are being impacted by these activities. The performance should be measured on dimensions that are simple, realistic, and meet the priorities of the blacks in South Africa.

The American companies should take highly visible measures that demonstrate their abhorrence to the apartheid system. The primary focus of these measures would be to challenge the outer limits of the apartheid laws with a view to constantly confront the government into admitting that these laws are unwarranted and must be changed. Another measure in this direction would be to test the sincerity and commitment of the South African government by constantly pushing the compliance levels of those apartheid laws that have supposedly been suspended or repealed.

These could be undertaken in a variety of ways.

Dismantling Apartheid

- Encourage workers to break the laws that on the face of it are hard to justify, thereby putting the South African government in an awkward position if it insisted on their compliance. General Motors' promise to pay the legal expenses of its black workers who violated the segregated beach laws in the area of GM's operations illustrates this approach.

• Acquire housing in predominantly white segregated areas and assign it to the company's black workers of similar socioeconomic class.

• Assign blacks franchises and other operational privileges in company-owned premises or business activities that are primarily located in white areas or cater to a white clientele. Be very open and aggressive on the company's objective in doing so, and be prepared to take some losses as a consequence of loss of white patronage in some of these facilities.

• Locate corporate facilities in areas where it is easy to commute for the black employees, thereby making it easier to hire and promote more blacks in supervisory and managerial positions.

• Encourage white-owned companies that do business with U.S. companies to voluntarily implement Sullivan Principles in their enterprise. Reward those South African companies that implement non-discriminatory policies through channeling more of the U.S. companies' business to those firms.

Exploring Alternative Avenues for Achieving a Peaceful Transition to a Democratic Postapartheid South Africa

• U.S. companies, in cooperation with other like-minded firms from South Africa and other countries, should create forums for bringing together leaders of *all* political segments with a view to discuss possible ways of creating a more democratic South Africa, provide avenues for negotiating transition arrangements between the South African government and opposition groups, and build higher threshold levels of trust among various groups whose cooperation will be necessary to develop and implement a viable plan for power-sharing in South Africa.

• Similarly, U.S. companies should also take the initiative and leadership position in disseminating the ideas generating through these forums, as well as their opposition, to the current form of apartheid-based and minority-dominated government, through news media and paid advertising, to make the black people in South Africa aware of the commitment of the U.S. private enterprise toward equality and fairness for all the people in South Africa.

Increasing Black Stake in the Private Enterprise

• Create an employee stock-ownership plan where a company would allocate a certain amount of funds based on either annual sales, profits, or asset value that would be used to assist a company's employees to buy stock in the company. The fund would be a partial recognition of the company's excess earnings in South Africa that resulted through lower wages and other discriminatory exploitation resulting from the apartheid policies of South Africa. Both the employee and the employer would contribute toward the purchase of the company stock. However, the company's share of the purchase price would be weighed more heavily toward the lower end of the wage spectrum. Although black employees will be affirmatively favored under such a plan, it is recommended that the stock ownership plan should be available to all of the company's employees. This is one of the necessary ingredients for a peaceful transition to a postapartheid South Africa and should create a harmonious work environment.

• Create affirmative plans for encouragement of black entrepreneurship through allocating a certain proportion of a company's business to black-owned companies. Experience in the United States shows that such a plan can be highly successful if a company's purchase agents are encouraged, through salary increases and other forms of recognition, to seek out and nurture black-owned enterprises.

Community-Support Activities

• In the area of education, companies should provide scholarships and fellowships to different schools that are tied directly to an institution's level of achievement in integrating their educational facilities above and beyond those considered acceptable by the South African government. Thus an institution's level of support per student would be increased when that institution increases its nonwhite enrollment above 20, 25, or 30 percent within a certain period of time.

• Emphasis should be placed in creating greater black enrollment in professional schools — law, engineering, business, and medicine.

• To the extent possible, scholarships and university support programs should be clearly identified with individual companies. This would provide the participating students, the institutions, and the community-at-large with a recognition of U.S. companies' commitment to South Africa and its black population. Furthermore, it will also create in people's minds a better association between private enterprise and public good.

ACTIONS OF CHURCH GROUPS AND OTHER SOCIAL
ACTIVISTS AGAINST APARTHEID

The churches, along with other critics of conscience, have been at the forefront of the public action in the United States against apartheid. The Sullivan Principles against which the performance of U.S. firms in South Africa is measured were initiated by the Reverend Leon Sullivan. The National Council of Churches and the Interfaith Center on Corporate Responsibility (ICCR) have led the movement of "shareholder actions" seeking corporations to comply with the Sullivan Principles.

During the last three years, the protest movement of the U.S. Christian churches against apartheid has taken a more ominous form. It would appear that the notion of U.S. corporations being a source of positive good in South Africa is being increasingly rejected. Instead, according to Arie Brouwer, General Secretary of the National Council of Churches, the U.S. corporate presence in South Africa is tantamount to "their support for apartheid." Consequently, church groups have been mounting pressure to have institutional investors such as endowment and pension funds divest their portfolios of all stocks in companies that do business in South Africa, and to require that all U.S. companies pull out their investments from South Africa.

These actions are motivated both by a frsutration at the lack of progress to date, and also by a desire to dissociate oneself from an action that is patently immoral and reprehensible, while at the same time punish the wrong doer. It is presumed that these actions would bring enough economic pressure on South Africa, that when combined with similar actions by multinational corporations in other parts of the world, would force the white minority government of South Africa to end their apartheid policies and bring about a more democratic political order.

I do not need any urging to support actions that would bring about a speedy end to the apartheid system. However, I find myself in strong disagreement with the strategies and tactics of the church groups and other critics of conscience as far as they relate to the issues of divestment and disinvestment. The problem is not doing what is right but knowing what is right.

Unfortunately, both these tactics are riddled with internal inconsistencies and faulty logic. Like economic sanctions, they are quite likely to be counterproductive and to harm those they are designed to help.

Moreover, because so much energy would have been consumed by these strategies, they would distract from other efforts with better long-term prospects for yielding positive results both against apartheid and in creating a democratic postapartheid South Africa.

The stridency of the church groups has had two other unfortunate consequences.

. . .The church imprimatur, or the halo effect, has led the more radical and ideologically motivated groups to simplify the issue in a manner that divestment and disinvestment are viewed not as a means to end apartheid but as an end in itself. Issues are presented as good and evil with social activists defending the good and the poor against the evil and the unscrupulous. Doubters are viewed as naysayers. Those who are just as adamantly opposed to apartheid but are equally convinced of the futility of divestment and disinvestment, are labeled as condoning apartheid and therefore supporters of the white South African regimes. This has the unfortunate result of suppressing discussion and debate and breeding intolerance among people who agree with ends but disagree as to means.

. . .The absolutism of the assertions and proclamations of ultimate success of these strategies, which they must know are unlikely, have created the impression among the blacks in South Africa that the white regime is about to fall and that salvation is just around the corner. Ignoring for the moment the point of what this "salvation" actually means to different people, it has created a false hope and has contributed to a series of actions whose inevitable outcome must be more deaths and injuries for the blacks of South Africa. As Helen Suzman, one of the most vocal South African critics of apartheid, and also a strong dissenter of the U.S. churches' strategy of disinvestment, states:

It is manifestly true that blacks, especially young blacks, are demanding liberation now. "Liberation before the next school term" was one slogan heard toward the end of the last year. Indeed, among the worst side effects created by outside pressures for sanctions is the delusion among young blacks that the transfer of power is imminent. Nothing is further from the truth, yet that sort of false impressions kept the unrest at fever point, has kept hundreds of thousands of black pupils out of school for months on end, and has led to the deaths of more than 1,000 black people over the last sixteen months, some through vicious vigilante gang wars, some through gruesome "necklace" murders, and most by police action.

People living 6,000 miles away from the scene who think they can judge the situation accurately have no idea whatsoever of the strength and ferocity of the police and military inside South Africa. Indeed, not only is victory not around the corner, it is not even within sight. Not only is the transfer of power not imminent, it isn't even under consideration. Change, however, is. And that is what should be encouraged — attainable objectives — as a forerunner to creating a climate for negotiation about the total dismantling of apartheid and black participation in the political power structure.

FLAWS IN THE STRATEGY OF DIVESTMENT

The divestment strategy has been designed to persuade institutional investors to divest their holdings in companies doing business in South Africa and thereby bring pressure to bear on those companies to "end their support of apartheid" by completely pulling out of South Africa.

An act of divestment simply means that an institution sells stock to someone else and thus does not directly influence the company whose stock is being divested as this company is not a party to the transaction. The only influence of such a strategy on the company is at best indirect and as we shall see, in this case it is not likely to be even remotely effective.

In the first place, contrary to the assertions of the supporters of the divestment strategy, the statements of success are so fogged with ambiguities and wishful thinking, that had they been made by a corporate spokesperson he would be immediately charged by the Securities and Exchange Commission with misstatement of material facts and thereby guilty of misleading the public.

The total number of actual divestment actions are infinitesimally small both in relation to the institutions involved and also within the scope of total investments available in the stock market. For example, the activists suggest that the states, cities, colleges, and universities, that have so far adopted policies of divestment, represent over $95 billion. However, more precise facts would likely give one a very different impression. According to Christopher Coons of Investor Responsibility Research Center (IRRC), less than $6.0 billion in "holdings *has been or is committed* to be divested" (emphasis added). This represents approximately 1.6 percent of $352 billion held by public employee pensions funds. In the case of universities, the stocks earmarked to date for divestment represent only 1.2 percent of the approximately $33 billion held by college and university endowment funds. It should be remembered that even these miniscule numbers do not represent actual divestments but stated intention of divestment to be implemented gradually over a number of years so as not to adversely affect the value of the stock for the divesting institution. Coons also points out that whereas most large church funds have at least issued statements on investments in South Africa, few unions have even seriously discussed divestment. Largely untouched by the divestment movement are over $1.0 trillion held in corporate pension funds, and other trillions held in mutual funds managed on behalf of individual and corporate investors.

The sale of stock by one institution represents an assessment on its part that alternative investments offer a higher potential for rewards commensurate with risks. Conversely, an individual or institution buying such a stock views the new investment as a better investment opportunity than other alternatives available to an investor. The fluidity of the stock market reflects these opposing assessments. The sale of stock on political grounds, and in the absence of underlying financial or economic considerations, simply offers an *improved opportunity* to someone else to acquire a financial asset with a potential of superior future returns. Given the market's ability, a divestment drive contemplated at the current rates will have no effect whatsoever on the price of the stock of these companies. Even if the rate of divestment is appreciably accelerated, its impact on the market, in the absence of any deterioration in the underlying economic factors, will be negligible given the tremendous fluidity in the market. Moreover, foreigners have billions of dollars that would easily move in if these stocks present suitable investment opportunities.

A company's stock price influence its behavior when the price is low compared to its underlying value and also when compared to other similarly placed companies. A low stock price will affect a company's ability to raise capital for further growth and expansion. Given the present set of circumstances, the amount of funds involved in relation to overall value of the companies' stock and the willingness of other investors to buy these stocks, such a course of events is totally inconceivable.

The advocates of divestment further weaken their argument by indirect admission of the low appeal of their strategy. They argue that a portfolio free of South Africa-related investments can indeed be managed without any significant transaction cost. In other words, one can easily salvage one's conscience without any sacrifice. If divestment is such an important moral issue, why should the short-run cost even be considered as a factor? Moreover, gradual divestment negates the influence of such an action on the value of the stock, thereby under-mining the very source of the pressure that is supposed to be brought to bear on the companies involved.

Moreover, it is not clear that substantial short-run costs could in-deed be avoided if a large number of institutions were to decide to unload their investments in companies doing business in South Africa. This would of necessity create a short-run imbalance in the demand and supply of those stocks and therefore depress their prices. Further-more, the long-run impact on the portfolio performance of the divesting institutions cannot be ignored. The companies doing business in South Africa are among the corporations with the largest capitalization and industry representation. Exclusion of these companies would serious-ly imperil a balanced portfolio and expose it to greater risk.

The advocates of divestment have also protested against the trustees of pension funds seeking the views of their beneficiaries regarding in-vestment decisions based on political or moral criteria. It is argued that the broad mandate of the trustees encompass such a criteria. When it cannot be so clearly defended, it is also suggested that these com-panies operate in a politically unstable environment and carry a higher financial risk compared to the companies without any South African operations. It is therefore no wonder that most of the stated policies of divestment have been adopted by political bodies or public institu-tions who are either legally protected from being sued by the beneficiaries or are under political pressure to response to the concerns of the social activists. If the strategy of divestment is so critical to the apartheid issue, why are the activists not working hard enough to per-suade the beneficiaries of these pension funds to ask the trustees to vote their conscience? Furthermore, why is it that the individual holders of stocks in mutual funds have not flocked to the companies offering South Africa-free investment funds?

FLAWS IN THE STRATEGY OF DISINVESTMENT

The strategy of disinvestment is equally flawed but with potentially far more serious consequences, in the wrong direction than in the case of divestment. Disinvestment requires that all U.S. companies withdraw their investments or "get out of South Africa" if the South African government does not change its apartheid policies.

Left quite unclear is the little matter of how the two actions are related. Or even what the disinvestment or withdrawal means in practical or implementable terms. Ford and Coca-Cola have recently announced a substantial reduction in their investments in South Africa. In practical terms this has meant that both the companies have sold their majority interests to South African businesses controlled by whites. Does it mean that South Africa now has less plant capacity for automobile manufacturing or that they cannot quench thier thirst for Coke? Far from it. This action shows only one thing, a blatant attempt at creating a positive public relations gimmick. We are told that the new owners of Ford and Coke have promised to continue to comply with the Sullivan Principles. But what if they don't?

Most foreign enterprises in South Africa are overwhelmingly managed by the South Africans who are perfectly capable of operating and managing these enterprises without the enlightened guidance of two or three representatives of the foreign owners. When a company chooses to disinvest, it cannot simply lock hundreds and millions of dollars worth of plant and equipment. Even if it could do so, there is nothing to stop the South African government from expropriating the plant, under international law, by paying a "reasonable" compensation to its former owners. It could even be in the form of South African rands that would be payable in installments over a long period of time. In any case, the purchase price will most likely be lower than the value of that enterprise as a "going concern" and, therefore, would represent a significant loss to that company's stockholders.

Alternately, the company would sell its investment to another foreign investor or a domestic South African investor. Given the presence of time and circumstances, the new buyers would realize that the American seller is under tremendous pressure to unload its investment and is, therefore, in no position to bargain for a fair price. Thus these plants are likely to be sold at fire sale prices.

And what is the impact of these acquisitions at bargain basement prices on the South African government? I would say, highly positive. Suppose for the sake of argument that a plant that would ordinarily cost $300 million has been acquired by a South African company for $150 million, thereby effectively reducing its capital costs by half. Now suppose that general economic sanctions against South Africa make it more expensive for this company to acquire foreign technology and spare parts because they have to be bought on the black market. However, the higher prices of those parts are more than offset by the lower cost of capital plant leaving the South African company in a good competitive position. The only losers are the original owners—the foreign companies — and the black workers who would not have the protection of the Sullivan Principles.

The scenario is not as farfetched as it might appear at first glance. The South African companies are loaded with money that they cannot invest overseas because of government restrictions and at home because political turmoil has reduced investment opportunities. Thus these investments are likely to present a lifetime opportunity for them. I am also sure that the South African government would extend them a willing hand in order to insulate more of its domestic economy from the whims of the meddling foreign (read American) corporations.

The proponents of the disinvestment strategy also assert that the impact of U.S. corporations on the black employment in South Africa is negligible and therefore their withdrawal will not impose intolerable burden on the local black population. And yet they seek withdrawal precisely because it would impact the South African economy. The inconsistency and mutually conflicting logic of this argument should be apparent with even a rudimentary analysis.

Congressman Howard Wolpe argues that

there are 70,000 blacks employed in U.S. firms in South Africa which is less than 1 per cent of the entire black labor force.

Beyond that there are 26 million non-whites in South Africa, and I think it should be apparent that to focus even more than a moment of discussion about South Africa upon the fortunes of 70,000 workers or 45,000 workers at the expense of the 26 million has, again, an extraordinary ludicrous ring to it from a South African vantage point. It misses the reality of what South Africa is today.

In the first place a loss of 70,000 direct jobs means a loss of perhaps twice as many jobs lost to businesses who depend on the patronage of workers with earnings from their employment with U.S. firms. So the total number of lost jobs would be far greater than 70,000. Second, as part of extended families, and in many cases the only wage earners, each black worker's income probably feeds four to six people in a family. Thus a complete shutdown of U.S. owned plants would most likely impact between 1.0 to 2.0 million black people.

Moreover, economic theory tells us that overall wage rates in a market are determined at the margin, by the workers who are employed last and laid off first. Since workers in the U.S. firms have traditionally been paid higher wages than other firms and have worked under a more integrated environment, these companies have been exerting competitive pressure on the firms to follow similar practices or risk losing skilled workers or workers in high demand to their U.S. competitors.

In the long run the disinvestment will have an adverse effect on the South African economy and retard its growth rate. This would result because the South Africans would be forced to produce those goods and services that they were hitherto importing from abroad and for which they do not have a comparative advantage. If it were not so, these goods and services would already be produced in South Africa. Thus it would be an inefficient use of resources. Moreover, since South Africa, like all developing economies, would not be able to generate enough domestic savings for investment, its economic growth would be retarded to the extent that foreign capital and technology would not be available. This would be especially so if the disinvestment strategy is pursued on a massive scale involving significant players from other industrialized countries as well, notably those from the United Kingdom and West Germany, a scenario that at this stage appears unlikely.

The biggest gains made by the blacks in South Africa have been made invariably during the periods of rapid economic growth. At present, black South Africans account for almost 50 percent of gross domestic product and therfore a tremendous purchasing power which, if used judiciously, can be an important instrument of change. The recent consumer boycott in Port Elizabeth succeeded precisely because blacks had incomes and purchasing power which they could deny the white businesses in the absence of significant reforms. They would have no such leverage without economic power.

Therefore, it is callous to say that a strategy of disinvestment would not have a serious impact on the black population of South Africa. One should also not forget that a slowdown in the South African economy would also adversely affect its black neighbors. Botswana, Lesotho, Swaziland, Zambia, Malawi, and Zimbabwe all depend on South Africa for trade, employment, transportation, and a host of other services.

The logic of the proponents of the disinvestment strategy grossly underrepresents, if not totally ignores, the costs and sacrifices that would be imposed on the black majority in South Africa. Even if we overlook the suffering that must befall on the black population, we should not underestimate the resiliency of the white minority in holding onto power.

If all else fails, there is the ultimate argument of "taking a moral stand and sending a message to the South African government." Even here the empty rhetoric might be easily dismissed were it not for its frightening impact on the people in whose behalf we are being asked to take a moral stand.

I am not sure there is anyone who thinks that the South African government, the white minority, or for that matter anybody else in the world is unaware of our opposition to apartheid and that we would like to see it dismantled forthwith. Therefore, sending a mesage must mean that if the other party refuses to take any action, certain consequences would follow. I fail to understand the potency of such a message if the South African government knows it is coming, has been preparing for it for a long time, and has good reason to believe that such a message carried little potential clout.

And what about the morality argument? As Helen Suzman points out,

by divesting or disinvesting,. . . any influence that might have been exercised in South Africa, such as setting an example to others regarding adherence to fair employment practices and exercising their social responsibilities, also disappears.

Retribution when it comes is not selective. Indeed it falls more heavily on those it is meant to help than on those it is meant to punish.

It is not the businessmen who put the National Party regime in powers. Most of them support the official opposition party. . . .The government is kept in power by civil servants, programmed over forty years to implement apartheid. About 40 percent of the gainfully employed whites are directly, or indirectly, in government employ.

Herman Nickel, U.S. Ambassador to South Africa, is even more blunt in his denouncement of the "moral stand" argument. He states:

But perhaps the shabbiest argument of all is also the one that is the most pretentious. This is the "moral gesture" rationale and goes something like this: Even if general economic sanctions and disinvestment do not work, it will at least be a symbolic move to put the United States "on the right side." The callousness of this position is staggering. Its proponents openly admit the futility of their gesture. They knowingly advocate a path leading to actions that would inflict suffering and would be at best ineffective and at worst positively harmful — all in order to stand on some imaginary pedestal of moral purity. This kind of feel-good moralism, in fact, falls into the realm more of self-indulgence than of morality.

PROPOSALS FOR ACTION

The problems confronting black South Africans are indeed enormous and they need all the help we can give them. The religious community has condemned apartheid as evil and morally reprehensive. The Christian church is a powerful force for creating world opinion and for keeping up the pressure on the South African government. However, this pressure must be used in measured terms and in full regard of its potential consequences lest we dilute this moral authority. In our desire to do something we should not fail to connect actions with outcomes. Our agony over the plight of blacks in South Africa should not trap us into taking actions that are more pronounced in their symbolism than in their capacity to bring about substantive changes. Otherwise, rather than controlling and shaping events, we would be shaped by them.

In India, during the great migration following the partition of that country and the ensuing communal riots, there was an enormous loss of life and extreme cruelty and misery visited upon the losers on both sides. Those who advocate a faster timetable for sharing political rights in South Africa and clamor for making all the necessary sacrifices do not quite comprehend the bloodshed and the death that such a strategy could cause, nor whether those who would be losing their lives had anything to say about the course of action chosen for them.

There is no question that the church can be a tremendous force for bringing about change in South Africa. Among the steps it can and should take would include

•Pressure on the governments of the industrialized West to increase aid to the South African blacks. This should be accompanied with promise of greater economic cooperation or lack thereof, with the South African government in return for reform measures that are feasible given the political and social reality of both the black and white South Africans.

•Work aggressively to publicize the human rights violations and suppression of other basic freedoms in South Africa in order to create a sense of moral outrage so real and abhorrent that it would energize not only the world opinion but also the whites with South Africa to discard their inhuman system of apartheid.

•Work in cooperation with the business community, both foreign and domestically owned businesses, to create a stronger and more viable economic base for the South African blacks so that they can use their economic power as a positive instrument of change.

•The church leaders should lend their moral support and active encouragement to those foreign corporations who are willing to incur the wrath of the South African government by testing the limits of apartheid laws by constantly challenging them and thereby risking their investments and operational autonomy in South Africa.

•Above all, the church should encourage the process of change, in terms of attainable objectives, both in time and in scope, and to create the necessary preconditions for building a democratic postapartheid South Africa. It would be a real tragedy if in the process of gaining black power, the South African economy were to be seriously damaged. The demands for economic improvement on the part of poor blacks in a postapartheid South Africa will be very high and ordinarily beyond the scope of even the most robust economy. Let us not play a cruel joke on South African blacks by taking them to the Promised Land only to find that it was a mirage and an illusion.

Part I

POLITICAL PERSPECTIVES

CHAPTER 2

Promoting True Democracy in South Africa

by RICHARD G. LUGAR

The United States faces a serious foreign policy challenge in South Africa. Our goals are simple, but the choices we have to make are difficult. The United States wants an end to apartheid. We want democratic rights for all South Africans. We want an economically strong South Africa. And we want South Africa to achieve these goals peacefully. In 1985, the President and Congress reached a consensus on the direction of our policy toward South Africa. This was not done easily, and it will take work to maintain it.

A review of what happened in 1985 is instructive. South Africa burst back onto the political scene in the weeks after President Reagan's landslide reelection in November 1984. Beginning on Thanksgiving Day, black Americans began a year-long protest at the South African embassy in Washington. Many black political leaders saw in South Africa a cause to reassert their influence. Blacks were about the only group in American society that had not supported Ronald Reagan. The policy goal of this protest campaign was U.S. disinvestment from South Africa. Black leaders attacked the Reagan Administration's policy of "constructive engagement," contending that it amounted to nothing more than a wink at apartheid.

Constructive engagement was devised by the Reagan Administration in response to the South African policies of the Carter Administration. The Carter Administration publicly attacked South Africa for its racist policies and attempted to separate the United States from it. The Reagan Administration argued that the Carter approach ignored the geopolitical importance of South Africa as a bastion of anti-communism in Africa. The best way to influence South Africa to change its ways on apartheid was to stay engaged.

The concept of constructive engagement was good, but its implementation was not. Soon after I became chairman of the Senate Foreign Relations Committee, I joined Senator Nancy Kassebaum in writing a letter to President Reagan urging him to speak out against apartheid. The President did so in December 1984, but the political calls for disinvestment continued to mount in Congress. I concluded that disinvestment would be bad policy in that it is an isolationist approach. The United States should instead try to effect reform in South Africa. Washing our hands in moral outrage over apartheid might make us feel good, but it would cause us to lose our influence.

U.S. LEGISLATION

The legislation drafted and passed by both houses of Congress eventually represented this perspective. It was not a disinvestment bill but a bill that attempted both to express U.S. outrage and to exert U.S. influence to encourage reform in South Africa. The legislation imposed some sanctions against South Africa, mandated that all U.S. companies in South Africa follow nondiscriminatory practices, and directed U.S. foreign aid to black community groups in South Africa.

Most of the press attention over this legislation centered on the rather dramatic way in which President Reagan, after opposing the bill, adopted it in the form of an executive order. The sanctions dominated the political discussion, although I believe that what we did to channel aid to black groups was the most significant development for U.S. foreign policy.

Democratic reform is our primary goal in South Africa. Democracy, in fact, is the strongest suit of U.S. foreign policy. Promoting and protecting democracy are in the best interests of the United States. Democratic countries celebrate human rights, they enhance our security interests, and they are good trading partners.

But democracy is not easy. Too often in the past, the United States has naively called for democracy in developing and Third World countries only to see these elections fail. We have tried to prop up self-proclaimed democrats only to see them turn into petty despots. Democracy requires the development of institutions that work against the consolidation of power and open up a society to free political discourse. Political parties, labor unions, business associations, churches, a free press, and citizen groups concerned about the sanctity of the ballot are all required in order to achieve these goals.

American foreign policy should work to develop these democratic institutions throughout the world. We must defend and promote the process of democracy. That is what we did in the Philippines, and that is what we need to do to encourage reform in Nicaragua, Angola, Chile, and South Africa. Each country is different and the politics of each has to be taken into account. But the goal of U.S. foreign policy should be constant: democracy. Once we reach a consensus on that goal, we can go about implementing it within the cultural and geopolitical circumstances of each country.

PHILIPPINES CRISIS

When the Philippines emerged as the next foreign policy crisis point after South Africa in late 1985, there were some members of Congress who argued that we should reject Ferdinand Marcos's call for elections and just cut him off. As with disinvestment, to cut off Marcos would have been an isolationist approach. I feared it would lead to a bloody civil war, growing communist insurgence, and possible U.S. military involvement to protect our bases.

I argued that the United States should support the election process in the Philippines. The election process worked in the Philippines because of U.S. support. Thousands of volunteer poll watchers risked their lives to defend the right to vote and to have a fair count in the Philippines. They set democratic participation and performance standards by which the election could be judged both by Filipinos and by the world. Marcos lost the election. When he tried to claim a fraudulent victory, he lost his legitimacy to rule. The United States was able to help the Filipinos transfer power in a peaceful way because it had positioned itself as a defender of the democratic process and not as a backer of one of the candidates.

In a very simple but powerful way, the Philippines experience points the way to a new U.S. foreign policy based on free and fair democratic elections. This is a corollary in some respects to both the Kirkpatrick and the Reagan doctrines.

The Kirkpatrick doctrine, on which constructive engagement has some basis, argued that there is a difference between authoritarian regimes led by anticommunist dictators and totalitarian regimes led by communist dictators. Kirkpatrick argues that the United States should be tough on communist dictators and help the authoritarian rulers evolve toward democracy. The Reagan doctrine argues that the United States should actively back freedom fighters struggling against communist totalitarian regimes. The corollary to these two doctrines is that the United States should be promoting democracy in these dictatorships. I believe there should be free and fair elections, not only in the Philippines but also in Chile, Nicaragua, and South Africa.

Actively supporting democracy offers a consistency and an element of consensus that our foreign policy has lacked since Vietnam. President Reagan has led this country past the Vietnam syndrome. He is not afraid to act, and the American people are again proud of our role in the world. However, we are still debating how we can be both effective and true to our beliefs as we deal with the many crises of the world.

One of my distinguished predecessors on the Senate Foreign Relations Committee, J. William Fulbright, criticized the foreign policy that led this nation into the Vietnam War. He called it the "arrogance of power." But after the fall of Vietnam, our foreign policy became the "abdication of power." It was a policy of moral outrage but no action. The United States withdrew from the world.

Disinvestment from South Africa is such an isolationist policy of moral outrage without action. The United States will have to make some hard choices in South Africa, but it needs to maintain its influence in a hands-on manner to support those commerical and legal interests in South Africa that are working for equal opportunity and the development of democratic institutions.

The United States cannot force a one-man, one-vote government on South Africa. Although this has great emotional appeal in our country, in its pure form it is a truly nonnegotiable situation in South Africa. Our demands for fundamental human rights, economic and political freedom, and citizenship must include universal individual voting and yet maintain an atmosphere in which a unique constitutional system for one-man, one-vote principles could be utilized by an equitable South African government.

We should use our influence to keep open as many options as possible. Political polarization and economic decline cripple all efforts for a peaceful solution in South Africa. An attempt to be a trusted and stable friend to both white and black South Africans, and to encourage their progress (because it also promotes our progress), is the only practical road to democracy. We cannot risk being pushed off a tightrope by righteous and emotional persons in either country. They may claim to be comfortable with events leading to civil war, but the effects would be devastating and grave, serving neither black nor white. We need to stay involved and help pave the way to peace, before, and not after, war.

CHAPTER 3

Caution Signs on the Road to Reform

by NANCY LANDON KASSEBAUM

The year 1986 has turned out to be crucial in South Africa's history. Black protest against apartheid and demand for political rights have risen steadily and show no signs of subsiding. The country is experiencing the highest level of violence and economic disruption ever. The intentions of the government for the future remain unknown — is it willing to begin a process that could lead to power sharing, or does it hope to hold the line against fundamental change?

The current crisis in South Africa, I think it is vitally important that the United States consider its own role carefully. American emotions on the South African question have run high in the past years (for understandable reasons). Nevertheless, if we are to have a positive impact on that troubled land, we must let reason and not emotion guide our actions.

Although the debate about U.S. policy in South Africa is highly polarized, I think there is substantial agreement on what the basic goal of our policy should be. It is to move South Africa toward more rapid and real change and to maximize the chances of achieving political justice without catastrophic violence. The question is how best to do this. I believe that a prudent American policy in South Africa has to be based on a realistic understanding of the forces at work in South Africa as well as the sources and limits of American influence.

I am not one who takes a sanguine view of the reform momentum of the National Party and the leadership of State President Botha. President Botha has made some significant reforms, particularly in comparison to the apartheid paradigms that were in force when he came into office. But these paradigms were already self-evidently obsolete.

The labor restrictions, the lack of trade union rights, the notion that urban blacks were temporary sojourners in the white areas, and other restrictions of the late 1970s were at odds with the requirements of South Africa's industrial economy. Changing these things was not a concession to blacks but a recognition of economic rationality that benefited both blacks and whites.

The one political initiative that the Botha government has taken — the granting of representation to coloureds and Indians in multiple parliaments — is ambiguous in terms of its implications for the future. The government has portrayed it as a starting point for further change that will include blacks, but blacks have viewed it as an expansion of the white laager to incorporate everyone but themselves. And, of course, this black perception was a key factor in the beginning of the current unrest.

That unrest has raised the ante of acceptable change. Whereas about two years ago it appeared that the South African government was in control of events, and that blacks had no choice but to accept the pace and shape of reform dictated by the government, the situation now is different. By their willingness to put their lives on the line and to accept the costs of social and economic disruption, blacks in the urban areas, particularly the youth, have brought about a change in the balance of political power in South Africa, which has put the government on the defensive. "Reform" can no longer be defined solely in terms of what whites are willing to give; it must also take into account what blacks are willing to accept.

This new dynamic creates a challenge for the Nationalist government that is quite different from the challenge that President Botha faced in 1978. Incremental reform on socioeconomic issues remains important, but political issues can no longer be put off for the indefinite future (or for "our children's children," as Botha once said). Blacks are now insisting that the political question be addressed and are refusing to participate in the normal activities of the economy and education until it is.

The question for the Botha government today is: Having taken one step to deal with the socioeconomic aspects of apartheid, can it now take a second step to deal — or begin to deal — with the basic question of political power? I don't think we should be excessively optimistic about the prospect of the government taking this second step. Not only would it require Afrikanerdom to confront its most basic assumptions about group protection and the dangers of black power, but it would also require a degree of political vision and energy that the Botha government does not appear to possess at this stage. Nor is there any dominant figure waiting in the wings who offers a great deal more promise. One positive sign is the recent efforts by whites outside the government to explore options for negotiation, symbolized by a series of visits to the ANC in Lusaka. This suggests that there may be some hope for a more flexible government position in the future.

BLACK UNREST

Meanwhile, black disaffection and unrest continue at a level that few thought possible two years ago. As in the Soweto unrest of 1976, the protest has been led by a youthful vanguard, but the resulting repression has had a radicalizing impact on blacks of all ages. Unlike the situation in 1976, there have been signs of the new militancy extending even to many rural areas, which in the past have been relatively quiescent.

It is hard to say where black resistance is heading. Many feel that the costs of continued unrest will eventually force a downturn of protest. But that has not happened yet. Indeed, in some ways militancy is being institutionalized in the complex of community organizations and groups that exist in the townships, making it irreversible.

The role of the economy should not be underestimated. Businessmen have always argued that economic recession and unemployment play a key role in black unrest, and that seems to be the case in the current unrest as well. Black youth are in the streets for political reasons, but they have been influenced by the limited opportunities that would be available to them if they were to stay inside the system.

The ANC does not control the urban unrest, but it has gained in political weight and influence as a result of it. Progressive whites feel that the ANC is the only body that has the potential of exerting overall leadership of blacks of the kind that will be required if serious negotiation is ever to take place. This is one reason that the question of Nelson Mandela's release is so important. Mandela is the only individual who can claim the mantle of leader of all black South Africans.

Recently, there have been some indications that the ANC would be willing to consider a negotiation course if it felt that the South African government were serious about power sharing. This relatively moderate position represents an asset and an opportunity, which South Africa should not ignore.

AMERICAN POLICY

The debate about the appropriate U.S. response to this situation is vigorous and vocal, not the least in Congress. Some have criticized the Reagan Administration's policy of constructive engagement from the beginning. But in the past year, in response to the unrest in South Africa and vivid images on American TV screens, dissatisfaction with that policy and demand for tougher pressure have multiplied rapidly.

This was the motivation for the congressional legislation of last summer, which imposed limited restrictions on American dealings with South Africa, focused on the South African government. President Reagan's reluctant endorsement of these terms (implemented in an executive order) constituted at least a partial shift from the assumptions of prior policy. Many in Congress wanted to go farther. And if there is a new deterioration of the situation in South Africa, I have no doubt that calls for stronger pressures will be renewed with broader support. The earlier legislation observed a boundary between penalties aimed at the South African government (which were included) and restrictions aimed at the South African private sector (which were not). Whether to cross this threshold and, if so, how will be the main issues if events in South Africa cause Congress to take up this matter again. This could take the form of partial or total restrictions on American investment and/or bank loans.

My own feeling is that such restrictions should be approached with caution. I feel this way for several reasons. First, the desire to restrict economic relations is often driven by an impulse to sever links with a repugnant country or regime rather than by an assessment of practical results. We may reach a point in South Africa where things get so bad and the prospects for the future so hopeless that we conclude that the only defensible response is to get out. But until that point is reached, I believe that the United States must resist the temptation to withdraw and stay focused on using its leverage for positive influence.

There is a real trade-off between withdrawal and influence, because the latter depends on the leverage of existing ties. I believe that the U.S. aim should be to exert positive influence as long as there is hope of progress in South Africa. I think that the burden of proof should be on those who want to withdraw, not on those who want to work for influence. Unfortunately, political reactions are likely to go the other way.

Second, I have always been skeptical of the value of economic sanctions as a vehicle for influencing the actions of another country. I think the evidence is pretty clear at this point that sanctions seldom if ever cause the target state to say, "OK, I see that you don't like what I have been doing, so I will now change my ways." What usually happens is that the target state does nothing different, relations become more adversarial, and both the imposing and target states bear costs. In the case of South Africa, this would be particularly unfortunate because of the capacity of the government to shift costs disproportionately to blacks.

Sanctions can be useful for showing our moral or political opposition, and for "taking a stand." But we should not confuse this with foreign policy influence. The threat of economic penalties can play a role in influence, but if one gets to the point of actually imposing the penalties, the game is usually over.

Third, we already have a threat of economic cutoff by private forces that is quite powerful. Proposals for official governmental restrictions have to be considered in light of private pressures that already exist. Two types of private economic cutbacks have occurred. One is the halt of nearly all bank lending by Western countries, which began in August 1986. This was a purely market phenomenon, which reflected the banks' uncertainty about South Africa's future. Recently, the banks have agreed to limited rescheduling of debt, but no new loans have been granted.

CORPORATE BAILOUT

The second cutback is a modest reduction of the U.S. corporate presence in South Africa over the past several years and active questioning by a large number of businesses of the wisdom of remaining in South Africa. The investment reduction also occurred primarily because of market forces. Little new investment flowed in because of the political uncertainty and the recession, and several companies cut back their scale of operation or sold out entirely. Recently, many U.S. firms have begun to seriously question South Africa as an investment environment, because of the political risk and the low level of return.

The lending cutoff has had the most dramatic impact on South Africa. It has reduced the value of the rand to unprecedented levels and cast a pall over business confidence within South Africa. The disinvestment trend to date has been modest, but the South African government is quite aware of the doubts about South Africa as an investment environment and knows that this feeling affects other Western investors as well.

Thus, today, we have an effective halt of new lending and investment as well as a threat of investment reduction by private action, both linked (at least indirectly) to the issues of political stability and reform. This exerts a very tangible form of pressure, which has had a substantial impact on the political environment in South Africa and especially on the attitudes of the white business community.

With these pressures in place, one has to ask what the value of official economic restrictions would be. A ban on new investment might have symbolic value, but it would not alter the status quo. Legislated threats of disinvestment might reinforce the existing private trend, but they could also prompt a defiant response on the South African side. Historically, South Africa has tended to respond pragmatically to threats of private withdrawal, such as the beginning of capital flight during the Soweto unrest, but defiantly to governmental threats and criticisms, as in the case of the Carter administration's pressures. Actual disinvestment would only convert an existing threat that exerts leverage into a fait accompli that does not.

Thus, even if one believes that real influence requires tangible pressure, a persuasive argument can be made that we have an effective form of economic pressure in place, as a result of private mechanisms. Those who want to add official restrictions should show how their proposals would increase tangible pressure and not cause a backlash.

A case can be made that the whole issue of official economic restrictions has been overtaken by events. With private pressures in place, we should be worrying more about other aspects of the problem — how to push the South African government over the line to negotiation, how to facilitate leadership on the black side, and how to prepare ourselves to play a mediation role. Arguments about disinvestment are less relevant than such questions as whether the United States should give greater recognition to the ANC, what initiatives we should press South Africa to take in the next six months to establish a modicum of trust on the black side, and how the United States can better present its political position to black South Africans.

South Africa is at a vulnerable and sensitive stage. It is undergoing intensive strains from within and without. History suggests that a country with such deep divisions and inequalities has a high risk of breakdown into major conflict. In such a situation, the United States must act carefully and with foresight. We will need all the wisdom we can muster if we are really to have a positive effect. Above all, we should not add our own emotional impulse to a situation that is already supercharged.

CHAPTER 4

The Double Standard of American Foreign Policy

by HOWARD WOLPE

The situation in southern Africa is a critically important matter that requires the urgent attention of all Americans. It is no secret that Africa, for most Americans, is a very different and distant continent. There is a whole series of mythologies, of stereotypes, of feelings, of attitudes about race, about people of color that has very dramatically affected the way we have looked at Africa. It should be no surprise, therefore, that U.S. foreign policy toward the African continent, not only in the Reagan years but literally for decades, has frequently been counterproductive because it is based against a backdrop of some of that mythology, of that attitudinal set that we, as a society, have brought in the way we approach the continent.

There has been a tendency, as people look at South Africa, to project the American experience with race, racism, and with the civil rights movement onto the South African scene. The argument usually advanced in terms of facilitating nonviolent, evolutionary change is a referencing of the American experience: It takes time; attitudes must change; there must be a process in the economy and the society that will eventually trigger political change. But the important point is to understand that in two critical respects the South African experience is not like the American experience and, consequently, politics based on the assumptions of similarities is doomed to boomerang and to be counterproductive.

The first key distinction is that South Africa is, in fact, not a liberal democracy but a totalitarian police state. It is also one of the most brutal, repressive societies in the world.

I had the opportunity to spend one night in the black township of Soweto right outside Johannesburg, South Africa some years ago. This area has a densely concentrated population of about 1.25 million people who are housed within 100,000 living units. It's illegal under South African law for a white person to stay in a black area even for one night. (As visiting members of Congress, we were allowed certain privileges.) But I will never forget black Sowetians describing to me their perception that one out of every ten of their neighbors was a police spy, the reason being that the women and children who are living in Soweto are, for the most part, there illegally. They've come to join their men who are working in the mines. They do not have work permits and if they fail to cooperate with police, they're immediately subject to deportation to the so-called homelands or Bantustans.

You cannot comprehend the South African reality unless you understand the penetration by the police into every element of South African society. It creates levels of distress, disunity, suspicion, and paranoia that only a police state could fuel. The fact is that to protest, to dissent, to challenge the system of apartheid in any respect is literally to put one's life and liberty into jeopardy. That is why it sounds ludicrous to the South African ear when well-intending Americans talk about evolutionary change occurring as more blacks receive education and employment.

Second, and equally critical, majority-minority relationships are reversed. In the United States, whites are the majority; the excluded are the black minority. The white majority could countenance full political rights for the black minority without ever fearing they would lose ultimate control of the national political system by virtue of their control of the majority.

That is not so in South Africa. Clearly, political rights for the entire population will mean a loss of political control and of special economic privileges for the white minority. Political change need not mean the exclusion of whites from the political process any more than it has meant exclusion of blacks from the political process in the United States. However, it will mean a loss of political control and a loss of special economic privileges. So the political dynamic is very different and needs to be understood.

The second mythology that has underpinned much of the debate that has occurred in this country over many years about South Africa is that somehow economic change is inevitably linked to a process of political liberalization and democratization. Indeed, it is that argument that underpins those who would advocate that we should give great emphasis to the importance of the Sullivan Principles and seeing to it that U.S. companies become signatories. The notion is that the presence of U.S. companies constitutes a positive model of desegregation and that the skills that are being acquired by blacks in the industrial workplace will ultimately facilitate political change as well.

First of all, there is no question in the limited respects that I have just described that the Sullivan code has been positive. Indeed, there is a different kind of model of labor-management relationship, desegregated workplaces, and, for some very limited number of people, improved economic conditions. There are a total of 70,000 blacks employed in U.S. firms, which is less than 1 percent of the entire black labor force and at this time the "Sullivan" firms represent only about two thirds of that 70,000 population. Beyond that, there are 26 million nonwhites in South Africa, and I think it should be apparent that to focus even more than a moment of the discussion about South Africa upon the fortunes of 70,000 workers or 45,000 at the expense of the 26 million has, again, an extraordinarily ludicrous ring to it from a South African vantage point. It misses the reality of what South Africa is today.

There is, moreover, clear evidence in history if we look at Nazi Germany, Stalinist Russia, and indeed at South Africa itself, that economic change need not be accompanied by increased democratization and liberalization but may well be accompanied by increased repression. Over the past couple of decades, despite all the industrialization, all the economic change in process in South Africa, repression has intensified. Apartheid has been consolidated. It has not been weakened in any respect.

There is finally a third proposition to be offered up: We need to understand clearly how racial considerations have distorted our perception and understanding of the South African experience. If, in fact, the racial complexion of minority and majority were reversed in South Africa and you had a black minority imposing this horrendous system of apartheid on a white majority, do you really think that, over the past several decades, this country would have engaged in a long and tortuous debate about the ethics or wisdom of the application of sanctions? Would we be engaging in a very involved discussion of the efficacy and ethics, if you will, of nonviolence?

If we are honest with ourselves, the answer is clearly in the negative.

Indeed, if we were to look at other parts of the world where we have had somewhat similar experiences, whether we talk about the Soviet invasion of Afghanistan or the actions by the Polish state government in suppressing the Polish trade union movement, we would have clear instances where the United States not only responded instantly with sanctions, but that question was not even very controversial within our own society, Congress, or within the executive branches of our government no matter who the President was at the time. We have even gone so far as to extend, in the case of Afghanistan, moral as well as material support to people who were resisting Soviet oppression. We have characterized those who are engaged in the struggle for liberation in Afghanistan as "freedom fighters" and, in the Polish case, our President appeared on television calling on all Americans to light a candle in our windows at night as a symbol of our solidarity with the Polish trade union movement.

How different our response has been when it comes to South Africa. The subject of sanctions is enormously emotive and controversial, as well as the whole texture of the language that we use in discussing the subject of changes. Instead of talking about people fighting for liberation, suddenly we are discussing terrorism and the terrorists of the African National Congress.

DOUBLE STANDARD

We have to look at that because the rest of the world understands clearly that the United States, indeed, is applying a double standard in its approach to South Africa in contrast to its approach to these other situations around the world. When that double standard is so manifest, it clearly has important ramifications for U.S. interests around the world.

The policies of constructive engagement, indeed, I would argue, the policy of Sullivan code advocacy, is a direct consequence of the application of some of the mythologies described. And because that advocacy and these policies are based on mythology, they've had some terribly counterproductive consequences both in terms of the process of change in South Africa and in terms of U.S. national interests. These initiatives have been justified as the means of facilitating nonviolent, evolutionary change, yet the principal consequence of the policy of constructive engagement has been to signal to the Afrikaners and to the regime that they have a much freer hand to do what they will, both internally and within the region. What the policy essentially said, not only implicitly but actually explicitly, was that no matter how repressive the regime is in its internal policies, no matter how much aggression is launched against neighboring states, there will be no cost imposed in terms of the South African-American relationship. There would be no significant measure of international isolation that would flow from those initiatives by the South African government.

What has happened as a consequence of constructive engagement is greater repression, more violence, and more bloodshed. In the past five years, not only has there been a massive increase in police brutality in South Africa but also a massive escalation of the forced removal of urban blacks to so-called Bantustans or homelands. Over the last eighteen months, South Africa has experienced a great intensification of mass protest followed by severe state repression. More than 1,200 people have been killed, mainly by the government's security forces, and over 36,000 women, children and men have been arrested.

Further, in the region itself, South Africa has occupied the neighboring country of Angola for most of the past five years. It has launched brutal raids, violating international law, into Mozambique, Lesotho, and Botswana. It has attempted to overthrow the government of the Seychelles; it has sought to destabilize the government of Zimbabwe. As a consequence of constructive engagement, not only have these developments flowed from the South African knowledge that there would not be any penalty imposed and no American reaction, but the U.S. is now implicated in those developments.

The abandonment of apartheid and a commitment to negotiations will occur only when the white minority regime concludes that there are more costs than benefits to be derived from maintaining the system of apartheid. That calculation will be a product of both the internal pressures that are building within the country and the pressures from the international community.

BUSINESS AS USUAL

Every time the United States, our international leaders, or our President engages in temporizing statements verbally condemning apartheid on the one hand but allowing business as usual to flow on the other, claiming that there is progress taking place—when most reasonable people do not see progress taking place—those statements bolster the Afrikaners in the belief that they can maintain the system indefinitely without fundamental economic cost. The Afrikaaners want to believe that the United States' current interest in South Africa is only a temporary passing phenomenon. They want to believe desperately that the repression they are mounting now will eventually produce political quiescence within South Africa. When we provide the kinds of statements that reinforce the belief that they can, in fact, hold on indefinitely without fundamental cost and without significant isolation, we thereby prolong the decision point and the struggle. And just as important, we delay negotiations and the effort to seek a political accommodation.

Second, not only has constructive engagement encouraged greater repression and violence, but it has also alienated the black majority liberation movements within the region. We are told constantly that South Africa is anticommunist and we therefore must understand that too much pressure cannot be applied for fear of losing an important ally in the struggle against communism. The reality is that South Africa itself is an open invitation to communism. As long as the system of apartheid is in place, as long as South Africa maintains its illegal occupation of Namibia and continues to be a regional aggressor, there will be a struggle for liberation. If we do not want those who are struggling for their freedom to turn to the East, to the Soviets, or to others, then we had better not be ambivalent or ambiguous in the way in which we identify ourselves with that process of liberation.

Third, policies that we have pursued up to this point have clearly compromised American moral authority. We simply cannot approach the rest of the Third World with credibility as long as we maintain the kind of double standard that we have applied in the South African case. In short, current policies that have been applied, at least up until recently, not only have compromised American national values but have very significantly compromised American national interests.

LEGISLATIVE INITIATIVES

Against the backdrop of worsening internal repression and regional crisis in southern Africa, along with the failure of constructive engagement, I and a number of my colleagues are closely examining recent developments in South Africa in an effort to develop a legislative strategy that recasts our foreign policy toward South Africa.

Last year, the House of Representatives passed the Anti-Apartheid Act of 1985 — Conference Report. The major components of the bill included an immediate ban on Krugerrand imports, a ban on bank loans to the public sector, strengthened prohibitions on any kind of nuclear cooperation, and sanctions within one year of enactment of the bill if the South African government had not shown signs of dismantling apartheid. Before the compromise effort could be completed, the President issued Executive Order 12532 on September 9, 1985. The Executive Order was significantly weaker than the House-Senate Conference Report. The only sanction incorporated from the Conference Report was the ban on Krugerrands. While the Executive Order does send a signal to the South African government, weak as it may be, most of my colleagues and I in Congress do not feel that it is strong enough.

LEGISLATIVE STRATEGY

Thus, the overall legislative strategy for 1986 will be pressure for increased economic sanctions to convey to both the white minority South African government and Africans that the United States opposes apartheid. New sanctions could include most of those in the Anti-Apartheid Act of 1985, which contained bans on both new investment and bank loans on imports of South African coal and uranium and restrictions on nuclear-related exports to South Africa and exports of computers to the South African government. Other possible sanctions include bans on U.S. military attaches in South Africa, landing rights for South African Airways, and a consideration of conditional disinvestment in a strategic industry if apartheid is not dismantled by a specified time. It is critical that the legislation of 1986 should reflect our understanding that the situation in South Africa has worsened considerably.

Congress realizes that this legislation will impact on the corporate community, but we must be concerned with the ethical and political implications of corporate decisionmaking in the South African context. One of the things that needs to be understood is that the U.S. business community does have enormous impact within the South African setting, not only directly economically, but even more psychologically and politically. We have witnessed recently, with the decision by the United States to impose limited economic sanctions, with U.S. banks' decisions in August 1985 to demand repayment of loans, with the collapse of the rand and the extreme vulnerability of the South African economy, a sudden emergence of more pragmatic voices within the minority, African-speaking as well as English-speaking, calling on the government to abandon apartheid and begin the process of negotiation with the leadership of the African National Congress. None of that would have occurred were it not for the pressures and the economic, psychological, and political fragility of the regime.

GO IT ALONE?

There is a myth the South African government likes to propagate which is, "They can go it alone; there is nothing that we could do that would have any impact upon that society." Let me suggest that they would not be investing the enormous dollars that they do in America, in public relations and lobbying, if that were really a valid proposition. The Afrikaners care deeply about American public opinion and American political response.

That is not to say that the application of economic sanctions of disinvestment, in and of itself, is going to bring down apartheid. It is not. It is to say, however, that we are into a process where the regime will, in the end, be responding to a combination of both internal pressures and pressures from the external community.

We need to understand that there may be a decision made for narrow corporate profit reasons to stay in South Africa, but please understand that the decision is not facilitating the process of change; it is sustaining apartheid. It is sustaining Afrikaaners in the belief that this is a system that is economically viable over the long haul. When we argue that blacks would be hurt by sanctions and that they are the people we're trying to help, let me suggest that it is the black response in South Africa itself that is the most eloquent rebuttal to that concern.

BLACK PROTEST

Blacks every day are exposing themselves not only to the loss of their jobs and enormous economic risks but to loss of life by demonstrations, by economic boycotts, and by the petitioning that is in process within that society. For black South Africans, ameliorative economic progress within an overall system that denies them political power to protect and expand their gains and even deprives them of their citizenship is completely unacceptable. Black leaders acknowledge that sanctions may well cause economic pain to some blacks, but they are persuaded that the longer apartheid continues, the greater will be the economic and human costs.

An excellent example of black South Africans' commitment to this position occurred last year. Mine workers were called together by their leaders asking them to decide whether they wanted to support the Krugerrand prohibition that was part of the congressional sanctions legislation that the President has since imposed. These were the people who were most directly impacted by the Krugerrand legislation. They voted unanimously to support the Krugerrand prohibition, not simply because they recognize that there are no real short-term economic costs that might flow from the imposition of sanctions, but because they are persuaded that it is the only hope to avoid greater long-term costs, both economically and in terms of life itself. The economic and diplomatic pressures, in combination, represent the only alternatives to trying to move the regime as quickly as possible to the point of negotiations with the black majority.

We must act now to recast our foreign policy toward South Africa. In southern Africa, human, political, economic, and social rights are being trampled on every day, and the United States, all of its rhetoric notwithstanding, is still seen as a party to South Africa's ultimate purpose to dominate and control southern Africa politically and economically and to maintain racial supremacy at all costs. It is hoped that the legislative actions will send the correct signals to the South African government. That government should have no doubt concerning the U.S. government's stand on apartheid, on the question of Namibia's independence, and on South Africa's regional aggression. It should know that its continued intransigence on these matters will precipitate changes in its relationship with the United States and that those changes will prove costly.

American foreign policy interests in Africa, in the long and short term, require a redirection of U.S. policy toward South Africa. We cannot continue to struggle to achieve a just society at home and equivocate on our international obligations abroad. The racism and the denial of political rights we will not tolerate at home must not be condoned by our posture overseas. Our national interests dictate that we act on South Africa before it is too late.

CHAPTER 5

The Limits of American Influence

by J. DOUGLAS HOLLADAY

Churchill's memorable description of the Soviet Union equally applies to South Africa: "A riddle wrapped in a mystery inside an enigma." South Africa is a deeply troubled land riddled with numerous internal contradictions. Americans are concerned about events within the Republic of South Africa. The issues there engage our sympathies and test our resolve as well as our patience.

In the United States, the South African question has assumed a prominent profile. The domestic debate is highly charged and emotional. Perceptions rather than substance seem to dictate one's understanding of this volatile issue. Yet, on one matter all Americans are clear and unambiguous: Apartheid is wrong and the process of change must be accelerated.

South Africa continues to be a polarized nation. Blacks and whites are highly suspicious of one another and look at their country from two very different vantage points. For white South Africans, the pace of change has been monumental, even revolutionary. Power sharing and negotiations are called for by the white leadership; the state of emergency has finally been lifted; apartheid has been branded as "outdated" by the State President; the government has announced that political domination, petty discrimination, economic and educational inequality, and even the hated pass laws are to be eliminated. An undivided South Africa has been called for with a common citizenship and a universal franchise. These are statements of intent previously unthinkable by the National Party government. For some whites, such proposed changes inspire fear; in others they provoke resistance; to still others they offer the promise of a more just and peaceful society.

Observing these same events, many black South Africans see matters very differently. They view the changes that have occurred as marginal and cosmetic at best, failing to address the fundamental issues of injustice and power sharing. Regardless of the concessions that have been made or promised, the realilty is that blacks still lack full citizenship. They cannot vote for national leaders. They must send their children to inferior schools. They are confined to exclusively black areas where crime, intimidation, and the presence of security forces are far too commonplace.

In such an atmosphere, where after twenty months of violence there have been more than 11,000 recorded detentions and 1,300 deaths, it is hardly surprising that politics are further polarized. Nor is it surprising that the South African government should find apartheid considerably more difficult to dismantle than to impose.

FIVE ASSUMPTIONS

This article outlines the assumptions behind U.S. policy toward South Africa and the concrete actions the United States government is taking to aid South Africans in reaching a political settlement in the midst of great political strife. First, South Africans alone should determine their country's destiny. Whatever political arrangement emerges over time in South Africa, it must be the result of negotiation, compromise, and statesmanship by the people of South Africa, both black and white. No settlement can be imposed from outside, by the United States or by any other country. We have no formula for social and political change in South Africa beyond the firm belief that a just system of government exists only with the consent of all the governed.

Second, the "South African problem" is really a southern African problem. South Africa is an economic giant closely tied to all of southern Africa. For reasons of geography, history, and economics, all the nations in that region form a matrix that manifests itself in a symbiotic relationship. South Africa's mines, factories, and cities magnetically attract people from as far away as Malawi in pursuit of hard currency. Once employed, these citizens of neighboring African countries send their paychecks home. Such remittances play a considerable role in the cash-poor economies of southern African countries.

Similarly, a well-developed transportation network links southern Africa from north to south and from east to west. Minerals and other products originating in Zaire, Zimbabwe, Zambia, and Botswana are sent by rail to South Africa from which many are then exported for processing or consumption in other parts of the world. In turn, manufactured goods, food, and energy resources from South Africa and abroad are sent by rail, pipeline, and power line back to the surrounding countries through South Africa. If South Africa's political drama deteriorates into a bloody racial quagmire, the violence and instability will no doubt affect — deeply and adversely — South Africa's regional neighbors.

Third, U.S. leverage, while significant, is limited. The United States, although a global power since World War I, did not play a role in Africa's colonial period. It lacks the ties of kinship and history that, for example, Britain and France have had on the continent. Less than 1 percent of all U.S. investment abroad is found in South Africa. Foreign investment overall accounts for only 10 percent of capital investment there. The U.S. portion — less than $2 billion — is less than 2 percent of total direct investment in South Africa. This hardly represents the kind of economic leverage that could by itself bring apartheid to an end.

Our influence is principally moral, political, and diplomatic. But our greatest leverage is perhaps psychological. The United States is a nation that has derived strength from its diversity to become a democracy of unrivaled global power. This fact stands as a reproach to the exclusionary policies of South Africa. Nonetheless, many Americans and South Africans believe that U.S. power to bring about change in South Africa is virtually limitless. This misperception is naive and dangerous.

STRONG NATION

Fourth, South Africa is not weak. South Africa is not an inconsequential third-rate power or a client-state of the United States. It is a nation with vast natural resources and a highly developed economic infrastructure of highways, railroads, and electrical power lines. It is a resilient country that has risen above embargoes and trade restrictions placed on it over the past twenty-five years. In the face of an oil embargo against it, South Africa became the world's technological leader in extracting oil from coal. In the face of the United Nations arms embargo, which the United States fully supports, South Africa became self-sufficient in munitions and weapons production. In fact, South Africa is now among the top ten exporters of arms to the rest of the world. We are dealing with a strong, productive nation not easily susceptible to external pressure or sanctions.

Fifth, a growing economy can be a force for change. The main impetus for change in South Africa is internal. The greatest enemy of apartheid is a functioning, growing economy and an expanding work force which requires skilled labor, regardless of skin color. Black labor unions and purchasing power are giving the black majority additional political leverage and the white business and industrial community clearly supports the peaceful advent of political equality.

Economic growth over the past twenty years and desire to maintain it provoked South African authorities to increase the money spent on black education (still woefully inadequate), legalize black and multiracial trade unions, and repeal the job reservation laws that restricted certain occupations to whites or blacks only. Economic growth has affected the way in which laws restricting the free movement of blacks within the country have been enforced and interpreted by the courts.

Economic growth does not automatically or inevitably lead to political liberalization, but it clearly expands the prospects for peaceful change, just as economic decline diminishes them. In South Africa, economic growth has without a doubt accelerated the pace of change in a constructive direction.

In recent years, the South African black consumer has played an increasingly important role in the economy. South African merchants and manufacturers now look more carefully at their domestic markets and provide greater choices for black consumers. The most important factor is the enhanced purchasing power provided by higher wages; blacks now buy more goods and services than whites do. It can be argued that the success of recent black-led consumer boycotts against white-owned businesses in the Eastern Cape stemmed directly from the fact that blacks had money to withhold. Increased purchasing power brings with it the power not to purchase, a potent force in influencing social change.

The U.S. government and individual U.S. citizens and institutions can assist in concrete ways those most disadvantaged by the exclusionary policies of South Africa. Over the next two years, $45 million will be allocated by the U.S. government to address the humanitarian dimension of this problem. For example, the U.S. government has established a human rights fund, which amounted to $500,000 in 1984 and $1 million last year, to help support important, but underfunded, anti-apartheid groups within South Africa. Grants distributed through the

U.S. embassy in Pretoria have been used for seminars on human rights, education in resettlement areas, and legal books and aid for lawyers who are challenging apartheid laws in the courts.

The U.S. government provides scholarships for black South Africans to help address the enormous need for education. Last year, we spent almost $5 million to bring South African students to American universities and colleges. This year, scholarship aid will be expanded to $10 million, including a program to help pay the tuition and expenses of 200 black students attending South African universities. These schools were formally segregated but now admit students of all races. An additional $2 million was used to assist black high school students preparing for university admissions tests.

The U.S. government has spent $1.9 million to train black labor leaders in negotiation, organization, and other important skills necessary for their success. The AFL-CIO has been instrumental in guiding this program.

Taking advantage of recent changes in the apartheid laws that now allow black businessmen to operate their concerns in downtown business districts (formerly restricted to white-owned firms), we have provided $3 million to train black entrepreneurs desiring to begin businesses in urban areas. A special fund of approximately $250,000 annually has aided self-help projects since 1983 in black townships and rural areas. These projects are helping black South Africans improve their communities' facilities in medicine, education, and employment expansion.

PRIVATE EFFORTS

Such activities are also financed and run by individual U.S. citizens and organizations. Dozens of U.S. universities and colleges, for instance, are recruiting promising South African students for study in the fields of engineering, medicine, law, and other subjects. One charitable group collects funds for scholarships at the University of the Western Cape, a school attended primarily by students of mixed racial descent. Another group funnels new and used books to the library at Vista University outside Pretoria, which provides on-campus and correspondence courses for South Africans of all races. In addition, American church groups have initiated clergy exchange programs.

Add to the efforts of private organizations the positive role U.S. corporations are playing in South Africa. American companies with operations in South Africa clearly understand that working in South Africa differs substantially from running a business in Mexico, Belgium, or Japan. Therefore, the great majority, more than 200 of these companies, have signed the Sullivan Principles of fair employment practices. They have pioneered the way in South Africa by desegregating facilities, giving equal pay for equal work, organizing training programs to upgrade skills of black employees, and helping improve the lives of disadvantaged black South Africans outside the workplace. Since 1978, U.S. firms have spent more than $145 million on such housing, education, and social welfare projects.

For example, the Gillette Company has established a legal clinic to assist its own employees as well as other members of its community in confronting apartheid laws. More recently, General Motors publicly committed financial support for legal assistance to any black employee arrested for violating "whites only" beaches in Port Elizabeth. That highly publicized action spurred the Port Elizabeth City Council to end segregation of that city's beaches. American firms have been, and continue to be, an important force for change in the increasingly polarized South African context.

REJECT SANCTIONS

Imposing punitive economic sanctions on South Africa is a lot like the old magic trick where you pull the linen tablecloth out from under an elegant dinner setting. If it works, it is wonderful. If it fails, the fine china and crystal are destroyed; the silverware may be dented but not seriously harmed. Similarly, economic sanctions, if they are potent enough, threaten to harm the most fragile elements of South African society—the disadvantaged and disenfranchised black workers and their families—while having little or no real effect on the stronger, more economically viable members of society.

Those who advocate punitive economic sanctions believe damage must be inflicted on the South African economy to force a political settlement. The U.S. government does not share this simplistic view. The history of economic sanctions demonstrates that they are slow to work, easy to circumvent, and unlikely to achieve the intended results. Were they effective, however, in destabilizing South Africa's economy, economic growth would be blunted and a whole generation of South Africa's young would be condemned to unemployment, hunger, and despair. Many young black South Africans are already educated, politicized, and unemployed—an explosive combination. Indeed, three years of economic recession in South Africa have exacerbated frustrations and bitterness under apartheid. This despair and resentment serve only to alienate participants in the political struggle and forestall chances for peaceful negotiation.

Past experience with economic sanctions casts doubt on their utility; they have seldom worked as their proponents hoped. The authors of *Economic Sanctions in U.S. Foreign Policy* state: "[E]conomic sanctions have not necessarily altered the positions of the targets and in the long run have been ineffective in the fulfillment of their objectives." One reason for this—isolation—may apply particularly to South Africa. Researcher Margaret Doxey found that in every case she examined, economic sanctions failed because international ostracism limited communication with the target country and made understanding more difficult to achieve. Isolating the South African government insulates it from international opprobrium and other subtle means of nudging it toward further reform.

Moreover, it is unlikely that U.S. disinvestment would have the profound effect its advocates have claimed. As mentioned previously, U.S. direct investment in South Africa represents less than 20 percent of total foreign investment and only about 2 percent of the total capital invested in the South African economy. The European Community accounts for 57 percent of foreign investment in the country; any successful economic boycott would require the participation of South Africa's European trading partners as well as Japan. Presently, most allies agree with the U.S. government position that sanctions are destabilizing measures and ill-advised.

Even the strongly antiapartheid British Labour Party, when in power from 1974 to 1979, refused to pull British firms from South Africa. Aside from the adverse effect that disengagement would have on black workers within South Africa and the region, the Labour government recognized that disengagement would cause at least 70,000 Britons to lose their jobs. The prospect is similar for other European countries and for individual foreign investors as well.

There is, moreover, the near certainty that U.S. firms, pressured to disinvest, would sell their assets to eager foreign or South African entrepreneurs. "One can almost hear managing directors in other countries holding their collective breath in anticipation of windfall profits brought by an American pullout," said marketing professor Robert Weigand in *The New York Times* recently.

Further, there is a basis for concern that employment policy toward blacks would be less enlightened after non-American ownership took over, and that the American initiative toward fair labor practices would be significantly eroded.

NEGATIVE CONSEQUENCES

A final point here: We should take note of the negative consequences that would be felt throughout southern Africa should Western business undermine the South African economy. South Africa trades with every nation in the region and has investments in every country except Angola. South African foodstuffs are exported to Mozambique, Zaire, and Lesotho. In short, South Africa is the hub of a vast economic network, supporting the bulk of the national economies of several countries. For example, more than three quarters of the wage earners of Lesotho work in South Africa. Altogether, one million foreign workers work in South Africa and send their wages home to countries where hard currency is sorely needed. Moreover, some of these countries rely on South African transport networks — railways, highways, and ports — to ship their products to and import goods from markets abroad. A breakdown in the transportation grid caused directly or indirectly by well-intended but poorly conceived sanctions from abroad would reverberate throughout the southern African subcontinent.

It is clear that the South African government is under greater pressure to move away from apartheid today than at any period since the National Party took power in 1948. Our television screens and newspapers have dramatically demonstrated how black communities have erupted in protest almost daily since late 1984. The state of emergency decreed by the South African government last July and only recently lifted did little to stop mass demonstrations against injustice. There have been black consumer and school boycotts. Many South Africans — black and white, English- and Afrikaans-speaking, rural and urban — believe that change must occur.

The Reagan Administration agrees that change must come and come rapidly. The Executive Order signed by the President last September forcefully underscored America's collective repudiation of apartheid and our unhappiness with the slow pace of reform. This order applied limited sanctions directed specifically at the South Africa government's apartheid-enforcing apparatus; the measures were designed to send a clear political message to Pretoria that genuine reform was long overdue.

To reject punitive sanctions is not to convey support for the South African government's policies but to protect the economic gains and standard of living of the black majority in their struggle for change. It makes little sense to turn our backs on the victims of apartheid by disengaging U.S. business and government interests from South Africa. That would be wrong. The principles that have guided our nation in the pursuit of freedom, justice, and domestic tranquility dictate that we should be assisting all the people of South Africa during this difficult period of transition in their nation's history. The United States intends to exert as much influence as it can to help those who must bear the burden of forming a just, peaceful society in South Africa.

On a practical level, the United States can provide material and moral support to the victims of apartheid and to those who are struggling to incorporate democratic practices in daily and long-term political activity. This means we must reject violent means of struggle in favor of raising the level of political discourse so that both sides can grow in confidence toward one another. We urge the South African government to negotiate with credible black leaders on the future of South Africa. We will continue to assist those groups and individuals who work for peaceful change and who form the backbone of a democratic state—labor unions, churches, civic associations, entrepreneurs, educators, and community leaders.

United States policy toward South Africa hopes to make a difference by encouraging peaceful reform and change without contributing to racial polarization or economic hardship. Our policy is practical, moral, and faithful to the American tradition.

CHAPTER 6

Finding a Formula for Constitutional Reform

by JAN CHRISTIAN HEUNIS

Apartheid is one of the most controversial aspects of South Africa's domestic and foreign policy: apartheid. It is significant to note that the State President committed the South African government unambiguously to depart from the outgrown and outdated concept of apartheid. The question, however, remains as to the nature and extent of the reform agenda, even though the principles on which it is to be based have already been spelled out by the government.

The perceptions of people inside and outside of South Africa regarding the government's commitment to reform are a reality we dare not ignore. Unfortunately, such perceptions are sometimes quite erroneous. Therefore, this article provides a much needed perspective on the situation through a brief elaboration of the reform agenda in terms of the past, the present, and the future. A better understanding of the complexities involved will enable governments and business alike to better judge the course of reform in South Africa and how they may be affected.

The government's mission is to establish a democratic political order that will be internally and externally legitimate, as indicated by the increasing popular support for the emerging dispensation among all South Africans. I am confident that a new South Africa can be achieved, despite the political, economic, and social instability that is inevitably associated with thorough reforms. The commitment to a democratic future for South Africa is further reinforced by an unqualified rejection of all forms of discrimination.

Like peoples in other parts of Africa, South Africans experienced a most traumatic and arduous period in their fight against colonialism.

In fact, the Boer Wars of 1880 and 1899 were fought and eventually lost to the British Empire. It left an enduring impact on the Afrikaners who took the lead in the ensuing decolonialization effort, which was to last several decades. A significant aspect of decolonialization was that black communities did not participate in the process almost until its completion in 1961.

Though the issue of participation of black communities was not completely ignored, the attitude at the time of the National Convention in 1909, shortly before the Union of South Africa came into being, is vividly illustrated by the following statement made by General J.C. Smuts (the man who wrote the preamble to the United Nations Charter): "The native question is bound up with the future of this continent, not only for the black races, but for the white races in a way none of us can today foresee properly. Let us gather wisdom and leave as much of this problem as can be left to posterity."

The current governing National Party, which beat General Smut's South African Party at the polls in 1948, inherited this "posterity." Not much happened in terms of accommodating blacks politically between 1910 and 1948, a time characterized by the impact of two world wars, a crippling depression preceded and followed by extreme poverty among whites also, violent rebellion of groups of white citizens against their white government, as well as the growth of the South African Communist Party, particularly among English- and Afrikaans-speaking workers.

Yet, apartheid had already been fully established in South Africa by 1915 as a policy of dealing with black communities through segregation. The demographic realities of that time made it easy. In the tumultuous thirty years that followed, conditions changed drastically. Whereas an insignificant number of black communities had been living outside their traditional areas (also known as homelands), more than half were living outside these territories by 1948, increasingly outnumbering the whites settled there.

The major reason was the urbanization that took place because of enhanced industrial, mining, and commercial activity, resulting from South Africa's war effort as an active supporter of the allied forces. These changes greatly complicated the policy of apartheid (as it was known then) because they involved the segregation of people in a way not foreseen earlier in an attempt to prevent integration, given the emerging demographic realities. It should be noted that apartheid had not been devised to accommodate these circumstances.

WAVE OF HUMANISM

Immediately following World War II, a wave of humanism caused unprecedented worldwide reaction against any form of discrimination, of which apartheid was perceived to be one. In addition, colonial powers rushed to grant their African possessions independence precisely at the time that South Africa had to come to grips with the political accommodation of the black communities, bearing in mind the legitimate fears of whites at that time.

In little more than ten years after the National Party came to power in 1948, the focus had shifted from a Boer-Brit conflict to one that appeared to be a white-black conflict. South Africa was branded a polecat because it entrenched the policy of apartheid in its laws. Given the circumstances, little understanding for South Africa's dilemma and trauma was forthcoming from the international community.

South Africa's decolonialization from the British Empire came to an end with its withdrawal from the Commonwealth in 1960 and its establishment as a Republic the year after, perhaps partly as a protest against the international community's lack of appreciation for the implacable realities that faced the government. Apartheid was promptly revised in 1960 by H.F. Verwoerd, the prime minister at the time, to become the policy of separate development.

It was decided to grant the ten traditional black areas (now known as self-governing states) independence. These sovereign national states would not be dominated by the whites of South Africa. The remaining apartheid measures, which drew so much criticism, were considered transitory arrangements that could be justified by the results anticipated from the "grand design" of separate development as conceived in the Verwoerdian era.

For a number of reasons, this policy proved to be only a partial solution, as the government has acknowledged explicitly in recent announcements. Nevertheless, four of the ten states within South Africa have accepted independence in recent years. Even though their sovereign status is not acknowledged internationally, their right to self-determination cannot be negated.

The current dilemma with the reform agenda is to find the other part of the solution, something not as simple as it may appear to governments and businesses that are not familiar with the South African situation. The reform agenda is as an ongoing process involving a significant historical background, and a better understanding of the realities may serve to correct the foreign attitudes that have become stereotyped and remain largely devoid of fair judgment.

In the final analysis, politics is about people, their hopes, and their fears. South Africa, therefore, cannot afford the devastating fire of mistrust and despair to be fueled, even by well-meaning friends. Although we can understand why there has been such vehement reaction to events in South Africa in the past, that is not sufficient cause to doubt the commitment of this government to finding a genuinely equitable solution to our country's political problems.

Furthermore, it is no solution to withdraw or withhold support (even only moral support) if the intention is to assist a peaceful transition to the emerging new society. It may not be apparent, but once South Africa has rid itself of the shackles imposed on it (mostly arising from misinterpretations in regard to apartheid), it is destined to attain a leading role on the African continent and in the Southern Hemisphere. The enemies of South Africa are not likely to be thrilled by such a possibility.

In view of the meaning that is currently attached overseas to apartheid, the government cannot and does not intend to justify policies derived thereof. As the State President has declared, apartheid is indeed an outdated concept. However, this realization does not resolve the hard realities of our situation which are as real today as they were when the National Party acceded to power thirty-eight years ago. Whites feared that blacks would dominate them, simply because of their numerical majority, should the British system of Westminster government be continued. This fear of domination and the corresponding need for the protection of minorities (also numerous black minorities) constitute a legitimate concern which has preoccupied reformists until this day. It should be noted that Westminster democracy, characterized by a winner-takes-all mechanism, was the only accepted norm for Anglophone African countries at the time of decolonialization. As a consequence, the secession of independent states encompassing parts of South Africa's black population was considered inevitable and justifiable by the South African government, especially since it was a reflection of what was happening elsewhere in Africa. Unfortunately, the policies relating to separate development were not perceived as justifiable by a growing contingent of people within and without South Africa. It was said that South Africa did not have the right to decolonialize itself in order to solve the problem of "one man, one vote." Some opponents of the government's policies were genuinely concerned about the problems associated with them, whereas others merely exploited the opportunity that was created by the widespread condemnation of South Africa as a means to achieve particularistic political or economic aims. The result has been that the South African government's commitment to peaceful reform became suspect in the eyes of many. Possibly more than any other issue, such doubt constitutes a major impediment to reform because the establishment of a certain level of international support is necessary for the creation of a new South Africa.

CONSTITUTIONAL OPTIONS

To some extent, the exact nature of the constitutional dispensation that may evolve through negotiations among South Africa's communities is of less importance than the perceptions of those who partake in its making. This is why the government is so opposed to attempts to polarize our society at a time when it is on the threshold of achieving the ideal of a democratic South Africa. Moreover, the recent rethinking of constitutional options, both inside and outside government circles, has resulted for the first time in a wide rejection of the winner-takes-all type of democracy, which has bedeviled reform for so many years. The government considers it essential for a winner-takes-all situation to be avoided. This is a prerequisite for meaningful future negotiation. The dilemma is, however, that significant parties inside and outside South Africa do not agree with this view. They are insisting that a form of minority rule be replaced by a form of majority rule that would be equally, and possibly more, undemocratic given the realities of the heterogeneous population. In some cases it is probably not because these parties wish us to fall prey to radical forces of the left or right, but simply because they do not realize the complexity of the matter. Reform does not happen with the stroke of a pen. It takes time to shape attitudes and mobilize the resources on which reform depends.

It often happens that our critics demand results rather than declarations about what we intend. But what is the reality of the government's track record? Whatever the imperfections of the policy of creating the independent homelands may be, at least the policy recognizes that distinct groups and areas have interests that should be protected by granting autonomy within an appropriate system of regional government. Irrespective of the nature of the group or the area, recognition of its particular vested interests and the need to protect those interests within an acceptable framework cannot be regarded as discriminatory. A new-style regional approach to protect the vested interests of groups and areas concerned is not the same thing as or even related to apartheid. It is indeed the bottom line in making reform work in South Africa. By now, it should also be clear that what is generally understood overseas by the concept of apartheid bears no relation to the current agenda of reform in South Africa.

Even though the constitutional dilemma is often presented in general terms, as a case of blacks versus whites, this is not an accurate representation of the situation. South Africa is composed of a multitude of groups and areas whose distinctiveness demands constitutional accommodation. I do not for one moment seek to support the "divide-and-rule" approach, because South Africa is, as the State President has clearly stated, one country and one nation. We must find a way to combine unity and diversity in a stable balance, however vulnerable it may be. South Africa has already progressed along this route with the constitutional reform initiatives that commenced in 1977.

In 1983, the government tangibly demonstrated its commitment to an enhanced democracy by including the previously disenfranchised Indian and coloured population groups as equal partners at all levels and in all branches of government. The government considered this achievement a major milestone in guiding the white electorate toward an understanding of how unity and diversity can be accommodated simultaneously, but unfortunately the policy became the subject of grossly distorted propaganda. A strong backlash, developed among both whites and blacks, preceded the current situation. The government had to endure the painful process of losing those members within its own ranks who resisted reform and seeing the radicalization of some black moderates. All has not been in vain, however, because these steps helped to convince many people that there must be a way to establish a democracy involving all the peoples of South Africa, even though it may be a most difficult quest.

Having completed this phase simultaneously, and with a reasonable measure of success, we turned our attention to the issue of including the black communities in a sysem of genuine power sharing. Enfranchising those black communities that are not accommodated in one of the independent states deserves top priority. In this regard, it is not merely a question of establishing a mutually acceptable constitutional dispensation but also essential that the process by which it is arrived at should be legitimate.

First and foremost, a significant mainstream of all population groups should support a new dispensation as being fair and workable. Toward this end the government has stated its commitment to a system of universal adult suffrage. Furthermore, it has emphasized that no group or area shall be excluded from an equal say in the governing of South Africa.

If this were to be achieved, the international community would not be able to reject a solution, even if the eventual dispensation does not match their particular vision of democracy. One should nevertheless be realistic. South Africa is bound to experience a measure of conflict due to the discrepancies inherent in a dualistic and heterogeneous country that shares characteristics of both the First and the Third Worlds. In its political, social, and economic structure, South Africa is very much a part of Africa, despite its uniqueness on the continent.

It is important for South Africa to be recognized in its rightful role as a member of the international community that has successfully embarked on the road to comprehensive democratization. The international pressure that has and is being applied on political and economic levels has indeed been counterproductive. It has, for example, already succeeded in impoverishing the most susceptible part of the population and in increasing the revolutionary climate among them. The likelihood of negotiating a mutually acceptable dispensation under conditions of stability, progress, and goodwill has, therefore, been impeded. Only if we succeed in establishing a conducive environment will negotiations provide tangible results.

Opposition to the government's policies are often rationalized as being justified because of the alleged discriminatory content of these policies. Allow me to stress again that discrimination on whatever grounds is totally rejected in principle and in practice and that it has no place in a future dispensation. This refers not only to its removal from our legislative and executive actions but also to its active eradication from society. The government professes its aversion to discrimination and its adherence to the equality of all human beings, regardless of race, class, religion, ethnicity, or the like.

PRETORIA WATCHERS

For many of the Pretoria watchers abroad, discrimination equals apartheid. In that sense, I can understand their vehement reaction. Nevertheless, I would like to point out that differentiation between groups and areas in an attempt to protect their legitimate interests is not the same as discriminatory apartheid. The universal condemnation of discriminatory policies and their corollary of apartheid should therefore not be confused with this government's concern for the recognition of the interests of all segments of society, which will be regarded as constituent parts of a future dispensation. Finding the means of protecting the rights and interests of constituent groups and regions is no easy task. The major obstacle in our way is the perception that any constitutional dispensation would involve the majority ruling the minority. This is, of course, based on the erroneous assumption that such a simplistic analysis could accommodate the dynamics of a society characterized by deep-rooted differences in terms of the group and areas involved in negotiations.

Protagonists of the winner-takes-all type of democracy argue that any deviation from this classical principle would constitute a nondemocratic political order. I reject such a statement in the strongest terms possible. It is parochial and myopic and it does not reflect the demands of the conditions actually prevailing in South Africa. This does not imply that South Africa is the only one of its kind in the world, because that would be presumptuous. Rather, it is a case in which deep cleavages in a society result in the many minorities not being prepared to accept to dominance of other groups.

In terms of the traditional paradigm that governs the national sovereign state approach, the automatic response is to call for the secession of the dissenting community. In South Africa, the situation has been slightly different, though based on the same principle. We allowed the acceptance of independence by the self-governing territories even before nationalism had reached the same level of development as elsewhere in Africa. Solving the problem by granting independence may not always be possible, as was shown in the case of South Africa. If the seceding entity cannot be regarded as a self-sustaining state from within or without its borders, for example, because it merely duplicates the conflict present in the larger whole, another solution has to be found. Even if the self-governing territories had all become sovereign national states, it would not have solved the problem of diverse groups living in adjacent areas that cannot be subdivided into homogeneous communities and viable governmental entities. This dilemma is probably the major cause of the failure of grand apartheid as the only solution. At the same time, it demonstrates the challenge of reform in South Africa.

Unfortunately, clear guidelines for a democratic dispensation, operating on a different basis from that of numerical minorities and majorities, are not readily available. To avoid making positional statements regarding the nature of a future dispensation, the South African government declared its intention to negotiate the form of a new dispensation. In a sense, it will have to be custom-designed and home-grown. It cannot be an imposed blueprint based on the classical forms of federalism or unitarism that have been popularized today. On the other hand, we realize that there is a strong tradition of statecraft which must be respected. In order to facilitate the negotiations, a common frame of reference will have to be found to serve as a model from which a mutually acceptable political order can be realized through negotiations.

Despite all the technicalities involved, the attitude and perceptions of those taking part in the negotiations and of their constituencies are probably decisive. In this regard, the government seeks to demonstrate its commitment to building a new society that will reflect the true South Africa and the promise it holds.

NATIONAL COUNCIL

To facilitate the formal process of negotiation, the government has proposed a statutory body known as the National Council. The purpose of this council is to lay the foundations of the new dispensation. One of the major impediments to the reform agenda at present is the radicalization of black communities which should be part of the reconstruction process. We are convinced that many reform-oriented black leaders do realize the importance of their role in bringing about a peaceful and prosperous South Africa. We understand the predicament that many black leaders find themselves in. The government will do everything within its power to make representative negotiations succeed, even if certain black leaders persist in advocating violence in some form or another. Pressure on any party to future negotiations that encourages a definitive position in private or in public is bound to damage attempts to reform.

Despite the importance of attitudes, a discussion of the reform process would be incomplete without considering the technicalities involved. For example, what are the implications of a dualistic economy, including both First and Third World elements, for the nature and extent of reforms? South Africa is a heterogeneous society for a number of reasons, apart from different levels of development and the presence of diverse ethnic groups. Right or wrong, the fact is that there are groups and regions in South Africa that are unwilling to accept the dominance of others. Often, a typical response is that we should simply remove the distrust and stress the commonality of interests. Granted, that is the ideal to be strived for, but in the meantime the government is faced with the hard reality of providing for a smooth transition into the new society. Given the political uncertainty and social instability of recent times, our task will most definitely remain extremely complicated.

Despite insistence that we should be left alone to solve the problems as South Africans who share a common destiny, we are not ignorant of our interdependence with the rest of the world. We recognize that foreign powers may have genuine concerns about the nature, extent, and timing of reforms. On the other hand, the negative pressure that has been applied thus far has proved to be counterproductive.

Therefore, we call for greater understanding and constructive involvement. This is not meant to thwart reform or promote the maintenance of the status quo. South Africa's reform program has suffered from the internationalization thereof, but international interest can also be turned into a positive force for viable and feasible reforms. Reform involves political, economic, and social dimensions which need to be addressed simultaneously. Regardless of the peculiar nature of the South African situation, the process of modernization always makes exceptional demands on the resources needed to effect the envisaged reforms. The argument that direct and indirect constructive involvement by foreign governments and businesses serve to maintain the status quo is sheer fallacy. Without economic development, the conditions favorable for democratization in the political arena are reduced, if only because the rising expectations created by reform initiatives cannot be satisfied.

Nobody denies that time is of the essence for South Africa. However, accommodating the many conflicting interests while keeping the tenuous balance between stability and instability does not allow us to gamble with the future of all South Africans. That the realities of the situation preclude immediate results in several spheres cannot be interpreted as a lack of commitment on the part of the government. The actions we have taken and the intentions we have stated thus far testify to this fact. It is not intended to prescribe the agenda of reform to the black communities which are about to share power. The agenda remains open in order to ensure that the dispensation to be established will achieve the maximum internal and external legitimacy.

The black citizens of South Africa will have to share the challenge of creating the new society. This new nation will be a diverse one, whose minorities demand the constitutional protection of their interests. But it will also be a united nation with a major role to play in international affairs. Apartheid is being dismantled, but in a manner that will strengthen rather than weaken South Africa.

CHAPTER 7

The Outdated Concept of Apartheid

by COLIN W. EGLIN

South Africa is rushing toward an unprecedented political crisis. For generations, black South Africans, in spite of their frustration, their anger, and at times their bitterness with the policy of apartheid, have accepted, albeit grudgingly, the authority of the white government of the Republic of South Africa.

In recent years, and increasingly in recent months, black South Africans are beginning to challenge and even resist that authority. The result: confrontation, violence, repression, and counterviolence; bannings, boycotts, bombings, burnings, and shootings; polarization, radicalization, and increasing militancy, especially among young black citizens.

To date, the government has not used the awesome power available to it should it decide that "the unrest is starting to get out of hand." To date, the turbulence has taken place primarily in black and coloured townships. It has not spilled over into either the white residential suburbs or the multiracial industrial and commericial areas in and around the big cities. Nor has it had a significant effect on the economy, except in those regions where black consumer boycotts have hurt and in places even crippled white traders.

Nevertheless, the authority of the government is being challenged in many areas. Black education has been brought to a standstill at times, with students boycotting classes for weeks on end and students themselves organizing programs in "education for liberation." The civil adminstration in many black townships has collapsed. Members of community councils — the local authorities in these townships — have been killed. Others have resigned en masse. Indeed, many of these townships are "no go" areas for government officials, except when they are escorted by armed police. Many blacks refuse to pay rental increases for houses provided by the state.

Many openly defy provisions of the government's twenty-six-year-old ban on the African National Congress. Often, at the funerals of the victims of violence, ANC T-shirts are worn, ANC banners are carried, and the crowds chant ANC freedom slogans.

It would be a dangerous oversimplification to suggest that the conflict situation is intensifying simply because the South African society is not moving away from apartheid or because the South African government is not prepared to change. South Africa is changing; so too are certain aspects of government policy.

Regardless of the government and its apartheid laws, the South African society is in a process of fundamental restructuring, away from apartheid and discrimination and toward a new South African society involving greater social freedom, economic opportunity, and political power for all South Africans. The most important impetus for this process of restructuring is undoubtedly the dynamics of South Africa's economic development, with its consequential urbanization of rural blacks, the creation of a new urban community infrastructure, the upward mobility of people within the urban environment, and the increasing economic muscle—especially in the consumer and labor fields—of the newly established and voteless black urban communities. The Nationalist government has responded to this surge of black importance in economic and political fields with "reforms" of its traditional apartheid policy.

SUBSTANTIVE REFORMS

Some of these reforms have involved changes in substance—for example, the recognition of full labor union rights for black workers, the granting of freehold property rights to blacks, and the repeal of racially based job reservation. Other reforms of traditional Nationalist policy such as the repeal of the Mixed Marriages, the Immorality, and the Prohibition of Political Interference Acts have been seen by white supporters of the government as a major step forward.

The harsh reality is that blacks, and especially young blacks in the cities, many of whom are unemployed, perceive no real improvement. Many of the harsh apartheid laws, including the pass laws, remain. So does the disparity in wealth and economic opportunity. Their education, although in the process of being upgraded, remains inferior. They remain trapped in the urban ghettos allocated to them in terms of the Urban Areas and Group Areas Acts.

Thus far, the reforms introduced by Botha's government have been too little to undo the damage done by decades of apartheid and too late to accommodate the rising tide of black frustration, anger, and determination. It is against this background that on January 31, State President P.W. Botha spoke at the opening of the 1986 session of South Africa's tricameral parliament. This speech has been dubbed "Rubicon 2" following his disastrous "Rubicon" speech at the National Party Congress in Durban last August.

NEW DEAL?

On the face of it, it was an encouraging speech. It dealt with such lofty concepts as "the sanctity and indivisibility of the law," the protection of "dignity, life, liberty and property," and "a democratic system of government." It committed the government to move on such practical issues as "a socioeconomic plan for the less developed areas and communities," freehold property rights for black citizens, the removal of the present influx control system, the restoration of citizenship, and negotiation with black leaders on possible new constitutional structures. Hopes of a genuine "new deal" rose high when the positive aspects of the State President's speech were reinforced by a massive government-sponsored advertising campaign.

But, within a week, hopes were dashed. Botha publicly reprimanded Foreign Minister Pik Botha for suggesting that the consequence of the government's new policy was that a black South African could possibly become State President. Added to this, Botha endorsed the conservative views of F.W. De Klerk, the National Party's Transvaal leader, who returned to National Party orthodoxy when he stated that in terms of the government's new deal, there would still be "separate structures and separate systems for each of the racial groups." This is where the so-called reform program has become bogged down. On the one hand, the Nationalist government clings stubbornly to the concept of reform within the framework of separate structures on the basis of compulsory race group members. On the other hand, black South Africans, together with a considerable number of whites in a political party like the Progressive Federal Party, insist that apartheid structures must go and that a workable nonracial constitutional alternative must be negotiated on the basis of freedom of choice.

RECIPE FOR CONFRONTATION

South African society is moving — and dragging the government along behind it. This is simply not good enough. It is a recipe for confrontation, for conflict, and for escalating violence. This need not be. South Africans in overwhelming numbers would prefer peace to violence. They would prefer to talk rather than to fight. They are pragmatists rather than ideologists. They are intensely South African.

A settlement acceptable to the vast majority of South Africans of all races is possible. However, there can be no start to achieving that settlement until the Nationalist government comes to realize that one can't reform apartheid. South African society can be reformed, but only by eliminating apartheid lock, stock, and barrel. The National Party, slowly and hesitantly, is escaping from its apartheid past. The question is whether it is going to have the courage to embrace a nonracial future in time to prevent the violence that has now become part of the South African scene, rising to unmanageable and destructive levels.

As one who has fought the National Party and its apartheid policy for the past twenty-five years, I refuse to give up hope. When I look at my country, its people, its resources, its achievements, I cannot accept that this is going to be destroyed for the sake of what Botha himself has described as "the outdated concept of apartheid." The next few months will tell.

CHAPTER 8

A Democratic Blueprint for South Africa

by AREND LIJPHART and DIANE R. STANTON

Both outside and inside South Africa, there is strong and widespread opposition to the continuation of the white minority regime and to its policy of partitioning the country into a set of small black homelands and a residual white-ruled state (separate development or grand apartheid). There is probably just as much agreement that the optimal alternative would be a fully democratic government in an undivided South Africa. It should be noted that even the South African government itself has joined this consensus. In his address on January 31, 1986, President P.W. Botha declared that "we have outgrown . . . the outdated concept of apartheid," and that "we accept an undivided Republic of South Africa . . . one citizenship for all South Africans [and] a democratic system of government."

Since democracy is almost everyone's ideal, we should consider the question: What *kind* of democratic government should South Africa adopt? We recognize that the responsibility for writing a new constitution belongs mainly to the South Africans themselves when they eventually sit down to negotiate a solution, and our input is merely intended as friendly advice. We shall start with an outline of what we believe to be the optimal constitutional principles for a democratic South Africa. We shall then offer our justification for these suggestions and assess the possibility that such a constitution will be adopted and will be able to operate satisfactorily. We feel that a cautious optimism is warranted and, in particular, we want to warn against the grave danger that undue pessimism will become a self-fulfilling prediction: If the South Africans and other interested parties assume that democracy is impossible, they will not even try to attain it — thereby in fact making it impossible. Let us not allow the future of South Africa to be shaped by such debilitating pessimism.

POWER-SHARING CONSTITUTION

We believe that a democratic constitution along the following lines is optimal for South Africa:

• The democratic principles of equality and liberty will be fully respected. All discriminatory rules and measures will cease. There will be complete freedom of association, individual freedom of affiliation, and free electoral competition.

• There will be a bicameral federal legislature. The lower house will be elected directly by the voters by means of the list form of proportional representation, which is the most widely used electoral system in contemporary democracies; it allows any group to nominate lists of candidates and to have its candidates elected in proportion to the share of the total vote that the list receives. The upper house will represent the states in the South African federation and will be elected by the state legislatures.

• The federal cabinet will be a power-sharing cabinet in which all parties of a specified minimum size in the lower house can participate. This can be accomplished by having the lower house of the federal legislature either elect the entire cabinet on a proportional basis or elect the prime minister who in turn will appoint the other ministers on a proportional basis. In the former case, the prime ministership can rotate annually among the members of the cabinet.

• Proportionality should also be the target for all federal civil service appointments, including the armed forces and the police, and for the judiciary.

• In the federal legislative process and in the cabinet, decisions will be made by consensus as much as possible. Consensus will be encouraged by requiring extraordinary majorities instead of simple majorities for most decisions; this means that minorities will have a veto power. Probably the best way to institute such a veto is to make it an absolute veto on the most vital matters, such as cultural and educational autonomy, and a suspensive veto on all other matters. Constitutional amendments will also require approval by extraordinary majorities. The exact percentage of the minority vote that will count as a veto may vary for different types of issues.

• Ethnic groups that wish to run their own cultural and educational institutions may establish cultural councils for this purpose. These councils will be officially recognized public institutions whose activities will be publicly funded on an equal per capita basis.

• The state boundaries will be drawn in such a way as to form states that are natural economic units and that have relatively homogeneous populations. Most experts agree that these criteria will yield ten to twelve states — a considerably larger number than the current four provinces.

• The federation will be a decentralized one with as much power as possible delegated to the state governments.

• The organization of the state governments will be along the same lines as specified above for the federal government: The state legislatures will be elected by proportional representation, the state executives will be power-sharing cabinets, the state civil services will be composed on as proportional a basis as possible, and the principles of consensus and minority veto will apply to all decisionmaking processes.

COMPROMISE AND CONSENSUS

The justification of these constitutional principles which we believe to be optimal for South Africa will proceed in four steps. First, we want to emphasize that much of what we propose is completely normal and ordinary in democratic countries. For instance, most of the world's democracies use proportional representation for parliamentary elections and have relatively rigid constitutions that can be amended only by extraordinary majorities, many are organized as federations, and most cabinets in those democracies that have such collegial executives operate by consensus instead of majority vote, usually as an informal but nonetheless firm rule.

Second, the proposed constitutional principles reflect the special needs of deeply divided societies. The tensions between the groups in such societies are too severe to be accommodated by majorities outvoting minorities. The only way to manage these societies is by the search for compromise and consensus and by the recognition of minority rights and minority autonomy. South Africa is, of course, an extreme case of a divided society. It is important to recognize that this is so not just as a result of the black-white differences. Even if there were only whites in South Africa, the split between Afrikaners and English-speakers would make the country as ethnically divided as Canada, Belgium, and Switzerland. And even if there were no whites, coloureds, and Asians at all, South Africa would be as ethnically divided as Zimbabwe, Angola, Zaire, and many other African countries.

TERRITORIAL FEDERALISM

The accommodation of these deep differences requires that decisions affecting the whole country be made by the representatives of all significant groups and that all other decisions be left to the groups or regions affected. Specifically, this means that the federal cabinet, legislature, and civil service should be as broadly representative of the entire population as possible (power sharing and proportionality), that executive and legislative decisions should be made as much as possible on a consensual basis (for which the minority veto provides a strong stimulus), and that decisions that mainly concern particular geographical areas or cultural groups should be delegated to the state governments and to the cultural councils. All of these rules are incorporated in our proposed constitutional outline. Our suggestion that group autonomy be implemented by the dual device of territorial federalism and the system of cultural councils is based on the high degree of intermixture of the South African population. While the states can be drawn in such a way as to make them *relatively* homogeneous — certainly much more so than the country as a whole — they cannot be made completely homogeneous. Hence, federalism has to be supplemented by the nonterritorial cultural councils. Structurally and functionally, these councils may be compared to the familiar local boards of education in the United States, although the councils will operate both at the national and local levels. Each cultural council will consist of representatives elected by a self-identified cultural group and supported by a civil service, and each will make decisions about education as well as matters like subsidies for literature, the theater, and so on, for this group.

HISTORICAL PRECEDENTS

We concede that these rules and institutions are somewhat unusual, but they are not unprecedented. For instance, the Belgian constitution stipulates that the cabinet be composed of equal numbers of Flemings and French-speakers, and the Swiss federal executive has traditionally been a power-sharing body in which the country's complex diversity of political, linguistic, religious, and cantonal divisions is faithfully reproduced. Belgium also provides a good example of nonterritorial Flemish and Francophone cultural councils with autonomous authority over all educational and cultural matters. The minority veto, in addition to its role in constitutional amendments, is frequently applied to nonconstitutional matters as well. In the United States, national legislation requires the approval of three institutions elected by different methods (Senate, House, and President) which can veto each other's decisions — certainly a far cry from straight majority rule. In California, the state budget must be approved by two-thirds majorities in both houses — giving minorities of slightly over one third of the members of either house an absolute veto.

RACIAL GROUPS

The third step in the justification of our constitutional proposals concerns a problem that is peculiarly South African: the disagreement on exactly what the constituent groups of the South African divided society are. In most other divided countries, the main groups can be identified and officially recognized without difficulty and controversy. In Belgium, for instance, there is no disagreement on the fact that the two major cultural communities are the Flemings and French-speakers. Hence, these two groups can be explicitly named in the articles of the constitution that provide for power sharing and autonomy. Similarly, the Lebanese agree on very little, but there is no disagreement on the existence of a Christian-Moslem split and on the further sectarian subdivision into Maronites, Shiites, Sunnis, and so on. And everyone recognizes that Malaysia is divided into separate Malay, Chinese, and Indian communities.

The principal reason why it is so difficult to identify the basic groups in South Africa's divided society is that the government's apartheid policies have been based on racial and ethnic criteria. The official four-fold racial categorization is the rationale behind the tricameral parliament established in 1983: separate chambers for whites, coloureds, and Asians, and no representation of the African majority. Ethnic criteria were used to set up the so-called homelands for Zulus, Xhosas, Tswanas, and other African ethnic groups. These widely despised policies have made the use of racial and ethnic categories for any purpose very distasteful for most South Africans.

In our view, ethnicity will remain an important factor in the foreseeable future, and it will be considerably more important than race. One reason is that ethnic and cultural differences form deep cleavages within the main racial groups, such as the Afrikaner-Anglophone split in the white community and the Zulu-Xhosa-Tswana-etc. split among the Africans. Moreover, cultural identity may transcend racial divisions; for instance, the Afrikaans language and culture are common to both the Afrikaners and the majority of the coloureds.

At the present time, ethnicity among nonwhites is muted by the shared dislike of the white minority regime and its discriminatory policies, but we believe that it will become strong again as soon as white minority control ends and free elections take place.

However, because of the controversial nature of ethnicity, ethnic groups cannot be explicitly identified in the constitution. For example, the constitution cannot state that the Zulus, Xhosas, and Afrikaaners—who form about 20, 20, and 10 percent of the population respectively—should have 20, 20, and 10 percent of the ministerial positions in the cabinet or that there will be state-funded Zulu, Xhosa, and Afrikaans schools instead of, or in addition to, ethnically neutral public schools. Therefore, instead of predetermining the groups that constitute the South African divided society, the constitution should permit these groups to define themselves. The main methods that we propose for this purpose are proportional representation and the system of cultural councils. The former is ideally suited not only to guarantee minority representation but also to be completely neutral on the question of which particular minorities deserve to be represented. By defining executive power sharing in terms of the parties elected to the lower house of parliament, we achieve broad participation in the cabinet of the groups that the electoral process has shown to be salient without having to identify these groups in advance. And by permitting and encouraging cultural minorities to form cultural councils if they wish to have autonomous authority over schools and related matters, we achieve cultural autonomy—again without explicitly naming any particular group.

DETRIBALIZATION

The fourth and final step in the defense of our suggestions is closely related to the third. The controversy over ethnicity concerns not only the question of the identity of the constituent groups in the South African divided society but also the question of whether South Africa is a divided society at all. The thesis that South Africa—or at least the African majority in South Africa—should be regarded as relatively homogeneous is based on two arguments. The first is that the processes of modernization, industrialization, and urbanization, and the consequent mixing of people with different ethnic backgrounds, have "detribalized" them; instead of Zulus, Xhosas, and Tswanas, they are now primarily South Africans or black South Africans. Second, the ethnic differences that are still apparent today were artificially created and are artificially maintained by the government's ethnically oriented policies; hence, these differences will disappear when the white minority government comes to an end.

In our view, both arguments are incorrect. The government's insistence on ethnic differences has clearly been counterproductive. Instead of strengthening ethnic feelings, it has generated feelings of solidarity among nonwhite groups that have softened the differences dividing them. But this is only a temporary phenomenon. As soon as white minority control is ended, and as soon as free group formation and free electoral competition are instituted, we predict that ethnic divisions will strongly reassert themselves. Furthermore, a quick comparative glance at the effects of modernization in divided societies elsewhere in Africa, in Europe, and in Asia shows that ethnicity is an extremely persistent and tenacious force. Industrialization and urbanization have not eliminated ethnic divisions or appreciably reduced their salience in Canada, Belgium, Nigeria, and Malaysia. There is nothing that makes South Africa so different from these societies that we should expect a totally different outcome.

However, one of the advantages of our constitutional proposals is that they do not hinge on the accuracy of the above analysis. Those who assume that South Africa is a deeply divided society and those who question this assumption do not have to reach a prior agreement on this matter in order to agree on our constitutional principles. Proportional representation does not favor any particular majority or minority. Hence, if the critics of the divided society assumption are right, they have the chance to be proved right by seeing nonethnic instead of ethnic parties emerge. If this turns out to be the case, these nonethnic parties may agree that the power-sharing requirement for cabinet formation can be softened, and they can do so by amending the constitution. If there are no groups that desire cultural and educational autonomy, the constitutional provision regarding cultural councils can remain a dead letter.

Let us be perfectly clear: This is not what we expect and predict. On the contrary, we expect that ethnically based parties and groups will predominate. But the important point is that people on opposite sides of the issue can agree to disagree. Whether South Africa is really an ethnically divided society and which are the salient groups will become clear by the election results.

CHANCES OF ADOPTION

Will a power-sharing constitution be adopted in South Africa? The chance of this depends primarily on the preferences of the South Africans themselves, but encouragement and support from outside will also be helpful. We feel that the United States and other democratic countries should urge all parties and groups in South Africa—from the ruling National Party government to the African National Congress—to be willing to negotiate and compromise and to accept the principle of power sharing as the point of departure in their negotiations. Since a democratic solution is undoubtedly the optimal solution, it is worth a serious and committed effort even if the chance of success is only slim—which we are convinced is not the case. Let us examine the attitudes and intentions of the South African government and the African National Congress, the two major parties that appear to be the farthest apart.

In spite of President Botha's promising pronouncements cited at the beginning of this article, the government's actual implementation of reforms has been minimal. In particular, its refusal to begin negotiations with the other South African groups has been very disappointing. A new constitution cannot be written by unilateral decisions; it has to be jointly negotiated. Nevertheless, the government is now clearly aware that white minority rule may be maintained by force for a few more years but that it will become untenable in the relatively near future. This means that the government cannot choose between holding on to exclusive white power and sharing power; the only choice is between sharing power and losing power. The logic of this is inescapable to any realistic observer of or participant in the South African political scene.

Moreover, the government has shown itself to be quite realistic and pragmatic—and obviously self-serving—in the past. It is wrong to interpret its actions as those of ideological and racist diehards. For instance, the new 1983 constitution cannot be criticized on the ground that it is simply a continuation of racial exclusiveness because, in fact, it provides for participation by coloureds and Asians: Representatives of these two groups now sit in parliament (albeit in separate chambers), in the cabinet, in the advisory president's council, and in the presidential electoral college with white representatives. What the 1983 constitution can and should be criticized for is that it is a clever and complicated arrangement to keep the National Party in control. It does so by excluding the African population from the system and by parlaying the Afrikaner minority in the remaining white-coloured-Asian population into a political majority by a series of institutional tricks. In other words, it can be regarded as an opportunistic and cynical means to maintain power. But cynicism and opportunism are the pejorative equivalents of pragmatism and realism. In the choice beetween racial segregation and power, the government has clearly opted for the latter. When the ruling white majority can no longer avoid choosing between sharing and losing power, it is unlikely that it will forfeit the opportunity to keep at least some power.

WILL BLACKS BARGAIN?

There are many signs that the African National Congress will be willing to compromise on a power-sharing solution, too. Quite understandably, the ANC has not been willing to formulate detailed proposals before there is a definite prospect of serious constitutional negotiations. But its general policy statements are certainly compatible with the power-sharing idea. The goal of majority rule does not exclude minority rights and usually refers to true democracy instead of the pseudo-democracy in which only a minority has political rights. The goal of "one person, one vote, in a unitary state" is also perfectly in line with power sharing, since "one person, one vote" is the general democratic standard, and a "unitary state" in South African parlance means opposition to the homelands policy instead of to the principle of federalism.

African leaders are legitimately concerned about the operation of the minority veto. Obviously, the veto should not be used to maintain white economic power and privileges. That is why we propose to apply an absolute minority veto only to cultural and educational issues. Moreover, we believe that power sharing in South Africa can work only if it is accompanied by a strong affirmative action program in order to drastically reduce the country's vast economic disparities. Such a program should be part of the constitutional bargain.

CAN IT WORK?

Once a power-sharing constitution is in place, will it work well? Nobody can guarantee this, of course, but there is no reason for pessimism. The divisions in South Africa are deeper and harder to reconcile than those in Switzerland, as the skeptics frequently point out. But in Malaysia, where the racial and socioeconomic differences are as great and the cultural differences much greater than those in South Africa, power sharing has worked satisfactorily for a long time. The frequently cited negative example of Lebanon is at best only partly relevant: Its power sharing government collapsed in 1975 under the weight of foreign pressures and interventions, but before 1975 it operated quite well for more than three decades. Above all, we should remember that power-sharing democracy is the only kind of democracy that has any chance of working in countries like Malaysia, Lebanon, and South Africa. These countries do not have the luxury of being able to choose between different types of democracy; their choice is between power sharing democracy and no democracy.

In the final analysis, both the successful drafting of a power sharing constitution and its successful operation depend mainly on the political will and commitment of South African political leaders. But democrats elsewhere have the moral duty to give maximum support and encouragement to the efforts of their democratic friends in South Africa.

CHAPTER 9

Is Democracy on the Political Horizon?

by GERRIT C. OLIVIER

There is an old adage that South Africa has developed economically by windfalls and politically by disasters. Reviewing the economic and political developments in South Africa over the past few years, there seems to be an element of truth in this characterization. Somehow, as the adage infers, South Africa has always managed to use crises productively. But what about the present crisis? Although it is quite different from any other crisis South Africa has experienced in the past, it is essentially a "developmental crisis," too, in the sense that it has precipitated the withering away of institutionalized apartheid and at the same time opened the door for the emergence of a participatory democracy in South Africa. Thus the caterpillar may indeed turn into a butterfly!

Nobody will deny that this historical metamorphosis will be a very difficult process. Right now the process of change in South Africa is erratic, complex, and even dangerous; there is a race between reform and revolution. Should the forces of extremism prevail, South Africa will lapse into the familiar Third World syndrome of concentrated power and economic decay. Reform, on the other hand, holds out the real hope that power will be shared equitably and that economic improvement, and the distribution of wealth that goes with it, will continue to enhance conditions for the emergence of a stable democratic order in South Africa.

DEPENDENT VARIABLES

In view of the ever-shifting boundaries of the political conflict in South

Africa, it is impossible to foretell whether the politics of revolutionary conflict or the politics of democratic reform will prevail. Both revolution and reform are dependent variables, and in the end, the outcome of the conflict will depend on the amount of social energy that will be fed into both these respective causes. From the perspective of reform, success depends, more than anything else, on the ability of the reform mongers to expand their support base on the one hand and on the other hand to overcome certain developmental crises, particularly the crises of participation, legitimacy, and distribution. Revolution feeds on the failures of reform. It is also a well-known fact that there is an inverse relationship between reform and stability. One could hypothesize that without the reform initiatives of the government, South Africa would have been a much more stable country than it is today (a fact that in itself puts a lie to the assertions by activists that there has been no change). Therefore, depending on prevailing circumstances, reform could be either a substitute or a catalyst for revolution.

Obviously, should the situation continue to deteriorate as a result of external intervention and internal unrest, the South African government could at any time fall back on its formidable power base and embark on strict authoritarian means to control the situation. At the same time, to immunize itself from external intervention, the isolation option could be chosen. However, such a desperate situation has not arisen in South Africa and the mode the government has chosen to address these crises is to share power and to expand democratic participation in the country.

DISMANTLING APARTHEID

When the Verwoerdian apartheid doctrine turned out to be a failure, the energy previously spent on trying to make this doctrine work became redirected toward finding an alternative for political accommodation. This transformation has been characterized by various chronological stages. At first there was the notion that apartheid could be "modernized" by effecting changes within the system. The most significant aspects of this modernization effort were the abolition of "petty apartheid" (i.e., apartheid in elevators, at railway stations, public conveniences, post office counters, etc.), the scrapping of job reservation for whites, the granting of ninety-nine-year leasehold rights to urbanized blacks, and the doing away with the color bar in sport. The second discernible phase in the movement away from apartheid was the introduction of the 1983 constitution which provided for the inclusion of coloureds and Asians in the central decisionmaking process. This development effectively marked the end of the color bar in South African politics but retained the notion of group autonomy and white hegemony. The hegemony principle was entrenched in the 4:2:1 proportional formula for parliamentary representation (of whites, coloureds and Asians, respectively) and the exclusion of blacks from the new three-chamber parliament, while group autonomy was assured by the differentiation on legislative and executive levels of government between "own affairs" and "general affairs." During this second phase, the government still maintained that the homeland policy was an adequate device for addressing the political needs of blacks, and it also believed that the political future of blacks could be decided without involving them in the decisionmaking process regarding this goal.

The third phase was characterized by the government's formal acceptance of the permanence of the so-called urban blacks in South Africa. The acceptance of this reality led to the introduction of a number of measures aimed at giving blacks political rights on the third- and second-tier levels of government in erstwhile "white" South Africa. These measures were specifically aimed at facilitating black mobility outside the traditional homelands, at enhancing democratic development at the grassroots level, and at encouraging black participation in the free market system. Perhaps the most important characteristic of this phase was abandoning ideological apartheid and starting a process for the systematic abrogation of institutional apartheid.

The fourth phase, which South Africa is moving into at present, was precipitated by the political unrest during the latter half of 1985 and the international reaction to it. In a series of speeches from August 1985 to January 1986, the State President made a number of announcements that, in essence, amounted to the dismissal of apartheid and the start of a process toward power sharing with blacks. Thus, in a period of about six months, the South African government made a dramatic break with the past. This was confirmed by President Botha when he said in January: "We have outgrown the colonial system of paternalism as well as the outdated concept of apartheid." At the same time, he cleared the way for a political renewal in South Africa when he declared that the government had accepted a framework for the future based on the development and the broadening of democracy, the concept of one nation in an undivided South Africa, universal citizenship, the sovereignty of law, and the protection of basic human rights ("life, liberty and property") regardless of color, race, creed, or religion.

How can a democratic state be created in South Africa? Whereas, on the one hand, political institutions "are the work of men," they, on the other hand, do not act of themselves. Mill lays down three conditions:

The people for whom the form of government is intended must be willing to accept it.... And they must be willing and able to do what it requires of them to enable it to fulfill its purpose. They must be capable of fulfilling the conditions of action, and the conditions of self-restraint, which are necessary either for keeping the established polity in existence, or for enabling it to achieve the ends, its conduciveness to which forms its recommendation.

Mill concludes: "The failure of any of these conditions renders a form of government, whatever favorable promise it may otherwise hold out, unsuitable to the particular case."

This triple test may well be applied to any new form of government in South Africa. Would the people of South Africa accept it? Would they support it and keep it standing? Would they help it to perform its functions? The answers to these questions depend very much on the conditions that make democracy possible, because this is the road South Africa has embarked upon. The obvious question is therefore: How favorable are conditions not only for the introduction of a veritable democracy but also for the perpetuation of democratic rule in South Africa?

In considering this triple test, one is faced with severe problems because of the uncertainty as to whether radical black leaders in South Africa will accept a nonmajoritarian variety of democracy. If it cannot be convinced of the wisdom of an alternative course of democratic development, South Africa will face the same fate as countries elsewhere in post-colonial Africa. Although Mill does not explicitly say so, his models imply that the development of legitimate democratic institutions is a *dialectic* process and not a "one process" or singular event as in many Third World countries where the democratic process really came to a standstill, or was reversed, as a result of one-partyism or the concentration of power in the hands of the leader or the executive. Thus, whereas majoritarianism may be a necessary condition for immediate political order, it is by far not a sufficient one for lasting and stable democracy.

STABLE DEMOCRACY

If South Africa wants real and lasting democracy, the temptation to seek the "political kingdom" via majoritarianism should be strongly resisted. The South African situation seems to require that control and consociational engineering should go hand in hand, with the former continuously diminishing as the latter gains ground. Hence a strong democratic infrastructure providing for a viable system of checks and balances must be developed to enhance movement from apartheid to democracy. Majoritarianism could be a natural development of this dialectic process toward democracy.

The problem is, of course, that this long view of democratic engineering in South Africa is not reconcilable with the immediate demands of the black majority, which boil down to one person, one vote in a unitary state. Democratically minded South Africans would not have regarded this as an outrageous demand were it not for the fact that the ANC, Bishop Tutu, and other black activists point blank refuse to commit themselves on the structuring and operationalization of democratic procedures once majority rule is achieved. What about the voting system, the role of political parties, division of powers, the role of the judiciary? What about individual rights and freedom of expression? Would American activists in their penchant to be on "the right side" accept responsibility for the aberration of these rights and freedoms? For the ANC and other activists, it is simply not good enough to say the "people will decide" or that there will be "horse trading." Democratically minded South Africans want democracy to be a continuous and sustained experience and not a moral pretense for the grabbing and monopolization of power by the strongest group. This is not an outrageous demand bearing in mind the example set by a large number of ex-British, Dutch, Belgian and French colonies which have not sustained democracy in spite of the example set by the metropolitan states.

The straightforward replacement of white-dominated authoritarianism by black-dominated authoritarianism with all the bloody consequences would draw South Africa into the same spiral of decline and decay as most other African and Latin American countries. The alternative to replacement is transformation. According to Huntington, democratic transformation occurs when

the elites within an authoritarian system conclude that, for some reason or another, that system which they have led and presumably benefited from no longer meets their needs or those of society. They hence take the lead in modifying the existing political system and transforming it into a democratic one. In this case, while there may be a variety of internal and external pressures favoring change, the initiative for such change comes from the rulers.

Democratic transformation requires skillful maneuvering by political reformers. Thus it is a slow and combersome process, but if successful it is invariably more enduring than power achieved through violence. According to Robert Dahl: "In the future as in the past, stable polyarchies and near-polyarchies are more likely to result from rather slow evolutionary processes than from revolutionary overthrow of existing hegemonies."

BALANCING OF INTERESTS

Thirty-eight years of Afrikaner hegemony should not be used by radical opponents of the government as an excuse for introducing perpetual black domination in South Africa. In terms of the democratic ideal, this would be no progress at all. The challenge is to change the political game in South Africa from the zero-sum approach of radicals at both sides of the political spectrum to an accommodative approach where the focus will shift from power to interests. Here one is reminded of what Charles A. Beard said of the constitutional proposals contained in the *Federalist Papers*. The aim of these proposals, he said, was "to guard one part of the society against the injustices of the other part. Different interests necessarily exist in different classes of citizens. If the majority be reunited by a common interest, the rights of the minority will be secure."

South African society comprises many parts, and if cognition is given to the variety of interests that exist over and above racial differences, a dynamic equilibrium could be established in South African politics. Then, indeed, as the authors of the *Federalist* have wisely pointed out, security will lie "in the multiplicity of interests" and the degree of security "will depend on the number of interests."

The South African government has declared its willingness to negotiate with black leaders for the purpose of working out a framework for power sharing in the country. To set the ball rolling, State President P.W. Botha has promoted the idea of a National Constitutional Council under his chairmanship, where white and black leaders can negotiate for constitutional change. Should black leaders be willing to serve on this council, it could be the most important step in South African history toward establishing a veritable democracy. A major stumbling block in the way of realizing this ideal are the deliberate efforts by revolutionary activists to polarize the South African population. Familiar revolutionary rhetoric such as "sellouts" and "collaborators" proliferate in the radical political vocabulary. Therefore, there should be no illusions about the great difficulties moderate blacks have to face if they wish to cross the line. True to the pattern prescribed by revolutionary theorists such as Mao Tse Tung, Giap, and Ho Chi Minh, radical revolutionary elements in South Africa conduct a campaign of terror against all blacks who cooperate with the government because, in their revolutionary terminology, they are "enemies of the people." From their Vietnam experience, American people in particular remember the many thousands of local officials, landlords, and informers who were killed on the grounds that they were appointees of the Diem regime. Furthermore, trying to emulate other African factions like Frelimo, SWAPO, the Patriotic Front, and the MPLA to which the international community officially or tacitly accorded the status of "sole and authentic" representators of the people, the ANC leaves no stone unturned to achieve the same prize. At the same time, the ANC refuses to spell out the nitty-gritty of its constitutional plans for South Africa. Its philosophical pro-Marxist stance and its use of violent means point to nothing else but an undisciplined game of power politics should the ANC gain control. Obviously, this will bring unparalleled hardship, suffering, and decay to South Africa and the region.

Surely, if the choice were between this uncertain political future under ANC rule and gradual democratization, a coalition of moderate South Africans would be seen as the more effective instrument for bringing about a just society in South Africa. Under these circumstances, the present role perception of the South African government is not difficult to understand. If only the apartheid stigma and what goes with it could be shed at a faster pace and South Africa could be left in peace in its search for a veritable democracy, the results would be far more productive and durable than in most Latin American and African countries which in spite of overwhelming external acclaim and support have achieved very little.

As South Africa is poised to move into the postapartheid era, I can think of no better way to describe the rationale and to underline the imperative for a durable democracy than by quoting the well-known lines from Reinhold Niebuhr's book, *The Children of Light and the Children of Darkness*: "Man's capacity for justice makes democracy possible; but man's inclination to injustice makes democracy necessary." Let us therefore hope that the worldwide fervor to get rid of apartheid will be followed up by an even stronger urge to restore democracy to South Africa. This will be the real challenge to all of us who wish to see apartheid smashed, because South Africa's capacity for perpetual conflict and violence will not disappear with the removal of apartheid — it could be exacerbated.

CHAPTER 10

Reform or Revolution: Political Forecasting for Postapartheid South Africa

by PATRICK O'MEARA and N. BRIAN WINCHESTER

The one certainty in South Africa in 1986 is that the state ideology of apartheid is no longer the guiding principle for government and for individual thought and action. Apartheid is under serious internal and external attack and has begun to lose its effectiveness as public policy. The laws of apartheid, always repugnant to millions of blacks, are becoming increasingly unacceptable even to some segments of the white population. Far from being an intentional course of action by the government and its officials, it has become a floundering, contradictory, and reactive process. The disintegration of apartheid is accelerating and the likelihood of significant change is increasing.

The unity of the Afrikaner people is now splintered and the base for the ruling National Party's (NP) power and legitimacy is diminished and shifting. Laws, public statements, and official regulations still pay lip service to apartheid but are contradicted by conflicting official interpretations, for example, while the Mixed Marriages Act and pass laws are being repealed, the Group Areas Act and segregated education remain intact. While some government ministers are using slogans such as "Apartheid is dead" or admonishing whites that they must "Adapt or die," simultaneous efforts are made to mollify the extreme right wing and crush black opposition and resistance.

Government policies in the past, particularly those associated with separate development, were part of a grand design that was intended to change the geopolitical face of South Africa by stripping millions of blacks of their citizenship through their forced relocation into so-called black homelands. This would have created a white majority, for the first time, while maintaining a supply of cheap black labor for the white economy. Apartheid was seen as more than political expediency because whites believed in what they perceived to be its moral justification. At the same time, the government was able to rely on an array of restrictive laws, such as the Suppression of Communism Act (1950), to maintain law and order. Today, there are no grand schemes but rather a reliance on draconian measures to maintain law and order in the black townships although there is an increasing awareness that bannings, treason trials, and detentions are no longer effective modes of control for the 1980s.

For most white South Africans, there continue to be a number of nonnegotiable areas for reform despite the seriously deteriorating situation. President P.W. Botha recently made this clear: "But what I do say is that if the Whites' way of life is affected, if their right to raise their children as they choose, if their language is endangered, if their residential areas, if those things — if the wealth which they have accumulated, if that is taken away, then I say to you, you are looking for trouble."[1] Since the issue is one of political power, merely removing the visible manifestations of Petty Apartheid, or even implementing significant reforms will not bring about lasting order and stability, if the substance of white power remains intact. It must not be forgotten that the history of Afrikaner racial exclusivity has virtually conditioned the government and most Afrikaners against accepting a common, nonracial citizenship.

Historically, the white rulers of South Africa, with police and military support, have imposed their views and philosophy on black South Africans. In the last few years fundamental shifts have begun to occur; blacks have become increasingly aware of their labor power, of their buying power, and of their ability to induce change and affect the political system. Today in South Africa, nearly all who are not white consider themselves black and through such tactics as strikes, boycotts, and violence have injected demands into the political system to which the government has been forced to respond. Together these may be seen as a central part of the whole process of black liberation.

For black South Africans these are not only practical ways of expressing political discontent but are also a means of hurting those institutions that they see perpetuating the ongoing system. In addition, the black organizations are at the same time establishing their legitimacy and a stake in the liberation process which could be of importance should a national convention ever be called. Unions have become particularly relevant. There are now more than eight black trade unions in South Africa with a total dues-paying membership of well over 500,000. They are not simply concerned with demands of labor since political issues and labor concerns are intertwined and hence most black unions have as their primary purpose the transforming of the political environment. Most of these articulate strident political goals; some, such as the congress of South African Trade Unions (COSATU) express similar goals to those of the African National Congress (ANC). Not surprisingly, the powerful Metal and Allied Workers' Union recently demanded that factories in which its members were employed should cease to produce goods for the police and the military. Thus since the black unions became legal in 1981 they have increased in size, importance, and in their politicization. Large numers of blacks now forcibly demonstrate their opposition to the power and strength of the white system and their opposition may well increase in intensity and scale. Individuals and groups may differ in ideology, strategy, and leadership but their hostility is the central motif of modern politics in South Africa. Legitimate channels of opposition are absent and so groups are forced to adopt the politics of unconventional tactics since these have become the most available and tangible ways of expressing opposition. With the end of apartheid's grand design and no viable scheme to replace it, the roles are slowly reversing; blacks have seized the initiative to which whites seem merely to react.

POLITICAL FORECASTING TOWARD POSTAPARTHEID SOUTH AFRICA

Any attempt at political risk forecasting about South Africa must take into account the major political actors and organizations involved, the changing contexts in which these actors make choices and the strategies and tactics that they employ. Given the extreme fluidity of the situation, the political capital of black and white actors continues to rise and fall; new actors and unlikely alliances cn be expected to emerge. For example, there is speculation that the Progressive Federal Party (PFP) could form an alliance with the left and center of the ruling National Party (NP) in order to stem the inroads of the conservatives or the PFP might just as easily form an alliance with moderate blacks. In either case participants in such coalitions run the risk of losing credibility with their constituents because they might be perceived as having sold out.

Two current examples of the rapidly changing situation in South Africa are Winnie Mandela's emergence as "the mother of our nation" from relative obscurity and Frederik Van Zyl Slabbert's recent resignation from the PFP and as leader of the parliamentary opposition in favor of working for a more broadly based alliance of black and white democrats. Slabbert concluded that the government was not committed to pursuing fundamental change and he was therefore unwilling to add legitimacy to it by his presence.

The range of possible scenarios for the political future of South Africa must include (1) a continuation of the current pattern of limited reforms with the likelihood of escalating violence, (2) the capture of white power by the radical right or by the military with a return to greater repression, (3) a negotiated settlement with the possibility of a major transformation, or finally, (4) a protracted, black war of liberation. Within each of these scenarios there is, of course, room for substantial variation and it is also possible that more than one of them could be operating concurrently. For example, at a time when the white system is offering limited reforms, black liberation movements would likely continue to gain momentum and consolidate their strength among the masses.

CONTINUATION OF THE CURRENT PATTERN OF LIMITED REFORM

The government seems willing to compromise on certain principles but not apparently on what it sees as nonnegotiables, including the maintenance of residential segregation, separate education, and, above all, white political control. South Africa has been adept at the politics of stalling and equivocation. The years of aborted settlements for Namibia provide ample evidence of its ability to protract and hamper deliberations to its advantage. Its goal of trying to appease black discontent and yet sustain its own power is in the long run impossible to achieve. Nonetheless, if economic conditions improve and black unemployment decreases it might be able to maneuver an even longer delay, particularly through some form of constitutional fabrication. Only a few years earlier, under similar circumstances, white Rhodesians attempted such constitutional mechanics, at first with voters' rolls of different weights and later with efforts at power-sharing with those blacks who were persuaded to collaborate, such as Bishop Abel Muzorewa. South Africa's constitutional experimentation in 1984 and its subsequent proposal for black councils in 1986 are reminiscent of the inability of white Rhodesians to recognize that because they were dealing with system blacks, rather than legitimate black leaders, their efforts were doomed to failure.

If the Herstigte Nasionale Party (HNP), the conservative Party, and the right of the National Party combine to become the official opposition, this could prompt a new ruling configuration between the left of the NP and the PFP. It is interesting to note that the PFP has agreed to take part in the 1989 general election as a multiracial party and to contest seats in the different Houses of the tricameral parliament. Any rearrangement involving the PFP would imply a more liberal and open political process and reforms that would be based on a federal reordering of the country but still within the prevailing political system. The new leader of the PFP, Colin Eglin, summed up its perspective recently: "The nature of South African politics is changing—from a small, largely white political arena dominated by a white Parliament to a largely non-racial political arena in which Parliament is a very important, but not the only site on which political actions or decisions are taking place. . . .The PFP must use the base it has in Parliament to hammer the Government when it is wrong—but more than this, it must use its base in Parliament to persuade the Government and the voters of South Africa to dismantle apartheid—and to do so before it is too late."[2] The PFP is holding itself open to interaction with a wide range of different organizations that are working for "peaceful change," some through persuasion, others through confrontation. Any changes implemented by a ruling NP-PFP Coalition would of necessity be of an interim nature and might spark greater black pressure for full political participation by the very opening up of the political process. But this type of coalition-building, with the inclusion of authentic black leadership, is the only possiblity for nonviolent change.

Despite the escalating violence of the recent past it should not be forgotten that whites are still firmly in control in South Africa and they are unlikely to surrender their privileges easily. The South African government still seeks to keep black discontent in check rather than to relinquish political power, although its room for maneuvering is becoming increasingly circumscribed as evidenced by its recent loss of control of some black townships. Indeed the government's reliance on the military to maintain a semblance of order in these townships points to their increasing ungovernability. However, far more lies behind the concept of ungovernability than the breakdown of white imposed law and order. More than simply a case of widespread and leaderless rioting, a strategy of alternative structures of black rule is emerging, for example, in the Eastern Cape where "People's Committees" have begun to replace the former black local authorities, which many blacks saw as government surrogates. Militant and mostly young blacks have injected into this vacuum tenative structures that represent a new strategy of resistance.

Who are the young black militants who now actively seek to control South Africa's black townships? Tom Lodge and Mark Swilling refer to those in the Eastern Cape as Amabuthu, the young lions, named after Xhosa warriors who resisted the settler invasions during the frontier wars of the nineteenth century. Lodge and Swilling are correct in their assumption that "For the last ten years, black South Africa has experienced a cultural revolution, a metamorphosis in values and conventions of the profoundest type. . . .The youngsters are the frontline cadres in an army of freedom. How the youth will respond if the fighting ever stops and the talking ever begins may not be such a simple question to answer."[3] While the link between the banned African National Congress and the youth councils in the township is presumed, it is more accurate to see parallel strands of revolutionary activity; the ANC with its new emphasis on soft targets and the youth of the townships, uncompromising yet capricious, quick to impose their own system of harsh justice, engaged in creating conditions of ungovernability as a new strategy of resistance. There is increasing evidence, howver, that the tie with the ANC is tenuous and in some instances the young radicals are highly critical of what they perceive as the comfortable life-style of the ANC leadership in exile. This may prove to be less problematic for the ANC than convincing the youth that they have not sold out at that point when negotiations with the white power structure becomes necessary.

Parts of some townships are now seen as "semi-liberated zones," an indication that these "people's committees' can provide an alternative to anarchy or to rule by so-called "system blacks." Notwithstanding these "islands of ungovernability" there is a widely held white view that the security forces will be able to control the situation for years to come. The recent alleged arming of conservative black vigilante groups by the South African authorities as a way to neutralize these young black radicals is but one strategy to deal with them and a tacit recognition that they are a force to be reckoned with.

A "RETURN" TO ORTHODOX APARTHEID

A second scenario must take into account the possibility of a drift to the right, either by the white electorate or a sudden seizure of power by the military. Faced with continuing upheaval and no end to the stalemate in sight, white voters in large numbers might be ready to switch support to the regressive proposals of a possible Conservative Party-Herstigte Nasionale Party (HNP) alliance. Fearing an end to white privilege and vehemently opposed to black majority rule, such an alliance between extreme right-wing splinter parties would stop all change and attempt to return the country to orthodox apartheid; a more rigid enforcement of police and military controls, greater repression, press censorship, the banning of organizations such as the United Democratic Front (UDF), and the imprisonment of black leaders. Internal black opposition would be forced underground and the power of moderate elements within the ANC compromised.

An even more extreme right-wing reactionary group, the Afrikaaner Resistance Movement (Afrikaaner Weerstandsbeweging, or AWB), increased its popular support in 1986, in the rural areas of the Transvaal and Orange Free State and among working-class urban Afrikaaners. The AWB capitalizes on white fears with a blatant appeal to white racism and a call for the reestablishment of the old, independent Boer Republics of the nineteenth century. Eugene Terre' Blanche, the leader of the AWB, sees members of the organization as "true freedom fighters" defending the heritage of the Afrikaner *volk*. While the National Party remains firmly in control of the white Parliament and no general election is scheduled until 1989, the radical right with its increasing support cannot be discounted. indeed, the extent of apparent right-wing support has led to speculation that if the election were held much earlier, the Nationalist Party might not be able to win a majority.

The National Party faces an internal challenge from its "left" as well. More liberal elements within the party, the so-called "new Nats," have gone so far as to advocate the possibility of negotiated black rule, an ironic recognition of President Botha's admonition that white South Africans must adapt or die.

In a variation of this scenario it is also possible that the military and security forces could stage what they see as a preemptive coup d'état. The politicization of the military as a result of its growing preoccupation with maintaining law and order might well affect their disposition to intervene and sensitize them to the opportunities to do so. Heightened fear of an expanding internal threat provides a powerful motive. If they perceive the civilian government as unwilling or unable to reestablish order or to govern effectively, the disposition and motive are reinforced. In the specific case of South Africa the circumstances are creating an environment conducive to military intervention; the state's diminishing ability to control events as a result of the escalation of black-white confrontation, the increasing incidence of "black-on-black" violence and the intensification of the white, right-wing, extremist challenge to the Botha government suggest the possibility of a disintegration into anarchy. Military intervention would come as no surprise under such circumstances. It could act with a decisiveness that civilian regimes lack. Brutal repression of opposition violence would likely follow but while a semblance of stability in the short run is enforceable, a return to chaos and instability is just as predictable; internal and external opposition have come too far to surrender to a return to orthodox apartheid.

NEGOTIATING CONSENSUS

A growing number of whites, part of a fragile consensus in favor of step-by-step black enfranchismenet, realize that they cannot hold back three-quarters of the population forever. They share many of the views expressed in a recent article in *The Economist*, "Reinventing South Africa," that "earlier, voluntary, reform is preferable to later, involuntary upheaval."[5] More and more, Afrikaner businessmen, English-speaking liberals, and blacks with different ideological perspectives who support either Chief Mangosuthu Buthelezi's Inkatha movement, Nelson Mandela's African National Congress, or the United Democratic Front (UDF), which is loosely aligned with it, subscribe to this approach which views consensus as preferable to dividing South Africa into geographic or ethnic entities suggested by some other constitutional formulas. On the other hand, fear of black domination or a nation besieged by racial and ethnic conflict continues to lead most whites to insist that "a continuation of law order under a white-dominated army and police force is the essential safeguard against collapsing into anarchy."[5] As such, negotiating a settlement to avert either a return to orthodox apartheid or a black war of liberation is an increasingly attractive option for many. Of course, the extent of any changes and their ultimate acceptance or rejection will depend on who is empowered to negotiate and what constraints, if any, would be imposed on the process. The government proposes a National Statutory Council which would consist largely of hand-picked system blacks but the alternative of a national convention, of all parties with no preconditions, is preferred by many others as the only solution with any real chance of success.

National Statutory Council

In a reversal of past National Party philosophy, President Botha said in January 1986 that South Africa had outgrown the outdated concept of apartheid and that the proposed National Statutory Council would prepare a new constitutional dispensation for the country.[6] In perhaps his most radical departure from the past, or a veiled attempt to split the ANC, he subsequently invited noncommunist members of the banned organization to return to South Africa to participate in the reform process. Despite all his rhetoric, the process is flawed by an underlying assumption of a continuation of some form of white power and privilege, and by the likelihood that the proposed Council would consist primarily of homeland leaders and other black leaders chosen by the government, inevitably the majority of whom would be seen as opportunists prepared to collaborate simply in return for limited gains. As a result, legitimate black leadership would reject the process, thus undermining any chance for success. The final result would not be unlike the rejection of electoral politics by an overwhelming number of so-called coloureds and Indians at the time of the 1984 elections for the newly created tricameral legislature. In explaining the failure of the new parliamentary experiment, former leader of the opposition PFP, Frederik Van Zyl Slabbert said: "If the Government extends the principle of co-optive domination to blacks as it has done to Coloureds and Indians, violence and conflict are inevitable. The search for consensus does not lie in finding co-optive clients. It lies in genuine negotiation with those who can deliver the goods."[7] Slabbert went on to challenge the very basis of the reformist philosophy. "The dismantling of apartheid has nothing to do with negotiation. It is simply the first step towards negotiation. Apartheid is not up for negotiation, it has to go completely. . . reform or constitutional change will never be successful as long as this Government insists that it takes place on the basis of compulsory group membership."[8]

Whether the pressure for change can be translated into constitutional reform is now the central issue, particularly since the concept of "one person, one vote" in a unitary state is ultimately the only one which black South Africans find acceptable and since it would necessitate white abdication of political power. While whites demand absolute assurance of the protection of minority rights and blacks will settle for nothing less than full unqualified political and economic rights, both must contend with those unreconstructed whites who want to maintain white supremacy and with those blacks who oppose any power-sharing at all with whites.

National All-Parties Convention

The one best hope for long-term stability is a National Convention in which there would be the full participation of all the primary political actors and principal business, labor and religious organizations white and black; leaders of the ruling National Party and opposition Progressive Federal Party and right-wing conservative parties, the African National Congress and the Pan African Congress, the United Democratic Front, Inkatha, the Black Consciousness Movement and its related organization, the Azanian Peoples' Organization (AZAPO), the National Front, representatives from the various labor movements, religious leaders, among others. The convening of such convention might require the moderating influence if not the active intervention of outside states or organizations such as the Commonwealth's recently formed Group of Eminent Persons. The outcome of such a convention could lead to a totally new constitutional configuration culminating in an election in which there could be alliances and alignments including the possibility of a fragile and tenuous coalition between the ANC and one or another of the liberal white political organizations. A convention of this sort would not necessarily open the way for the ANC to assume political paramountcy, although an open political process in which free elections took place would provide a real indication of its popular support.

Possible Outcomes of a Negotiated Settlement

Once negotiation has started in earnest, much of the constitutional discussion would likely focus on the issue of a universal franchise and on whether elections should take place in a unitary, federal, or consociational system. A compromise constitutional settlement might be acceptable as an interim measure as in 1979 in Zimbabwe when all of the parties involved agreed to negotiate an end to the guerrilla war with a constitution that guaranteed majority rule but also parliamentary representation and a limited veto for the white minority for a fixed number of years. Such a measured approach toward ultimate black rule might be reassuring to whites in South Africa but would only be acceptable to blacks if a clear timetable for majority rule was to be carefully spelled out. The ANC might accept this route to majority rule if it perceived the process as a significant wedge to full black political self-determination.

A consociational model, arguably less democratic, would involve a governing coalition of the political leaders of all significant segments of South Africa's plural society, each with a veto ostensibly to protect vital minority interests, with a high degree of segmental autonomy and political representation and allocation of public funds based on the principle of proportionality. The new 1984 constitution, with its tricameral legislature for whites, so-called coloureds, and Indians is a variation of this model and appeals to many whites who see it as a means of giving up apartheid, if they must, without relinquishing real power and privilege. While such a model cannot be dismissed, the acceptance of the consociational option in South Africa is doubtful given black insistence on universal and unqualified enfranchisement in a unitary state. A further, major limitation in the context of South African political reality, is its potential to bring the governing process to a standstill since all major decisions affecting the larger consociation would require the consent of all constituent minorities.

At talks initiated in March 1986 by Mangosuthu Gatsha Buthelezi, Chief Minister of Kwazulu, and the Natal Provincial government and other civic leaders discussions were held about regional power-sharing among blacks and whites. The first of South Africa's four provinces to consider an integrated form of provincial government, the so-called Kwa-Natal option is considered by some as a possible model for integrated administration in a larger federal system of government. Even though conservative white groups and most blacks declined to participate in the discussions, such a political arrangement might provide the South African government, which sent observers to the meetings, with the opportunity to institutionalize a more limited form of power-sharing. The backing of the Natal Provincial government, the South African government and Kwazulu might be sufficient to implement this model, which could then serve to encourage similar regional solutions.

Partition, as the ultimate solution to South Africa's racial and ethnic problems has been suggested from time to time, most recently, by the Afrikaaner Resistance Movement (AWB). The central issue for any planned partition would be the equitable reallocation of land and other natural resources and infrastructure, inherently, some of the least amenable issues for negotiation. This approach is, in addition, unacceptable for many of the same reasons that the government's homelands policy has been rejected; it would continue to define citizenship narrowly, restrict access and movement and would ignore the real contribution made by generations of black South Africans to the country as a whole.

ON THE POSSIBILITY FOR BLACK REVOLUTION

There seems little chance of a full-scale and decisive black revolution in the near future. First, while there has been, and will no doubt continue to be widespread violence, it seems likely to continue to be localized and sporadic and not systematic and nationally coordinated. It has so far been largely restricted to black townships and the ability of the miltary to continue to contain it is unquestioned. Second, there seem to be significant elements within the black community, such as the conservative black "vigilantes" who would, at the least, refuse to be part of a revolutionary movement and might even actively oppose it. Finally, the one group seemingly capable of conducting a black war of liberation, the ANC, has had its ability to sustain such a war increasingly circumscribed by South African Defense Force raids on ANC offices, training camps and lines of supply. Even though it is estimated to have 10,000 men and women in training outside of South Africa, its unchallenged, direct access to the country has been diminished because of the South African government's diplomatic and military efforts to intimidate neighboring countries from giving it sanctuary and support. Currently, Angola provides the only access route which is readily available but it is not as convenient a base for operations as were Lesotho, Botswana, Mozambique, Swaziland, or Zimbabwe. Unlike the Zimbabwe African National Union (ZANU), in Rhodesia in the 1970s, the ANC does not have an adjacent, friendly, independent African nation on its borders, such as Mozambique, from which to launch the war of liberation.

Should a full-scale, black war of liberation become a reality in South Africa it would differ from the liberation war in Rhodesia and the current level of violence in South Africa in scale, intensity, duration, and mode of operation. The liberation war in Zimbabwe was waged primarily in the rural areas with cities such as Salisbury (now Harare) and Bulawayo relatively untouched. The peasants in Rhodesia were the support of the ZANU guerrillas. In South Africa the strategies would differ. While there have been isolated attacks in rural areas, urban targets would be the focus of guerrilla fighting and the black townships would be central to the liberation process. In part, this is a result of topographic factors and patterns of settlement. Even South Africa's most isolated farms are part of more densely populated regions than was the case in Rhodesia. Furthermore, the sophistication and size of the South

African police and military forces preclude the type of guerrilla activity that was so successful in Rhodesia, although the size and power of the black industrial working class with its capacity to cripple the economy might offset this white advantage. South African conditions call from small groups of highly trained guerrillas operating in congested urban areas in which they cannot be easily identified or detected. In many ways, the bombing of strategic and urban targets would have more devastating effect than targets attacked during the Rhodesian war. The climate of chronic instability that would result coupled with a deterioration of the way of life for white South Africans would have far reaching ramifications. International investors would see South Africa as a risky investment and the uncertainties in the quality of life would lead many whites to emigrate from South Africa with little likelihood of new white immigration from Europe. This does not preclude many whites from remaining in South Africa but it could lead to a greater polarization because those who remained might be more strongly comitted to the politics of resistance and intransigence.

CONCLUSION

Conditions in South Africa seem to be evolving such that no one group or faction can be said to be controlling events, although prevailing opinion strongly suggests that the white South African government possesses the military and economic strength to maintain itself in power for the foreseeable future. Despite white ability to hold on, perhaps because of it, violence and counterviolence will undoubtedly continue and likely escalate. The question then seems to be at what point do the human, psychological, and financial costs of maintaining some semblance of order in a society in crisis become so high that the majority of the white population is willing to "sue for peace." In this particular case, suing for peace means entering into sincere negotiations with authentic black leaders over significant and meaningful political, economic, and social transformation. The superficial transformation of existing institutions and relationships and the government's insistence on dealing only with system blacks is doomed to failure because its ultimate aim is still the maintenance of white power. The creation of black advisory councils to appease the discontent of urban blacks and President Botha's proposed National Statutory Council are simply inadequate to the task because, like the 1984 constitution, they too lack widespread credibility from the outset. The outcome of limited change will inevitably be continued chronic social, political, and economic instability because, to paraphrase Bishop Desmond Tutu, blacks do not want their chains to be made more comfortable, they want them removed.

Where South Africa is going over the next few years is all the more unpredictable because of the uncertainty of a number of major factors. For the moment, the military, whose political influence is increasing, remains loyal to the government, in part, through the Minister of Defense, Magnus Malan, a former chief of the South African Defense Force. However, there are knowledgeable blacks and whites who privately assert that renegade elements within the military may have been responsible for subverting the Nkomati Accords, a nonaggression pact with Mozambique signed in 1984 and might pose a threat to some future government action as well. Similarly, there is speculation that the allegiance of at least some of the police might be severely tested if they were to be called upon to control the activities of the white radical right since it is alleged that an undetermined number of them are members of such right-wing organizations as the Afrikaner Resistance Movement. The surprising strength of the reactionary right over the past several years has in fact concerned the ruling National party. While right-wing opposition remains divided, its combined political potential suggest that the balance of white power may be shifting to the right. Nonetheless, with only an estimated 20 percent share of the vote, unless events precipitate a more dramatic shift to the right, the Botha government is in no danger of losing its parliamentary majority.

Significantly, black opposition is also divided, but for different reasons. There is a conspicuous absence of black leadership at the national level, in large part the result of a concerted effort by the white government over a number of years to imprison and exile and otherwise intimidate and compromise all potential black leaders perceived as a threat to the status quo. They have been quite successful in this effort and in their attempts to exploit differences among blacks, to "divide and conquer." White efforts to sow disunity have been aided by ethnic and ideological antagonisms between blacks and the generation gap between the very young black dissidents, some as young as twelve or thirteen, and other black opponents of apartheid who have struggled longer. How these very young and independent political actors will be reintegrated into a more conventional political process in a postapartheid era is an imponderable. Experience in Zimbabwe illustrates that the guerrilla forces, which many analysts thought would be a challenge to the stability of the state after independence, were integrated into the armed forces because of the legitimacy accorded to ZANU in an open and independently supervised election. A governing ANC would have to reestablish authority in a similar way.

Just as the nature and duration of the current crisis in South Africa sets it apart from previous periods of unrest, so too has the external response been measurably different from the antiapartheid campaigns of the past twenty-five years in Europe and North America. The ambassadors to South Africa from more than a dozen nations were temporarily recalled in 1985 to protest the declaration of the state of emergency; the voluntary codes of corporate conduct for U.S., Canadian, and European Community businesses in South Africa have all been strengthened; and laws and binding resolutions prohibiting or restricting investment in South Africa are proliferating. Numerous lobbying groups, churches and student organizations have intensified their antiapartheid activities and in the United States, Canada, Europe, and elsewhere, South Africa has become a major domestic political issue. The call for sanctions against South Africa in the U.S. Congress in 1985 was supported by Republicans and Democrats alike and persuaded President Reagan to reverse his policy never to impose sanctions against South Africa, an indication of the changing U.S. political climate. The effect of sanction and calls for divestment is hard to calculate. In Rhodesia, for example, there were many corporations and nations willing to break sanctions imposed by the United Nations. On the other hand, as long as they are in effect and the threat of additional action exists, they create and sustain an image of political instability and economic risk which has, and will continue to influence the white power structure. Former Prime Minister of Australia, Malcolm Fraser, speaking on behalf of the Group of Eminent Persons in June 1986 maintained that the only path left to a peaceful resolution of South Africa's crisis was an economic boycott to force the South African government to the negotiating table.

What are the implications of black rule for South Africa? In what ways would an ANC government transform the country? Would whites and blacks coexist as they have done in relative amicability in Zimbabwe since independence in 1980? If there is one lesson from the Zimbabwe experience it is that liberation movements behave very differently from governments. The rhetoric and strategies of the Zimbabwe African National Union changed overnight when it became the ruling party of an independent nation. There is a need for a more measured approach when leaderhsip shifts from a unified liberation movement to governing a diverse nation. A ruling ANC government would have to temper its policies to the pragmatics of governing and would no doubt have to make conciliatory gestures to convince whites that life would be secure under black rule. There is no question that the ANC wuld come to terms with business interests because it fully realizes the need to sustain South Africa's economic and industrial productivity. While it has been suggested that it would be unrealistic "to expect an ANC government, once in power, to be any keener on western-style democratic pluralism than any other African nationalist movement,"[9] its size and diversity might just as well lead it to experiment with different models of democratic pluralism. It should not be forgotten that contemporary South Africa has been virtually a one-party state since 1948.

The willingness of the ANC to negotiate and coexist with whites is predicated on a relatively speedy transfer of power. If the struggle is a protracted one, the more militant members of the leadership of the ANC may predominate, and given its radical orientation and links with the South African Communist Party, would result in a different scenario.

Whatever the problems and difficulties of transition to black rule and the subsuequent hazards of self-determination, they are preferable to the repression of more than 27 million Africans, so-called coloureds and Indians by less than 5 million whites. The real problem that a postapartheid South Africa will have to face involve the dismantling of the legacy of apartheid. Separate public facilities will be easily desegregated but the psychological damage to the dignity of generations of black South Africans as well as social and economic inequities will be much harder to eradicate. The tragedy of white South Africa is that it has not learned the Rhodesian lesson: that earlier, voluntary, negotiated settlement is much preferable to a later, rampant, maelstrom. Remarkably, after all that has happened, blacks still think that negotiations are possible and can save South Africa from a wider war.

NOTES

1. Transcript of a taped, private conversation (November 25, 1985), *South African Digest*, February 28, 1986, supplement, p. VII.
2. Interview with Colin Eglin, "New leader spells out his priorities," *Deurbraak*, March 1986, p. 3.

3. Tom Lodge and Mark Swilling, "The year of the Amabuthu," *Africa Report 31*, no. 2 (March-April 1986): 4-5.
4. "Reinventing South Africa," *The Economist 299*, no. 7445 (May 10, 1986): 11-12.
5. Ibid., p. 11.
6. "A new beginning," speech by President P.W. Botha on the occasion of the opening of the third session of the eighth Parliament of the Republic of South Africa, January 31, 1986.
7. "The time has come for me to go," excerpts from the final speech made by former leader of the PFP opposition, Frederik Van Zyl Slabbert, in Parliament on February 7, 1986, in *Deurbraak*, March 1986, p. 5.
8. Ibid.
9. Xan Smiley, "A Black South Africa?" *The Economist 298*, no. 7431 (February 1, 1986): 40.

Part II

AN OVERVIEW AND HISTORICAL PERSPECTIVE

CHAPTER 11

The Legal Structure of the Apartheid State

by LAURENCE BOULLE and JACKY JULYAN

Apartheid in South Africa has been developed and sustained by many social institutions and forces. The most enduring has been the technological superiority of whites, which has enabled them to construct and dominate a coercive economic and political system. In addition, white control of the means of production, cultural and religious factors, historic experiences and geographic realities, the social psychology of whites and the dominant social ideology, and international investment and support have come to reinforce the system. Particular attention has recently been given to the factor of capitalist economic development. The revisionist interpretations of the country's political economy emphasize the historic function of segregation and racial discrimination in promoting the accumulation of capital and the control of the labor force, so that in time deep structural forces came both to rely on and sustain the apartheid order. Whatever the disputes about the relative significance of these various forces and institutions, they have in combination produced the system of deep economic exploitation, political subjugation, social differentiation, and residential and educational segregation which characterizes the modern South African social order.

The legal system has also played a prominent part in sustaining the apartheid order, but its exact role has fluctuated over time. While the early expressions of apartheid were founded on coercive labor and social prejudice, the first apartheid laws can be identified in the seventeenth century. Their frequency increased with the growth of public administration and local lawmaking in the next two centuries, and in particular in the early decades of the twentieth, but it was only in the period between the late 1940s and early 1980s that law was used comprehensively and pervasively to reinforce and accentuate prevailing patterns of segregation in most facets of social intercourse. The State's extensive use of law in this period can be understood both in terms of the need to provide the administrative and regulative infrastructure to cope with the growing complexity and extent of the apartheid system, and in terms of the State's need to legitimize its coercive actions through the ideology of legalism and proclaimed independence of the judiciary. In both respects the use of law was an inviting and successful strategy. More recently this trend has been reversed with the apartheid "reforms," and there is now less reliance on legal structures than before.

In this chapter attention is given to the principal statutes and regulations which have reinforced the apartheid system, mainly during the last four decades. The material includes laws that overtly discriminated against blacks, such as the Land Acts and Influx Control measures, and those that were nominally nondiscriminatory but were intended to be used against blacks in administrative practice, such as the Group Areas Act and laws permitting the segregation of public amenities. Limited attention is given to a third category of statutes, which were not intended to be administered differently but have developed a profound bias in practice, for example, security legislation, censorship, and the criminal law, the use of which has been crucial in upholding the apartheid system. Where necessary, reference is made to the judicial interpretation of the measures dealt with. Attention is given to matters of land use and movement, constitutional and political ordering, and social and economic segregation. In view of the discrepancies usually encountered between the normative structures of law and the way in which they operate in practice, an attempt is made to indicate the extent to which various statutes were actually utilized. An account is also given of the recent attempts to "delegalize" apartheid by deracializing the public domain. Finally it is suggested that apartheid must be redefined in the light of the state's attempts to modernize it by relying less on discriminatory statutory arrangements.

The focus on legal measures must be seen throughout in the light of the dominant principle of the constitutional-legal system, namely, the legislative supremacy of the sovereign parliament. There are no substantive limitations on its competence and no countervailing system of judicial review, a predicament compounded by a tradition of legal positivism and an ideology of mechanical jurisprudence. Furthermore, the parliamentary executive system has enabled the dominant political group to utilize legislative supremacy to institutionalize its social designs with the backing of the state's coercive power.

LAND USE AND MOVEMENT

Geographic segregation has deep roots in South Africa. At the time of Union each of the four colonies had established reserves for black people. Consolidation of land segregation measures was achieved by the 1913 Land Act. This provided for the demarcation of tracts of land for the exclusive use of and occupation by black people, and restricted blacks to using and occupying those areas only. The 1913 Act was intended as a temporary measure only, but it served, ironically, as a basis for the Land Act of 1936. The object of the 1936 Act was to add further land to the areas set aside in terms of the 1913 Act. The combined effect of the Land Acts of 1913 and 1936 was to divide the land of South Africa between white and black and to restrict black people to some 13 percent of the country's total area.[1]

In addition to the geographical division accomplished by the Land Acts, the system of "Influx Control" further ensured the segregation of white and black. Influx Control was designed to keep blacks out of towns and functioned as a means of controlling the supply of labor for agriculture and mining. Unable to support themselves in the areas allocated for black use and occupation, blacks were attracted to urban areas in search of higher wages. This created a readily available and cheap labor force. However, the white working class felt threatened by the vast numbers of blacks flooding the labor market, and the curbs on the entry of blacks into urban areas were meant to protect white workers. Subjected to controls and restrictions on urban residence and employment, black laborers could be used in the development of the economy to the advantage of whites.

Restrictions of varying degree and kind had been placed on the entry of blacks into towns by local legislation. The first step to a national system of Influx Control was the promulgation of legislation in 1923, empowering the government to regulate matters pertaining to blacks in urban areas, and, importantly their entry into those areas. The enactment of 1923 was the forerunner of the Black (Urban Areas) Consolidation Act of 1945. This Act controlled the rights of movement and residence of blacks in urban areas. In terms of section 10 of the Act blacks were restricted from remaining in a "proscribed area" (in effect, and "white" urban area, including all industrialized parts of the country) for more than seventy-two hours. Certain exemptions to the seventy-two-hour provision allowed blacks to obtain "section 10 rights" in urban areas. These exemptions were based on residence in the area from bith, or employment for a period in excess of ten years (with one employer) or fifteen years (with more than one employer). The wife or unmarried child of a qualified person was also entitled to section 10 rights. In addition, a black person granted a permit issued by a labor bureau was exempted from the seventy-two-hour provision. Labor bureaus are state-run agencies for the recruitment of laborers in the rural black areas and for the control of recruited laborers in urban areas. The Act made the registering of contracts of service entered into by male blacks obligatory; hence control through the labor bureau constituted an important restriction on the employment of blacks and their influx into urban areas. Furthermore, an amendment to the Black (Urban Areas) Consolidation Act in 1952 sanctioned the removal of black vagrants from the towns.

While it was expedient to allow blacks entry into urban areas in the interests of the economy, segregation within the urban areas was still maintained. Prior to 1910 it had been practice within the colonies to provide separate residential areas for those blacks who were permitted to remain within an urban area. This policy was continued after the Act of Union. The 1923 legislation provided for the establishment of "locations" and "native villages" as residential areas for blacks. This created division within division: the country was divided into land for the exclusive use of blacks, and, land from which blacks were excluded by the Land Acts of 1913 and 1936; while within the "nonblack" part of the country separate residential areas for blacks were established. Even nicer distinctions based on race and ethnicity were introduced by the Group Areas Act of 1950 and its amendments of 1957 and 1966. The general purpose of this Act has been to create separate "group areas" for whites, blacks, and coloureds, the coloured group being divided on "ethnic" lines; in practice, separate group areas have been declared for whites, coloured, and Indians. Only persons belonging to the relevant group may own or occupy property situated in a group area.

The pass system reinforced Influx Control. The pre-Union colonies had created pass laws, requiring blacks to carry documents in order to move into, out of, or within any specified area. These enactments persisted after 1910, although the details differed from province to province, as did their application. In the Transvaal and the Orange Free

State the pass laws were stringently enforced, while they were largely disregarded in the Cape and Natal.[2] The Nationalist government introduced uniform regulation of passes for blacks with the promulgation of the misnamed Blacks (Abolition of Passes and Co-ordination of Documents) Act of 1952. All blacks over the age of sixteen were compelled to carry "reference books," or passes, with details such as the older's identity, race classification, place of birth, and fingerprints. A pass contained also a record of the holder's employment and reinforced the provisions of the Black (Urban Areas) Consolidation Act of 1945 requiring a labor bureau to sanction every contract of employment entered into by a black person. Consequently passes became the mainstay of every black person's life. They conferred both the right to remain or reside in a place and to work there.

Territorial segregation was one aspect of the state's divide-and-rule strategy. Physical demarcation of the land supported the development and entrenchment of political, economic, and social segregation. The measures restricted black persons severely, confining them to certain parts of the country and allowing them into urban areas only insofar as this was necessary to minister to the needs of whites. These curbs on movement of black persons gave rise to the system of migratory labor that persists today, and fostered the economic supremacy of whites. Geographic partition performed important ideological economic, and political functions.

THE SEGREGATION OF POLITICAL INSTITUTIONS

Since the earliest forms of settler administration in southern Africa access to the institutions of government has been determined by factors of race and ethnicity. This was first formalized in constitutional documents in the nineteenth century. In the colonial systems of Natal and the Cape the franchise was nominally nonracial, but the educational, property, and income qualifications rendered it predominantly white in the Cape and almost exclusively white in Natal. In the Afrikaner republics the constitutions not only restricted political rights to white citizens but also forbade equality between whites and blacks in the public domain. Although these British and Afrikaner variations on the racial theme were relatively minor, they were regarded as highly significant at the convention preceding Union in 1910. The perceived differences of principle resulted in a franchise "compromise" among the exclusively white convention delegates: each unit of the Union could retain its existing franchise arrangement in the new system, but only whites would participate in the central institutions of government. In effect the majority of blacks could neither elect nor be elected to the new political institutions. It was assumed by the liberal delegations, however, that the franchise based on "civilization" would eventually be extended to the other provinces. The new parliament was empowered to change the franchise qualifications, subject to the requirement that if any existing voter was disenfranchised the bill would require a two-third majority of the two legislative houses sitting unicamerally.

Since Union, successive governments have retracted the franchise on a racial basis, mainly through legislative amendments. In the 1930s the nonwhite vote was devalued when white women only were enfranchised without any qualifications, and shortly thereafter the qualifications for white men were abolished. Various administrative practices discouraged potential nonwhite voters from registering themselves. Then in 1936, the year of the second Land Act, the government removed all black voters from the common rolls and registered them on separate rolls from which they could elect four white representatives to the legislature. This step was supported by a two-thirds majority and was sanctioned by the courts. In the early 1950s a similar strategy was pursued in respect of the coloured voters still registered on the common rolls, but on this occasion the new National Party government could not muster the special two-thirds majority and the courts twice invalidated amendments enacted in the normal bicameral manner, thereby creating a constitutional crisis. After the white voters had furnished an election mandate for its ultimate objectives, the government packed the upper house of parliament and the Supreme Court, and following intense political pressure from the state the court relented and sanctioned the various legislative measures and the retrospective disenfranchisement of coloured voters. In token compensation for this deprivation coloureds were given four white representatives in parliament. However, in 1959 the first step was to taken to preclude all nonwhite influence in parliament when the white representation of blacks was discontinued. The process was completed in 1968 when the four seats of the white representatives elected by coloureds were also abolished. Thus by the late 1960s the central legislature was exclusively white in composition and representation, and as the South African executive has always been drawn from parliament it had been exclusively white throughout.

To justify the retraction of the parliamentary franchise, separate institutions for the various excluded groups were established. In all cases these bodies were predominantly nominated, had mainly advisory powers, attracted little credibility, and were politically insignificant. The first was a council for blacks created in 1936. It operated hesitantly for a few years (during which it was dubbed the "toy telephone") then went into stagnation, and was finally abolished in the early 1950s. At about this time a similar council was established for coloureds. It later became predominantly elective and was delegated some policymaking and executive powers from the central government, but without relinquishing its political, financial, and administrative subordinacy. When the elected component was increased in the 1970s the majority party rendered the council ineffective through noncooperation tactics and the government was compelled to reclaim its delegated powers. As its legitimacy was by now irrecoverably lost, the government abolished the council in 1980. An equivalent council for Indians existed from 1964 to 1983; it was less politically prominent, but no more effective.

Another line of constitutional development for blacks commenced in 1951. An enactment of that year provided for a hierarchical structure of authorities in the rural areas based on tribal affiliations. After several delays, caused mainly by the reluctance of traditional leaders to participate in the new system, it eventually came into operation in most parts of the country. At the apex of the system were territorial authorities which had delegated administrative and financial powers and which were eventually transformed into the legislative assemblies of the homelands.[3]

The basis of the homeland system was more firmly established in 1959 when the principle of ethnic differentiation was introduced into black constitutional structures. For the first time the system came to be justified by the state in terms of concepts of self-determination, self-government, and even independence. By 1970 ten homelands had been established with their own governmental infrastructure and territorial jurisdiction, but the main policymaking bodies were in all cases either unelected or unrepresentative. However, the homelands did function administratively under central government control and supervision, and in the mid-1970s and early 1980s parliamentary enactments rendered four of them independent in terms of South African municipal law. One of the most crucial aspects of this process was that all blacks statutorily associated with a particular homeland were denationalized when it became legally independent, and they became aliens in South African law regardless of their place of permanent residence or employment. In several judicial decisions the courts, both directly and indirectly, upheld the independence program and the denationalization of black South Africans despite their nonrecognition by the international community. The system not only served to deflect black political energies into relatively insignificant, and often remote, institutions but it also divided the black constituency into rigid tribal divisions.

Segregation also characterized the subnational institutions of government. At the regional level the provincial councils in all four provinces were elected on the same basis as parliament and were in practice exclusively white, save for the Cape Provincial Council, which had two nonwhite members during its seventy-year existence. As far as local government is concerned South Africa has always had a developed system of municipal authorities in both urban and rural areas. The organic statutes have ensured that these have been elected and staffed exclusively by whites, except in the Cape privince where as late as 1960 there were several coloured councillors on the Cape Town city council. The white councils had local powers over black, coloured, and Indian residential areas within their territorial jurisdiction and for the first fifty years after Union there were no separate local authorities for these groups. In furtherance of the separate develoment blueprint the Group Areas Act first provided the statutory basis for separate coloured and Indian local authorities, but few were ever established and fewer were viable since they had little jurisdiction over ratable industrial or commercial property. In some cities coloureds and Indians attended white council meetings in advisory capacities. In 1971 the control over black urban townships was removed from white local authorities; it was centralized in Pretoria and came to be exercised on a regional basis by administrative boards, subsequently transformed into development boards. Control over most matters of daily life for urban blacks vested in the boards despite the existence, since 1961, of advisory black councils. The state eventually used these largely ineffectual councils as a basis for the upgrading of black local institutions, in particular through the elective community council system introduced in 1977. In 1982 yet further legislation made provision for a comprehensive system of local government for blacks, similar to that for whites save that greater controls, or potential controls, over their activities were retained by the central government. It was contemplated that these bodies would assume more and more of the functions exercised by the administration and development boards. However, for the now predictable reasons segregated black local authorities of all descriptions lacked credibility and were frequently boycotted, and in the civil disturbances of the 1980s the councils and their members were often the targets of opposition strategies.

The new constitution of 1983 was in several respects a culmination of the political segregation of the previous decades. Most significantly it continued to exclude all blacks from the central government, endorsing by implication the homelands system and its citizenship arrangements. Furthermore, the provisions of the Population Registration Act, in terms of which all constitutional developments since 1950 had taken place, were incorporated by reference into the Constitution Act itself. Although the new system introduced coloureds and Indians into the central political institutions its design, including voting procedures, default mechanisms, and public finance system, ensured that they would permanently be junior partners of the dominant group. One of the most striking features of the constitutional transition in 1983 was the continuity of personnel; no fewer than fifteen members of the new eighteen-person cabinet had been members of the predecessor, which indicated that the same core of white policymakers continued to dominate the new political system, although the constitutional framework within which they operated had altered. Moreover, the functions over which coloureds and Indians acquired nominal sovereignty comprised those matters of social and economic life in which segregationist policies had been most discriminatory for them: housing, education, health, and social services. The internal logic of the new constitution compelled coloured and Indians to operate and provide separate and unequal services in these matters for themselves. They were designated the "own affairs" of the three statutorily defined groups accommodated in the new constitution, and "own affairs" became a new euphemism for apartheid.

Segregation in the constitutional-political system of South Africa ensured that the state's monopoly of legitimate violence was at the exclusive disposal of the dominant white group. The enforcement of political segregation not only between white and nonwhite but also among different nonwhite groups provided all the benefits of classic divide-and-rule tactics. Moreover since 1968 the Prohibition of Political Interference Act had precluded any member of one statutorily defined population group from being a member of, or providing political or financial assistance to, a political party from another group, thereby proscribing multiracial parties. The two most important principles of the constitutional system, parliamentary sovereignty and legislative supremacy, entailed that there was no policymaking rival to the white parliament and that its legislative decrees were immune from judicial review or invalidation. This provided a convenient method for the statutory aspects of the apartheid state to be implemented, and for the executive, which effectively controlled parliament, to legitimize through law the prerogative powers that it needed to implement the administrative and coercive aspects of the system.

THE ENTRENCHMENT OF ECONOMIC AND SOCIAL SEGREGATION 1950-60

A spate of discriminatory legislation followed the National Party's election victory in 1948. The Population Registration Act of 1950 underpinned the sophisticated system of discrimination and segregation that was to be developed. All persons are classified according to racial or ethnic groups, the three main groups being white, coloured, and black. The coloured group is divided into seven subgroups, including Cape Coloured, Indian, and a catch-all "other Coloured." The criteria for classification are appearance and social acceptance, but these are subject to the overriding criterion of descent and the classification of the natural parents.

As the American Supreme Court was denouncing the "separate but equal" notion, in *Brown v. Board of Education of Topek*,[4] the South African government initiated "separate and unequal" legislation. South African courts do not have the power to review acts of Parliament, but they do have jurisdiction over subordinate legislation. In 1934 the Appellate Division ruled that the provision of separate post office counters was not invalid, as the facilities, although separate were substantially equal (*Minister of Posts and Telegraphs v. Rasool*).[5] This corresponded to the decision of the U.S. Surpeme Court in *Plessy v. Ferguson*,[6] both being predicated on the assumption that separate can be equal. In subsequent decisions, notably *R v. Adurahman*,[7] the courts quashed subordinate legislation whereby substantially unequal facilities in railway coaches and premises had been provided for different race groups. To counteract these "separate must be equal" rulings, the Reservation of Separate Amenities Act was introduced in 1953. This provided for separate buildings, services, and conveniences for people of different racial groups. The legislation declared that the separate amenities need not be substantially equal, thus expressly neutralizing the courts' power to invalidate the provision of separate and unequal facilities. The provisions of the Act have affected almost all aspects of life, and have been especially apparent in the social sphere. Transportation, recreational facilities, art galleries and libraries, restaurants, and theaters were all segregated during the 1950s through to the 1970s.

The Group Areas Act, together with the Reservation of Separate Amenities Act was vital in the achievement of extensive residential and social segregation. Often both Acts covered the same situation: for instance, restaurants were racially segregated in that they were "amenities" under the latter Act, while patronizing a restaurant was regarded as "occupying" it for purposes of the former Act. The Group Areas Act also proved a powerful obstacle to economic integration. Entrepreneurs were confined to conducting business within an area zoned for use by their racial group. Effectively, nonwhite businessmen were excluded from the central business districts. Precluded from living in the same suburbs, sharing recreational facilities, enjoying holidays at the same resorts—in short, from having almost any common ground on a social level, the statutory race groups became deeply segregated. A pattern of social life was created that complemented the political segregation.

Job reservation served even more obviously to effect economic segregation. The origin of statutory job reservation in South Africa was the Mines and Works Act of 1911, in terms of which only whites and coloureds might qualify to take up skilled mining occupations. This measure was reenacted in 1926 and again in 1956. Job reservation was statutorily extended to the building trade in 1951 when blacks were prohibited from performing skilled building work in urban areas.

A key enactment was the Industrial Conciliation Act of 1956. The Minister of Labour was empowered to reserve any specified class of work for persons of a specified race as a "safeguard against inter-racial competition." The trade union provisions in the Act supplemented job reservations. The Act created a system of collective bargaining, but one in which blacks were to have no part, and which moreover extended job reservation beyond its statutory framework. First, the Act provided that "employees" might form trade unions, yet expressly excluded blacks from the definition of "employees." Second, the white trade unions used their bargaining strength to bar the employment of any blacks in a variety of skilled occupations far wider than those reserved by statute. This was responsible for the exclusion of blacks from apprenticeship to qualify for a trade.[8]

Love and lust were also destined to be racially regulated. Marriages across the color-line (but here only the divide of white and nonwhite) were forbidden by the Prohibition of Mixed Marriages Act in 1949. A marriage entered into between a white and nonwhite was deemed void and any marriage officer performing such a marriage ceremony was guilty of a criminal offense. Persons who had sexual intercourse or committed any "immoral or indecent act" where one party was white and the other nonwhite were penalized in terms of the notorious section 16 of the Immorality Act of 1957.

Segregation and unequal education has a long history in South Africa. Prior to 1948 primary and secondary education for blacks was provided by mission schools. Soon after coming to power in 1948, the Nationalist government appointed the Eiselen Commission to inquire into black education. As a result of the Commission's recommendations the Black Education Act was passed in 1953 and control of black education was transferred to a State department. Subsidies to mission schools were terminated, forcing most of them to close. All black schools, including night schools, had to be registered.[9] Separate syllabi were devised for the black schools. Mother-tongue instruction was permitted at primary school level, but at secondary school level an official language, either English or Afrikaans, had to be used as a medium of instruction. Arrangements for the financing of black schools underscored heavily the discriminatory nature of schooling. In 1955 the amount of expenditure on black education from the state's general revenue account was pegged at a certain amount.[10] Communities were responsible for establishing and maintaining schools in their area; students were required to purchase their own textbooks and writing materials. From the mid-1950s, when teachers of black students were required to teach double sessions, school hours for each class were reduced. For coloured pupils, schooling was initially controlled by the provincial administrations, but the Department of Coloured Affairs, created in 1950, increasingly assumed control. Segregated schooling for coloureds was given the final legislative stamp in 1963 by the Coloured Persons Education Act. Again, financing of schooling was determined according to race: expenditure on schooling for coloureds was much lower than on white although higher than on blacks. For Indians, education was provided by the provincial administrations until the Indians Education Act of 1965. In the Cape they attended provincial schools for coloureds, and in Natal and the Transvaal the provinces either admitted Indians to coloured schools or established separate schools for Indians. State expenditure on Indian schools was also lower than on white schooling. The all-pervasive Group Areas Act ensured that schools remained segregated, as not even private schools (that is, schools not funded by the State) could admit students of other race groups.[11]

In 1959 tertiary education was also statutorily segregated. The Extension of University Education Act provided for the creation of separate universities for blacks, coloureds, and Indians and restricted the "open universities" (those that had admitted students on academic merit regardless of race) from admitting nonwhite students.

This sketch of the legislative measures designed to enforce economic and social segregation affords an idea of the elaborate structure created to sustain the apartheid state.

APARTHEID LEGISLATION IN PRACTICE

Inevitably only a limited insight can be provided into the application of the apartheid laws, as even the statistics used quantify the dependence of the apartheid system on legislation in only the crudest way. However, it is possible to show that some apartheid statutes were applied consistently and comprehensively whereas others were applied only selectively and with fluctuations over time. The latter category were the first to be repealed in the early 1980s. An extreme example of this category was the "church clause," which was never enforced.[12] The executive was empowered to prevent the attendance of blacks at any religious service in a white area but this was widely opposed at the time and in 1978 the responsible minister announced a change of policy: attendance at church services by blacks was a matter for the churches to decide.[13]

The basic defining status of the apartheid system, the Populaton Registration Act, has been applied consistenly since its enactment in 1950. All identification documents were issued in terms of its statutory categories and these became the access keys in many areas. So basic is race identification to the system that the statute itself has become unobtrusive and its existence is taken for granted. However, the following figures give an indication of the recent attempts made by individuals to change their classification, and the relative success rate of the applications.[14] The vast majority of applicants were seeking white status.

Year	1983	1984	1985
Applications	1,139	1,057	1,565
Successes	237	262	398
Failures	902	795	1,167

Other legislation that has been rigidly applied is that regulating access to political institutions, as indicated above. The constitutional documents, in combination with race classification, succeeded in producing a rigidly stratified and constrained political system that defined all interests and issues in terms of the statutory group definitions imposed by the white government. This was to cause considerable difficulties for the government when it attempted to make the political process more inclusive.

The Land Acts of 1913 and 1936 have produced an obvious disparing in land distribution, and the latter Act has resulted in forced removals of communities from "black spots." A black spot is land owned by blacks before 1936, falling outside the areas designated for black owners by the two Land Acts, and surrounded by white-owned land. The state is empowered to expropriate the land constituting a black spot and the implementation of this provision has resulted in misery, suffering, and humiliation. The Land Acts have been rigorously enforced, but there is uncertainty as to how many people have been actually relocated. According to the Surplus Peoples Project over 3.5 million people were forcibly removed from their homes by the state between 1980 and 1983.[15] Statistics provided in parliament show that 1,993,794 people were moved between 1960 and 1984, but of these only 456,860 for "ideological reasons" — presumably a reference to "black spot" removals. The others were removed for reasons such as "infrastructural development schemes" and "strategic or military purposes."[16]

The legislation that prevented blacks from forming registered trade unions was unable, from the 1950s, to restrict the growth of collective consciousness among black workers, and by 1976 there were twenty-six black trade unions. Although they enjoyed no legal recognition, these unions represented some 126,000 workers.[17] However, real development in black union strength only occurred in developments after the Wiehahn Commission referred to in the following section.

Labor legislation had a more pernicious influence on the position of black workers than merely the deprivation of bargaining power. Although the Apprenticeship Act of 1944 did not itself discriminate on grounds of color, white trade unions were represented on apprenticeship committees and were able to bar blacks from being apprenticed to qualify as artisans.[18] This effectively maintained the status of blacks as unskilled laborers, and the resultant dearth of black artisans is an indication of the effects of apartheid legislation. Black artisans formed 5.9 percent of the total number of artisans in 1981. In 1983, out of a total of 12,485 new aprenticeship contracts, only 656 were registered for blacks.[19]

Influx Control legislation, by its very nature, could only be applied selectively. To trace any accurate pattern in the application of the legislation is impossible. Statistics on the number of arrests made in terms of Influx Control legislation must be collated from two separate government departments; furthermore the increase in the size of the black population has to be borne in mind in an evaluation of such statistics as are available. Both the police and the administration or development board officials are empowered to arrest blacks for infringement of Influx Control regulations. The following figures on pass law arrests by South African police and administrative officials are offered as an indication of the system's application:[20]

1981	160,000
1982	206,022
1983	269,904
1984	163,862

However, in the period preceding their repeal, the regulations appear to have been less severely applied,[22] and the courts mitigated the effect of some provisions, as indicated in the following section.

The statutory prohibition on sexual intercourse or immoral or indecent acts between white and nonwhite persons gave rise to reprehensible policing practices, and the figures on investigations into alleged offences and prosecutions are inevitably misleading. The dark figure for these contraventions can only be guessed at, as conceded by State President Botha when he said: "There has been mixing since Jan van Riebeeck arrived here . . . these laws were introduced in 1927, so what happened between 1652 and 1927?"[22] The ministers' replies to questions on the enforcement of the Immorality Act are contradictory, but by reconstruction of various sources it is possible to give the following figures for the 1981–1985:

Section 16 of the Immorality Act

Year	Investigation	Prosecutions
1981	249	199
1982	225	185
1983	189	141
1984	107	171
1985	223	191

The inequalities in the provision of education reveal the effects of statutory segregation of education reveals tellingly the inequalities segregation in this field. According to an investigation by the government-funded Human Sciences Research Council[23], disparities existed in respect of the *per capita* costs of education, the qualifications of teachers, the proportion of students obtaining standard 10 (the highest secondary qualification), and the percentage of students obtaining this qualification with university entrance. The following figures present an impressionistic picture:

Per Capita Costs of Primary and Secondary Education[24]

Year	Black	Coloured	Indian	White
1953-54	R17	R40	R40	R128
1969-70	17	73	81	282
1975-76	42	140	190	591
1977-78	54	185	276	657
1980-81	139	263	13	913
1982-83	146	498	711	1211
1983-84	203	722	1105	1591

Pupil/Teacher Ratios[25]

	1979	1984
Black	47.6:1	41:1
Coloured	29.6:1	26:1
Indian	26.2:1	23:1
White	19.6:1	19:1

THE RETREAT FROM STATUTORY APARTHEID: 1976-86

The decade between 1976 and 1986 witnessed a retreat from the highpoint of statutory apartheid that had been attained in the previous thirty years. This coincided with intense internal resistance to the system, commencing with the uprisings in Soweto in 1976, international political and economic pressure, the state's fiscal crisis and economic problems, and burgeoning social forces. It has also been accompanied by a change in the rhetorical and ideological justification for the South African social order: concepts of racial inferiority and white domination have been replaced by ideologies of self-determination, free market, privatization, technocratic administration, and political power-sharing.[26] While these developments have lead to significant social adjustments in South Africa, neither the changes nor the new rhetoric have affected the fundamental nature of the apartheid order in relation to the political dominance of whites or economic subjugation of blacks. However, the restructuring of the public domain has changed the legal-institutional framework within which this domination and subjugation take place.

Some of the earliest changes have occurred in the economic field and these have the greatest potential significance. In the wake of the Wiehahn Commission investigations into labor law, the state allowed blacks for the first time to join registered trade unions and to participate in the system of collective bargaining. This led to a resurgence of union activity and by 1983 the black membership of registered trade unions totaled 469,260.[27] In late 1985 a large federation of mainly black unions, the Congress of South African Trade Unions, was formed. Over the same period many forms of statutory job reservation were abolished, theoretically creating more employment opportunities for blacks, but coinciding in time with a severe economic depression and high general unemployment.

The extension of trade union rights was part of a begrudging acceptance by the state of the permanence of blacks in the white urban areas, in contradiction of purist apartheid theory. Other manifestations of this change were the provision for a ninety-nine-year leasehold system for blacks in some areas and the abolition of regional labor preference policies that had disadvantaged blacks. In early 1986 it was announced that some urban blacks would qualify for freehold rights under prescribed circumstances, a complete about-face on the urban black policy.

In the political domain there was also some blurring of the racial divide. The advisory President's Council, introduced in 1980, was the first institution to provide for the common participation of whites, coloureds, and Indians. In 1983 it became an extension of the executive with quasi-legislative powers and the majority of its members are now indirectly elected. The 1983 constitution drew coloureds and Indians into the tricameral parliament, although deliberations with whites can take place only in the joint legislative committees. In 1985 provision was made for Regional Services Councils, comprising nominated members but with no racial qualification, to coordinate local authority activities within their jurisdiction. In 1986 the State President announced the intended formation of a permanent National Council under his chairmanship to deliberate on a new constitution; although it makes provision for black participation it does not cater for constituency elections as the State President can nominate all the members of the Council, except for the ex officio homeland ministers. Shortly thereafter it was announced that nominated executive committees will take over the functions of the former Provincial Councils and will also be nominally open to all races. Again the principal of democratic representation has been avoided and other exigencies suggest that authentic black leaders will not participate widely on the new bodies.

In 1985 much publicity was given to the repeal of three prominent apartheid statutes. The Prohibition of Mixed Marriages Act was repealed in its entirety, with provision for the retrospective recognition of marriages previously affected. The clause of the Immorality Act that proscribed miscegenation was also repealed. However, mixed couples, whether married or unmarried, were not relieved from the restrictions of laws prohibiting integrated residence or use of public amenities. Shortly thereafter the prohibitions on intergroup political organizations and cooperation were also removed, but not the requirements for separate electoral rolls and constituencies.

Other changes in this period came about through administrative concession or judicial interpretation. Among the former were the concessions in terms of group areas legislation, which provided for open trading areas in the central business districts of most cities and major towns; other concessions resulted in blacks for the first time being allowed into all hotels or public liquor outlets without their requiring the fictitious international label, and being allowed access to places of recreation and entertainment and sports facilities. Among the latter the most significant were a series of court decisions expanding the rights of blacks to obtain urban residence rights, in some cases in clear contradiction of state policy. The administration boards responsible for administering Influx Control had interpreted the provisions of section 10 (referred to above) as conferring on blacks only an exemption from prosecution for being in the urban area concerned. The Appellate Division in 1980 ruled that the section conferred a right on any qualifying black to remain in the area, and such person was not dependent on administrative goodwill (*Komani NO v. Bantu Affairs Administration Board, Peninsula Area*.[28] Another administrative strategy was for labor bureaus to issue employment contracts for only one year at a time in order to prevent blacks from qualifying under the continuous employment requirement of section 10. Even if employer and employee agreed to renew the contract, the labor regulations required them to go through the formalities of signing-off the employee; the employee obtained a call-in card from the labor bureau and returned to the rural area and the bureau through which he was first recruited, and then entered into a further contract for one year with the former employer. The administration boards viewed this as an interruption of employment. In *Oos-Randse Administrasieraad v. Rikhoto*[29] the Appellate Division held that the call-in card system was designed to defeat the purpose of section 10(1)(b), and that it constituted an abuse of power. The procedure did not in fact interrupt the period of employment, and the applicant therefore qualified to remain in the urban area. The effect of these judgments is to entitle black workers formerly regarded as "migrant workers" to qualify for permanent residence in the urban area in which they are employed. Despite threats to reverse the decisions through legislative amendment, the state left them intact and they had positive consequences for thousands of affected blacks. From the time of the Rhikoto judgment to May 31, 1984 some 54,679 applications by migrant workers for urban rights had been received, and of these 38,9078 had been granted.

In late 1985 and early 1986 a further series of intended reforms was announced. Among the most significant were the indications that blacks who forfeited their nationality when the homelands became legally independent will have it restored, provided that they reside permanently in the Republic of South Africa. Pass laws and influx control will also be repealed. The state has committed itself to the introduction of a system of equal education over a ten-year period and expressly disavowed the Verwoerdian concept of inferior black education. However, as with all other ameliorations of the apartheid state these changes involved hidden or indirect exceptions. Thus the repeal of the pass laws is to be succeeded by the establishment of a nominally similar identification document for all persons, but one that will probably include a racial categorization in terms of the Population Registration Act, which will by implication be retained. In the case of influx control the state proclaimed a nonracial urbanization policy that will allow rural blacks into urban areas, but this will be dependent not only on the group areas legislation but also on the availability of housing, which even on the state's admission is in acutely short supply for blacks. Categories of citizenship can be and are still used to enforce Influx Control policies. The state has also threatened to use nominally nonracial statutes, such as the Trespass Act and Slums Act, to restrain and control black urbanization. Even an announced moratorium on forced removals has not deterred the state from redrawing homeland boundaries to achieve a similar purpose.[31]

In the educational fields legislative and administrative developments have resulted in the partial integration of universities and private schools; in both cases threatened quota systems, on which state subsidies would have depended, were not implemented after extensive opposition from the institutions concerned. However, the state insisted that there would be neither a single ministry of education nor integrated state schools, in defiance of professional, political and private sector pressure on the point.

This brief survey indicates the attempts of the state to deracialize the public domain. In some cases the changes were made because the legal provisions could no longer be implemented and in others because they were no longer functional to the apartheid order. They had the effect of restructuring the apartheid state and tempering some of its harshest aspects without undermining its essential political and economic features. In the result they necessitated a new understanding of the apartheid state to take account of its decreased reliance on laws and regulations.

CONCLUSION

This chapter has shown the role of the legal structure in reinforcing and sustaining the South African apartheid system. So extensive has the legal enforcement of apartheid been that the system has often been identified with statutory race discrimination. This is, however, to view it in only one dimension and the partial "deracialization" of the apartheid system in recent times has revealed its multidimensional nature: if measured by factors of state coercion, political domination, control of the economy, or residential and educational segregation, the apartheid of 1986 is as structurally entrenched as in previous decades, despite being more blurred at the edges. So deep is its structural nature that years of reformist measures have not materially affected its defining characteristics, namely the political subordination and economic exploitation of most blacks by most whites. The collateral safeguards, in the form of nonracial statutes that facilitate state control and coercion, remain at the disposal of the dominant group and are extensively used: detentions without trial in 1985 exceeded the total number of detentions for the previous ten years, and two states of emergency have been declared within a year.[32] Reform of the statute book has exposed the coercive and structural features of the apartheid system, and in the civil disturbances beginning in 1984 and running through 1985 and 1986 the significance of geographic apartheid became apparent, the activities being confined mainly to black localities.

Partial deracialization of the public domain has, however, served to draw more people into the apartheid system. This development is designed for two purposes — first, to enlist more elites from subordinate groups in operating the system, and second, to increase the number of its beneficiaries. However, the process has not always been internally consistent and coherent and it has created not only strategic problems for the dominant group but also tactical opportunities for subordinates.

In one respect the legislative reforms have clarified the issues relating to the abolition of apartheid. As it has become clearer that the deregulation of miscegenation, mixed theaters, or integrated sports facilities has done little to affect the defining characteristics of the apartheid system, so the attention has turned to the remaining instances of legislative discrimination. These include the race classification laws, group areas legislation and, most pertinently, the racially based political system. It has become obvious that the abolition of apartheid in the political dimension is a necessary, albeit not a sufficient, precondition for its disintegration in the economic and social spheres. This is partially recognized in the state's contemporary references to the need for a new constitutional dispensation based on "power-sharing." However as all state attempts at constitutional reform are based on racial or ethnic building blocks and imposed group membership, they have self-evident limitations as far as the system's legitimacy problems are concerned. The resolution of the apartheid predicatment will ultimately be found not in state reform but in a political settlement.

NOTES

1. Page 100 of M. Robertson, "Land Law in South Africa until 1936," *Natal University Law Review 3* (1984): 81ff.
2. G.R. Munro, "Influx control: a re-examination of the position of the urban black," *Natal University Law Review 2* (1980-1981): 382.
3. L.J. Boulle, *Constitutional Reform and the Apartheid State* (New York: St. Martin's Press, 1984): pp. 89-94.
4. 347 U.S. 483 (1954).
5. 1934 AD 167.
6. 163 U.S. 537 (1896).
7. 1950 (3) SA 136 (A).

8. S. Van der Horst and J. Reid (eds.), *Race Discrimination in South Africa: A Review* (Cape Town: David Philip, 1981), p. 49.
9. H. Perold and D. Butler (eds.), *The Right to Learn: The Struggle for Education in South Africa* (Johannesburg: Ravan Press, 1985), p. 55.
10. M. Horrell, *Race Relations as Regulated by law in South Africa 1948-1979* (Johannesburg: SAIRR, 1982), p. 119.
11. See in general ibid, pp. 115-45.
12. R. Omond, *The Apartheid Handbook* (Harmondsworth, England: Penguin, 1985), p. 185.
13. Horrell, *Race Relations as Regulated by Law in South Africa*, p. 52.
14. *House of Assembly Questions*, vol. 10, col. 1230, April 18, 1986.
15. L. Platzky and C. Walker, *The Surplus Poeple: Forced Removals in South Africa* (Johannesburg: Ravan Press, 1985), p. 9.
16. *The Weekly Mail 2*, no. 44, p. 4.
17. Human Sciences Research Council Investigation into Intergroup Relations, *The South African Society: Realities and Future Prospects* (Pretoria: HSRC, 1985), p. 43.
18. Van der Horst and Reid, *Race Discrimination in South Africa*, p. 49.
19. South African Institute of Race Relations, *Race Relations Survey 1984* (Johannesburg: SAIRR, 1985), pp. 249-50.
20. Ibid., p. 348.
21. Centre for Applied Legal Studies, *South African Journal of Human Rights* (Johannesburg: Ravan Press, 1986), vol. 2, pt. 1, pp. 121-22.
22. *The Star*, November 30, 1985.
23. Human Sciences Research Council Investigation into Intergroup Relations, *The South African Society*.
24. Perold and Bulter, *The Right to Learn*, p. 98; Human Sciences Research Council Investigation into Intergroup Relations, *The South African Society*, p. 31.
25. Horrell, *Race Relations as Regulated by Law in South Africa*, p. 115; Human Sciences Research Council Investigation into Intergroup Relations, *The South African Society*, p. 31.
26. Boulle, *Constitutional Reform and the Apartheid State*, p. 1.
27. Annual Reports, Department of Manpower, South Africa.
28. 1980 (4) SA 448 (A).
29. 1983 (3) SA 595 (A).
30. South African Institute of Race Relations, *Race Relations Survey 1984*.
31. Centre for Applied Legal Studies, *South African Journal of Human Rights*, pp. 164-65.
32. Ibid., p. 109.

CHAPTER 12

The Religious Rationale of Racism

by OLIVER F. WILLIAMS

One of the most surprising features of South African political life is the vitality and strength of the opposition party, the Progressive Federal Party. Until early 1986, the party was led by a talented and articulate Afrikaaner, Dr. Frederick van Zyl Slabbert; the party has long championed the cause of the blacks and argued for immediate negotiations to end apartheid. Slabbert's strong criticism of the government is regularly reported in the press in South Africa. His trenchant analysis goes to the heart of the current unrest.

Nothing is a greater threat to the rights and protection of minorities than to entrench racial and ethnic groups in a new constitutional dispensation. This is one of the fundamental shortcomings of the Government's constitutional reforms, both in the tricameral parliament and in the latest constitutional initiatives between Black and White. If racial and ethnic groups, as defined in law by the Government should form the building blocks of a new constitutional dispensation for South Africa, then a future picture of siege and conflict will become a reality.

What the criticism highlights is that the doctrine of separate development continues to be an important assumption in the policies of the ruling National Party. For example, separate schools, housing areas, and hospitals are the guiding assumption. What many outside South Africa may not realize, however, is that this doctrine has long been firmly rooted in the teachings of the Dutch Reformed Church (DRC). This article outlines the history of the DRC, its present theological rationale for the doctrine of separate development, and the prospect for the DRC's taking the lead in the movement to form a multiracial society.

HISTORICAL NOTES

The ancestors of today's Afrikaners first came to southern Africa when the Dutch East India Company located its refreshment station at the Cape of Good Hope in 1652; Jan van Riebeeck and 125 men established a colony there. Five years later, a number of the men were released from the company in order to farm and tend cattle for the station. In 1688, the Dutch East India Company brought some 150 French Huguenots to the Cape with the promise of free land for cultivation. Although the native Khoikhoi could not be taken as slaves by order of the Dutch leaders, their grazing and hunting lands were slowly appropriated by the new arrivals from Europe. To augment the meager labor force, slaves were brought in from East and West Africa and Malaya. Intermarriage between the Dutch and freed slaves or the Khaisans was not uncommon in the early days, and the resulting population is what is known as the "Cape coloured" today. By the late seventeenth century, mixed marriages were officially discouraged, however, so that the mixed-race population is a relatively small group in South Africa today.

The eighteenth-century life in the Cape colony saw the population rise to almost 15,000 persons. Although life was difficult with ongoing guerrilla warfare with the Khoikhoi and increasing strife with the Xhosa population, the Trekboers, as they came to be called, survived with their strong Calvinist faith and their great spirit of self-reliance. They likened their own situation to that of the patriarchs of the Old Testament, facing untold hardships with nothing but their faith in God and their own resources. As the Boers (farmers) moved further into the wilderness and expanded their land holdings, life became more fraught with danger, but these were hardy people who possessed a passionate conviction that God was on their side. Although the first Dutch Reformed Church minister had arrived in 1665, missionary work among the slaves and Khoikhoi was discouraged. The "heathen" could not be baptized, although there were some exceptions in cases where a white person guaranteed the Christian training of a candidate. Not until 1786 did missionary work become a full-scale ministry.

Missionary activity increased with the arrival of members of the London Missionary Society and the Wesleyan Methodists. The Methodists made the journey with some 5,000 British immigrants in 1820. This large influx of new arrivals from England added many former city dwellers to the Cape colony. With increasing missionary activity among the Africans, a tension began which is still present to-day. A scholar at the University of Cape Town, John W. de Gruchy, expressed it well in *The Church Struggle in South Africa*.

The basis reason that Dutch and English settlers alike resented the presence of some missionaries was thus precisely because the missionaries not only evangelized the indigenous peoples, but took their side in the struggle for justice, right and land. The missionaries, being white, regarded themselves as the conscience of the settlers and the protectors of the "natives." . . . The church's struggle against racism and injustice in South Africa only really begins in earnest with their witness in the nineteenth century.

There was a constant tension between the Boers and the British over how to deal with the race issue. The Boers were not in favor of freeing the slaves. Whether, in fact, racial discrimination was subtly based on economic reasons, that is, the need for land and cheap labor that could be met only if slavery perdured, is an intriguing question. In any event, the trekker republics were all governed by the principle that there would be "no equality between black and white in church or state." As early as 1839, the white members of a Dutch Reformed congregation in the Eastern Cape petitioned to have separate communion based on race. Although their General Synod would not hear of it in 1839 for scriptural reasons, in 1857, acknowledging the weakness of whites who could not accept blacks and coloureds, the Synod allowed separate communion and services. The so-called daughter churches for coloureds, Indians, and Africans followed in short order from this separatist policy.

SEPARATE AND UNEQUAL

Scholars have noted that in the nineteenth century, the seminal period in the development of what would become the Republic of South Africa, there were at least two distinct theories of what constitutes an appropriate approach to missionary work with the Africans. One approach argued that tribal life and culture should be infused with Christianity but not merged with white, Western culture. Separateness was thought to be essential to promote and protect the way of life of the African. This theory was congruent with the political vision of those who saw separateness as the only way to ensure the safety of the white communities. Another group advocated the acculturation of blacks into the white communities as the most appropriate way to convert to the Christian way of life. The practice of separate churches for the races grew to be standard not only for the Dutch Reformed Church but also for other Protestant denominations such as the Baptists and the Lutherans. Roman Catholics and Anglicans, on the other hand, in *principle* could never accept the requirement of separate churches, although in *practice* the typical congregation was, for the most part, of one skin color.

AFRIKANER NATIONALISM

Although the Afrikaners comprise about 60 percent of the 5 million whites in South Africa today, they have not always dominated the politics of the country. Those of British descent, the "English-speakers," long held the power and many Afrikaners still harbor bitter resentment over the brutal treatment by the British in the Anglo-Boer War at the turn of the century. The Nationalist Party under James Hertzog finally won control of the government in 1924 and an era of Afrikaner dominance began to take shape. Whites were protected from African competition through new legislation, and a number of measures were taken to help alleviate the poverty of Afrikaners. Export quotas, import duties, and minimum price controls were enacted to assist white farmers. In 1925, Afrikaans replaced Dutch as the official language, and with this move, bilingual competencies were enforced for all civil service employees. This gave Afrikaners a decided advantage, for many of the English-speakers had never bothered to learn the language of the Boers whom they disdained. Gradually, Afrikaners moved from farms in the rural area to the cities, at first taking a subservient role to the English but finally becoming full-fledged colleagues in business and industry.

Hertzog enacted what was called the "civilised labour" policy. This meant that the government would hire "civilised" (i.e., white) workers in preference to "uncivilised" (i.e., black) workers. The effect of this policy was dramatic. For example, among railway workers, in the first ten years of the Hertzog administration, the percentage of blacks dropped from 75 percent to 49 percent, while the white percentage rose from 9.5 percent to 39 percent. In 1936, Hertzog passed the Representation of Natives Act which took the 11,000 Africans in the Cape off the common voters' role. He also strengthened the pass laws and authorized the government to exercise "forced removals" of blacks when necessary for the convenience of white areas.

During Hertzog's administration, there was a strong current of

Afrikaner nationalism brewing. Hertzog was never an advocate of melding the two white cultures, but rather had a vision of "twin streams" of English- and Afrikaans-speaking South Africans who could live together in harmony. In 1933, Dr. Daniel Malan broke away from Hertzog's approach to form the "Purified" National Party, which would champion the cause of an Afrikaner Republic. Malan was a member of the famous *Afrikaaner Broederbond*, an organization founded in 1918 to safeguard Afrikaner interests. Initially, its role was to promote the culture and language and strengthen the Afrikaner identity in the face of an overwhelming British presence in urban and business life. In a short time, however, the *Broederbond* became a secret organization, its chief aim being Afrikaner domination rather than preservation. Still active and most influential today, the *Broederbond* now has 800 branches and 12,000 members. The Afrikaner exclusivity of Malan's new Purified National Party seemed to be a carbon copy of the *Broederbond*'s agenda. Malan would soon have the opportunity to implement that agenda, for he won the election for Prime Minister in 1948.

Malan, departing from all the administrations before his, chose a cabinet comprised completely of Afrikaners. To be sure, Malan's policies during his six-year tenure did not introduce segregation to South Africa, but they did begin a process, carried to term in successive Nationalist governments, that transformed a segregated way of life into a rigid ideology enforced by legal and theological sanctions. From 1948 until the 1960s, the major pieces of legislation that set the contours of what is known as "apartheid" were passed. Over 300 laws were passed to regulate the apartheid system.

In 1978, P.W. Botha assumed the role of Prime Minister. Botha, compared to previous leaders, was a reformer (*verligte* or "enlightened") Nationalist. He told his white constituency that they must "adapt or die." He dramatically increased the education budget for Africans, dismantled more of the color bar legislation in the workplace, granted Africans the right to form and join unions, abolished the Mixed Marriages Act and the Immorality Act, and provided the franchise for Indians and coloureds. However, his critics in the Progessive Federal Party, the opposition party, continue to point out that all his reform measures assume the legitimacy of Grand Apartheid, that is, of a society based on ethnic groupings enforced by law. Is P.W. Botha really willing to move toward genuine power sharing with the Africans? Is he willing to form a new constitution through negotiations with all ethnic groups? To answer these questions, it is essential to examine the teachings of the Dutch Reformed Church on apartheid. Does the DRC today provide a religious rationale for this system of separate development?

RELIGIOUS SANCTIONS

Among the white members of the Dutch Reformed Church today are the power brokers of government policy in the Republic. Almost all of the top government officials, parliament members, provincial council members, police, and military officials as well as town council members worship in a church of the DRC. Although most mainline Protestant churches and the Roman Catholic Church are openly critical of the policy of separate development, this has not been the case with the DRC. A brief outline of the DRC position is helpful, for it is only a slight exaggeration to state that, in large measure, the future of South Africa lies in the hands of this church.

An important distinction in analyzing the teachings of a church is the difference between official teaching and what in fact is taught and believed by the people in the pews. There is no question that the DRC has functioned in the past as a civil religion par excellence, providing the people with a religious sanction for a bold Afrikaner nationalism. The Afrikaners understood themselves as struggling for dignity and identity in the face of oppression from both the British and the Africans, and they found a vision, a rationale, and a source of strength in the Dutch Reformed Church. However, for this article, the interesting question is: What is the official teaching of the DRC today on separate development? Is this official teaching still able to provide a religious sanction for current Nationalist government policies on matters governing the races?

In 1974, the General Synod of the Dutch Reformed Church promulgated a document detailing the DRC's position on racial matters. Titled *Human Relations and the South African Scene in the Light of Scripture*, the document builds its case from Scripture, focusing on the creation narratives and the protohistory of *Genesis* 1-11. The twin themes of the unity and equality of all peoples and the ethnic diversity among peoples are both taken to emerge from Scripture and thus to be in accord with the intentions of the Creator. Consider, for example, a text from the Acts of the Apostles:

From one single stock he not only created the whole human race so that they could occupy the entire earth, but he decreed how long each nation should flourish and what the boundaries of its territory should be. And he did this so that all nations might seek the deity and, by feeling their way towards him, succeed in finding him.

While the unity of all peoples is the ultimate destiny of ethnic groups, human sin has made diversity a fact of life that finally can be overcome only in the next world in God's Kingdom. The story of the tower of Babel in *Genesis* tells of the results of sin.

Now Yahweh came down to see the town and the tower that the sons of man had built. "So they are all a single people with a single language!" said Yahweh. "This is but the start of their undertakings! There will be nothing too hard for them to do. Come, let us go down and confuse their language on the spot so that they can no longer understand one another." Yahweh scattered them then over the whole face of the earth, and they stopped building the town. It was named Babel therefore, because there Yahweh confused the language of the whole earth. It was from there that Yahweh scattered them over the whole face of the earth.

To be sure, the 1974 document of the Synod acknowledges that the message of the Gospel has social significance. Although, for the DRC, rather than blurring "all distinctions among peoples," the Scriptures mandate that Christians insure that diversity does not degenerate into estrangement. The document, however, in what seems to be a fatal flaw, equates "diversity" with "separation." Thus, for example, the document states: "In specific circumstances and under specific conditions the New Testament makes provision for the regulation on the basis of separate development of the co-existence of various peoples in one country." While the Christian task of avoiding estrangement in the midst of *diversity* is a manageable one, it is quite another story to overcome estrangement in the face of a rigid government policy of *separation*. The facts are that the policy of separation has brutally increased injustice and systematically destroyed the African family.

The DRC document, while clearly rejecting racism and discrimination on the basis of skin color, advocates the policy of separate development. Since apartheid is often associated with racial discrimination, this term is avoided. As indicated above, there is concern in the document that the policy of separate development be implemented in accordance with the biblical norms of justice and love. In the face of ample evidence that this is an impossible task, the DRC refuses to abandon the policy. Why? Could it be that it is not biblical principles but the survival of Afrikaaner power and identity that is controlling the DRC theology? The policy of separate development has required a plethora of legislation that is demeaning to the human dignity of blacks. In fact, the one clear advantage of the legislation is that it maintains the power and privileges of the whites. To be sure, some of the most incisive criticism of the Dutch Reformed Church in South Africa has come from its own theologians. There is a growing conviction in the DRC that Dutch Reformed practice is "more determined by the interests of the Afrikaner than the word of God."

To understand how such a fundamentally religious people as the Afrikaners could subsume the word of God to their own interests, it is well to remember that civil religion is an ever-present temptation, a temptation to which we in the United States have often succumbed. The Afrikaners, in the face of great adversity, triumphed over enemies in the major events of their history—the Great Trek, the many wars, the 1948 National Party victory, and the 1961 founding of the Republic. Through these events, many came to believe that God was acting in their history as he had done in Israel. They are a chosen people destined by God to bring an abundant life to all of southern Africa. God is believed to be on their side, guiding their policies and their destiny. With this sense of divine calling and mission, central policies such as separate development are not simply strategies devised on the basis of prudential judgments. Rather, they are thought to be part of the very order of creation and hence not easily altered. As mentioned above, however, this overarching world view is losing its compelling power for the DRC as it becomes more and more apparent that separate development is impossible to reconcile with a biblical vision of justice and love.

PROSPECTS FOR CHANGE

One step many see as essential to the process of eroding the theological sanction for apartheid is the dismantling of the racial structure of the Dutch Reformed Church—in Afrikaans, the Nederduitse Gereformeerde Kerk (NGK). The racial structure of the church is reflected in the sister churches of the NGK: for coloureds there is the Nederduitse Gereformeerde Sending Kerk; for Africans, the Nederduitse Gereformeerde Kerk in Africa; and for Indians, the Reformed Church in Africa. Since the NGK would not condemn apartheid as a sin and a heresy, as the nonwhite branches of the NGK with some 1.7 million members had done, the World Alliance of Reformed Churches suspended it from membership. To be sure, there is a growing minority of members of the NGK who want to move toward a multiracial church and society. Some NGK officials are hopeful that the 1986 General Synod will begin the moves necessary to bring structural unity to the church and end the color bias. Although only a few NGK theologians are presently arguing to open the white churches to all races, there is no question that the theology of separateness is increasingly under attack. Before Slabbert's critiques find resonance in the Afrikaner way of thinking, the Dutch Reformed Church will have to mend its ways.

HOPEFUL NOTE

One of the most hopeful notes that indeed the process of dismantling apartheid is under way is a statement released from the August 1985 annual meeting of the Presbytery of Stellenbosch of the DRC. It is worth quoting.

We recognise that, in the South African society, racial discrimination plays a fundamental role in both structural and personal matters; we confess that this is contrary to the biblical principles of love of one's neighbour and justice.

We also acknowledge that the ideal of apartheid did not succeed in creating social justice but has, on the contrary, led to human misery, frustration and injustice.

We confess that the Nederduitse Gereformeerde Kerk has often insensitively and uncritically tolerated the negative realities and consequences of apartheid.

'We therefore hereby declare ourselves prepared

a) to assess the apartheid system in all its consequences truly honestly and critically:

b) With all other people in our country, to seek prayerfully for a meaningful alternative for our land, and to do whatever we can to alleviate the suffering caused by the system."

To this, all people of goodwill throughout the world can only say, "Amen."

This chapter is excerpted from *the Apartheid Crisis*, forthcoming from Harper & Row.

Part III

THE DEBATE ON
ECONOMIC SANCTIONS

CHAPTER 13

A Plea for International Sanctions

by DESMOND TUTU

In 1976, out of a growing and deepening apprehension about the mood in Soweto, one of increasing anger and bitterness and frustration, I wrote an open letter to then Prime Minister, B.J. Vorster. In it I warned him that unless something was done, and done rapidly, to remove the causes of black anger, I was fearful of what was likely to erupt because black people were growing increasingly resistive under the oppressive yoke of apartheid. For young people it was represented in the insensitive determination to enforce Afrikaans as a medium of instruction in their inferior schools in a system of education that had been designed by its author, Dr. Verwoerd, for inferiority. My letter was dismissed contemptuously by Vorster as a propaganda ploy somehow engineered by the Progressive Federal Party. He did not think I could as a black person have the intelligence to know the grievances of my own people or the ability, if I did, to compose a letter to express those grievances.

I refer to this first effort to show that for over ten years I have attempted to alert the authorities in this land to the dangers to which their misguided and iniquitous policies were exposing our beloved country. In that 1976 letter, I referred to some of the minimum conditions necessary to allow blacks to feel that their plight was being taken seriously. I have made many public statements urging the government to act decisively and to give blacks hope.

Since then, I have often intervened in delicate, volatile situations to try to help diffuse them. With other black and white leaders I have gone to Turfloop and Fort Hare Universities to offer our good offices to resolve the perennial problems relating to student boycotts on those campuses. This was the action of someone who believes that problems can be solved by people sitting down together to discuss their differences. I have spoken to various white groups and addressed audiences at all the white university campuses. I was criticized in the black community for doing so because it was said I was just wasting time. I was ready, as I still am ready, to talk especially to young whites to help them see that by thinking independently they will come to reject this horrendous policy.

1980 PROPOSALS

In 1980, on my initiative, some of the leaders of the South African Council of Churches and of member churches went to see P.W. Botha, who was then Prime Minister, and his senior cabinet colleagues. We were trying to make them understand that unrest would be endemic in South Africa unless its root cause was removed — and that root cause was apartheid.

We declared then that we knew that politics was the art of the possible and did not want to suggest they do anything to erode their support among their constituency. And we put forward four actions which, if they were carried out, would be a dramatic demonstration of the government's intention to effect real political change leading to political power sharing. Remember, this was in 1980, six years ago. We said:

- Declare a commitment to a common citizenship for all South Africans in an undivided South Africa,
- Abolish the pass laws (even a phased abolition to avoid chaos), detention without trial, and arbitrary banning,
- Stop all forced population removals immediately, and
- Establish a uniform educational system.

These were not wild, radical demands and if the government had implemented them, we would have been saved a great deal of anguish, bloodshed, and loss of property and an increase in bitterness, hatred, and anger. We were criticized in the black community for going to the government. These were much of the same conditions in my 1976 letter to Vorster. But do you know what happened? They were ignored. In fact, we later discovered that the government had dealt dishonorably with us, for while we were discussing with them in good faith, they were employing the Christian League as a front organization in their nefarious efforts to subvert, malign, and discredit the SACC. Actually, the government intensified its efforts to undermine the council and me personally by getting its sycophantic South African Broadcasting Corporate and others of its media lickspittle supporters to denigrate and vilify us. That ended up with the government's being embarrassed, and the SACC and I received global vindication by the award of the Nobel Peace Prize. And the government was thoroughly hoisted by its own petard because our member churches and overseas supporters rallied to our support in an unprecedented way.

NEW CONSTITUTION

In 1984, far from heeding our calls for negotiation leading to power sharing, the government introduced a constitution that was the climax of the policies of exclusion to which blacks had been subjected since 1910. Seventy-three percent of the population was excluded from any participation in this monumental hoax designed to hoodwink the international community into believing that apartheid was being reformed.

Apartheid is not reformable. It must be destroyed before it destroys our country. That constitution was meant to entrench white minority rule with the coopted help of so-called coloureds and Indians, collaborators of their own and our oppression and exploitation. The people have rejected it unequivocally.

Despite all this, I tried again in 1985 to see the State President to talk with him as one South African to a fellow South African, as one grandfather to another, as one Christian to another. I hoped that he would act as only he could, the one white South African who would have gone down in history as having presided over the dissolution of apartheid and the emergence of a new, more equitable, just, nonracial, and truly democratic South Africa. He turned me down.

Little or nothing in South Africa has changed without pressure from the international communities. The sports policy changed only as a result of the sports boycott which I have supported and continue to do so as a nonviolent method to bring about change. I have called on the international community to exert pressure on the government— political, diplomatic but above all economic pressure—to persuade it to go to the negotiating table with the authentic representatives of all sections of our society, and I have said for blacks this would mean those in jail or in exile. I have said this umpteen times. I have been accused of advocating sanctions and I said I have not yet called for sanctions. I have said each country should surely decide for itself the nature of economic pressure it wishes to apply.

Most Western countries have rejected economic sanctions because, we are told, they would hurt blacks most of all. I hope that those who use this argument will drop it quietly and stop being so hypocritical. It is amazing how solicitous for blacks and such wonderful altruists everybody has become. It is remarkable that in South Africa the most vehement in their concern for blacks have been whites. Few blacks have repudiated me for my stance. This is very odd. They are not stupid. They know whether they are going to suffer and they would reject out of hand one who wanted to bring that suffering on them. And, yet, in the black community, my standing is very high. And, even more remarkably, two recent surveys have shown that over 70 percent of blacks support sanctions of some sort. Blacks have carried out consumer boycotts. They have staged massive stayaways to make a political statement.

Nothing that Botha has said has made me believe that he and his government are serious about dismantling apartheid.

I have no hope of real change from this government unless it is forced. We face a catastrophe in this land, and only the application of pressure by the international community can save us. Our children are dying. Our land is burning and bleeding and so I call on the international community to apply punitive sanctions against this government to help us establish a new South Africa, nonracial, democratic, participatory, and just. This is a nonviolent strategy. There is still a great deal of goodwill in our country between the races. Let us not be so wanton in destroying it. We can live together as one people, one family, black and white together.

CHAPTER 14

Discerning the Divestment Debate

by MANGOSUTHU G. BUTHELEZI

Why does a black South African oppose divestment? Why, in the face of the overwhelming support many prominent Americans are giving this antiapartheid tactic, am I saying thanks but no thanks?

The answer is really quite simple. The majority of black South Africans don't want divestment. They see investment as a strategy for liberation. They know that jobs will give them economic and political muscle. Without a means for survival—because blacks in South Africa are cash-dependent—their grinding poverty and degradation will continue unabated. They are aware of this, too: Divestment will not help the struggle for liberation; it will hinder it.

An average black wage earner, working for a company dependent on foreign investment or the ripple effects of healthy international trade, will not appreciate that following a divestment squeeze he has lost his job for his own good because activists in the United States and elsewhere say so.

Can you name a campus spokesman in the United States or any other campaigner for divestment who is prepared to come to South Africa to face black workers and tell them he supports their losing their jobs? If he doesn't fear for his life I can arrange a rally in any of our black townships—where unemployment is rampant—at any time. I would like to hear how he would explain to these men and women that divestment is in their best interests; that it will help liberate them; that he has decided what is best for them. Find me anybody who is brave enough to spell out to a mass meeting of black South Africans what divestment is really all about.

Quite frankly, I think the arrogance and the insensitivity of many divestment debate stalwarts is beyond decent description. I am appalled at how many of your politicians have cynically used this issue for their own political ends within the United States.

Does the United States know how long it is going to take before there is power sharing in South Africa? Has the West any idea of the sort of time scale involved? Have proponents of this so-called tactic really thought about the consequences of divestment? About who it will really affect? About whether it will really force the government to its knees? And, finally, if cornered, how the whites of South Africa will react?

LIFE-AND-DEATH ISSUE

In many ways the divestment debate can be likened to well-meaning citizens trying to free innocent prisoners by throwing a bomb into the middle of their cell. What the West often forgets is that it is the lives of ordinary blacks they are dealing with. This is not a dry, academic debate. Divestment is a life-and-death issue. We are talking about blood, sweat, and tears. About poverty, ignorance, and disease. Apartheid is condemned, quite rightly, for the evil that it is. We are grateful for that condemnation and we urge you to keep it up.

Just because there are blacks like myself who exercise their democratic right to oppose divestment and sanctions, the word has gone out that we are "tools of the system"; that we are "apologists for the South African government." This is, as you so descriptively say in the United States, hogwash. I have spent my life fighting apartheid and will continue to denounce the racist policies of the South African government for as long as it is necessary. None of us will know peace until there is justice in our beloved country. Until there is power sharing in a free and united South Africa. But please allow us to conduct the struggle for liberation in the manner in which we see fit. I am always amazed when well-meaning foreigners inform me that black South Africans are prepared to undergo even more pain in the struggle.

ZULU HOMELAND

Kwazulu is the area set aside for South Africa's seven million Zulus. I lead a political liberation movement called Inkatha, which has 1.2 million paid-up members. Nobody has to tell me about pain and suffering and the struggle for liberation.

Do Americans know that children die of malnutrition in this country? That starvation is permanently, mentally, damaging others? Thousands upon thousands of children will never learn to read and write because there just isn't the money to educate them. Thousands more fathers and mothers who have lost their jobs in the present economic recession will probably never work again. Some 60 percent of all black South Africans live in the rural areas. Years of drought and then successive cyclones and floods have devastated much of the overcrowded, eroded countryside allocated to them.

When we talk about subsistence farming we mean millions of people who barely manage to scratch enough food out of depleted soil to exist in the most primitive of circumstances. South African black society has been forced to develop in such a way that many of those who work in the cities send home money to their dependents in the farms and villages.

It might be hard for Americans to grasp, but a law called influx control has, for decades, forced wage earners to leave their families back in their traditional areas when they have sought employment in towns and cities throughout the country. Some figures calculate that for every wage earner in the city, there are at least nine dependents in the country.

The effects of the economic recession, coupled with the obvious political ramifications of divestment and sanctions, are beginning to tell in South Africa. The jobless are moving from the cities back into the countryside. In Kwazulu, for instance, old-age pensions are a primary source of income for entire families. The hardships being endured are staggering.

And on top of all this, 50 percent of all blacks in South Africa are under fifteen years of age. If the economy is ground to a virtual standstill by divestment and sanctions, how will any leader in a postliberation government ever recreate the infrastructure required to provide these young people with jobs — let alone the education to equip them to work? The economy of any country cannot be switched on and off like a tap.

BRINK OF RUIN

The reality is that successful divestment and sanctions strategies will, step by step, drive this country to the brink of economic ruin. And this will create a situation of ungovernability, which is precisely what proponents of the armed struggle want.

The African National Congress (ANC) Mission in Exile openly exhorts black South Africans — in its radio messages and publications — to create chaos. The ANC has stated time and again that the country must be made ungovernable. It sees itself as a de facto, postliberation, government. It doesn't talk of elections, just of "the will of the people" — as it dictates. The ANC Mission in Exile, after twenty-five years in exile, has a slick international propaganda operation. The members argue their cause persuasively. The trouble is, they haven't been home for so long they are out of touch.

That is why I argue differently. I know that the majority of blacks in this country will support me when I say we yearn for peaceful change. We don't want the ongoing misery that the ANC Mission in Exile has in store for us. We want negotiation and national reconciliation in a united South Africa. We want to build a multiracial society in which there is power sharing; in which there is hope for the future. How can we build a new society if the economic foundations of our country have been destroyed? What wealth will there be left to share?

Of course, you have read or heard of South Africans like Bishop Desmond Tutu and Reverend Allan Boesak calling for sanctions. I say they have no mandate to do so. I address audiences of tens of thousands at a time throughout South Africa. I am an elected constituency leader, and each and every time I have asked ordinary black South Africans whether they favor the tactic of divestment they have answered with a resounding "no."

This is why I respect the stand taken at present by the U.S. government. Considering the pressure placed on him, the decision by President Reagan was restrained and civilized. We applaud moves to alleviate black suffering. To attempt, as he has indicated, to assist in educating our children is a step in the right direction.

International audiences of the South African drama must be aware that there are two struggles taking place in this country: One is against apartheid and the other is for the establishment of a meaningful democracy. Support for divestment plays right into the hands of those who, as I have already noted, seek their political goals through violent means. It is a simple truth that men who use terrorism as a means to power usually rule by terror once they are in power. Just what do Americans want for South Africa?

Of course, we support moves to put the squeeze on foreign companies operating in South Africa that do not actively work for the elimination of apartheid. If they are simply in South Africa to exploit South Africa and her people, we do not need them now and we won't at any time in the future.

The work started by the Sullivan signatories must continue. We welcome any pressure brought to bear to ensure that companies that do operate in South Africa increase their efforts for change. I believe that foreign investors should search for selective new opportunities in South Africa — selective investment that will add to the pressure for change and, at the same time, add to opportunities for black South Africans.

They will find black South Africans who want to build, not burn; who want peace, not bloodshed; who are ready to work hard and who are anxious to learn. These are the people who need to be given a chance to change South Africa their way. They see the free enterprise system as the only system man has yet devised that is capable of fostering sustained economic growth. They have looked at what has happened in the rest of Africa where the glories of socialism have been extolled and the misery has continued. I must try to hammer home here that it is too simplistic to regard any action meant to harm the economy of South Africa as something that will do just that and nothing else.

ECONOMIC REALITIES

South Africa is a net exporter of food and energy to Africa and elsewhere in the world. The economy of this country is already integrated with the vested interests of the Western industrial world and with the developing economies of Africa.

Any harm to the South African economy will reverberate in these countries. Divestment may well shake South Africa's economic foundations, but it will pulverize the rest of southern Africa. These are the realities.

Wave your banners. Write to your congressmen. Shout about apartheid until you are blue in the face. We are grateful for your anger and your activity.

But when it comes to divestment, think again. It's a recipe for disaster. You will watch, on your television screens, blacks trying to achieve their political rights on empty stomachs, without roofs over their heads.

Just remember that it is we blacks who are burying our dead.

CHAPTER 15

Plenty of Propaganda to Prop Up Pretoria

by MICHAEL O. SUTCLIFFE

Increasingly in South Africa, various factions of the government and business have used conventional social science (and its protagonists) to provide rationalizations for reform initiatives and bargaining positions. Typically, this involves the appropriation and subsequent publication of surveys that evidence "popular" support or opposition to particular socioeconomic or political positions. As the work of distinguished social scientists laboring in "independent" institutions, these surveys are hailed as objective and definitive.

A recent example is Lawrence Schlemmer's survey of black workers. This study undertook to examine the attitudes of black workers about a range of issues such as capitalism, the role of trade unions, and worker militancy. The most significant finding — and certainly the one most widely publicized — was that only 25 percent of black workers were in favor of disinvestment, whereas the majority supported a policy of conditional investment along the lines of the Sullivan code. The immense propaganda value of this simple conclusion is immediately apparent. Specifically, it undermines the legitimacy of the divestment campaign by questioning the assumption that it enjoys a popular mandate from black workers. Not surprisingly, then, the report has been cited extensively by interest groups opposed to disinvestment, both in South Africa and overseas. Moreover, notwithstanding the fact that the largest black trade union federations — COSATU, AZACTU, and CUSA — have adopted resolutions expressing their support for divestment, Schlemmer's survey continues to be regarded as the definitive statement on black worker opinion.

DISINVESTMENT POLLS

Although Schlemmer's remains the most influential survey conducted to date, a number of other surveys have been conducted. On the one hand, support for his general conclusions may be found in four other surveys. The Human Sciences Research Council, for example, conducted surveys during July 1984, February 1985, and May 1985 and found that, respectively, 82, 65, and 76 percent of the black respondents were against economic boycotts. Schlemmer's survey noted above and another more widely conducted survey in November 1984 suggested that 75 and 84 percent of the black respondents were against disinvestment. On the other hand, more recent surveys have indicated that blacks would be in favor of applying punitive economic sanctions against South Africa. Mark Orkin found during September 1985 that 73 percent of his black respondents were in favor of economic sanctions, and in a poll of urban blacks conducted for the London *Sunday Times*, 77 percent supported economic sanctions. In addition, a poll of 406 blacks living in Durban was conducted in March 1985 for the *Ilanga* newspaper. A substantial 44 percent of those interviewed thought that U.S. companies should take their money out of South Africa.

Although it is impossible to compare these results from different surveys, it is quite clear that apparently similar questions (relating to disinvestment, economic sanctions, etc.) have produced different responses. As one might expect, black workers generally do not wish to lose their jobs as a result of disinvestment, but at the same time the majority appear to feel that punitive sanctions would force the government to abandon apartheid.

More important, however, what has become clear is that social surveys may be used to make highly effective political interventions. This is especially true of situations (such as South Africa) where social surveys are popularly but erroneously perceived to be necessarily "scientific," where individuals with sufficient training to challenge social surveys on a scientific basis are scattered thinly and unevenly throughout the population, where the subjects of social surveys are denied the opportunity to question the methodology or the conclusions that are drawn from the results, and where high-profile social scientists of particular political persuasions enjoy privileged access to the media through which to disseminate and legitimatize their work. Under these conditions, social science has become a means whereby the government and business can advance (white/reformist) social scientists as spokespersons for the (black/progressive) working classes.

It must be a source of great irritation to workers and their unions to see their "views" debated in the media by remote academics on the basis of flimsy survey data. But it is not enough merely to dismiss these studies as irrelevant or reactionary, since this will do nothing to challenge their "scientific" credentials. A more effective response is to examine critically the methodologies that are supposed to guarantee the "scientific" basis of social surveys. This has been accomplished in detail elsewhere, but it is important to address some of the sources of bias that may have been introduced into these essentially political intervention. The Schlemmer survey is selected for such analysis simply because it is the one instance in which a survey result has been used to support policies of the governments of the United States and South Africa when in fact the results contrast markedly with the official views expressed by almost all significant black-led South African organizations.

A potential source of bias in research is the relationship between client and donor. In the case of the Schlemmer survey, the extent to which the donor (the U.S. State Department) may have influenced the results is difficult to assess. Schlemmer would probably defend his claim to be "independent" of donor bias. However, it seems likely that the U.S. State Department, which has already adopted a position on South Africa, would be particularly interested in obtaining results endorsing its policy of "constructive engagement." Certainly the way in which the disinvestment issue was portrayed to workers suggests that donor bias may have been important to the process of questionnaire design. The questionnaire, in fact, reflects a very biased conception of "constructive engagement." The policy is not presented to workers as one related to the abstention on votes against apartheid in the United Nations, negotiation with the South African government ("quiet diplomacy"), and the like, but as one that leads to the provision of jobs and, implicitly, good fringe benefits for workers. There appears to be no corresponding attempt to predict worker support, for example, for Representative Stephen Solarz's (D-N.Y.) formulation of the divestment issue.

SAMPLING BIAS

Certain aspects of sampling bias also need to be discussed. First, the survey is not regionally representative of all black workers. Second, there is no statistical basis to the claim that the sampling frame accords with the regional distribution of multinational industrial concerns (in terms of black employees). Third, Schlemmer's reasoning for overrepresenting the Port Elizabeth and Durban-Pinetown areas appears to be tautological. Finally, it is worth noting that this was a survey of black male production workers (not "black male workers," not "black workers," and not "blacks" in general), since that fact is generally overlooked in media broadcasting of the results. The *Sunday Times*, for example, headlined its report on the survey "Most S.A. blacks want investment from overseas." However, only 20 percent of black workers are employed in the manufacturing sector (and 19 percent of these are women), so the survey focuses on the attitudes of a group that accounts for 16 percent of black workers — perhaps 12 percent if unemployed workers are excluded.

A third source of bias relates to the design of the questionnaire schedule. Here, a number of points must be borne in mind. The first concerns the difficulty of obtaining truthful responses to the questions. It should be taken into consideration that many of the issues examined in Schlemmer's survey are highly sensitive, and it is clearly naive to assume that assurances of anonymity will guarantee that responses are genuine. A second problem lies in designing questions that generate meaningful responses. One common predicament is ambiguity. A good example of this in Schlemmer's survey was the statement that "whites are strict but honest and fair — blacks would not be happier under their own people," to which respondents were asked to agree or disagree. For a variety of reasons, this makes no sense, whatsoever. In fact, the statement consists of four distinct questions, and considerations of the second half cannot be made independently of the first, which is loaded in favor of whites.

A further difficulty stems from inviting respondents to answer under conditions and alternatives that may at present be only vaguely and subjectively imagined. Related is the problem of collapsing complex political opinions into multiple choice or yes/no categories. There are two dangers here. The first results from incorporating a wide range of opinion into one or two statements or questions. This often obliges respondents to associate themselves with attitudes they would not articulate in open discussion. The second arises from a biased or inadequate conceptualization of the issues under investigation, which "forces" responses to assume a certain shape. The fact that none of Schlemmer's respondents appeared to be undecided about any of the questions dealing with highly complex issues (capitalism, constructive engagement, disinvestment, etc.) suggests that the survey suffered from both of these tendencies. Respondents were given no option other than to agree or disagree with preselected statements that were loaded in particular directions.

This is most evident in Schlemmer's treatment of the disinvestment issue. In each of the three questions dealing directly with disinvestment, U.S. investment is equated with the building of factories, whereas disinvestment is associated with the closing down of factories or an inability to build new ones. It is hardly surprising, then, that production workers did not come out in solid support for a strategy that they are told will lead to retrenchments. Alec Erwin of COSATU comments, for example, that the Schlemmer survey "basically posed a question of whether workers would be prepared to lose their jobs as a sign of support for disinvestment. Even such deliberate simplification did not elicit total rejection for disinvestment, although workers were quite justified in being opposed to disinvestment if the problem was posed in this misleading way."

The important point, then, is that the disinvestment issue was presented to workers in terms that are both misleading and unbalanced. For example, the impression given in the survey was that the contribution to jobs locally by *direct* U.S. investment is quite considerable and that the involvement of U.S. capital in South Africa is almost exclusively in the private manufacturing sector. Both views are incorrect; nevertheless, it appears to have been accepted as a basic assumption that U.S. disinvestment will result in a drastic increase in black unemployment. Another assumption that appears to underlie Schlemmer's conceptualization of the disinvestment issue is that South Africa's domestic savings have traditionally been insufficient to satisfy its capital needs, and that U.S. investment therefore comprises a central element in ensuring and maintaining a satisfactory growth rate and the creation of sufficient job opportunities in the long term. This is also misleading; both assertions are gross exaggerations and serve to deflect discussion from factors that are more central to the processes of economic growth and job creation in South Africa.

Schlemmer himself admits that "the debate about disinvestment and trade sanctions is, to say the least, very strongly informed by preconceived notions and ideas based on a variety of ideological positions." It is ironic, then, that if the questions on investment and disinvestment are examined more closely in the South African context, Schlemmer's very simplistic and unacceptably biased conceptualization of these issues is immediately apparent. In his report, the disinvestment question is presented as a simple either/or dilemma: Either one frightens the South African government or there are more jobs for black workers. It not only misrepresents the issue but also fails to acknowledge the strategic and symbolic value of the campaign and the fact that it incorporates a variety of options. For this reason, the disinvestment issue could have been presented to workers in terms quite different from those used in Schlemmer's questionnaire. One wonders, for example, what the response might have been if workers had been asked their opinion of the sale of computer technology to the South African police or restrictions on loans to the South African government. One wonders, also, what the reaction might have been if workers were asked whether they supported a ban on private invest-ment *if* the investors did not encourage democratic trade union organization and subscribe to a basic charter of workers' rights.

In the introduction to his report, Schlemmer states quite correctly that "rank-and-file black people are seldom if ever consulted [while] a great many people speak on their behalf." Of course, Schlemmer is one of the most important of these "great many people," but he argues that in his role of spokesman he is only proffering the views "of the people" as they are articulated through his social surveys. Because these surveys are supposed to be "objective" and "scientific," his utterances are generally considered unbiased and reliable. Given this perception, it is not surprising that the work of reformist social scientists such as Schlemmer is often appropriated to legitimatize government policies.

WEAK AND IMPRECISE

What is lost in this process is that social surveys are subject to a host of biases and methodological deficiencies, and they are not the reliable and efficient monitors that most people believe them to be. As Schlem-mer himself acknowledges in an earlier publication, attitude surveys should be "recognized for what they are—very crude, weak and im-precise instruments. . . ." Whereas they may be "useful guides to the interpretation of large social scenarios," he continues, they "should never be read as social facts." Since this is not generally appreciated, social surveys may be used to make political interventions with considerable effect. The political appropriation of Schlemmer's survey is an obvious example.

This brief analysis suggests the inappropriateness of surveys, such as the ones conducted by Schlemmer, as indicators of black attitudes toward disinvestment. In fact, one might argue that since the issues are so complex and since they are essentially political in nature, it would be impossible to construct a social-scientific procedure whereby black South Africans (or anyone for that matter) could objectively assess the contending positions.

The majority of South Africa's whites and major trading partners have not, for obvious reasons, called for effective punitive sanctions. However, these groups have found only limited support from black South Africans for this position. In particular, only Bantustan leaders such as Buthelezi of Kwazulu have been outspoken black critics of sanctions. As a result, it is difficult to gauge the actual extent of support for this position among blacks. In the case of Buthelezi, it is interesting to note that a survey conducted by a newspaper that favors his policies found that almost 50 percent of those interviewed were happy to see the withdrawal of all U.S. assets from South Africa.

The antidisinvestment lobby usually suggests arguments revolving around the extent to which sanctions might affect the general welfare of black South Africans. However, proponents of disinvestment have been quick to point out that "this view reeks with hypocrisy and insincerity . . . that it is a dishonest attempt to protect the vested interests of the West." In particular, they note the following:

- A substantial amount of foreign investment is in (black) labor-saving devices.
- Many multinational firms locate in South Africa simply because of the cheap labor power available.
- In fact, massive outflows of South Africa's wealth, produced by black and white South Africans, have occurred over the past five years.
- Major Western countries have avoided even limited sanctions and therefore do not have the interests of South Africa's blacks at heart.
- Proposed disinvestment measures do not touch the mainstream of economic relations between South Africa and its major trading partners and therefore would not affect blacks to any great extent.
- Blacks have continued to suffer in spite of the so-called Botha reforms.
- Some overseas corporations provide strategic technology, know-how, and contacts that help maintain the apartheid structure.

The argument that sanctions will hurt blacks more than whites is most commonly heard, but it has been supplemented recently with a more insidious form of paternalism which verges on downright racism. Helen Suzman, for example, has argued that sanctions must be opposed because they create a delusion among township blacks that the transfer of power in South Africa is imminent. In contrast to the arguments presented by spokespersons (usually white) for black South Africans, most black-led organizations in South Africa subscribe to the principle that pressure brought to bear on the South African government through the campaigns for sanctions is far more important than any possible side effects this may have on the overall welfare of individuals. The substantial support for the disinvestment campaign given by groups such as COSATU, UDF, ANC, and CUSA makes it difficult to believe, as Schlemmer's survey suggests, that only 25 percent of black workers support disinvestment.

Three general points are made by the pro-sanctions groups in developing their positions vis-a-vis sanctions: that investment in South Africa is undertaken for profit and not for the improvement of black living conditions, that strategic technology imported from the West is used directly in the repression of South African blacks, and that investment is not democratically controlled by black South Africans. For those advocating support for sanctions, the choices are quite clear. Either one supports the continuation of apartheid or one works for its dismantling by forcing the government to acquiesce to the demands made by the disenfranchised for equal political rights in a unified South Africa. Support for investment and contact with the racist government is regarded as a continuation of the status quo and not as the means whereby black living and working conditions may be improved and black political rights granted.

CHAPTER 16

Will Sanctions Harm the Oppressed or the Oppressor?

by HERMAN NICKEL

A striking feature of the mounting campaign for disinvestment and general economic sanctions against South Africa is how little effort is spent in explaining how the campaign will bring about its ostensible goal: the peaceful replacement of apartheid by a democratic society in which the rights of the individual are protected without regard to race, religion, or national origin. Perhaps this glaring omission reflects the extent to which the South African drama has been presented to the American public in terms of a morality play—black and white in moral as well as racial terms, with the just demands of the black majority pitted against the repression of the white minority. Morality plays, of course, do not allow for the subtleties of tragedy, in which the real or imagined equities of the antagonists are pursued to the point of mutual or self-destruction. They are about crime and punishment.

The morality play version of what is happening in South Africa uses a simple syllogism. Since apartheid is evil, and sanctions (or disinvestment) are aimed against it, every right-minded foe of apartheid must support sanctions, and anyone who doesn't must therefore be at least a closet supporter of apartheid. Of course, this is a preposterous position, but it is being used with considerable effect to silence politicians and others who do not want to be tarred with the brush of being "soft on racism." One is inevitably reminded of an unhappy era in the not-too-distant American past when anyone who did not accept Senator Joseph McCarthy's brand of anti-Communism found himself labeled as "soft on Communism."

In a morality play, the curtain falls when the villain has met his deserved fate. History is not like that. It goes on, and the prime task of politicians and diplomats is not to punish but to lay the foundation for a better future. And that is why their moral responsibility must be to think through and anticipate, as well as they can, the results of their actions. In the case of South Africa, moral responsibility cannot be only the destruction of apartheid but the establishment of a more just order. A policy that would merely achieve the former without the latter could easily mean the replacement of one evil system by another—hardly a moral result.

BLUNT INSTRUMENT

The problem with general punitive sanctions is, of course, that they are a terribly indiscriminate and blunt instrument which hurts the oppressed as well as the oppressor, not to mention a lot of more or less innocent bystanders. We are told that we needn't worry too much about that, since it is the oppressor who stands to lose the most. This argument seems to ignore the obvious fact that the margin of safety that separates the more prosperous South Africans (*i.e.*, the whites) from deprivation and starvation is much wider than for people who live dangerously close to the subsistence level even now. Proponents of sanctions scoff at this solicitude for the poor. This may be a fair point with respect to those who never showed much solicitude for the victims of apartheid before, but hardly so with respect to such implacable and life-long foes of apartheid as Alan Paton or Helen Suzman, not to mention countless South African blacks who oppose disinvestment and sanctions. Blacks, we are assured, "are prepared to suffer"—as if this absolves those who mete out the suffering from making their own moral judgment.

The credibility of this position suffers somewhat from the fact that it is taken most vocally by South African spokesmen whose jobs, income, and immediate families would be the least affected. It carries even less weight when uttered from a long and safe distance by outsiders.

The substantive flaws of the "blacks are prepared to suffer" argument are even more glaring. In the first place, what data we do have cast grave doubts on whether the majority of blacks really agree that more suffering will be good for them. (And even if a majority were to agree, what about those who do not?) It is interesting that Professor Fatima Meer of the Institute of Black Research in Durban, who was one of the most vocal detractors of the 1984 survey by Professor

Lawrence Schlemmer of the University of Natal, has recently published the findings of her own survey, financed by the Ford Foundation, which strikingly resemble Professor Schlemmer's findings. No more than 26 percent of Dr. Meer's respondents would support disinvestment if it meant that "many people lost their jobs." ("Many" jobs implies that among the jobs lost might be your own.) As a supporter of the United Democratic Front, no one could accuse Dr. Meer of an anti-disinvestment bias.

Furthermore, the organizations that are most directly concerned with black jobs (i.e., the black trade unions) are more than just a little ambivalent on the whole question. Some unions have argued for "selective" disinvestment. Others are on record as wanting foreign companies to remain in South Africa because they have become part of the "social fabric." Still others have taken a strong public line in favor of general disinvestment. But if we probe beneath the surface, what most of these unions seem to be saying is that foreign firms can pull out as long as they "leave the wealth in the hands of the workers." How many multinational corporations can satisfy these conditions remains obscure.

The second problem with the "blacks are prepared to suffer" position is its tacit implication that the additional suffering will indeed be rewarded by political liberation. But just how this is supposed to happen is never clearly spelled out. Instead, we are being asked to accept more or less on faith the assertion of well-intentioned people, among them prominent clerics in South Africa, that general economic sanctions and disinvestment represent "the last chance of peaceful change." Their sincerity and motives need not be questioned, but their infallibility should be. Chances are that they are, in fact, quite wrong.

Assuming the inevitability of change, how peaceful is that change likely to be when a government dependent on the support of white voters defends the living standards and the political power of these constituents and—in the process—polarization deepens and the vicious cycle of revolt and repression spins still further out of control? As a general rule, reform anywhere is easier to achieve when the socioeconomic pie is growing, and harder when it is shrinking.

SIEGE ECONOMY

We have been told that even Afrikaner businessmen understand the disastrous consequences of a siege economy and will therefore work alongside their English-speaking colleagues to force their government either to forestall sanctions in the first place or to take the political steps necessary to get them lifted. This is a half-truth. Afrikaner businessmen have indeed worked very hard to stave off the sanctions-disinvestment threat. Nevertheless, one should take note of the warning from Dr. Fred du Plessis, chairman of the giant Sanlam group, who, pointing to Rhodesia's paradoxical sanctions boom, warned in March that, if necessary, "we will get by without foreign relations." Dr. du Plessis's view may not be shared by most South African businessmen, the majority of whom see a siege economy as a disaster. But what matters more is whether he reflects the view of the leadership of the ruling National Party and their perceptions of what the political traffic will bear in their Afrikaner constituency.

Ironically, the very maximalism of the demands of the sanctions-disinvestment movement has weakened its political effectiveness vis-à-vis the South African government. Self-sufficient in food, rich in coal and minerals, and with a formidable industrial capacity (developed, in part, as a precaution against sanctions), South Africa is less vulnerable than many or most other countries. However painful, sanctions tied to maximalist conditions which are perceived by most whites as political suicide are not likely to have the desired effect — and it is the perception that matters. Human experience tells us that people prefer almost any other form of death. The lesson of the sports boycott is that there must be some equivalence between what one side is withholding and what it is demanding. The sports boycott was no doubt effective in getting South African sports to move toward integration, but it is not likely to be very effective when the ante is raised to the demand of black majority rule.

On the black end of the political spectrum, the maximalism of the disinvestment-sanctions camp is to create the illusion that negotiations with the white regime are no longer necessary, and that with international support one can wait until the fortress of apartheid surrenders. The result, the maximizing of intransigence on both sides, would seem to be neither helpful to conflict resolution nor in the U.S. national interest in peaceful change toward a South African order based on consent. Our own ability to bring the parties together under those circumstances would be reduced to next to nothing.

HIDDEN AGENDA?

Of course, there may be some people who have quite a different hidden agenda, and that is to use economic pressure precisely because they think it will hasten a violent, revolutionary struggle. Those who pursue this hidden agenda should be forced to put their cards on the table. In the United States, there is a broad consensus for the abolition of apartheid and the establishment of a truly democratic society in South Africa. But there is certainly no popular support for a scenario of violence and indiscriminate terror, let alone the emergence of a totalitarian dictatorship which is so often the result.

Two of the less serious arguments that are popular with the sanctions and disinvestment lobby should be dismissed as the humbug they are. As of late, the United States is being exhorted to adopt general economic sanctions against South Africa as a matter of "consistency." This would carry more conviction if those who pleaded for consistency were, in fact, equally fervent supporters of sanctions against Nicaragua or Libya or, for that matter, against such a massive and systematic violator of human rights as Ethiopia, which seems to have given the concept of forced removals a new and brutal African meaning. Of course, they usually take exactly the opposite position, on grounds that range from ineffectiveness to immorality. In fact, an economic weapon that may be effective in one case can be quite ineffective and positively harmful in another, depending on the circumstances and the political objectives. The question is pragmatic, not dogmatic.

But perhaps the shabbiest argument of all is also the one that is the most pretentious. This is the "moral gesture" rationale and it goes like this: Even if general economic sanctions and disinvestment do not work, it will at least be a symbolic move to put the United States on "the right side." The callousness of this position is staggering. Its proponents openly admit the futility of their gesture. They knowingly advocate a path leading to actions that would inflict suffering and would be at best ineffective and at worst positively harmful—all in order to stand on some imaginary pedestal of moral purity. This kind of feel-good moralism, in fact, falls into the realm more of self-indulgence than of morality.

The Reagan Administration's approach is decidedly different. It should go without saying that the Administration, too, accepts that the system of apartheid poses a profound moral challenge. But it proceeds from the premise that in social morality, good intentions are not enough. As we all know, the path to hell is paved with them.

In our actions, we must weigh the likely consequences for the future welfare of the people—all the people—of South Africa and the southern

African region as a whole. The criteria that we must put to ourselves is whether U.S. policy will effectively promote conditions conducive to peace, justice, and welfare in southern Africa, whether it speeds the process leading away from apartheid to a full sharing of power by all the people of South Africa on a mutually acceptable and nonracial basis. That apartheid is doomed we take as a given. What truly matters is how it goes and what follows it.

The Administration's policy rests on a number of fundamental prepositions:

- Apartheid is not only a moral affront. It is a prime source of internal and regional instability in an area of great importance, which opens up targets of opportunity for our global adversary.
- The Administration opposes violence from whatever source. This goes for official repression as it goes for terrorist activity. It was *The Washington Post* that put it well in a recent editorial: "A new rule needs to be engraved in everybody's mind: Nobody who uses terrorism as a means is entitled to have his political purpose taken seriously as an end."
- The Administration realizes that South Africa is inextricably intertwined with and, indeed, is the powerhouse of the rest of the southern African subcontinent. Therefore, it recognizes the need for regional stability and security in southern Africa. Improved relations between South Africa and her neighbors and the internal reform process are mutually independent. Particularly critical is the need to create the political context in which Security Council Resolution 435 can at last be implemented and Namibia can achieve independence. By necessity this will require the withdrawal of Cuban forces from Angola and the deinternationalization of the internal conflict in that country.
- The Administration realizes that the principal impetus for change in South Africa is and will continue to be internal.
- It accepts that U.S. influence in and on South Africa, although important, is limited. When added to the forces for change that are already at work in South Africa itself, it can help create a "critical mass" or, in a different metaphor, help tip the scales. The Administration does not intend to lessen or lose that influence by taking our chips from the table and walking away from the problem.
- The Administration does not accept the notion that the role that U.S. investment has played in the development of the South African economy has merely "undergirded" the system of apartheid. On the

contrary, it is the collision between the requirements of a growing industrial society and an essentially preindustrial political ideology that accounts for much of the reform process that has already taken place. There is no constructive benefit to weakening this dynamic, which has strengthened black economic and political clout and in which U.S. investment has played its part. Its attitude toward sanctions and disinvestment is a function of this pragmatic analysis of U.S. interests and goals.

This is why the present Administration is committed to resisting a course that although advertised as moral in intent is, in fact, morally unacceptable in its likely consequences. It will continue to oppose punitive sanctions that would damage growth prospects of the South African economy, hurt the people they are ostensibly intended to help, and lead to further political polarization and violent conflict.

DEMOGRAPHIC TIME BOMB

We must also look to the future. The notion that once the investment tap has been turned off it can be turned on again at will after the political objectives have been reached requires more than the normal dose of economic naivete. In South Africa, a demographic time bomb is ticking away. Job creation is falling woefully behind the entry of young blacks into the labor market. By the year 2000—just fourteen years from now—the number of black South Africans living in urban areas will have doubled. Merely to accommodate these new entrants into the labor market, the South African economy would have to create a quarter million new jobs each year—to say nothing about combatting the already frighteningly high level of unemployment in the black community. It is doubtful whether the South African economy by itself has the capital resources to achieve the twin tasks of creating additional employment opportunities and making up the enormous backlogs that exist in black education, housing, health, and other public services. This has ominous implications for the future political stability of that country—no matter who governs it.

Nor can one ignore the effect that a policy of deliberately damaging the growth of the South African economy would have on the even more precariously poised economies in that region. So far, at least, there does not seem to be much enthusiasm in Congress to compensate the neighboring countries of South Africa for the disastrous consequences they would suffer from sanctions. The United States has had to warn these governments quite bluntly not to look to us in this regard.

As a corollary to this outline of the basic framework of the Administration's policy toward South Africa, it is necessary to trace briefly the most recent fine-tuning of that policy: President Reagan's Executive Order of September 9, 1985. It is true that the order placed further restrictions on certain types of trade with South Africa. But—contrary to what some commentators have said—this does not represent a change in U.S. policy. Restrictions on certain types of U.S. trade with that country have been in place for many years. For example, the United States has taken part in the U.N. arms embargo against South Africa and for years has had restrictions on equipment that can be sold to the South African police.

The Executive Order is a codification of a long-standing U.S. policy. Its measures are not punitive in an indiscriminate way. They are aimed specifically at the machinery of apartheid, rather than targeting the entire economy and people of South Africa. Briefly, the Executive Order bans bank loans to the South African government, terminates the sale of Krugerrands, prohibits the export of computers or computer technology to that government's military, police, or apartheid-enforcing agencies, bars nuclear technology exports, and requires sizable U.S. subsidiaries to comply with a set of Fair Labor Standards that are similar but not identical to the Sullivan Principles. That code, which dates from 1977, is a completely voluntary set of principles for U.S. subsidiaries operating in South Africa. The impact of the Executive Order may well be to increase the number of companies adhering to the Sullivan Principles, but these remain voluntary. The Executive Order, on the other hand, involves penalties for noncompliance with the Fair Labor Standards. Primarily, it would deny U.S. companies operating in South Africa intercession by the United States government with the host government regarding the export marketing activity of these companies. Although conditions may vary, this penalty can be substantial—especially for larger firms.

It is not surprising that the Executive Order of September 9, 1985 was not exactly greeted with universal applause in South Africa. That was hardly its intention. But anyone who has any familiarity with the realities of the political situation on Capitol Hill knows that the alternative was the passage of much more stringent and, in the Administration's view, counterproductive measures.

It seems clear that renewed political pressure to push through legislation of this kind this year is going to be tremendous. Representative

William Gray (D-Pa.), the powerful chairman of the House Budget Committee, has already served notice that he will introduce a bill that may ban all new investment in South Africa. The Reagan Administration will call on its supporters in Congress to oppose such measures, especially since they would preempt the findings of a broadly based Advisory Committee on South Africa to the Secretary of State, which is composed of twelve distinguished Americans. They are visiting South Africa on a fact-finding mission before submitting their report in January 1987. Their recommendations will carry considerable weight, and they should not be preempted.

RACIST STIGMA

With the congressional elections coming up in 1986, however, we must face the fact that South Africa will be an issue, especially if the news from there is not positive. Under such circumstances there will be great pressure on many candidates, even of moderate and conservative persuasion, to adopt a tough posture—if only to avoid the stigma of being "soft on racism." So this year will be as crucial to the relations between the United States and South Africa as it will be for South Africa itself. South Africans will have to keep in mind that what happens in the United States regarding their country depends very largely on the perceptions of the actions of the government over there.

The Administration has welcomed State President Botha's acknowledgement on January 31 that apartheid is an outdated concept. If the hated pass laws are scrapped, clearly and unequivocally, on July 1 as he has pledged, and if South African citizenship is restored to those South African blacks who lost it as a result of the policy of grand apartheid, clearly these would be significant steps away from apartheid. They should encourage representative black leaders to come forward to negotiate the political meaning of black citizenship in a post-apartheid order that reflects the consent of the governed. It should be added, however, that as long as the interface of blacks with the authorities is characterized by Casspirs and tearsmoke, it will be difficult for the South African government to put itself across as a government of reform, both internally and internationally.

We have also stated repeatedly that the release of Nelson Mandela and other political prisoners is an important element in creating the context for political dialogue. Americans know from their own political experience that long-ingrained attitudes do not change overnight. It took until 1954 for our Supreme Court to strike down the doctrine of "separate but equal." But today it is no longer a salable political commodity. Thus it does not seem likely that the important commitment to abandon "outdated" apartheid will be taken at face value in South Africa or abroad, as long as such basic aspects of life as where one can live, where one can go to school, and how one can exercise one's political rights as a citizen remain dependent on one's racial classification. Freedom of association and freedom of choice are rapidly emerging as the next key questions in the South African reform process.

How South Africa is seen to be tackling these issues will be critical to its political and economic future. The threat of sanctions and disinvestment legislation will continue unless progress is seen to be happening. What is probably more critical, however, is the possibility that international market judgment about the investment climate and the long-term stability of South Africa could come to coincide with the political judgment of those who would want to impose sanctions as a punitive measure.

Sanctions that run counter to market judgments normally do not work. Where sanctions and market judgment run parallel, they could reinforce each other. Keeping this from happening is a task for all who believe that the political and moral costs of sanctions are unacceptable.

CHAPTER 17

The Folly of Economic Sanctions

by HELEN SUZMAN

Recently at the Students Union at Oxford University, Dr. Chester Crocker and I opposed the motion "that economic sanctions are necessary for the abolition of apartheid." Not surprisingly, the vote on the motion went against us. But the important point is that the students at Oxford were prepared to listen to the argument. It is doubtful whether this would be the case on any campus in the United States, for there the issue has been reduced to a simple equation— if you are against sanctions you must be for apartheid— you must be a racist.

It should be made clear that the ultimate aim of the motion—the abolition of apartheid—was not at issue. There was consensus that there is no valid argument against the abolition of a system that has so much inherent cruelty and oppression. It was on the means to that end, on the strategy to be employed, that there was a difference of opinion.

Whether criticism of Pretoria constitutes outside interference with domestic affairs, whether there are double standards, or whether expediency is implicit in the strong sentiments presently evident in U.S. public opinion is irrelevant. It would be a sad day if countries like the United States, which cherish human rights as their basic philosphy, allowed apartheid to go unprotested. As for double standards, while it is true that many countries that practice oppression worse than that of the apartheid regime escape the wrath of the world, South Africa claims to belong to the community of Western democracies and therefore must expect to be judged by those standards and not by those observed behind the Iron Curtain or in some Third World countries.

Certainly, there is expediency in the opposition to apartheid in the

United States and elsewhere. No doubt, Citibank and Chase Manhattan pulled the financial plug on South Africa at the beginning of August 1985 because of threats of withdrawal by depositors rather than because of moral strictures against apartheid. And no doubt, too, the presence of black voters in their constituencies encouraged many U.S. congressmen to leap onto the antiapartheid bandwagon. Why not? Here was one of those rare occasions in politics when expediency and morality coincide.

Nevertheless, the two main factors that motivate people to support the imposition of sanctions are the moral factor and the punitive factor. Both are understandable. The moral aspect is a healthy impulse that makes one want to have nothing to do with the country that implements the repulsive system of apartheid — the "clean hands" syndrome. And that is fine, until it is realized that by divesting or disinvesting, which are two forms of sanctions, any influence that might have been exercised inside South Africa, such as setting an example to others regarding adherence to fair employment practices and exercising their social responsibilities, also disappears. The desire to punish South Africa, to use punitive measures like sanctions against the apartheid regime, is certainly understandable.

But retribution, when it comes, is not selective. Indeed, it falls more heavily on those it is meant to help than on those it is meant to punish. True, white South Africans would certainly feel the impact of sanctions, as indeed they are feeling the impact of the bank freeze and the drastic decline in the value of the rand. Businessmen in particular are now much more vocal than ever before in their opposition to apartheid. But business lobbies have far less influence, far less clout, with the government in South Africa than do their counterparts in the United States. It is not the businessmen who put the National Party regime in power. Most of them support the official opposition, the Progressive Federal Party. The government is kept in power by civil servants, programmed over forty years to implement apartheid. About 40 percent of gainfully occupied whites are directly, or indirectly, in government employ in South Africa. Many of them are likely to turn their backs on the government and veer right if it deviates too far from existing policy. The regime is also kept in power by the white artisan class, such as the mine workers and other skilled workers in industry, who are hardly to the forefront of the struggle for black advancement, and by the rural white electorate which is notoriously reactionary.

The brunt of such measures would be felt by blacks at home and in the heavily dependent neighboring countries in South Africa. Whatever harm is done to South Africa's economy will certainly harm the economies of the neighboring black states, all of which are dependent to a greater or lesser degree on South Africa for jobs, markets, and transportation. The former High Commission Territories of Botswana, Lesotho, and Swaziland are part of a Customs Union with South Africa and belong to the rand monetary area. South Africa's Escom is an important source of power for these countries.

They depend entirely on routes through South Africa for trade. Malawi, Zaire, Zambia, and Zimbabwe are also heavily dependent on South African transport and ports for their imports and exports. Trade between South Africa and the rest of Africa is substantial. Alternative sources of supply could only be found at greater cost.

Over a quarter of a million foreign blacks work in South African mines alone, earning $1.1 billion per annum, half of which is repatriated. A further 70,000 blacks are employed in other occupations in South Africa, plus an estimated 1 million "illegals."

At home, blacks are always the first to get fired during economic recession. Unemployment is no light matter in a country like South Africa, which has no social security safety net. A visit to Port Elizabeth, once a thriving industrial town in the Eastern Cape, would be instructive. Today, Port Elizabeth is dying, in the most painful manner. Ford and other assembly plants have closed down. Unemployment among black workers is up to 60 percent. The townships are in ferment; they are occupied by police and the army. Daily there are reports of shootings and tear gassing. Black-on-black violence is horrific, with kangaroo courts meting out rough justice. Eight murders in a week are not unusual. Transfer this scene throughout the country and anarchy results, with blacks the main victims of the strategy of making the country ungovernable.

To all this the response is usually, "But blacks say they don't care. They say they are suffering so much already, that more suffering, more unemployment, will not matter." Well, generally blacks who say they don't care either have nothing to lose, or they will lose nothing, or they want everyone to have nothing. Those in the first category have no jobs to lose; they are already unemployed. The second category—those who will lose nothing—are in sheltered employed: their jobs are not in jeopardy. And those in the third category—those who want everyone to have nothing—hope that unemployment will spur on the revolution and will lead to a swift transfer of power to the black majority.

COLLAPSE FEASIBLE?

There is little point in entering into arguments about the first two categories, but the third category deserves some attention. If it were feasible that sanctions would do the trick, that sanctions would bring down the Pretoria regime instantly or, at worst, within weeks rather than months, to borrow Harold Wilson's famous prediction regarding the demise of Ian Smith's government in Rhodesia (a demise, incidentally, that took a further fifteen years to be accomplished, and with it the death of some 30,000 people), if sanctions would swiftly rid South Africa of the system of apartheid and replace it with a nonracial democracy, no reasonable person could fail to back such action to the hilt.

But this proposition is, in fact, not feasible. The euphoric idea that the Pretoria regime would collapse within a short time following the imposition of sanctions shows a woeful ignorance of the intransigence of the nationalist Afrikaaner character, and indeed one might say also of many English-speaking South Africans and their determination to retain, as long as possible, the status quo of white domination. They will agree to, and indeed already have accepted, incremental change, some of it more than cosmetic. But the total dismantling of apartheid and removal of its foundation stones, such as the Group Areas Act, the Race Classification Act, and the Land Acts, are simply not on the cards in the foreseeable future. Nor is transfer of political power to the black majority.

The Pretoria regime will not fall because of sanctions. It will make the changes it intended to make, which will fall far short of what it believes is demanded of it by the undefined expression "dismantling apartheid and sharing power." Thereafter, if continued pressure is put on it, the Pretoria regime will retreat into the *laager*, bringing with it an even more oppressive system than has been experienced up to now in South Africa.

This is not just a gesture of defiance; it is to the Afrikaaner nationalist the essential for survival. He has no motherland to return to; he represents 75 percent of the white electorate that put him in power to implement the policy of apartheid, and he has formidable military and police forces to back him up. Indeed, part of the 75 percent has already been eroded by the white political parties to the right of the National Party, which oppose any deviation from the old Verwoerdian, pure apartheid dicta.

There is no swift capitulation in sight. There is no possibility that the South African saga will have a rapid and happy end, if only sanctions are imposed. Nor is there any guarantee that a total transfer of power to a black majority will result in the replacement of the existing regime by a democratic nonracial government that will respect the rule of law and ensure a free press, free association, and free elections. The basic premise, that sanctions are necessary for the abolition of apartheid, implies that nothing else will do the trick. This is not true.

INTERNAL FACTORS

Although external factors have played an important role in promoting change, internal factors are likely to be more effective in the future. It is not only defections to the right that are eroding the National Party's power structure. There are also an increasing number of white South Africans, among them Nationalist M.P.s, who realize that apartheid is the disaster that has caused turmoil at home and isolation abroad. In South Africa, it is fashionable these days to say that white politics are irrelevant. On the contrary, white politics are very relevant, because whites are in power. Parliament remains an important forum from which to hold the government accountable for its actions and from which to propagate alternative policies through the press gallery.

South Africa does not consist of only radical blacks on the one hand and pro-apartheid whites on the other. There are hundreds of thousands of white South Africans who abhor apartheid. At the last general election, 20 percent of the white electorate voted for the Official Opposition, which advocates universal adult franchise, the repeal of all racially discriminatory laws, and a bill of rights within a geographic federation.

In addition, within South Africa there are extra-parliamentary organizations whose actions could be very effective through black trade union action and black consumer boycotts. Both weapons will be much more effective when blacks dominate the skilled labor market and have increased their consumer power. Blacks will acquire this enhanced economic muscle only in an expanding economy, not in a shrinking market for black manpower induced by sanctions or disinvestment. It never seems to occur to the advocates of such punitive measures that success in their implementation would undermine the most significant power base that blacks could acquire.

The question may well be asked, "Why disapprove of disinvestment and sanctions and not of strike action and consumer boycotts, which are also a form of sanctions?" The reply is that strikes can be settled and called off, and consumer boycotts can be discontinued. They do not destroy the economy permanently. Repeal of mandatory sanctions can be vetoed by one vote at the U.N. Security Council. And once investors have withdrawn, they do not come back, as the experience in black African states has demonstrated.

SELF-DEFEATING SANCTIONS

Sanctions and other punitive measures are, in fact, self-defeating, for they blunt the cutting edge of the real weapons that blacks ultimately will be able to use against apartheid with which to make demands that will have to be accommodated. All this is long term, and it is manifestly true that blacks, especially young blacks, are demanding liberation *now*. "Liberation before the next school term" was one slogan heard toward the end of last year. Indeed, among the worst of the side effects created by outside pressures for sanctions is the delusion among young blacks that the transfer of power is imminent. Nothing is further from the truth, yet that sort of false impression has kept the unrest at fever point, has kept hundreds of thousands of black pupils out of school for months on end, and has led to the death of more than 1,000 black people over the last sixteen months, some through vicious vigilante gang wars, some through gruesome "necklace" murders, and most by police action.

People living 6,000 miles away from the scene who think they can judge the situation accurately have no idea whatsoever of the strength and ferocity of the police and military inside South Africa. Indeed, not only is victory not around the corner, it is not even within sight. Not only is the transfer of power not imminent, it isn't even under consideration. Change, however, is. And that is what should be encouraged — attainable objectives — as a forerunner to creating a climate for negotiation about the total dismantling of apartheid and black participation in the political power structure.

The Western democracies should keep up condemnation of apartheid; they should keep up pressure against apartheid, by all means, but not pressure that will lead to chaos and the wrecking of the economy. That is the strategy of despair — destroying the inheritance that blacks inevitably will one day share.

The system of apartheid — legally sanctioned racial discrimination — is an affront to people concerned with civilized values throughout the world. The eradication of apartheid would be an important gain for the civil rights movement and would increase the sum of human freedom, worldwide, but it should not be at the cost of more deaths, more poverty, more misery, more starvation, and more oppression.

CHAPTER 18

How Economic Sanctions
Could Cripple Reform

by SIMON S. BRAND

The merits of economic and financial sanctions against South Africa
as a way of bringing about desired changes in the political and social
conditions in that country are often debated in ethical terms. From
this perspective, such questions arise as to whether it is morally
justifiable to use penal measures to attempt to modify the behavior
of the South African government, well knowing that the negative impact
of such measures may fall primarily on the black population whose
interests they are supposed to serve. These questions about the moral
rightness or wrongness of economic sanctions are clearly important,
but they can occupy much energy and time without leading to any firm
conclusions. It is equally important to consider the issue of economic
sanctions from a more mundane perspective, namely, in terms of their
effectiveness in achieving the objectives ostensibly aimed at with their
implementation.

There can be little doubt that economic sanctions, whether in the
form of export or import boycotts, the withholding of new foreign
investment, or disinvestment, must have a markedly negative effect on
the South African economy. This is evident from the simple facts that
some 30 percent of the gross domestic product of the country is normally exported, that export growth is often the leading factor in
initiating and carrying forward periods of rapid growth in the economy,
and that imports normally constitute a similar percentage of gross
domestic expenditure. Furthermore, the historical record shows that
during periods of rapid growth, an imbalance between domestic savings and investments, reflected in a deficit on the current account of

the balance of payments, typically arises, and that the South African economy thus has to rely on a certain net inflow of foreign capital to sustain the kind of growth rate required to meet desired socioeconomic objectives such as the adequate creation of new jobs to accommodate the rapidly growing population.

Although one may accept the potential of economic sanctions to harm the South African economy, the first question that needs to be asked when judging their effectiveness as an instrument to bring about desired social and political changes concerns the length of time it may take for the impact of the sanctions to be sufficiently drastic to affect significantly the behavior of the South African government and other key decisionmakers in the country. The second question concerns the nature of the reactions that can be expected from the various actors on the South African scene. A third question concerns the effect economic sanctions against South Africa may have on the economies of other countries in the southern African region.

The recent experience with the withdrawal of certain short-term foreign loan facilities and the consequent standstill arrangement on South Africa's foreign debt certainly illustrate dramatically the effect that sanctions against South Africa's external financial relations can have in the short term. The effect of trade sanctions are, however, likely to be less dramatic in the short term. In addition, it is important to note that even the dramatic negative impact of the recent financial disruptions has not paralyzed the South African economy but rather has impaired its medium-to-longer-term growth potential — despite the obligation to repay a portion of the foreign debt, and therefore to maintain a surplus on the current account of the balance of payments, a moderate revival in economic activity has already started and is expected to continue through 1987. This observation can be extended to virtually any economic sanctions against South Africa that are foreseen.

STAGE OF DIVERSIFICATION

A crucial factor to consider in this connection is that the South African economy has reached a stage of diversification where it has the technical capability to manufacture virtually any essential requirements that are normally imported, including liquid fuels, and that as far as food and the general run of consumer goods are concerned, the economy is in any event normally self-sufficient. Apart from any inevitable slippage in the tightness of export or import boycotts aimed at cutting South

Africa out of international markets, it would be possible for the country through some shifting of resources to keep functioning at a relatively high level of activity, albeit a reduced level compared with its full-capacity performance. Moreover, the threat of economic sanctions that has overhung the South African economy since the early 1970s has led the authorities to make fairly extensive preparations for such a circumstance, especially as far as reducing the dependence of the country on strategically important imports. The stocking up of crude oil supplies and the erection of the Sasol oil-from-coal plants have, for example, put the country in a situation where it can withstand the effect of an oil boycott for a considerable period of time. Large investments have also been made in other strategic economic sectors such as the motor vehicle industry, including the most recent commissioning of a diesel engine plant. Similarly, the actual enforcement of an arms embargo has resulted in the development of a flourishing armaments industry of considerable scope and sophistication.

These precautionary measures have equipped the South African economy to withstand the effects of most forms of an import boycott for a considerable period of time. This means, in the first place, that the effect of sanctions is unlikely to be clear-cut and sharp and unlikely to force the hand of the South African authorities in the short term. Rather, it is likely to be a protracted period of below-capacity performance, artificially bolstered by further investments in strategic production capacity, during which the social and political status quo would be more likely to be entrenched than to be overthrown. The below-capacity performance that would be imposed on the economy for such an extended period of time would inevitably lead to a buildup of unemployment and increased potential for social unrest and would therefore tend to invite intensification of repressive measures by the authorities and to encourage a hardening of attitudes between the different population groups.

EFFECTIVENESS OF SANCTIONS

The precautionary investments that have been made to stave off the effects of economic sanctions illustrate another and perhaps more important point concerning the second question raised above, namely, the nature of the reactions of the various actors in South Africa to the intensified threat or the imposition of economic sanctions. During the 1970s, when the threat of economic sanctions first started to assume significant proportions, one of the principal reactions to such a course of events was to divert resources on a considerable scale to applications that contributed little to meeting the most urgent social needs — in other words, large amounts of savings, manpower, management, and other skills were directed toward such precautionary activities instead of being employed to improve housing, educational facilities, health facilities, and the expansion of those sectors of the economy that can create the largest number of jobs and produce the kinds of goods and services that will increasingly be in demand if incomes should become more evenly distributed. Already the recent intensification of sanctions threats has led to further decisions involving the expansion of so-called strategic industries, at the very time when the need is increasingly recognized for expanding the scope of social services to achieve a more just economic order. There is no way in which these two contradictory objectives can both be pursued effectively at the same time, given the development stage of the economy and the scarcity of resources, especially capital, skills, and management. In a situation of sanctions or even the serious threat of sanctions, the social objectives are sure to be the loser in the inevitable tug of war for resources.

There is still another, more subtle but certainly no less important aspect of the reaction to sanctions that must be considered. An overview of the interaction between economic development and social and political change in South Africa over the past three decades tends to lead to the conclusion that to the extent that they impair the performance of the economy, economic sanctions are more likely to frustrate than to encourage processes of social and political reform.

During the 1960s, when the South African economy experienced average annual economic growth rates of 6 percent and higher in real terms, the seeds were sown for the economic reforms that took place during the 1970s and 1980s, which inevitably led to reforms in the social sphere and also laid the basis for reform in the political sphere.

During the 1960s and early 1970s, it became increasingly clear not only to the business community, both English- and Afrikaans-speaking, but also to the established white-dominated trade union movement that the apartheid system was hopelessly incompatible with the requirements of an expanding economy. Pressures from business circles, increasingly supported by the white trade unions which realized that their interests were not being served by artificially restricting the economic growth rate as the only way of keeping blacks out of more advanced occupations, led first to gradual changes in labor practices and eventually to the systematic overhaul of labor and industrial relations legislation that crystallized in the adoption of key recommendations of the Wiehahn and Riekert Commissions.

Even before the appointment of the two commissions, the strict adherence to job reservation had been undermined to such an extent by the demands of economic expansion that the authorities had to change their stance on industrial and occupational training for blacks in the urban areas. This, in turn, led to the open acceptance by government, in direct contrast to its previously held positions, of the permanent presence of blacks in the urban areas and of their irreversible integration into the modern economic system. Once this had been acknowledged, it was inevitable that further reforms had to follow, as they did in the form of the extension of business rights of blacks in the urban areas and eventually the opening up of central business districts for blacks that is currently under way. The adoption of the ninety-nine-year leasehold system, and more recently of the principle of freehold title to residential land in the urban areas for blacks, and the change in housing policy toward meeting the housing needs of blacks in the urban areas were further inevitable consequential developments. And having finally accepted the permanent presence of blacks in the urban areas, their integration in the modern economy, and the need to address their social needs in these areas, the question of how their reasonable political needs were to be accommodated could no longer be avoided. To be sure, adequate answers to this crucial question have not yet been found, but the fact that it has risen to the top of the agenda of public discussion and debate has to do as much with the pressures created by economic expansion as with any other cause. This whole process took a long time to reach the point it has, but once it got under way it started to accelerate appreciably and in the last few years the tempo of change has become very rapid compared to earlier years.

RAPID GROWTH

The conclusion to be drawn is simply that social and political reform were promoted much more significantly by internal pressures created by the forces of rapid economic growth than by external pressures or even by the threat of such pressures. In fact, as argued earlier, these external pressures actually worked in the opposite direction and were therefore probably more of a brake on the tempo of change than an encouragement to it. Now that virtually the whole white body politic, with the exception of the extreme right wing, agrees on the need for drastic movement in the political arena toward a fair and just society that will accommodate and respect the rights of all the people of South Africa, it would be a tragedy if this process is brought to a halt by intensified actions to impose economic sanctions on South Africa. The results of this lengthy period of change, which has reached such a crucial point, would be undone, the process of change would be set in the other direction toward a hardening of attitudes and a denial of the community of interests that exists between the people of South Africa, and energies would increasingly be devoted to measures that would entrench the respective positions of the various groups in the camps that they would be building around themselves.

NEIGHBORING NATIONS

The third question that should be asked in relation to the effectiveness of sanctions relates to the effect that economic sanctions might have on neighboring countries. These countries are in various ways dependent to a significant extent on their economic relations with South Africa, and unlike South Africa, they have poorly diversified economies. They are therefore likely to suffer heavily from sanctions and all the indications are that they would receive little in the form of special assistance from elsewhere to overcome the impact that sanctions would have on them. Because of their much lower levels of income, unlike South Africa they have not been in a position to divert resources toward precautionary measures to enable them to deal with the impact of sanctions and they are likely to feel the impact in a much shorter time span than South Africa. It is therefore not surprising that spokesmen for most of these countries have at one time or another expressed serious reservations about imposing sanctions against South Africa, in light of the effect that it could have on their economies.

It is, however, not only from this negative point of view that the effect on other countries in southern Africa of sanctions against South Africa should be considered, but also from the more tragic aspect that the considerable opportunities for more constructive relationships between South Africa and its neighboring countries would be frustrated. The mutual benefits of trade for the countries involved, the benefits of joint use of expensive infrastructure, and the potential for drawing resources from abroad to the region as a whole rather than to each country separately would all go by the board. As in the case of the process of reform within South Africa, the process of building mutually beneficial relationships between the countries and thus contributing to stability and prosperity on the whole subcontinent would simply be brought to a halt.

In light of the above arguments, it seems clear that whatever the abstract ethical pros and cons concerning the imposition of sanctions against South Africa might be, such measures are in practice likely to be blunt and ineffective and to achieve in large measure exactly the opposite of what they are intended to bring about.

CHAPTER 19

Can External Leverage
Pressure South Africa?

by C. JOHN A. BARRATT

All countries are subject to external pressures of one sort or another, but the South African case is distinguished by the length of time (four decades) over which these pressures have grown and by their all-embracing nature. Measures taken by international organizations, governments around the world, and nongovernmental bodies now include diplomatic isolation, exclusion from most international conferences and organizations (including scientific ones), sports and cultural boycotts, trade boycotts, labor union action against transport links, a mandatory U.N. arms embargo, denial of loan facilities by foreign banks, some disinvestment by foreign-based corporations, and other relatively mild economic sanctions (both official and private). There is also some military and other material support by governments (mainly in Eastern Europe) and private organizations for political movements (notably the African National Congress) engaged in an armed struggle with the South African government. In addition, there has, of course, been mounting and now almost universal public and diplomatic condemnatory criticism of the government of the South African political system generally.

The main distinguishing feature of the South African case, however, is that these pressures have been and are aimed primarily at changing the internal order of the country and even at the overthrow of the government itself. A secondary aim has been to change the government's policies on the issue of Namibian independence and toward other neighbors in southern Africa. But the overriding emphasis has increasingly been on South African domestic policy, rather than on foreign policy. Moreover, it could be argued that South African actions in the southern African region are so closely related to its own domestic political situation that they cannot simply be classified as foreign policy matters.

This focus on the domestic political system and human rights may not make the South African case unique in contemporary history, if one considers such other cases as Spain, Chile, Poland, Uganda, and even Nicaragua, where external pressures have been, or still are being, brought to bear from one ideological side of the world or the other. But at least the distinguishing features mentioned previously make South Africa a rather special case in today's world, and this unfortunate status is underlined by the fact that the pressures come from both East and West, as well as the Third World.

TARGET OF PRESSURE

The various forms of external pressure are not intentionally directed at the country as such and all its people. The targets are claimed to be the political system in the country and the government which maintains and perpetuates that system without the consent of the majority of the people. Although some of these pressures are increasingly affecting the country as a whole, rather than only the government and the white population which supports it, it is important at the start to draw this distinction between government and country; the two are not synonymous. In South Africa's case there are clearly many people outside who do not make the distinction in what they say about the country, particularly in some of the punitive measures they propose. To do so would obviously make the problem of dealing with South Africa much more complex and difficult. This careless and simplistic thinking plays into the hands of the South African government which, for its own ends, also consistently identifies itself with the country as a whole.

In the government's view, the defense of its ideology, its policies, and the political system it has constructed is equivalent to the defense of South Africa. In public statements, government representatives never refer to external criticism of, and actions against, apartheid as an attack on the government but simply as an attack on South Africa. From this point of view, it is an easy step to the position that an attack on government policies is an unpatriotic act. This is probably the natural tendency of any government under threat, as it attempts to mobilize public opinion in defense of itself and its policies. In a democratic society, where the government has been elected by a popular majority, such identification of government with the people can have some legitimacy. But this is not the case in a society where there has been no clear expression of popular will—and one can think of many such cases in today's world—even if there is no doubt about the particular government's own legitimacy, as a recognized government, in terms of accepted international law norms.

In the 1970s, as the pressures increased, the South African government developed the concept of a "total national strategy" in response to what it perceived as a "total onslaught" against the country as a whole from outside, or at least orchestrated and manipulated from outside. This concept, clearly designed to mobilize public support, has worn thin during the past two years as the internal opposition and resistance have escalated and the level of external pressure has risen out of all proportion to its level at any previous period.

HISTORY OF PRESSURE

The problems for the South African government began after the conclusion of World War II. As one of the victorious allies and a founding member of the United Nations, South Africa could expect to play a significant role as a middle-ranking power in the shaping of the peace. But very soon the government of General Jan Smuts (himself a figure of considerable international standing) came under fire in the United Nations over its policy toward the mandated Territory of South West Africa (now Namibia) and over racial policies in South Africa itself. This negative change in South Africa's international fortunes was aggravated by the advent to power in 1948 of the National Party government with its winning political concept of "apartheid" (*i.e.*, the legalized separation of the races on all levels of society).

It was not so much that the political situation in South Africa had changed, because racial discrimination, including the denial to blacks and other "nonwhites" of a share of political power, was not a new phenomenon after 1945; it was rather that the world order was changing fundamentally, and South Africa was not adapting to this changing international environment. In particular, international revulsion against racism, following the experience of Nazi atrocities, together with increased concern for the protection of human rights, focused much greater attention on racial policies and practices in South Africa. Second, the mounting tide of anticolonialism led to a growing number of independent black-ruled states in Africa at a time when the new South African government's policies were clearly designed to deny any share of power to black Africans in the central political structures of the state. Thus the government and South Africa as a whole became increasingly isolated politically in the international community.

At first, the resulting pressures on the South African government were mainly confined to criticism of its policies, chiefly in debates of the United Nations General Assembly. The government defended itself on the grounds of article 2, paragraph 7, of the U.N. Charter, forbidding intervention in the domestic affairs of a member state. At first, the Western powers generally, and particularly the colonial powers, supported the South African case. But the turning point came in 1960, when serious and violent racial disturbances within South Africa (which began at Sharpeville) coincided with the peak of the African drive for independence. The Western powers, themselves under pressure from the strongly emerging Third World, now gave up their support of the South African government's case on domestic jurisdiction, and the South African issue became increasingly internationalized.

The international campaign against the South African government moved now from mere criticism to the idea of diplomatic and economic sanctions which were for the first time supported by a two-thirds ajority in the U.N. General Assembly in 1961. Although the Western powers generally still opposed sanctions — and the three Western Permanent Members of the Security Council were prepared to use their vetoes against mandatory measures — they did accept in 1963 a decision by the Security Council recommending an arms embargo, which was strengthened by a further resolution in 1964. Thus a new basis had been laid from which to develop more meaningful international pressures on the South African government.

END OF COLONIALISM

The next critical period occurred in the mid-1970s, when again a major change in Africa — this time in southern Africa itself — coincided with violent disturbances within South Africa. The overthrow of the Portugese government in April 1974 was followed in 1975 by the independence of Mozambique and Angola, fundamentally shifting the power balance in the region away from colonial and white political domination. This shift accelerated the process leading to the ending of white control in Rhodesia which became independent as Zimbabwe in 1980. The violent disturbances within South Africa in 1976-1977 were not unrelated to the wider disturbance of the status quo in the southern African region. In any case, the combination of all these events in the region served to focus attention again — and more sharply than ever before — on the South African government and its policies both internally and toward its neighbors. These events also encouraged a wider belief internationally, notably in Western countries, that the old order was now inevitably changing, that increased pressure on the South African government would help to effect the change more quickly, and that if the West took no action, its own economic and political interests in the region would suffer to the benefit of the Soviet Union and its allies.

Thus, in November 1977 the first mandatory sanctions against South Africa were adopted by the Security Council, with the necessary Western support in the form of an embargo on the sale of all weapons and related equipment to the South African government. Although there have been some breaches in this embargo by covert means, it has on the whole been universally applied. However, the results have been rather different from what its authors intended, because the embargo has contributed substantially to the growth within South Africa of a large arms industry which now provides almost all the requirements of the South African Defense Force.

Nevertheless, the arms embargo has caused problems in regard to more advanced technology and the higher costs of producing some weapons that could have been imported more cheaply. Even more significant, perhaps, the arms embargo showed that in certain circumstances Western powers would be prepared to give up their opposition to sanctions. In 1977, the circumstances included, as they did in the early 1960s, violent resistance on the part of blacks within South Africa, repressive security measures by the government in trying to reestablish control, related changes in the international or regional environment of South Africa, foreign and domestic pressures on the governments of the Western states themselves, and the presence of governments in Western states which were politically inclined to sympathize with black resistance.

REFORMIST PROGRAM

In the years immediately following the crisis of 1976-1977, two trends contributed to a reduction of the threat of further pressures. First, B.J. Vorster was succeeded as South African Prime Minister, after twelve years in office, by P.W. Botha, formerly Defense Minister, who came into office with a reformist program. His phrase "adapt or die" was widely interpreted, in South Africa and abroad, as indicating a new willingness to introduce changes that would help to accommodate and hopefully reduce the mounting internal and external pressures. The inclination in many quarters abroad, at least in the West, was to give Botha's government a chance to implement its reform program, and there were certainly significant developments away from discrimination in the social, economic, and labor relations fields.

Second, there was a trend in the major Western countries toward more conservative governments, notably in Britain, the United States, and West Germany—three of the four most important trading partners of South Africa (the fourth being Japan). These governments were strongly opposed to punitive measures against the South African government, and they preferred rather to encourage, even with incentives, the government's reformist tendencies. This approach has been embodied in the "constructive engagement" policy pursued by the Reagan Administration since 1981. These governments have been influenced by economic considerations, including, of course, their own economic interests in South Africa, but also by the view, as it has commonly been expressed, that sanctions, disinvestment, and other similar measures would hurt mainly the mass of South Africa's black people, the very people they were intended to help. They have also argued, with good reason, that damage to the South African economy would unavoidably cause serious damage to all South Africa's weaker neighboring states, damage that would not easily be repaired in the future.

Since the Botha government's reform initiatives appeared to gather momentum in the early 1980s, and since there was no widespread and openly apparent resistance among blacks, the Western policy of constructive engagement could be maintained and there seemed little need to change it. It was argued that Botha's determination to pursue reform had been demonstrated by his willingness even to pay the cost of a split in his own National Party, over the question of constitutional reform, and the resulting formation of the Conservative Party to his right.

By early 1984, there were also important signs that the government was willing to adopt a more cooperative policy toward its neighbors in southern Africa, and the Accord of Nkomati with the government of Mozambique was heralded as a dramatic demonstration of this new approach. Constructive engagement was given much of the credit, and P.W. Botha was in a sense "rewarded" with invitations to visit several European capitals in June 1984. There were rumors of a visit to Washington to follow, perhaps after the reelection of President Reagan at the end of that year.

END OF RECOVERY

However, the first half of 1984 proved to be the high point and the conclusion of this short period of recovery for the South African government. From mid-1984 there was a marked downturn in the government's international position and once again an escalation of external pressures. It is not the task of this article to analyze the extent and causes of the domestic crisis that have continued to plague the country since 1984, but it is necessary to acknowledge at least that the fundamental issue is the political and constitutional one of the exclusion of the majority of South African citizens from participation in the government of their country. This issue is at the root of the problems in all areas where disruption and violence are prevalent or threatened, including black education, labor relations, living conditions in black townships, conditions in rural "homelands," and economic inequalities generally. It is this basic issue, and the means of resolving it through negotiations, on which domestic and international attention is increasingly focused, more sharply than ever before.

The crisis of the past two years, with the combination of increasing internal and external pressures on the existing political and economic order of the country, clearly exceeds in degree the previous crises mentioned earlier. The question that cannot yet be answered is whether there will again be a recovery from this crisis and a reduction, even if temporary, in the growth of external pressures. At present, there are no signs of such a reduction, and some commentators believe that this crisis is qualitatively different from past ones and that, unless there are dramatic moves toward a negotiated settlement, black resistance to the established order will be sustained. Piecemeal reforms, without a change in the basic power structure, will only serve to raise further the level of aspirations and demands of those excluded from a meaningful share of power. In such circumstances, it can reasonably be argued, it is unlikely that international attention will easily be diverted from the South African situation and that external pressures on the government will be relaxed.

During the past year, the intensity of the negative reaction to South African events in the countries of the West has caused a conservative Republican Administration in the United States to take action, in the form admittedly of rather mild sanctions, because of the growing domestic pressures on it, particularly from Congress. President Reagan's Executive Order of September 9, 1985 may thus have resulted more from domestic political considerations than from foreign policy concerns, but, if this is the case, it means that the South African issue has in effect put down roots in U.S. domestic politics. Attention to this issue is therefore more likely to be sustained than in the past, and this factor of domestic political influences is becoming evident in other Western countries, too.

WESTERN ACTIONS

If one looks at the actions on South Africa taken in major Western countries in recent times, they fall into three broad categories. First, there are the official, albeit mild, sanctions adopted by Western governments themselves. President Reagan's Executive Order prohibited certain transactions with the South African government, including bank loans to the government; the export of computers, related goods, and technology to certain government agencies; nuclear exports; the import into the United States of any military equipment produced in South Africa; and export marketing support to U.S. firms in South Africa that do not adhere to certain fair labor standards. The Executive Order also led to a prohibition on the import of Krugerrands into the United States. On what may be described as the positive side, the order provided an increase in the amounts for scholarships for black South Africans and the establishment of an Advisory Committee by the Secretary of State, which would make recommendations on measures to encourage peaceful change in South Africa.

In addition to this American action, the members of the European Community agreed to impose certain restrictions on dealings with the South African government, after the French government had taken the lead with the announcement of its own measures. The Japanese government followed suit, adopting measures very similar to those of the United States.

Although all these measures do not amount to serious sanctions, they do indicate an acceptance of the principle of sanctions as a means of bringing influence to bear on the South African government, and they can be seen as a response to the foreign policy and domestic pressures on these governments, which built up so dramatically in 1985 in reaction to events in South Africa. It should be noted, however, that these mild punitive measures were designed, according to the governments concerned, to influence the South African government and, as far as possible, not to harm the South African economy as a whole. For instance, the U.S. Assistant Secretary of State for African Affairs, Chester Crocker, has recently said that American policy on South Africa "through several administrations...has sought to use our influence, limited as it is, against apartheid and for peaceful change, not against innocent people who are the victims of apartheid." This distinction between the government and its policies on the one hand and the country and all the people on the other is an important one, as indicated earlier in this article, but the question remains as to whether any sanctions can be targeted so precisely.

Although the governments of the major Western states and Japan are still publicly opposed to any drastic economic measures that would damage the South African economy and the economies of its neighbors, the opposition in principle to sanctions, as a means of effecting change in South African policies, has been breached. The threat of further measures along the sanctions road has therefore become greater if events in South Africa should continue to cause intense reaction overseas. Further, a change in the political complexion of the governments of any of South Africa's major trading partners during the next few years could result in very much less resistance to the use of sanctions (*e.g.*, in Britain, West Germany, or the United States).

The second area of pressures from the West constitute a more serious current threat. These are the measures taken by nongovernmental organizations, including banks and other international corporations, universities, trade unions, church groups, etc. These measures may be described as "private sanctions," and the most widespread and intense manifestation has been in the United States during the past year or more. The advocacy of disinvestment and economic withdrawal from South Africa by some of these private groups has now become a powerful force which has influenced many city and state governments, university administrations, and even the U.S. Congress. As a result, concerted pressure is being brought to bear on many U.S. corporations doing business in South Africa, and there is no doubt that the growing strength of this campaign in the United States in 1985 was a significant factor in the critical decision of banks at the end of August 1985 not to extend their loans to South Africa. That unexpected decision, the most serious of the "private sanctions," coupled with the inevitable South African response of imposing a "standstill" on repayments, created a new form of international pressure on South Africa, not only on the government, at a level never before experienced. It also demonstrated rather dramatically the country's vulnerability in an economically interdependent world. As H.F. Oppenheimer has pointed out, this decision also demonstrated "that we do not have to be concerned simply with possible sanctions by the U.N. Security Council or by individual governments, but also with the opinion and judgments of a wide range of private sector organisations on how their own interests are affected by their links with this country."

GROUP MONITORING

The third category of increased international pressure, indicating the growing concern particularly in Western countries over the South African issue, involves the appointment in recent times of high-level groups by both the private sector and by governments to monitor or investigate the situation. A Corporate Council on South Africa has been established by chief executives of major U.S. corporations, while more recently in Britain the British Industry Council on South Africa has been created. These important and influential groups aim to play a positive role in promoting peaceful change and development in South Africa rather than to bow to the growing demands on them to disengage. But this means that they are now paying much closer attention than in the past to political developments, rather than to the purely economic ones, since these developments are obviously affecting the economic environment in which they have to operate.

Two important official groups have also been formed, and their eventual recommendations to governments will have a significant influence on future policy toward South Africa. The first is the Eminent Persons' Group (EPG) established by the last Commonwealth Heads of Government Meeting at Nassau, which has already paid an extended visit to South Africa, meeting a wide range of leaders in all sectors of society, including government ministers and the ANC leader, Nelson Mandela, in prison. Although South Africa's economic links with most of the countries of the Commonwealth are insignificant, and in any case most of them have already officially broken all links, relations with a few Commonwealth countries, particularly Britain, are of great significance. Future relations with these countries are bound to be affected, one way or another, by the EPG's report due to be submitted in mid-1986.

The second important official group is the advisory committee referred to above, which has been appointed by the U.S. Secretary of State, in terms of the President's Executive Order. The members of this committee have not yet visited South Africa, but they have started their work. It is obvious that their report, due at the end of 1986, will have an important bearing on the further development of U.S. policy to South Africa, not only by the present Administration but also by its successors.

The South African government is clearly aware of the importance of these two groups and has been willing to facilitate their work, placing no obstacles in the way of their movement throughout South Africa and their access to all those they wish to meet. However, it still remains to be seen what effect the reports of these groups will have on government policies and on the attitudes of all South African political groups to the issue of negotiations.

INTERTWINED AFFAIRS

The foreign policies of most governments are strongly influenced by domestic political considerations, and this is clearly true for South Africa. But it seldom occurs, as it does in South Africa's case, that a government's domestic policies become the overriding issue in its foreign relations. The events of the past four decades show how this trend has developed and strengthened, so that now no aspect of the country's relations with the outside world—economic, diplomatic, cultural, sporting, security, etc.—is unaffected by domestic political developments. In fact, it is no longer possible to consider South African foreign policy and external relations generally separately from the country's domestic affairs; they are fully intertwined.

In these circumstances, there is bound to be a high degree of interaction between domestic developments and the international response. This pattern of interaction emerges clearly as one looks back over the events of the past few decades, especially the years since 1976. There are two sides to the interaction: the first relates to the impact internationally of events in South Africa; the second relates to the impact and effects within South Africa of the international reaction.

The impact abroad of South African events is clearly demonstrated in recent history, especially during the critical periods referred to earlier. It is evident from the intensity of media coverage and the statements of governments and other organizations. The impact and particularly the type of reaction vary, of course, from country to country and government to government, and the reaction in each case is affected by a host of foreign policy and domestic considerations related and unrelated to the South African situation. The United States case is a good illustration of this fact.

DO SANCTIONS WORK?

The other side of the interaction, namely the effects within South Africa of the foreign reaction, is much more difficult to see clearly. There is no doubt that international pressures — from mere criticism to sanctions threats — have had an effect, much of it positive in the sense of contributing to reform, some of it negative in that it has caused hardening of official and white attitudes. On the positive side, external pressures, often linked with developing pressures inside the country, have contributed, for instance, to the end of segregation in sport, to greater integration in higher education, to significant advances in employment practices and in labor relations, to the end of apartheid restrictions in many social and cultural areas, to the promised change of the influx control and "pass law" restrictions, and to the effort to end forced removals of people. But it is not possible to measure the extent of the role of external pressures in each of these areas against the internal pressures for change. One problem is, of course, that the government has never been able to admit explicitly that external pressures have to any great degree been responsible for changes in policy, and it often in fact denies that any changes are made to satisfy outside opinion or pressures.

On the more specific aspect of economic sanctions, it is impossible to reach any categoric conclusions about their possible effects on government policies, on the attitudes of whites or blacks, or even on the economy, because much of the speculation about sanctions is still hypothetical. There is probably no doubt that economic sanctions, if applied strictly for any length of time by South Africa's major trading partners, would have a disastrous effect on the economy, including also the economies of neighboring countries dependent on South Africa. But the effect that this would have on the government, and on the attitudes of whites who support it, is still a very open question. It is possible, as some black leaders and political movements appear to believe, that the government, under pressure from important sectors of its white constituency (particularly the business community), would move much more quickly to end apartheid and to enter into meaningful negotiations. Certainly the threat of sanctions seems to have had an effect in that direction. But it is equally possible that, in the event of the actual application of sanctions, the resistance to external pressures would instead increase among whites, resulting in greater support for strong government measures to try to ensure its survival and continued white control. In such circumstances, it is quite possible that a form of siege economy could be maintained for many years to come, based on stringent government controls and harsh security measures.

Those in South Africa and abroad, who appear to have an almost unquestioning faith in the ability of external pressures, particularly economic sanctions and disinvestment, to bring about the desired political change, need to be more specific as to how they think this will happen. There is also a need to face up honestly to the possible alternative consequences of punitive sanctions, both for the process of change and for the South African economy in the postapartheid era.

By the same token, the government and whites generally have to appreciate that the threat of sanctions is a reality and may not always remain simply a threat. To avoid such a development, with its probable disastrous consequences for all South Africans and many others in southern Africa (not to speak of the interests of the West in the region), the clearest alternative path available is that of meaningful and realistic negotiations to reach an acceptable political settlement. The need for negotiations is recognized in principle now by the government and by most political movements, black and white. But ways still must be found to bring the various conflicting parties together, and to this end there is doubtless a positive facilitating role to be played by external agencies, including Western governments.

Part IV

THE SOCIAL PERSPECTIVE INSIDE SOUTH AFRICA

CHAPTER 20

Education for Black People in South Africa: Challenges and Progress

by GERRIT VAN NIEKERK VILJOEN

South Africa is an intriguing combination of a Third World and an industrialized country. It has a multicultural population derived from different historical, racial, and cultural streams. People of diverse political, religious, and socioeconomic leanings and with different value systems are working, consciously and otherwise, toward an acceptable synthesis and symbiosis.

This diversity is also at the root of many of the challenges and problems facing education authorities in South Africa. On the one hand, the government has to satisfy a growing social demand for education and also has to provide skilled and trained manpower for commerce and industry, whose needs are becoming increasingly more sophisticated. On the other hand, it has to cope with typically Third World problems of development and growth and of transition from one world to another, from one development stage to another, with their often conflicting and different values and attituded.

A better understanding of the complexity and magnitude of the task and responsibility of the Department of Education and Training (responsible for education of blacks in the Republic of South Africa) and its ten sister departments (which are responsible for the education of black people in the self-governing and independent black states) is only possible when viewed against the following backgrounds.

LOGISTICS—THE PROBLEM OF NUMBERS

There is an overriding demographic factor that vitally affects the provision of education for black people who presently make up 75 percent of the total school population in South Africa: the explosion in enrollment at all educational institutions. The total annual increase in enrollment of black pupils in southern Africa is on the order of a quarter of a million.

The departments of education responsible for black pupils are faced with the formidable task of providing education to approximately 6 million pupils in order to prepare them to play a meaningful role in a modernized technological society. In addition there are 15 million adults, because nonformal adult education in the case of developing communities forms as much a part of the total education task as does education for children.

SPECIAL NEEDS—THE REALITIES OF DEVELOPMENT

There are special needs to be addressed at this stage in the provision of education for black children. Education is a fundamental means of assisting a transition at different levels, from traditional cultures to the highly competitive technoculture of modern society. Socioeconomic factors and general levels of development of a community are co-determinants which set the general level of achievement at which its children can be expected to perform. Although formal school education can never be a substitute for parental upbringing, it is the duty of education to identify and compensate, as far as possible, for such handicaps as a rise from lower development levels in the community and at home.

PROFESSIONAL CONSIDERATIONS— THE QUALITY OF EDUCATION

Although the standards set for all education departments are the same in terms of syllabuses prescribed and the level of the final (Standard 10) examinations, it is clear that the quality of teaching and education lag behind for various reasons. Although many schools are in fact maintaining a high level of performance, the majority unfortunately do not perform so well. It is therefore obvious that similar staffing, facilities, and equipment do not guarantee similar results. Obviously the factors influencing the standards and general level of achievement at a given school are varied and comples. They have to be identified and addressed.

HUMAN RELATIONS AND ATTITUDES

Positive attitudes and healthy relationships among all parties directly or indirecly involved in education are prerequisites for effective and successful education. There should be a general acceptance of the commitment of the education departments to offer the best possible education aimed at the full realization of the potential of every individual.

ECONOMIC CONSIDERATIONS

In the final analysis education has to be an economically viable investment in order to be affordable. It must yield its dividends in terms of human happiness and satisfaction, opportunity, economic welfare, and national prosperity in order to be a successful venture. Education is a public venture. The state is one of the partners who is investing heavily. Therefore the results should justify the investment.

The principle that the state, the individual parent, society, and the private sector shall share the responsibility for education has been accepted and included in the National Policy for General Education Affairs Act (Act 76 of 1984). This also implies shared responsibility to ensure that funds allocated for education are spent effectively and that education yields the expected dividends in terms of developing human resources and providing for the manpower needs of the country. This requires research into the manpower needs and the availability of job opportunities, and sound pupil and parent counseling based on these findings.

A formula is being developed to ensure parity in educational opportunities and equal financial provision among education departments. Such a formula will also provide for the elimination of backlogs. But it must be accepted that massive increases in expenditure do not provide an instant solution, and that natural evolutionary processes cannot be speeded up beyond certain limits, lest such pressure lead to waste and the unproductive application of human and financial resources.

POLICY

There are five vitally important statements of government policy which have intimately affected education and which will continue to influence its future development:

1. The government's White Paper on the Wiehahn Report (1980), which gave an important impetus to the provision of technical education
2. The Education and Training Act (Act 90 of 1979), which extended the scope and content of education and articulated policy clearly
3. The government's White Paper on the provision of education (1983), which followed on the De Lange Report and which can be regarded as a blueprint for educational reform in South Africa
4. The government's commitment to provide equal education opportunities and a single education policy for all inhabitants of the country has been reaffirmed by state president P.W. Botha in his opening address to Parliament on 31 January 1986
5. The National Policy for General Education Affairs Act (Act 76 of 1984) and the creation of the new Ministry and Department of National Education, which determine and monitor national education policy for all departments of education of all populations groups in the following vital areas:
   - norms and standards for the financing of education for all population groups
   - salaries and conditions of service of staff
   - the professional registration of teachers
   - norms and standards for syllabuses and examinations and the certification of qualifications

The new structures set up for policymaking and consultation on general education policy involve all departments of education as well as the various professional organizations.

The creation of a Ministry and Department of National Education, which determine national education policy and which serve all the executive departments of education, fulfill the strongly expressed need for one coordinating ministry and department to determine general education policy on a national level.

The facets outlined above are but a few indicators of the dynamic and ongoing nature of educational development, and they represent important milestones in the development of educational policy. Unfortunately, the speech made by Hendrik F. Verwoerd in the Senate in 1953 is still quoted by critics as being the "ideology" on which education for black people is based today, with a total disregard for radically changed circumstances, priorities, and needs, and for major and far-reaching policy developments and adaptations over the past three decades. Any implication in the Verwoerd statement of inferiority or of limitations and restructions on education for black children is firmly rejected by a series of government commitments to equal education opportunities repeatedly made in recent years.

Postponement of Examinations. Although 75,027 students elibible for taking matriculation examination did take their examinations in November 1985, special provision was nevertheless made for those matriculants who could not take their examination during November 1985, to do so in May 1986. More than 10,000 candidates (of which 5,439 are from Soweto) enrolled for this examination. Similarly, the internal examinations in Soweto and in some other affected schools were postponed until February/March 1986 in a desperate effort to enable pupils to continue normally with their education. The dates were finalized after consultations with all parties concerned.

Student Representative Councils (SRC). The possiblity for the establishment of democratically elected SRC does in fact exist. Educationally sound guidelines for the implementation of SRC have been widely publicized and such SRC have already been established and are functioning in a number of schools countrywide.

Excessive Corporal Punishment and Sexual Harassment of Female Students. Detailed regulations exist for the protection of the child. The department has also issued strict instructions that any malpractices should be reported immediately so that appropriate action can be taken. The department is thus assisting parents, school committees, and parent/teacher associations to give proper guidance to children on moral values in order to obviate many of these problems.

Reinstatement of Transferred and Dismissed Teachers. Dismissal of teachers is done on strict educational grounds, in accordance with the Act and regulations, and in the best interest of the pupils concerned. During the past year there have been fewer than 20 such cases out of the total of more than 46,000 teachers in the service of the Department of Education and Training.

As far as the other demands are concerned, it should be noted that the state of emergency has been lifted, all persons detained under emergency regulations have been released, and the deputy minister of defence and law and order gave the assurance to the SPCC that the defence force would withdraw from black townships as soon as peace and stability return to the affected areas. This has in fact already happened in many areas.

PROGRESS IN EDUCATION FOR BLACKS

Many developments which took place in regard to education for blacks over the past few years are not widely known because they are not properly acknowledged and often simply ignored. Such developments include the following:

- The government increased funding from R143 million in 1978-79 to R1,148 million in 1986-87 — an increase of 703 percent. This is tangible and incontrovertible proof of the government's commitment. It is also worth noting that the annual percentage increase in the department's budget over the past eight years has been consistently higher than the percentage increase in the total state budget.
- New schools have been built in the area under control of the Department of Education and Training. In the same period more than 9,000 classrooms were added to existing schools. Current building projects at 19 primary and 35 secondary schools will add a further 1,016 classrooms, while 33 new primary and 45 new secondary schools are being planned for the immediate future.
- Pre-school and out-of-school educational opportunities are now availble to ensure successful progress in the formal school year. The purpose of this new development is to ensure greater diversification, more meaningful subject and career choices, and better orientation to equip pupils for meeting the challenges of a highly competitive technoculture.
- Vast improvements have also been brought about in salary scales of teachers with lesser qualifications.
- The department is geared to meeting the challenge of training an additional 69,000 teachers by the year, 2002.
- The budget for teacher training has increased by 600 percent in the past five years.
- Two new colleges of education were established in 1985, two in 1986 and another six will be established during the next five years.
- More than R4.5 million was made available for 7,500 bursaries to student teachers in 1985-86.
- Courses aimed at improving the managerial skills of approximately 13,600 staff members in senior posts at schools were developed in conjunction with the private sector and introduced in 1985. This three-year project is the largest management development program ever attempted in South Africa.
- More than 50 percent of the department's 46,000 teachers were in-

volved annually in some form of in-service training during 1985.

- A specific program (Project Alpha) has been developed to improve subject knowledge and teaching ability, particularly of secondary school teachers. In this program free use is made of educational technology, including inter-active video. This is the first time that inter-active video has been used on such a scale by any education department.
- The pupil/teacher ratio in black schools has been brought down from 58:1 in 1968 to 38.8:1 in 1985. The goal is a ratio of 30:1.

POLITICS AND EDUCATION

Some organizations and persons are intent on disrupting education and abusing shoolchildren for political purposes. In this process widespread use is made of unfounded negative criticism and slogan-mongering (e.g., "Gutter Education"). There is also a total and deliberate disregard for any progress and positive development in education for blacks.

The education system in the RSA is based on educational principles accepted throughout the world and leads to certificates which are universally recognized and accepted.

It is also an internationally accepted principle that schools should cater for the full development of the potential of every individual pupil and for the education and training of every individual to take his or her rightful place in society to the benefit of the community and the country as a whole. For this to be achieved, it is essential that education should be offered in an atmosphere of discipline, peace, orderliness, and stability.

The government has accepted the responsibility to offer effective education and to work purposefully toward equal education opportunities in the shortest possible time. However, there is a great responsibility on every community to create an atmosphere in which effective education can take place and to ensure that all deliberations on education are based on sound educational principles and not on political emotions.

Against the background of slogans such as "Make South Africa Ungovernable," "People's Education," and "Freedom Now, Education Later," it is abundantly clear that there are political groups who are abusing education for ulterior political purposes to the detriment of the child who is to be educated.

COMMUNICATION

The government, and more specifically the Department of Education and Training, has maintained a policy of open communication with organizations and persons concerned about education. Extensive consultation takes place with the all-black Council for Education and Training, the African Teachers' Association of South Africa (ATASA), the Association of Inspectors in the RSA, as well as several delegations represnting local and regional viewpoints. Several meetings were held during 1985 with the Soweto Parent's Crisis Committee (SPCC) and the newly formed National Education Crisis Committee (NECC). During these meetings, and subsequent to the Johannesburg conference on educations held during December 1985 by the SPCC, several demands were put to the Department of Education and Training, including:

- Abolition of "school fees"
- Supply of free books
- Repair of schools damaged during incidents of unrest
- Postponement of examinations
- Recognition of "democratic" student representative councils
- Abolition of corporal punishment
- Sexual harrassment of female students
- Unconditional reinstatement of transferred or dismissed teachers
  Other demands which do not fall within the ambit of responsibility of the Department of Education and Training include:
- Lifting of the state of emergency
- Unconditional release of all detainees
- Unbanning of the Council of South African Students
- Withdrawal of the South African Defence Force from townships

The department's response, which has been conveyed and explained to the NECC, follows.

Books and Stationery. Text books in all subjects have been supplied free to all pupils by the Department of Education and Training since 1979. This year free stationery is also being supplied and free prescribed books (novels, plays, poetry) for the secondary schools will be supplied as of 1987.

Repair of Damaged Schools. The department is engaged in an intensive program for providing new schools for the increase in pupil numbers and the elimination of backlogs. The wanton destruction of schools is seriously retarding this program.

It should also be noted that the erection and repair of schools has been seriously hampered, and even prevented, by the continuing unrest in the affected areas.

The developments outlined above are just a few of the many programs and projects aimed at improving the quality of education efficiently, responsibly, and at the fastest possible rate.

THE FUTURE

It is clear that acknowledgment of progress attained as well as the cooperation of all concerned are essential ingredients for the above-mentioned projects to come to fruition. It is essential that the motivation and self-confidence of pupils to make optimum use of the opportunities available should be reinforced in order to promote successful education. On the other hand, boycott actions, unfounded negative criticism, and the abuse of education for political purposes will only retard progress and lead to stagnation.

Order in education and stability in the black communities is essential for progress on the road of political reform and the accomplishment of the ideal of equal education for all population groups. The key to quality education and to a brighter future for every individual in South Africa lies not in destroying but in building, not in confrontation but in cooperation, not in withdrawal but in communication, not in indifference but in commitment.

CHAPTER 21

The State of Education
for Blacks in South Africa

by A. J. THEMBELA

In considering educational problesm for black South Africans, it is necessary to look back at the historical determinants of the present situation briefly. We must also look at the social and cultural background. From these positions we may be better able to understand the influence of political and economic factors which cripple the education for blacks in South Africa in a very serious way. What follows is an account of the state of education for black South Africans during the first half of this decade.

BASIC PROBLEMS

Within the framework of separate schools for the different racial groups (namely whites, Indians, coloureds, and blacks) but one economy and one geopolitical space, blacks are at the bottom of the hierarchy. Even the black school leavers, with more relevant technical and other educational skills, are unlikely to possess credentials earned in black education having the same market value as those earned in the systems of education for the other racial groups. As a result of the sociopolitical order, black education, as a separate structural entity, lends itself to a labeing process in which employers interpret black school leavers as not having been sufficiently socialized into norms, values, and styles of thinking which they (the employers) value in a certificate. Some employers believe that the standard of black education is not comparable with that of the other racial groups. Deep concern is expressed about rote learning, lack of broadening of the mind, lack of encouragement given to pupils to develop initiative and skills of independent thought. Pupils have limited opportunity for problem-solving and thus they concentrate on abstract theory and verbiage. Black matriculants are viewed by employers as being overly compliant, docile and too dependent on structures of authority. This is the average perception of the products of the school system for blacks in South Africa.

HISTORICAL ANTECEDENTS

Schooling for blacks in South Africa is a foreign imposition that was grafted onto the social and cultural life of the various tribal cultural societies by the missionaries. This introduction of school education during the last half of the nineteenth century divided blacks not only into educated and noneducated classes, but also into Christianised and non-Christianised groups. When, later in the twentieth century, industrialization and urbanization gained momentum, all these groups were affected. These social processes set in motion a dynamic movement from stable norms of traditionalism to highly unstable conditions of modernism, all this occurring within a highly controlled and absolutely frustrating political and legal system which restricted not only the physical movement of blacks but also their socioeconomic and educational mobility.

Those groups or individuals who were favored by circumstances and who also possessed the ability to adapt quickly to new conditions moved faster through the process of social transformation. We now have a cadre of highly articulate and capable blacks who have moved up the social ladder in spite of the education system. A great majority, particularly in the rural areas but also in the urban areas, are at the various stages of social development. The complicating factor in South Africa is the political system which frustrates the free movement of black people.

During the missionary era in education (up to 1953) Christian norms were clearly and deliberately pursued. Schools were established in and around mission stations and pupils came mainly from families that had accepted Christianity. When mass education was promoted during the years of the Bantu Education system, pupils emerged from families which were at the various stages of transition from traditionalism to modernism. The heterogeneous social background of the pupils made it difficult for the teachers to uphold a consistent value system. The teachers themselves did not understand the educational implications of these social dynamics because of their own background and poor qualifications. The consequence of this situation was that school education became concerned merely with the imparting of dry facts of the subject matter which were hardly related to the daily lives of the pupils. The facts of history or geography, for instance were memorized without much understanding. The facts of science were taught without developing a sense of a scientific frame of mind.

The phenomenon of cultural discontinuity between the pupils' home background and school education was found in many countries in Africa. The agents of colonialism — civil servants, members of the armed forces, missionaries, explorers, or traders — ridiculed, criticized, and often humiliated Africa's cultural heritage. African religions were labeled primitive; works of art were described as crude and immoral, dances were seen as ritualistic and sensual. None of these age-old heritages was considered worthy of any respect for preservation and perpetuation within the education system. Europe of the nineteenth and twentieth century was seen as the standard by which all other civilizations were to be measured. This deliberate application of Western standards to Africa had the effect of making the black Africans admire Western culture with ritualistic fevor.

Whereas school education was part of their cultural development in the First World countries, there was a cultural discontinuity in Africa. This created the first obstacle to black Africa advancement. It is necessary to understand this background properly if any attempts at improving the quality of education are to be made. Anyone who desires to contribute toward improving the quality of black education in South Africa must acquaint himself with this historical, cultural, and socioeconomic background.

THE EDUCATIONAL PROBLEMS

The questions that come to mind are: How quickly and how effectively can modern technology be introduced into African environments, and how soon can indigenous populations assimilate this technology in such a way as to have full command over the intricacies of a technological world? If the blacks in South Africa were merely called upon to cope with a situation of adjusting a foreign system of education to their cultural and social circumstances, they would have enough homework to do. However black education has not even started to grapple with the problems of cultural discontinuities in a Western-oriented and technologically dominated world. No significant research is going on to clarify the position with regard to such issues as communication, a key problem in this situation where black children have to learn through the medium of a foreign language. The problems of curriculum development and cognitive and social development under these South African conditions have not even begun to be addressed through research.

The problems that are spoken of are peripheral to the core issues of education. Black education still lacks elementary facilities such as writing material, desks, finances, and properly qualified teachers. The phenomenon of underqualified teachers, poor teaching, high drop-out rates, high failure rates, and overcrowding creates a situtation in which black schools are functioning at a very low level of productivity.

The imparting of knowledge to enable pupils to gain real understanding and insight into the subject matter is, to a large extent, absent. The proper development of physical, mental, and moral skills and wholesome attitudes is absent. There are few means at school; the teachers have very little capacity; and the environment is not conducive to the development of creativity, original thinking, and reasoning powers. This does not mean that these capabilities are not developing in black children. What it means is that a lot of human potential is wasted. A great mass of people then become objects of manipulative politics apart from the great poverty and ignorance which the school system is not assisting to eradicate. The schools are not producing sufficient numbers of properly educated individuals who can hold their own ground anywhere in the world in science and art, literature and religion, industry and commerce. A paradoxical situation exists in South Africa where there is a great shortage of skilled manpower on the one hand and a high percentage of unemployment on the other hand amongst blacks.

Instead, schools are providing a powder keg of resistance as more and more people perceive the conditions at school to be an inevitable consequence of the general sociopolitical situation in the country. As far as the blacks are concerned, there is no such thing as educational problems per se. What we have in this country are sociopolitical problems. When pupils attack teachers and burn down school buildings, they are reacting against the immediate symptom of their frustrations. It is a suicidal syndrome of desperation. Many pupils, of course, may not be aware of the causes of their disomfort and may even be manipulated by some people for noneducational motives.

The discriminatory practices in the provision of education for the various racial and cultural groups in South Africa vindicate the assertion often made that black education is "education for slavery." Once this perception is filtered down to the consumers of this system of education, its credibility is reduced to zero. Anything that is done after that to try to improve the education system, without improving the sociopolitical system at the same time, will be rejected. The key question here is: What is the role of education and schooling in maintaining the domination of one class and culture over others? The sociopolitical arrangements in the country (not discussed in this article) are the main causes of dissatisfaction. Let it be understood therefore by anybody who wishes to contribute something toward educational advancement, that those contributions will have no effect at all if the prevailing sociopolitical situation remains unattended to. Many thinking blacks are not impressed by ad hoc educational projects calculated to "assist" blacks to improve the quality of their education either within South Africa or in the United States. The products of these programs become disgruntled individuals who have been taken out of context. It is accepted, of course, that something needs to be done now even before the political situation gets normalized. Any such project implementers need to understand the following issues.

OTHER ISSUES

The first issue which emanates from the traditional cultural background of the blacks in South Africa relates to adult-child relationships. In traditional black society a child is expected to obey his elders and superiors without question. In a school situation this tends to suppress the exercise of creativity, initiative, and drive. Teachers who do not understand the need to encourage these qualities will insist that pupils must do as they are told. In classroom practice this is translated into rote learning and teacher-centered instruction. This situation is compounded by the fact that many black teachers operate in a school system that is highly centralized and overly prescriptive. All instructions come from above and a team of school inspectors sees to it that those instructions are obeyed without question. This stultifying atmosphere reinforces the traditional norm of obedience without question and reduces everybody into a state of resigned docility that is antiethical to the development of the desirable state of self-assertiveness. When this condition is stretched to the limit, the students begin to rebel.

What is more, the whole education system is overwhelmingly examination-oriented. Departmental officers, teachers, parents, and pupils overemphasize the importance of examinations and certificates. On the other hand, there is a very high failure rate. This generates a high level of frustration and a loss of self-esteem. Pupils lose self-confidence and self-respect as they continue to be told that they are failures. When teachers try to enforce their authority by some form of military discipline through corporal punishment, pupils rebel.

The condition of a poor adult-child relationship is not assisted by the child's home background. In many rural homes for blacks, the father is often away from home and is at his place of employment for as long as ten to more months per year. The laws of the country have up to now not allowed rural blacks to come with their families to urban areas. Children grow up without the wholesome influence from their fathers. In the urban areas the situation is not much better. Children seldom see their parents because these parents leave home very early in the morning before children wake up, and come back home very late in the evening after the children have gone to bed. Many children come from homes with broken families. The social services to care for these children are totally inadequate. This social factor of the disorganization of many black families is bound to have a deleterious effect on the child's school life. Some children actually leave home and squat in shacks near the school. A decent place of study is not known to them and many are poorly nourished.

The second important issue of a cultural nature which affects the education for blacks is the language of instruction. There are several threads which come in to complicate this issue. First, there is a colonial mentality and hangover which made some blacks think that a really educated person was one who spoke English very well. Then there is an apparent contradiction between the desire for the development of national and cultural pride on the one hand and the desire for Westernization on the other. This conflict finds its manifestation in the language policy of the schools. A very strong argument for the use of English as a medium of instruction is that it is an international language; a language of commerce and industry, science and literature. A knowledge and mastery of the English language opens channels of communication with the wider world. The use of the various African indigenous languages as media of instruction, it is argued, would lock the blacks into their tribel cultural kraals from which they would not emerge. The pedagogically sound principle of using the home language as a medium of instruction at school is frustrated by nonpedagogical considerations arising from economic and political issues. Black children learn through the medium of their various home languages for the first four years (that is, up to grade four) and thereafter switch over to the use of English as a medium of instruction. This practice creates serious problems for instruction. Black pupils who reside in rural areas seldom hear or use English outside the classroom. Obviously the use of a foreign medium presents the child with a double problem of having to struggle with the language as well as the subject matter concepts. It must be pointed out that the subject matter is itself Western-oriented, selected and ordered from Western culture. The child learns about electricity for instance, when there is none in his environment. Even highly urbanized areas like Soweto have had electricity installed only recently. The extent to which the use of a foreign tongue as a medium of instruction affects the cognitive development of black children has not yet been properly investigated. It can only be imagined that a great majority of pupils struggle and give up schooling sooner of later. Add to this difficult situation the fact that the teachers who teach these pupils have themselves not mastered properly either the language of instruction or the concepts they are transmitting.

Since educational disability is found among socially and economically disadvantaged groups in all societies, we can conclude that there is a systematic relationship between social conditions and educational competence. The culturally deprived child is also retarded in cognitive skills by the time he enters school. Many black children in South Africa come from squalid slums on the periphery of large cities. These urban slums with their overcrowded apartments offer a limited range of stimuli to a child. The scarcity of objects to manipulate and the lack of diversity in the environmental content, in addition to the absence of individualized training (because the mother is busy looking after a large family or is away at work), give the child few opportunities to handle and organize the visual properties of his environment and thus learn to discriminate perceptually its nuances. What we are saying here is that the home background of many black pupils does not enable a child to get ready for schooling. School life then becomes a frustrating experience.

The issues raised up to now indicate that anyone who desires to contribute anything toward the improvement of the quality of education for blacks in South Africa must understand that a few thousand or even a few million dollars for a specific educational project are merely going to scrath the surface. The danger of such contributions is that they create and illusion that the problem is being attended to. What I am suggesting here is that a much more comprehensive and coordinated attack on all the cultural and socioeconomic issues needs to be undertaken. Any specific project must then fit in within this plan. Otherwise a lot of energy, time, and resources are dissipated and wasted on piecemeal attention to a few specific educational projects sometimes totally unrelated to the wider issues.

SPECIFIC PROBLEMS

What follows is a description of specific educational problems relating to teachers' qualifications, pupil-teacher ratios, financing of education, subject choices, drop-out rates and failure rate.

TEACHERS' QUALIFICATIONS

The issue of the poor qualifications of teachers constitutes a major obstacle to black educational advancement as the following table indicates.

Qualification of Teachers in Black Schools, 1982

(excluding Transkei, Bophuthatswana, Venda, and Ciskei)[1]

| | Number of Teachers | | | |
Professionally qualified, with	White	African	Total	%
Std. 6	—	7,911	7,911	9.4
Junior Certificate	6	40,592	40,598	48.5
Technical Certificate	47	63	110	0.1
Std. 10 with primary teacher cert.	334	10,770	11,106	13.3
Std. 10 with secondary teacher cert.	16	4,462	4,478	5.4
Degree incomplete	49	1,266	1,319	1.6
Degree	539	1,590	2,129	2.5
Special teacher certificte	7	279	286	0.3
SUBTOTAL	998	66,933	67,931	81.1
No professional qualification, but with				
Junior certificate or lower	29	11,336	11,365	13.6
Technical certificate	209	45	254	0.1

Matriculation or senior cert.	50	3,773	3,823	4.6
Degree incomplete	8	70	78	0.0
Degree	83	208	291	0.4
SUBTOTAL	379	15,432	15,811	18.9
TOTAL	1,377	82,365	83,742	100.0

If a properly qualified teacher is one who possesses a poststandard 10 diploma or certificate, the table above reveals that only 23.1% of teachers in black schools could be considered to have proper qualifications in 1982. The situation has not improved much since then although considerable effort is being expended to do so. In one education department for blacks (out of 11) in an area called Kwazulu, of the 22,041 teachers in 1983, 20,613 teachers had an academic qualification of not more than a standard 10 (*i.e.*, Grade 12) certificate. Only 5 primary (elementary) school teachers and 826 secondary school teachers had university degrees. The consequences of this situation for the education system are obvious. The 1981 report of the *Human Sciences Research Council* emphasized this situation:

Without a corps of well-trained and talented teachers any endeavour aimed at a system of education by means of which the potential of the country's inhabitants is to be realized, economic growth promoted, the quality of life of the inhabitants improved and education of equal quality provided for everyone, cannot be successful.

The area of teacher education and teacher upgrading manifests itself as deserving high priority for anyone who desires to contribute something. Assisting colleges of education to perform more efficiently and more effectively is one significant project. Another is to assist the well-planned and well-coordinated in-service programs for serving teachers.

TEACHER/PUPIL RATIO

The following comparative figures reveal the teacher/pupil ratio among the various racial groups in 1983:[2]

Whites	Coloureds	Indians	Black
18.2:1	26.7:1	23.6:1	42,7:1

Again, looking more closely at one region in Natal and Kwazulu, and comparing it with the other education departments in South Africa, the following picture emerges:

Pupil/Teacher Ratio, 1980[3]

	Primary	Secondary
Kwazulu Department of Education (black)	56:1	40:1
Education and Training Department (black)	47:1	30:1
Indian Education Department (Indian)	28:1	22:1
Natal Education Department (white)	19:1	13:1

If one looks at individual schools, one finds classes with over seventy pupils per class. This makes it very difficult for any teacher to handle this group effectively and for pupils to receive the necessary individual attention.

FINANCING OF EDUCATION

Despite the fact that a considerable amount of money has been poured into black education in recent years, the gap that exists between the amount spent on black education and that spent in the other systems of education for the other racial groups remains unacceptably wide as the following figures show:

Estimated Capita Expenditure on Education, 19832/83[3]

	Including Capital Expenditure	Excluding Capital
Whites	R1385.00	R1211.00
Coloured	R 871.87	R 711.16
Indian	R 593.37	R 497.59
Black	R 192.34	R 146.44

From the first column of figures above, it can be seen that the ratio of white to black is 7.2:1; Indian to black is 4.5:1; and coloured to black is 3.1:1.

If we are talking about equality of opportunity someone will have to insist that all the children of this country receive equal facilities. I repeat that an isolated amount of money here and there for specific projects does nothing to address the massive problems of black education.

DROP-OUT RATE

The various factors mentioned above the others not mentioned result in a high drop-out rate for black pupils:[5]

Grade	Original Enrollment in 1st Grade	Still at School in 1975	Percent
4 (Standard 2)	687,000	419,212	60.9
7 (Standard 5)	624,942	221,019	35.4
10 (Standard 8)	515,449	50,772	9.9
12 (Standard 10)	443,030	9,009	2.0

A relatively recent report by the Research Institute for Education Planning at the University of the Orange Free State, shows that the black drop-out rate continues to pose an enormous problem:

Number of Black Pupils Leaving School in 1982[6]

With less than Grade 1	156,558
With less than Grade 4	192,180
With less than Grade 7	130,272
With less than Grade 10	116,378
With less that Grade 12	63,659

Many black children are thus leaving school without obtaining sustainable literacy. The rapidly increasing number of pupils and the high drop-out rate means that unless there is urgent change made, there will continue to be a large pool of uneducated and undereducated people in South Africa for a very long time.

FAILURE RATE

Another consequence of poor teacher qualification, inadequate financing, and a high pupil/teacher ratio is the high failure rate.

Black Matriculants 1960–1983[7]

Year	Number of Candidates	Number Passed	Percent	Number Obtaining Matric Exemption	Percent
1960	716	125	17.9	28	3.9
1965	1,339	827	61.8	323	24.1
1970	2,846	1,850	65.2	1,013	35.6
1975	8,445	5,400	63.9	3,520	41.7
1976	9,593	7,996	83.4	3,404	35.5
1977	8,225	5,899	71.7	2,294	27.9
1978	9,804	7,468	76.2	3,806	38.8
1979	14,574	10,706	73.5	4,136	28.4
1980	29,973	15,935	53.2	4,714	15.7
1981	48,571	25,963	53.5	6,069	12.5
1982	60,108	30,541	50.8	6,336	10.5
1983	72,168	14,876	48.3	7,108	9.8

The 1977 and 1978 figures exclude the Transkei and Bophuthatswana; 1979 and 1980 exclude the Transkei, Bophuthatswana and Venda; 1981, 1982, and 1983 figures exlude the Transkei only.

The main features to be deduced from this table, and from the facts that were mentioned earlier, are that:

• There has been a tremendous increase in the number of black candidates for Standard 10 (Grade 12).

• There has not been a commensurate increase in the number of teachers and facilities to cope with pupil increase.

• Many of these pupils are simply not matric material, but because there are no other educational opportunities for them, they all aspire to matriculation.

• The actual number who passed and those who obtained matric exemption increased, but the percentage of passes gradually decreased, thus revealing that the quality of performance in black schools is deteriorating.

TECHNICAL TRAINING AND UNIVERSITY EDUCATION

To complete the picture it is necessary to indicate what happens to the ultimate few who are able to overcome these obstacles and obtain a matriculation certificate (Grade 12). The enrollment of black students at universities, technikons, and technical colleges has increased in recent years but remains proportionately lower than that for the other population groups. The number awarded (mostly in nonscience subjects) is very low.

The failure rate for all university students in South Africa, and particularly for blacks, is very high. The frequent disturbances and closures of black universities seriously disrupt the teaching process and reduce the academic success rate. The figures that trickle out of universities and technikons show that it is going to take a very long time for the indigenous populations to absorb Western technology to the extent where they will have full command of it unless other strategies are adopted to accelerate the process.

CONCLUSION

The historical development of school education for blacks in South Africa created a situation of cultural and social conflict. This conflict made it difficult for education to proceed smoothly. The South African sociopolitical arrangements place blacks at the bottom of the social structue and rigidly keep them there by constitutional and legal constraints. This creates tremendous obstacles for blacks which make it difficult for them to do well at school. The conditions which exist in black schools make effective transmission of knowledge, proper development of skills, and the acquisition of understanding and insight by pupils difficult to attain. The lack of internal efficiency in the schools for blacks forces these schools to function at a very low level of productivity. The absence of a proper home and school environment within which to develop wholesome attitudes and appreciations and the absence of means and lack of capacity of teachers to develop in their pupils the qualities of creativity, reasoning powers, and originality all add up to a situation where we can say black education faces serious obstacles to advancement. The result is that, with a few exceptions, black education is not producing adequately educated individuals who can hold their own ground in the commerical and technical world.

The purpose of this article was not to provide answers for people who want to know what they can do to assist. It was definitely not to ask for donations or bursaries or the like which can only scratch the surface. The purpose was to raise issues in order to emphasize that anyone who wants to assist must understand that the improvement of the quality of education and the quality of life for the blacks is not merely a matter of expanding physical facilities for learning and providing opportunities to study abroad, however worthwhile and desirable all these might be. I am calling for a wider attention to the speedy transformation of this society by deliberately attending to all those issues that constitute obstacles to the realization of educational goals. How that is going to be done is a matter for consultation and negotiation with the local people.

NOTES

1 *Survey of Race Relations in South Africa, 1983* (Johannesburg: South African Institute of Race Relations, 1984), p. 419.
2. Ibid., p. 421.
3. *Energos 8* (1983).
4. *Survey of Race Relations in South Africa, 1983*, p. 420.
5. *Energos 8*, (1983): 56
6. *Survey of Race Relations in South Africa, 1983* p. 430.
7. Ibid., p. 434.

CHAPTER 22

Black Education in South Africa: Parameters, Scenarios, Needs

by JOHAN G. GARBERS

Apartheid, a policy of partition based on the unilateral and statutory institutionalization of race/ethnicity as cleavage, has caused immeasurable harm to South African society. As a government policy it inspired prejudice, a negative tendency that is found among people universally. Instead of the constitutional accommodation of all cultural groups that it aspired to, the apartheid policy reinforced ethnicity in an attempt to handle diversity; it failed to establish a meaningful balance between individual and group association in society; it institutionalized inequality and in general led to the isolation and insulation of groups.

The dismantling of apartheid (to which the South African government has irrevocably committed itself), however, would amount to the revolutionizing of South African society because of the far-reaching structural changes that would be called for in a short span of time. The challenges — political as well as nonpolitical — facing education in South Africa in order to conform to a postapartheid society will subsequently be indicated, as well as the measures that would be required to minimize the negative effect of political change on education.

Certain groups in South African society regard the politicizing of education as one of the means of achieving their political ideals. Education appears to be an irresistible target for the revolutionary; hence the fear that political liberation in South Africa (as in Communist China, for instance) would be at the expense of education and that the ensuing educational backlogs would take generations to wipe out. The question now is whether South Africa will be able to benefit from the lessons of history or whether she is heading for the same fate.

INSURMOUNTABLE FORCES

The demographic forces to be taken into consideration include the fact that blacks have the highest growth rate of all the population groups and that they are a relatively youthful population (52.5 percent are 20 years old and younger compared with 36.5 percent of the whites). Hence the increase in the school-going population from 3.5 million in 1974 to 6 million in 1985. It should also be borne in mind that whereas 0.2 percent of the school-going population completed its secondary education in 1974, this percentage had increased to 1.7 percent by 1984. In order to accommodate this number of pupils, more than 10 percent of the 1979 matriculants would have had to qualify as teachers just to cope with the additional number of pupils. This is a considerable proportion, keeping in mind there is also an acute need for black doctors, dentists, lawyers, nurses, engineers, accountants, and the like.

The financial implications are far-reaching if one takes into account the upgrading of black education and the required expansion to meet the needs of the steadily increasing numbers of pupils. In recent years, the South African government has steadily increased the educational budget to its present level of about 16 percent of the state's total annual expenditure. The budget for the Department of Education and Training (responsible for education of all blacks with exception of the national states) alone has increased by 538 percent since the beginning of the decde..

To reach parity by the year 1990 in the provision of education on the basis of one teacher for every thirty pupils on average entails an expenditure of 29.2 percent of the state budget for education alone. Over $140 million is required annually to meet the school building costs for the period 1985 to 1990, to eliminate the educational backlog, and to provide for the educational needs of the black population. There is no way that these obligations can be met by the South African economy which is already straining under the effects of disinvestment.

TIME SCHEDULE

Realistic time schedules and target dates in educational development are difficult to reconcile with political pressure and people's aspirations. There is at present a widespread insistence in South Africa that parity in the provision of education be achieved in the shortest time possible. There is a difference of opinion regarding the target date, ranging from periods as short as three months to 1990, with some stipulating the turn of the century and others even later.

The demands as well as the target dates become increasingly unrealistic as more pressure is applied for political considerations to be placed before equal educational opportunities. The government has committed itself through legislation to the establishment of equal educational opportunities, including equal standards of education for all races. Equal opportunities, however, involve both the providers and the users of education, and the achievement thereof depends on many conditions, some of which are very difficult to realize. Americans should be familiar with the challenges that this issue poses since they have been grappling over the years with the problem of enabling the disadvantaged to benefit most from educational opportunities in the United States. These challenges should also be seen in the context of the severe deterioration in the quality of the intellectual performance of black pupils since 1974. The results of a particular standardized scholastic test have shown a decrease by more than one standard deviation in the achievements of black pupils, and this decrease was most marked in those scholastic skills dependent on school attendance. This deterioration can be traced back to a reduction of the school career from thirteen to twelve years to bring it in line with that of the other population groups, the inability to cope with the demands of a burgeoning population particularly in terms of the provision of sufficient qualified teachers, and the effects of the continuing school unrest.

The combination of First and Third World conditions that characterizes South Africa has created feelings of relative deprivation and a legitimacy crisis among blacks. There appears to be a strong feeling of relative deprivation among the disadvantaged. The educational system for whites is the most sophisticated and also makes the proportionally largest contribution to the provision of high-level manpower. Consequently, white education is regarded as the model for all education in South Africa. In view of the available resources and the sheer numbers involved, this is simply not possible. Also bear in mind that South Africa combines a First and Third World economy and that it cannot, for the sake of all its inhabitants, afford to risk jeopardizing the training and provision of high-level manpower.

The almost insurmountable challenge facing South Africa therefore is to continue maintaining educational standards while striving to train to the highest levels more and more manpower of the necessary quality drawn from the traditionally less school-oriented groups. This should be achieved by means of a fair redistribution of resources, taking into consideration political demands and realities as well as the fact that black education has the further problem of its legitimacy to contend with, since many blacks regard it as inferior. In view of South Africa's strategic resources, it is as much in the interests of the Western world as in South Africa's own that a fair and urgent solution be sought to this dilemma.

There are certain forces that inhibit educational developments but which appear to be surmountable to a greater or lesser extent: The expansion of the education provision in an affordable way—bearing in mind population growth and rising expectations—is of vital importance. Formal education alone cannot provide for present and future educational needs, and even the immediate abolition of segregation in schools would contribute little toward satisfying the educational needs of the black community. The following facets of the education provision are particularly important here:

• Synchronizing the skills and infrastructure available in the nonformal education provided by the private and public training sectors with formal education. Such synchronizing contains the possibility of an effective mass education program encompassing the ideals of compensatory as well as life-long education.

Synchronizing formal and nonformal education would be based on a system of nine years of compulsory education comprising six years of compulsory school attendance, during which a pupil would acquire literacy and certain other skills that facilitate training, and three years of compulsory training in either formal or nonformal education. Fortunately, the South African private sector has already established a fairly extensive and sophisticated nonformal educational system, the annual expenditure of which is twice that of the total formal educational sector. The greatest challenge, however, lies in making nonformal education acceptable to blacks over a broad base and in making it possible for learners channeled to nonformal education to gain entry to formal education at a later stage.

• The expansion-of-education provision through distance education, because of its proven cost-effectiveness and flexibility, is at present receiving particular attention in South Africa. The penetration of the radio in the black population is at present 76 percent and that of television approximately 19 percent. The percentage of black learners who use distance education (particularly correspondence courses with the exception of the educational radio and television services) in ordinary education is insignificant. Distance education has the potential to expand education considerably, provided one bears in mind the particular demands it would make on a nonschool-oriented or nonlearning supportive cultural milieu. Therefore, it does not always offer an easy solution.

• Educational technology as a means of expanding and raising the quality of education is regarded highly in all circles, including the government. Hence the impressive activity, openness, and expertise displayed in this field at all levels of education. In view of the backlogs that are experienced, in the field of educational technology in particular, assistance from outside the Republic of South Africa can be used to the great benefit of all. In this respect, one thinks particularly of the interactive video technique for the upgrading of inadequately qualified black teachers. The biggest obstacle, however, remains the provision of hardware that is not dependent on electricity and appropriate software.

• South Africa's manpower needs call for the large-scale conversion of education from its current "academic" nature to a dominance of vocation-oriented education. Education for whites is at present approximately 70 percent academically preparatory and 30 percent vocation-oriented. In black education, this imbalance is even more striking, with approximately 95 percent of education being academically preparatory. These relationships need to be converted at the secondary school level—with consideration of the available job opportunities and the required manpower structures. First, however, this conversion would require the elimiantion of strong prejudice toward vocational education—especially when economic growth is used as a supportive argument.

• The sharing of educational resources (physical facilities, personnel, and teaching aids) appears inevitable on account of the market differences between education for the different groups and as a token of goodwill and cooperation. Bearing in mind, however, that white children constitute 12.7 percent and blacks 74.3 percent of pupils in South Africa, it is clear that the sharing of services and resources would not be sufficient to achieve equilibrium between supply and demand in South African education. The solution obviously does not lie in lowering the standards of or dividing white education, but rather in using it as a model for the upgrading of educational resources for all children in South Africa.

CURRENT REFORMS

The current educational reforms based on extensive research are comprehensive and far-reaching and proceed in accordance with the following principles of education to which the present government has committed itself through legislation:

• That equal opportunities for education, including equal standards of education, shall be strived after for every inhabitant of the Republic irrespective of race, color, creed, or sex.

• That recognition shall be granted both to that which is common and to that which is diverse in the religious and cultural way of life of the inhabitants of the Republic and to their languages.

• That, subject to the provisions of any law regarding school attendance for a particular population group by a pupil who is subject to compulsory school attendance, recognition shall be granted to the freedom of choice of the individual, parents, and organizations.

• That the provision of education shall be directed in an educationally responsible manner to the needs of the individual and those of society, and to the demands of economic development, and shall take into account the manpower needs of the Republic.

• That a positive relationship shall be promoted between formal, informal, and nonformal education in the school, society, and family.

• That the state shall be responsible for the provision of formal education, but that the individual, parents, and society shall share responsibility and have a say in that regard.

• That the private sector and the state shall share responsibility for the provision of nonformal education.

• That in providing education, provision shall be made for the establishment and state subsidization of private education.

• That in providing education, a balance between centralization and decentralization in the administration thereof shall be strived after.

• That the professional status of the teacher and the lecturer shall be recognized.

• That the provision of education shall be based on continuing research.

In the educational system of South Africa something unique is taking place, namely the development of one coordinating education department (the Department of National Education) that neither owns any schools nor employs any teachers. The department sets general policy on norms and standards for financing running and capital costs in education, salaries and conditions of employment of staff, the professional registration of teachers, and norms and standards for syllabuses and examinations, and for certification of qualifications. These policies will apply to all educational authorities. In view of the slowness that characterizes all educational reforms and the resources that will be required, present inequalities in the educational dispensation cannot be expected to be phased out overnight.

A fierce debate continues to rage, however, on the issue of a segregated versus a desegregated educational system for South Africa. The supporters of segregation in schools (which for more than three centuries has been the circumstances in South Africa—with marginal exceptions here and there) advance the following considerations: the great differences between the various population groups in respect of language, culture, general outlook, home background of pupil populations, and the right of every individual to voluntary association or dissociation. The preceding form the basis of the present educational policy as contained in the 1983 constitution, namely that education at whatever level constitutes an own affair (i.e., that the different cultural groups are responsible for their own education in respect of which they accordingly have self-determination). The educational dispensation that is taking shape in educational terms certainly has a powerful rationale. The context of apartheid (with all its ramifications), however sincerely conceived, makes attempts to diversify education in terms of culture appear suspect. The vast majority of parents of all population groups would probably prefer culture-based education for their children provided they were convinced that their children were offered equal educational opportunities.

A further essential development is reflected in the implementation of the principle of voluntary association and dissociation as well as parental freedom in the choice of school. There is a need to create racially integrated educational opportunities that are subsidized by the state for the children of parents who desire such facililties. If such a development were to prove viable, it would develop a momentum of its own. In the long run, such schools could increasingly become the predominant form of education, while schools with a particular language or cultural or philosophical orientation could still be maintained on a state-subsidized basis.

An alternative scenario in which education in South Africa plays a key role has also been planned and is in the process of unfolding. In this scenario, certain groups by means of revolution aim to create

a new social order in which South African society would be characterized by even greater polarization, with education severly disrupted and
restrained in its development. Although these revolutionary objectives
are in almost direct conflict with the American way of life or value
systems, it appears that they are nevertheless supported particularly
by the American disinvestment initiatives. The only countermeasure
aainst this destructive force is a constructive plan of action in which
apartheid is dismantled according to a fixed time schedule and undertaking, domestic forces being accordingly directed, and education's role
being safeguarded solely for its educational task. There are no easy
or instant solutions to problems experienced in South Africa in general
and in education in particular. In addition, the situation in South Africa
is vulnerable in more than one respect.

CHAPTER 23

The Press in South Africa: Twilight of Freedom?

by ANTHONY H. HEARD

Free expression in South Africa can play a key supportive role in achieving a relatively peaceful, nonracial solution to the country's problems. Yet it remains to be seen whether press freedom, with sturdy roots in history, can withstand current onslaughts of both a political and an economic nature. By free expression I mean the elementary right of the public to say what is in their minds and, therefore, of the media to publish accordingly. It is accepted like mother's milk in free societies, but in South Africa free expression is in a twilight phase.

I have in mind the basic right of people to know, essentially, what is going on in their own country—unlike the white Rhodesians who were duped by official propaganda and censorship into not seeing the Mugabe hurricane tearing across the Zimbabwean veldt. It simply means that when critical choices have to be made, the public is better informed to take the right course and to accept reality. South Africans desperately need this public service. In South Africa there are two important realities: black majority and white fear. Both must be fully reported on to be understood and resolved.

The history of a free South African press goes back some 150 years to the days when brave colonists, representing the embryonic commercial classes, clashed with despotic rulers in the Cape, notably Britain's Lord Charles Somerset. They won their freedom to print, subject to the usual Western legal norms of defamation and sedition, though regrettably no provision was written into the basic law of South Africa when it became a union in 1910 to entrench free speech along the lines of the First Amendment in the United States. There is irony in the fact that freedom first had to be won from the metropolitan British, now has to be secured against the attentions of an Afrikaner nationalist government, and next might have to be maintained under a black-majority government. If press freedom can be preserved in the current crisis in South Africa, the better its chances are in a future dispensation.

Since the freedom to publish was won in the last century, there have been successive attempts by governments to restrain the printed word. Times of war and internal crisis put the freedom to publish under great strain, but the press managed to maintain a British-type degree of editorial independence until after World War II, though there had been unsuccessful attempts before the outbreak of war to curb what the then prime minister, General Hertzog, who was neutral on the German issue, felt were overcritical attacks on Hitler. Indeed, in a celebrated case, the editor of the *Cape Argus*, Dominick McCausland, was fired at the time of Munich for having dared to adopt the sort of hostility toward Hitler that went against the current appeasement consensus. By the time he was proved right, he had been fired.

The McCausland case was a warning to other editors that if they stepped too radically outside the currently popular assumptions favored by their mainly mining industry masters, they could get the chop. It was one thing to be right; quite another to be right too early. The same sort of thing happened years later, when one of the most perceptive critics of apartheid, Laurence Gandar, then editor of the *Rand Daily Mail*, took up a brave and uncompromising position which in today's conditions would be less exceptional, yet he was eased out of his job. This came after he lost a celebrated case over his paper's disclosure of alleged prisons abuses in the late 1960s, after which his liberal paper found itself increasingly shunned by the English business community. This, plus other factors including the secret government funding of a competitor newspaper, meant loss of advertising and eventual demise in 1985 for the *Rand Daily Mail*. Not many papers are left to carry on the tradition.

PRUDENT EDITORS

For these reasons, newspaper editors tend to be rather prudent — highly professional and independent-minded in a Fleet Street way, but with an ear cocked to the bark of the business community. It is the mining-financial interests that in effect control the English-language press, and it is the National Party and its business comrades that control the

Afrikaans press. Significantly, blacks have no substantial control or share in the established press, and those papers aimed specifically at black readers tend to be white- or church-owned.

Yet, in recent times a new bark, complete with bite, has emerged which editors and owners must consider very carefully—the growing clout of black buying power, gradually overtaking that of whites as living standards, in spite of apartheid, rise. Editors find their papers facing black reader boycotts if they fail to give coverage that, in the black view, is relevant. And when it is considered that roughly half the readership of the English newspapers (and in some cases up to a quarter or a third in the case of the Afrikaans press) is made up of people who do not happen to be white, the lethal effect of a black boycott can be seen for what it is.

At least one newspaper has had to publish a prominent page one apology for not having covered news concerning the mass antiapartheid movement, the United Democratic Front, to the satisfaction of the UDF. The apology did the trick in calling off a debilitating UDF boycott. Another newspaper headed off a boycott threat by some sensible editorial negotiation with a traders' group which felt neglected in its columns. The specter of boycott, therefore, threatens not only the shops of Main Street in this country but also newspapers run by whites that have a majority of black readers. And it is obvious that the boycott weapon can be used against the interests of free expression and an open debate, if done so in a reckless or partisan fashion. The extent to which black opinion is veering toward an advocacy view of the role of newspapers, which can only be described as "openly show your support for our cause in your news and comment," is worrying for those who favor the freest flow of news and opinion, but it is a measure of the frustration and bitterness in the black community after years of apartheid. It represents similar forces to those in the Third World advocating a new information order which runs counter to the traditions of Western media.

Nevertheless, established newspapers in South Africa are finding it good for news gathering and good for business to employ increasing numbers of blacks, who have behind them an activist and alert union called the Media Workers' Association which is extending membership to all departments of newspapers and not just to editorial.

There are people who believe that if the Rand Daily Mail had lasted into this intriguing new era of the black economic boycott, it could well have drawn the advertising—from businesses wanting to show the flag to the black community via a liberal newspaper—to survive. Perhaps a new *Rand Daily Mail* will arise and prosper in the conditions of the 1990s, when black buying power will be dominant. More likely, a black-owned press will emerge, with mass readership but also white business support—assuming government does not do what it did to two vigorous black newspapers, *The World* and *The Post*, some years ago. They were forced to close, though their roles have been taken over, to a degree, by *City Press* and *The Sowetan*. The problem is that if black journalists, accurately and with feeling, reflect the bitterness and frustration felt in the black townships, they incur official wrath, along with their newspapers.

RESTRAINTS ON THE PRESS

The pressures on newspapers (e.g., political, economic, commercial) are manifold. Indeed, one would look hard to find a South African editor who disagreed with the view that if one spends too much time poring over the restrictions in detail, the paper would never be published. The main statutory restraints are in the areas of defense, security, police, and prisons reporting. The ban on publishing unauthorized defense information is almost total. It does not include public statements by a foreign official or responsible person such as a prime minister or cabinet member or foreign press or broadcast reports as long as the source is given. The Defense Department is given prior opportunity to comment and the report does not deal with South African military weapons or arms supply. There is a total ban on publishing without authority any information about oil supply to the Republic and about certain strategic materials such as uranium.

The reporting of police activities is made onerous through a device that sounds reasonable but is not. It is an offense to publish untrue matter about police without having reasonable ground for believing it to be true, on pain of a fine of 10,000 South African rands (about $5,000) or five years in jail. The big question, "What are reasonable steps?" is left vague and will be tested only when a Port Elizabeth court gives judgment in an important case involving the *Eastern Province Herald* in mid-April. At present, the rather Delphic statement of a judge on the principle (concerning the Gandar case) is not overhelpful for journalists rushing to production with a good story: "On the circumstances of each case must depend what the reasonable steps are. Steps clearly reasonable in one case may well indicate excessive caution in another and be inadequate half-measures in a third." It is worth noting, too, that the onus rests on the accused to prove that reasonable steps were taken.

The Prisons Act contains a similar restraint to the one in the Police Act, and South African newspapers have not, since the Gandar case, been distinguished for publishing prisons exposès. There is, however, a degree of relaxation of the law at the administrative level, because the Prisons Department has made it known that as long as it has the chance to comment on the allegations in question and the reply is given suitable prominence, there will be no prosecution. But editors are still wary of relying on such administrative waivers. When the controversial section of the Prisons Act was introduced in 1958, newspapers had authoritatively been led to believe that the provision on publishing false information without taking reasonable steps to verify was designed only to stop nasty death cell reports (presumably of a sensational nature), but this did not help Laurence Gandar when he was charged and convicted. Judges in South Africa apply the law as it stands, and informal assurances by the authorities are of little use in court.

The list of legal restrictions on the press runs to 100 or more, with about a score of them bearing heavily down on journalists. But the fact that there is no censor in any South African newspaper office gives scope for creative decisionmaking by those editors who care or dare to try. Some go further than others and test the limits of the law. Some become a cropper. It's like playing Russian roulette.

COVERING THE UNREST

Almost three years of racial unrest (unleashed, many believe, primarily because the new South African Constitution of 1983 confirmed and dramatized the fact that blacks were locked out of the central body politic) have brought special pressures and restrictions. Covering the unrest has been hideously difficult, with reporters and photographers pressured by both demonstrators and police. Pulitzers, some aver, should be earned for paragraphs in South Africa, and when one considers the time and effort, danger, checking, supervision, thought, evaluation, and sometimes sheer guts that go into getting relevant information into the paper on a night of mayhem in the townships when up to a dozen people could have been killed, the point is driven home. Some reporters turn up to work in crisis times with bedroll and sleeping bag in case they have to sleep in the townships while getting the news.

The seven-month state of emergency in 1985-86 made it even more onerous for journalists, local and foreign, to carry out their duties. They were locked out of emergency areas and forbidden to take pictures or tape-recordings. Many were detained, whipped, warned off, and generally harassed by hard-pressed police. And some were stoned or petrol-bombed by demonstrators for their trouble. Some still face charges or official investigations (e.g., for trespassing on school property—while checking in the course of their duty on pupils' return to school—defeating the ends of justice, or taking pictures of prisoners in custody—an offense in South Africa). Some have been blackballed by police, who refuse to give them routine information because of what they feel is hostile reporting. Some have faced subpoenas to provide the names of sources or to produce pictures, including nonpublished ones, of demonstrators so that the police can pick out ringleaders for prosecution or action. This immediately endangers the journalist, who can face reprisals at the hands of demonstrators.

The lifting of the emergency was a welcome but not necessarily far-reaching development for the press. Pictures of unrest came back to the front pages, though police still possess a battery of powers to detain, warn off, close areas, etc., that predates the emergency, and the question now is whether any new measures will be written into the permanent law of the land, as foreshadowed by President Botha in lifting the emergency. A controversial measure of this nature would be an indemnity for the security forces in carrying out their duties, which critics charge amounts to giving them virtually carte blanche in dealing with unrest. Another permanent measure could be tighter control of the press, whether by way of a statutory media council to exercise discipline or an even more ominous measure, the registration of journalists. Either move would, in my view, tip the press under effective state control.

Through the years there have been several onslaughts on the press which have not, happily, borne fruit—for instance, two highly critical commissions of inquiry, a newspaper bill or two, and plenty of threats and warnings to the newspaper industry to put its house in order. The existence of a relatively free press is seen as a useful card, among government sophisticates and diplomats, in countering foreign criticism, and therefore constraint has frequently been applied by a government otherwise enraged by the press.

Other pressures on the press exist. Perhaps as important as the political pressures are those economic. The South African newspaper industry was for years a cosseted, comfortable comradeship of four main groups, broadly the English-language morning and afternoon groups and the Afrikaans-language morning and afternoon groups. Each had some access to the lucrative Sunday newspaper market, less lucrative now that television has eaten into national advertising.

NO TELEVISION

One reason for the comfort was that the government, in the 1950s and 1960s when it was more conservative than it is today, kept television away from South Africans mainly because it was seen as a decadent influence. The West was viewed as a morally decaying, declining factor in the world, and it was felt that the faithful at home in South Africa should be protected from seeing too much of this dangerous little box in the corner of the sitting room. Of course, there was also the belief that if whites and blacks in South Africa saw too much happy racial mixing abroad, they might try it themselves, which, then, was too ghastly to contemplate. The ultimate white fear in South Africa has always been the prospect of a daugher getting hitched to a black man. With interracial sex and marriage now legalized, at least the law cannot be invoked to check natural selection.

So the very newspapers that lambasted the government for its archaic attitude toward television ironically benefited by its nonintroduction, because that large slice of the advertising cake now taken up by television was kept for the press. Newspapers bought new full-color printing presses to handle the advertisers' insatiable demand for color and were among world leaders in color technology and use. They prospered. Then came television in the mid-1970s, and the picture changed. Newspapers, struggling under the double-digit inflation that has gnawed at the economy for a dozen years and facing serious economic recession, racial unrest (which affects newspaper distribution and business confidence), and a falling rand (which makes imported new equipment astronomically expensive), have found themselves in dire straits.

It is widely acknowledged that only one Afrikaans daily newspaper and only a few English-language newspapers make money at present. Sunday papers, traditionally very profitable, are no longer laying the golden eggs to underpin their more serious, less profitable daily cousins. This has led to a process of concentration of ownership and the death of many well-known titles.

These bloodlettings, with the partial exception of the *Rand Daily*

Mail, which is a special and very political case, were not caused by political action but by economic forces. It is cause for reflection that a powerful English-speaking business community, which presides over billions and is the repository for a priceless heritage of freedom in commerce and thought, is strangely reluctant to underpin enthusiastically one of the sinews of its success — a press based on the free market ideal of the last century which opened up South Africa after the discovery of diamonds. The press, which plays such a pivotal role in checking government excess, probing into dark corners, and risking life and limb to bring the world as it is to the breakfast tables of business people who cannot really do without a maximum number of versions of the truth, is strangely lacking in attention from its natural patrons. It requires leadership of the caliber of the captains of industry and commerce, yet it is strained of resources and manpower and has unimpressive training and staff development programs. Now that the halcyon days are over, the press has difficulty finding people of caliber, editorial and managerial, to continue the battle. The business community carries heavy responsibility here.

GRAY UNIFORMITY

Overconcentration of ownership probably threatens the press as much as political pressures. If not held in check, it could mean the reduction of the present four large groups (two English and two Afrikaans) to two (one of each), with the gray uniformity that that must entail, and a few small and embattled independent newspapers trying to fly the flag against heavy economic odds and competition from the giants. The government has for years watched newspapers growing frail without offering financial relief. One reason is probably the government's basic belief that it is the newspapers that cause most of the trouble in South Africa and that are not as reliable as the state-run radio and television services. On the other hand, the press has always been markedly reluctant to plead for special favors from the government, which could use this as a political half-Nelson around the neck of the press. The newspaper groups have been given limited access to certain minor television channels, but the press is precluded from influencing the news or current affairs content of these state-controlled channels, and the financial proceeds are likely to be small.

The outlook is thus not good for the cause of free expression. Yet, if the country is to carve a proper place for itself in the world as one of Africa's few working democracies, it is of critical importance that free expression should be underpinned. The tendency in some quarters to lump South Africa with the most unfree and chaotic countries of the continent can cause people to lose sight of the vital role of the press. It is arguable that South Africa (and certainly the Cape region) has more in common with the state of Mississippi than with Uganda in terms of racial makeup, lifestyle, history of contact between black and white, business, education, urbanization, communications, etc. It is unthinkable that Mississippi should be without a vigorous, independent range of opinions and newspapers. It should be equally unthinkable in South Africa, where there is a 150-year-old tradition of press freedom, where a nonracial vote was in operation in the middle of the last century in the Cape colony, where *The Cosby Show* and *Benson* have all races splitting their sides, and where there are powerful institutions such as churches, chambers of commerce and industries, universities, political parties, trade unions, and cultural groups that stand outside (and critical of) government and, combined, could play a transforming role in society in spite of a formidable-looking government.

The experience of Rhodesia was that when Mugabe came to power, he did not have to do much to control the press, because government control existed already; generally he could rely on Smith emergency decrees for some of his drastic actions. In South Africa, it seems important that any new regime should not be handed similar tyrannies on a plate. If the essentials of freedom have been maintained, the stage can be set for their retention and development rather than their retrogression. This is the real reason why white and black South Africans should value their free institutions, however impaired.

STRENGTHENING THE PRESS

It is difficult, having diagnosed the illnesses afflicting the press, to suggest what should be done to give this fragile plant more life. Of course, the local business community in South Africa should come forward and be counted and underpin the cause more effectively, not necessarily with cash handouts, which are demeaning and foster inefficiency, but by investing at least as much attention in an ailing press as in cooperating with government, worrying about return on investment and offshore ventures, or trying at great cost to win friends and influence people from abroad. Moreover, those who run the press must appreciate that South Africa must change fundamentally, which involves black participation not only in government but in the organs of free expression, at professional and board levels. The government, if it is sincere in its reform protestations, should see the press not as the messenger bringing bad news who requires a public hanging but as an essential element in the process of peaceful change, as a bridging communication point among the races. These are internal answers to the problem.

DIRECT AID

When the problem is viewed from abroad, an avenue exercising some minds in South Africa and in the United States would be direct and open aid from foundations, or other public-spirited sources, designed specifically to further the cause of free expression and perhaps administered through a board of trustees of impeccable credentials in South Africa with full powers to act. It would not be easy for existing established newspapers involved in the hurly-burly of political controversy to take money or other assistance from abroad, if only because their internal position vis-à-vis the government would be compromised. For this reason, minority and majority foreign shareholdings in certain South African newspapers have faded from the scene in past years. On the other hand, the official cry in South Africa is against disinvestment, and perhaps this is a preeminent area where investment would be justified — and could be defended in the United States where public opinion is so seized of the South African issue, and also in South Africa where the more enlightened elements in the government realize the value of a free flow of information. Those who agree that press freedom is still important in South Africa should think about this. If people are looking for avenues for clean investment, free expression is worth a try.

The current trend, if it continues unchecked, could well see the demise of an independent-minded press, and the damage politicians have done will be finished off by economic predations, as explained above. This will mean that when change inexorably comes to these shores, hopefully by peaceful routes such as a national convention and not as in Cambodia or Iran, little will be left of the precious heritage of press freedom to help the country reestablish itself in the appropriate power spot on the world stage. Communication, once conducted in the columns of the press, will have been replaced by bullets and rocks strewing the streets. Who wants that?

CHAPTER 24

The Afrikaner Press: Free to a Degree

by HAROLD PAKENDORF

Judging media performance can be like judging beauty—it is in the eye of the beholder. Thus, the government of the day in a beleaguered society will see the performance of its own and the foreign media much differently from the way an uncommitted outsider would.

It certainly prefers those in the media who tell it what it already knows or thinks to those who dare to put forward provocatively different approaches and to report that which those in authority would prefer to keep under wraps.

The media habitually sees its role as that of opposing or at least critically examining the actions of the power holders. Thus, this role is looked on with greater suspicion in a beleaguered society. This is more true in an ethnically divided society, where, to make matters worse, race enters into the picture too. Add to this mix that class differences to a large extent run along the same lines as the racial ones and a ready-made recipe for tension between government and media exists.

This was South Africa before the declaration of an emergency situation in June of last year. That declaration—despite its lifting in the meantime—has made matters worse. Reporting a revolution, an uprising, or unrest (the definition of the widespread violence and anti-government action depends very much on where one stands politically) is never easy. This is even more true when one's own future is deeply involved in the events of the day and one is not simply at a distance.

To judge the role of the media over the last year, and particularly since the severe escalation in violence, it is necessary that one at least try to stand at a distance.

Over the years, the press in South Africa has deservedly earned accolades for the high standards it maintains and for the manner in which it has kept the flame of press freedom burning.

Successive South African governments have claimed that they, too, are committed to freedom of the press, but always with the following rider: as long as the press reports responsibly. Therein, of course, lies the rub, since one man's view of responsibility is another's sedition.

Generally speaking, though, it can be said that despite severe restrictions, government and media have not lived in hostility. In fact, the majority of journalists go about their jobs without feeling under any pressure. It is only those who report on contentious issues who have to deal with repressive measures.

Those restraints have grown over the years and can roughly be divided into three categories. The first one touches elements not uncommon in Western society: protection for children, no reporting on divorce cases, libel, and the like. The second has to do with the particular circumstances the country finds itself in; thus no reporting on arms or oil procurement, troop movements, and such matters.

Although they are annoying, most reporters understand the necessity for such restraints. It is understandable that the state does not wish it to become public knowledge where it buys those arms it does not produce itself, where it buys its crude oil, or even with which African countries it trades so vigorously. Understanding, though, does not imply liking, and there is a constant battle with the authorities to get as much as possible of even this "verboten" list published.

It is the third category that is really burdensome because it largely touches the field of human rights as well as freedom of expression directly. There are organizations that are banned in South Africa — notably the South African Communist Party and the African National Congress — and the list is constantly being added to. Being banned means that a legal existence is not possible and nothing may be published that could be seen to "further the aims" of such an organization.

Equally, a banned person may not be quoted. Thus, Oliver Tambo of the ANC cannot be quoted directly unless special ministerial permission has been obtained. As a matter of principle, many editors refuse to apply for such permission. Others, though, feel that if they were allowed to publish a balanced version of what Tambo says, they would gladly do so. One editor has gone ahead and published without prior permission. As a result, he now faces a possible jail sentence, but there are indications that the state does not want to proceed with prosecution and the case may die.

Then there is the infamous article 27(B) of the Police Act. This makes South African law stand on its head because under it, the accused is presumed to be guilty until he can prove his innocence, whereas one is normally presumed to be innocent until the state has proved the contrary. This clause says that if any untruth about the police is published, one is liable to a jail sentence or a fine — unless of course one can prove one's innocence. Since this is frequently difficult, it is a severely inhibiting factor when it comes to reporting possible police misdemeanor.

Interestingly enough, there is a similar clause in the Prisons Act, but it has not been applied for the last two years. The cabinet minister concerned has suspended its application, feeling that it is too draconian, hampers cooperation with the press, and is bad for the credibility of the prison services.

This is only a short list of the acts and regulations inhibiting the free flow of information in the country; suffice it to say that there is no absolute freedom of news gathering or of expression compared with the United States and Western Europe. However, contrasted with most other countries, there is such freedom. But whichever way one looks at it and however one tries to explain it, newsmen work under severe restrictions and, consequently, the South African reading public cannot be said to be fully informed about its country and the flow of events and opinions within it.

Added to this, of course, is the fact that there is no authentic black voice in the country. There are papers aimed specifically at the black market, but they are mostly separate editions of papers that aim at the general, mostly white, market. There is no newspaper company presently publishing that has black shareholders, under black management, with black control. There are black editors and newsmen, but they work for publishing groups owned and controlled by whites. Any Afrikaans newsman will tell you that there is a distinct difference between an Afrikaans newspaper published by Afrikaaners for Afrikaaners and one published by an English company for Afrikaaners. There have been attempts at the latter but all have disappeared. It is not that black opinion is suppressed but that if blacks speak for themselves, it is simply not the same as somebody else speaking on their behalf.

Look, for example, at the established dailies catering to the black market and a number of small community papers, such as *Ukasa* in Durban, *Grassroots* in Cape Town, and *Speak* in Tembisa, and one realizes immediately what the difference in feel is. However, no paper in this country is neutral in its reporting, and anybody who looks for that journalistic myth "objectivity" will certainly not find it here. We all write from within our own subjectivity, although the degree to which we strive toward fairness in reporting and putting out the other view differs tremendously.

Before black politics came to dominate the country's conversations, it was the intra-white battle that dominated. In those days, English papers were by definition against the Afrikaaner-controlled government and Afrikaans papers sided with that government.

There is no reason to believe black-controlled newspapers will behave in any other fashion. One must accept that black papers in the present situation will be more vociferously antiestablishment than white ones. That black newspapers owned by whites will be more careful than black dailies would be if they were published by blacks also must be accepted.

Against this background, how has the South African reading public been served by its newspapers? The question cannot be answered fairly without another difficulty being presented. The violent, prolonged, and widespread unrest in the country; the state of emergency; and the general hardening of the state's attitude toward newspapers in this period have certainly made it impossible for papers to report quickly and correctly all developing stories.

The difficulty and frequent impossibility, because of police decisions, of getting into areas where there is violent unrest make it extremely improbable that South African newspapers will report and explain all such events. It should be remembered, too, that another element has crept in; that of black intransigence, of suspicion, of not wanting to talk to white reporters.

Couple these restrictions with the ones that have been long established, add heightened feelings of insecurity and increasing racial polarization, and it must be easy to see that it is well-nigh impossible for any newspaper to come close to doing an outstanding job. And so it has been.

On the whole, the press has been remarkably responsible in its attempts not to sensationalize the already sensational events in the country and also to continue to put out the other point of view. Yet, even if the reporting has not been complete, a change has occurred. Never before have newspaper readers been confronted by such a new mix. Black spokesmen are used as sources for stories, get their views published, and argue their case through the press; frequently the press is being used as a medium to complain about police harassment. There was some of this before, but in the last year there has been a noticeable increase. This is the case for English and Afrikaans newspapers.

Still, it is true that some Afrikaans newsapers reflect official government thinking much more closely than others — and look on this as part of their duty. This is particularly so of papers in the Nasionale Pers group and less so for the Perskor papers where the *Transvaler* is to the right of the spectrum and *Vaderland* to the left.

Now more than ever before readers of Afrikaans papers can learn of events and opinions in black South Africa. In fact, there are complaints from the Afrikaner right wing that it gets less publicity than radical blacks do. One result of the continuing unrest has certainly been that black opinion has been aired more than ever before. Because of legal restrictions, though, it cannot be said that South African newspapers do a complete job on events in their country.

Yet, it must be said that despite the severe pressure under which the state has found itself over the last eighteen months, there has been no move, apart from the action over the emergency situation, to make life more difficult for newsmen or to restrict the flow of information more than before. The continued violent unrest has, in fact, helped newspapers to do a better job than ever, to report more fully on the whole spectrum of events and views inside the country.

Part V

U.S. PRESSURES FOR SANCTIONS

CHAPTER 25

Church Groups Lead the Battle Against Apartheid: International Campaign

by EMILIO CASTRO

During the last two years in particular, South Africa has been engulfed in violence and conflict. Many churches and Christians around the world have prayed that peace with justice may be established in this racially divided and troubled land. For the people of South Africa, this is a time of great pain and deep suffering. Since September 1984, more than 1,300 civilians, almost all blacks, have been killed. Many townships and rural areas have become ungovernable. Police and army brutality and the highly emotional funerals have so politicized the masses that unless the South African government makes fundamental changes to accommodate black demands, there will be no peace in that nation.

Apartheid is not only a political system, it is an economic system as well. European, American, and Japanese investments in South Africa have, in effect, reinforced the economic base on which political apartheid rests and strengthened the military power of the government. As Louis Luyt, a leading Afrikaner businessman recently said: "Whether business likes it or not, it has benefited from apartheid."

So do transnational corporations, banks, and other organizations representing the economic interests of Western nations. Through foreign links, the white economy of South Africa secures further capital, sophisticated technology, oil, and other vital goods. The oppressive racist regime has created an ideal climate for foreign investors, providing them with advantageous incentives and using the "homelands" as reservoirs of low-cost black labor. The U.S. Department of Commerce has recorded that the average rate of profits on U.S. capital invested in South Africa was 18 percent in 1979, in comparison to about

13 percent in the developed economics and 14 percent in the so-called developing countries.

Transnational corporations do not look for high profits only; their concern is also with the medium- and long-range political stability of the country that will safeguard their investments. Medium-term stability is assessed yearly by the Business Environment Risk Index, produced in Switzerland. In the beginning of 1982, South Africa was listed in twelfth place, ahead of the United Kingdom and France. The two factors, high profits and low investment risks, have enormously stimulated foreign investments in South Africa.

Transnational corporations are engaged in strategic sectors of the South African economy—oil and coal, iron and steel, chemicals, nuclear technology, transportation, and electricity. At the same time, they are providing strategic military weapons to the oppressive forces in the country, the police, the army, the navy, the air force and the various government departments engaged in maintaining the racist apartheid system. Foreign companies are therefore co-responsible for the internal oppression of the black majority and the external aggression of South Africa against neighboring states.

Proponents of economic links with South Africa argue that these links offer the possibility of influencing the white regime in a positive way. (The Reagan Administration's policy of "constructive engagement" is based on this idea.) Moreover, these proponents claim that foreign investments improve conditions for blacks and that blacks themselves are in favor of these investments. But the belief that economic growth and foreign economic ties of this nature would bring an end to apartheid is contradicted by the facts.

Despite the strong economic growth in South Africa during the last few decades, the white regime has further refined and systematized the apartheid system. The homeland policy has caused unprecedented human suffering and oppression of the black majority has increased. Also, foreign industry is forced to work within the context of the racist South African laws. The National Supplies Procurement Act, for instance, can be used by the South African authorities to force foreign companies to manufacture on demand any product the government determines to be essential to the national security. If a company refuses to comply, the government can seize the goods in question and take over the company's production processes.

In addition, foreign investments in South Africa are on the whole capital-intensive: The jobs created are relatively few, considering the huge amounts of capital invested. Only a small number of blacks find jobs with foreign operations, and the possible positive effects of the codes of conduct benefit only a limited number of people. Foreign investors do not call for the abolition of forced migratory labor and the hated pass laws, and they cannot make demands for black political rights. In fact, by and large they ignore the fact that black impoverishment is the product of a legal structure set up to keep the white minority in absolute power. Consequently, economic links with South Africa and constructive engagement become in effect destructive engagement, which only reinforces the system of apartheid.

DUAL ECONOMY

Everything finally boils down to the fact that South Africa has a dual economy: a white-dominated "modern" sector, controlled by about 16 percent of the population, and a "traditional" sector, in which most of the nonwhites are working. Transnational corporations and foreign direct investments strengthen mainly the white sector and contribute to structural unemployment in the black sector. This type of economy is not suitable when the total work force vastly outgrows the number of jobs created. In fact, it shows the hollowness of the South African government's argument that economic sanctions will affect black employment and lead to the necessity of sending migrant workers back to their homelands. If the regime were really concerned about black employment, it would have to do away with its present monetarist policy.

As early as 1964, the late Chief Albert J. Luthuli, president of the African National Congress and Nobel Prize winner, stated: "I appeal to South Africa's strongest allies, Britain and America. In the name of what we have come to believe Britain and America to stand for, I appeal to those two powerful countries to take decisive action for full-scale sanctions that would precipitate the end of the hateful system of apartheid." The late Steve Biko, leader of the Black Consciousness Movement, repeated this appeal in 1976 when he said, "If Washington is really interested in contributing to the development of a just society in South Africa, it would discourage investment in South Africa. We blacks are perfectly willing to suffer the consequences: We are quite accustomed to suffering."

In 1981, Bishop Desmond Tutu, then general secretary of the South African Council of Churches (SACC), stated, "Those who invest in South Africa should please do so with their eyes open. They must not delude themselves that they are doing anything for the benefit of the blacks. Please let us at least get rid of this humbug. They must understand that they are buttressing one of the most vicious systems since Nazism. . . ."

Calling for an end to the apartheid system, the SACC said in 1984: "It is our belief that disinvestment and similar economic pressures are now called for as a peaceful and effective means of putting pressure on the South African government to bring about those fundamental changes this country needs." The SACC appealed to the churches of the world to campaign for all-out economic sanctions against South Africa.

BOYCOTT MOVEMENT

The United Democratic Front (Allan Boesak, general secretary of the World Alliance of Reformed Churches, is one of the founders and Bishop Desmond Tutu and Beyers Naudé, now general secretary of the SACC, are patrons) has also taken up this position. It has, moreover, organized the boycott actions of black consumers. Economic pressure can indeed produce some results. In several South African towns, black consumers who patronize shops owned by whites boycotted them until their demands — the lifting of the state of emergency, the withdrawal of troops from the townships, the release of local leaders from detention, and improvement of local services — were met. When the consumer boycott started hurting, the white shop owners organized meetings with the black leaders of the boycott, supported their demands, and called on the government to redress their grievances.

The United Democratic Front, which has a considerable white membership opposing apartheid, has also stressed the importance of trade unions. In fact, many black workers and a number of their unions — the newly formed Congress of South African Trade Unions (COSATU), comprising thirty-seven independent trade unions, among them the National Union of Mine Workers, FOSATU, and General Workers Union — have called for economic sanctions, discounting possible negative effects on their employment.

Leaders of the frontline states that border South Africa have also taken up the same position. They are willing to pay the price that the imposition of sanctions will entail. During the last five years, the frontline states have lost over $10 billion through South Africa's destabilization of their economies. Many development projects in

Mozambique and Angola had to be postponed because the governments could not provide security to foreign skilled workers and technicians. Frontline states support economic sanctions against South Africa despite the adverse consequences for the immediate future.

WCC POSITION

International organizations like the General Assembly of the United Nations and the Organization of African Unity have called several times for effective international sanctions against South Africa and the total withdrawal of corporate investments. In 1972, the Central Committee of the World Council of Churches resolved to sell existing holdings in corporations that were directly involved in investments in, and trade with, southern Africa and urged "all member churches, Christian agencies, and individual Christians outside southern Africa to use all their influence, including stockholder action and divestment, to press corporations to withdraw investments from and cease trading with these countries." The Central Committee adopted a similar resolution regarding bank loans to the South African government and its agencies. In 1981, the WCC acted on this resolution by terminating its business with three banks that are heavily involved in business in South Africa.

In 1980, the Central Committee called on its member churches and all Christians "to press governments and international organizations to enforce comprehensive sanctions against South Africa, including a withdrawal of investments, an end to bank loans, an arms embargo and oil sanctions and in general for the isolation of the state of South Africa [and] to cease any direct, and as far as possible indirect, financial involvement in activities which support the apartheid regime." The Vancouver Assembly in 1983 stated that "institutionalized racism in South Africa continues to be the central problem of justice and peace in the region." It condemned the "illegal South African occupation of Namibia" as "oppressive and generating many acts of terrorism against civilians."

A number of churches and national councils of churches have followed suit and devised similar strategies. In 1977, the Governing Board of the National Council of Churches of Christ (NCCC) in the U.S.A. decided "to withdraw all funds and close all accounts in financial institutions which have investments in South Africa or make loans to the South African government or business. . . ." Many individual Protestant and Roman Catholic churches and their agencies in the

United States now have comprehensive policy statements requiring that they cease doing business with banks involved in lending to South Africa. This involves several billions of dollars of church investments which are now being invested in line with these policies.

The Church Commissioners of the Church of England sold its shares in three companies that are heavily involved in South Africa, and Christian Concern for Southern Africa (CCSA) recommended in 1979 that churches and missionary bodies associated with it withdraw their funds from banks operating in South Africa. Also, churches and church-related organizations in a number of other countries of the world withdrew their investments, closed their accounts, and engaged in critical discussions with corporations involved in South Africa.

Two facts have become clear in the WCC and its constituency. Apartheid is a costly system, in human terms as well as in financial terms. To keep the oppressive system operating, South Africa needs a huge amount of foreign money. Because of the increasing criticism of foreign bank loans to the nation, the government has started to solicit foreign funds for "social projects" like separate black housing and separate black education. To defend their involvement, foreign banks use the argument that they are investing in those "social projects." It is obvious, however, that such loans strengthen the existing "separate development" policy, within the overall system of apartheid, and free funds for military and other oppressive purposes.

The other fact is that even comprehensive sanctions practiced by nations and churches outside South Africa are, finally, only of secondary importance. The primary problem is the duality of the South African economy; the white government, which controls all investments, decides who invests in what, and who will profit from the investments. The goals of equal employment and equal education, freedom of movement for all citizens, and respect for human dignity cannot be reached unless and until the system of apartheid is dismantled. The time to achieve this peacefully is rapidly running out.

PRESSURE IS EFFECTIVE

As the uprising in black towns has continued, creating instability for foreign capital, the world of international finance has at last taken notice. In August 1985, there was an announcement that banks would not renew loans to South Africa. From the end of 1980 to August 1985, the rand has dropped from $1.34 to $0.38.

South African businessmen seem to have received the message. A few of them went to the headquarters of the African National Congress (ANC) in Lusaka, Zambia to negotiate and to talk about the future of southern Africa. They called on the South African government to undo apartheid and to negotiate with the authentic black leaders. They also urged the government to lift the state of emergency, to withdraw troops from the townships, and to release immediately and unconditionally Nelson Mandela and other detainees. Still other demands were voiced. Until recently, these businessmen had considered the ANC a terrorist organization.

General secretaries of Christian councils in southern Africa met at Livingston, Zambia last October, and drew the attention of the world to the ever-present threat of nuclear disaster in the region. They expressed their conviction that "the apartheid regime would not hesitate to use its nuclear ability if pushed to the limits of its illegitimate rule." Churches were called on to support and encourage all groups involved in the struggle against nuclear weapons, for the sake of justice and peace. The meeting also emphasized the necessity of strong measures against the apartheid regime, including sanctions, disinvestment, the unconditional release of all political prisoners, and measures to bring about democratic rule.

In the light, or rather in the darkness, of recent dramatic developments in South Africa, the WCC sponsored a conference at Harare, Zimbabwe in December in which leaders of churches from Western Europe, North America, Australia, South Africa, and other parts of Africa, along with representatives of the World Alliance of Reformed Churches, the Lutheran World Federation, and the All Africa Conference of Churches took part. There were eighty-five participants. The gathering stated unambiguously that "the South African government has no credibility" and that "the transfer of power to the majority of the people, based on universal suffrage, is the only lasting solution to the present crisis."

Looking forward to a new democratic and representative regime in South Africa, the Harare Declaration said:

• We call on the church inside and outside South Africa to continue praying for the people of South Africa and to observe 16 June, the tenth anniversary of the Soweto uprising, as World Day of Prayer and Fasting to end the unjust rule in South Africa.

• We call on the international community to prevent the extension, the rolling over, or renewal of bank loans to the South African government, banks, corporations, and para-state institutions.

- • We call on the international community to apply immediate and comprehensive sanctions on South Africa.
- • We call on the church inside and outside South Africa to support South African movements working for the liberation of their country.
- • We welcome and support recent developments within trade union movements for a united front against apartheid.
- • We demand the immediate implementation of the United Nations Resolution 435 on Namibia.

BATTLE RAGES ON

But the battle continues. Although State President Botha, in March 1986, declared the end to the state of emergency that he had imposed in July 1985, South Africa is now entering an era of intensified political repression through supercharged security legislation that will confer permanent emergency powers.

The WCC's involvement in the struggle for racial justice in South Africa has been a costly one — in terms of tensions within the constituency, loss of support, bitter criticism, and alienation in the mass media. Its concentration on South Africa, however, has also been rewarding in the sense that, in spite of doubts and conflicts, the churches have been brought together. The fact that the South African government has singled out the council as one of its strongest enemies is significant and implies that the WCC has been in some ways effective.

Churches have recognized their imprisonment in international political affairs. They know they are part and parcel of existing economic systems, ideologically and financially. But they realize that the call for repentance can be no longer ignored. They know the extent of the sin of racism, the frustration over the violent and nonviolent struggles against it, and they know that the enemy is within themselves. The liberating gospel calls for imaginative and daring actions which will embody their vocation in economic life, especially in South Africa where oppression and exploitation cry out to heaven. Christian churches have no other choice than to hope that inclusive sanctions may prevent a bloody civil war in that nation and that peace and justice will be established at last.

CHAPTER 26

U.S. Church Groups' Efforts Against Apartheid

by ARIE R. BROUWER

The struggle against apartheid is not new to the National Council of Churches of Christ or its member communions. We have been raising our voices against apartheid almost since the inception of the South African state in 1948. Over the years, the NCCC and its member communions have maintained and broadened historic relations with our black sisters and brothers in South Africa and strongly objected to the sinful denial of their basic human rights.

In the late 1960s, the protest of U.S. Christian churches against apartheid began to take the form of what we now call "shareholder action." The churches sought to use their influence as stockholders in U.S. corporations that did business in South Africa by filing shareholder resolutions at annual stockholder meetings that demand that banks and corporations end their support for apartheid.

By filing those shareholder resolutions with some of America's large corporations, the churches highlighted the moral dimensions of U.S. involvement in, and acquiescence to, apartheid in South Africa. Although the churches' action with the corporations had limited impact on U.S. business in South Africa and did not bring about real change in the Pretoria regime, their witness laid the groundwork for later action.

The Interfaith Center on Corporate Responsibility (ICCR), a sponsored related movement of the National Council of Churches, has provided a forum and coordinating center where seventeen Protestant denominations and 220 Roman Catholic orders and dioceses have considered various approaches to U.S. corporations. The organizations that participate in this ecumenical coalition together have investment assets totaling more than $12 billion.

Over the years, it has become increasingly clear to the religious community that moral persuasion will not be enough to help bring about real change in South Africa. Beginning in the late 1970s and intensifying in 1985, a growing number of U.S. churches began to take more drastic measures to express their frustration with the glacial pace of reform in South Africa. Many churches appealed to corporations to quit South Africa. If and when they refused, some denominations began to divest themselves of holdings in such companies. Other churches continued to file shareholder resolutions urging corporations to leave South Africa.

Increasingly, the churches no longer hold to the view that continued presence in South Africa by U.S. business can be a force for reform or that economic benefit accrues to the majority of blacks as a result of that presence. We have noted that U.S. companies in South Africa hire under 100,000 black workers, blacks who are already within the economic mainstream of South Africa. The vast majority of black South Africans lie outside that mainstream, languishing in unrelenting poverty and despair, untouched by the American dollar.

CHURCHES DIVEST

A growing number of NCCC denominations have moved quickly to shed their investments in companies that have refused to leave South Africa. One of the earliest to do so was the Reformed Church in America, whose Dutch Reformed heritage has made it especially sensitive to the need for action against apartheid. In 1980, the RCA, at its General Synod, moved to "establish a denominational policy of not holding investments in banks or corporations that do business in South Africa." The Episcopal Church voted to divest during the summer of 1985 and will have done so by the end of 1986, except for its Pension Board. The American Lutheran Church, the Christian Church (Disciples of Christ), and the Church of the Brethren are similarly involved.

Last summer, the United Church of Christ voted at its General Synod to call upon all its church agencies to divest within two years from corporations that refuse to stop activity in South Africa. That denomination's two large mission boards and their directorates have decided to divest fully from such companies by the end of 1986.

Among other NCCC communions, the Presbyterian Church U.S.A.

and the United Methodist Church have developed a selective divestment policy and have sold stocks in carefully selected companies with South African ties in recent months. Churches, synagogues, and religious institutions have been joined by mushrooming numbers of municipalities and nonprofit organizations. A sign of the growing abhorrence of apartheid among U.S. religious groups is that some traditionally conservative church bodies, not known for their social action, have also begun to support the antiapartheid campaign.

Other denominations are utilizing shareholder resolutions to press U.S. companies to disengage from the land of apartheid. Among the church bodies using this approach in 1986 are the American Baptist Churches and the Lutheran Church in America.

In 1985, church members across the nation staged rallies and demonstrations and sit-ins, many of them leading to peaceful arrests, as witness to our conviction about the evils of apartheid. We will continue that witness in 1986, employing other forms as well.

The African Office of the NCCC is coordinating the efforts of the Churches' Emergency Committee on Southern Africa, an organization of twenty-five U.S. Protestant and Orthodox Churches which have responded to appeals from South Africa. In January, 1986, this group called on U.S. banks not to renew loans to South Africa or approve any new requests for funds "until apartheid is dismantled."

A telegram was sent to the heads of ten U.S. banks by several church representatives at the time that the U.S. banks were considering a "rollover," or continuation, of South African indebtedness totaling $13.6 billion. These billions of dollars had been lent to private South African banks and much of that money had in turn been made available to the government, providing necessary capital for the beleaguered regime to continue its apartheid oppression. That telegram read in part,

After prayerful consideration, we have concluded that economic pressure on South Africa is the most important nonviolent method for bringing an end to the apartheid system. We agree with church leaders in South Africa that the rescheduling of South Africa's debt should be made contingent upon the resignation of the present regime and its replacement by a government that represents all of South Africa's people.

SIGNIFICANT RESULTS

Already this campaign has begun to yield significant results. By April 1, four major banks — Chase Manhattan, Chemical, Bankers Trust, and

Barclays—had responded by announcing that they would not make any new loans to South Africa's private sector, nor would they renew any existing loans. More banks are expected to enact similar policies. Five banks will be presented with church-sponsored shareholder resolutions coordinated by the ICCR, which call for an end to all future loans.

Many prominent South African religious leaders have implored the faith community to strengthen its antiapartheid campaigning. Their pleas have not gone unnoticed. In 1977, the Lutheran World Federation, meeting in Dar es Salaam, Tanzania, judged apartheid to be an issue of *status confessionis*, or a matter of essential belief. In 1984, the LWF moved to suspend the memberships of the Evangelical Lutheran Church in southwest Africa and the Evangelical Lutheran Church in southern Africa because of their refusal to condemn apartheid and integrate their denominations.

In 1982, the World Alliance of Reformed Churches, meeting in Ottawa, Canada, judged apartheid to be contrary to the will of God and heretical. The memberships of two white South African churches that condone apartheid, the Nederduitse Gereformeerde Kerk and the Nederduitse Hervormde Kerk van Africa, were suspended. These dramatic actions were prophetic affirmations of support for Christians in southern Africa, who struggle against apartheid, as well as a sharp rebuke to those who acquiesce in the oppression of black people there.

AGENDA '86

Another facet of our witness will be "South Africa: Agenda '86," a program of the National Council of Churches that will center on information, education, advocacy, and fundraising. Its focus will include not only the churches that strive for justice in South Africa itself, but also the churches in neighboring Mozambique, Angola, and Namibia. Events are scheduled throughout 1986, and each will be geared to raise the consciousness of the U.S. public, through the U.S. churches. In this way, we believe we can help motivate an informed public to act concretely against apartheid and against U.S. policies that undergird the South African regime. We hope that a growing "African constituency" will emerge in the United States, partly as a result of our efforts. As part of this agenda, ICCR has announced a campaign focusing on twelve companies which are "key investors in apartheid." The ICCR also has spearheaded the campaign to end bank loans and to urge companies to withdraw from South Africa.

We plan to raise funds to support the justice and development ministries of churches throughout southern Africa. These programs require legal advice and material aid as their advocates confront apartheid directly through protests, strikes, and boycotts. For such persons, arrest and detention are a likely consequence. They could face death.

In 1986, the churches will also promote the national observance on June 16 of the tenth anniversary of the Soweto, South Africa uprising. A large interfaith worship service in Washington, D.C. is planned in memory of those who died a decade ago while struggling for their basic human rights.

The Executive Committee of the National Council of Churches, at its meeting in February, voted to endorse what has come to be known as the "Harare Declaration," which states in part:

We affirm that the moment of truth (*kairos*) is now, both for South Africa and the world community. We have heard the cries of anguish of the people of South Africa trapped in the oppressive structures of apartheid. In this moment of immense potentiality, we agree that the apartheid structure is against God's will, and is morally indefensible. The South African government has no credibility. We call for (1) an end to the state of emergency, (2) the release of Nelson Mandela and all political prisoners, (3) the lifting of the ban on all banned movements, (4) the return of exiles."

The declaration, first approved by church representatives convened by the World Council at a special meeting in Harare, Zimbabwe, December 6, 1985, goes on to say:

The transfer of power to the majority of the people, based on universal suffrage, is the only lasting solution to the present crisis. We understand and fully support those in South Africa who are calling for the resignation of the government. We regard this as the most appropriate and least costly process of change. . . as we await a new democratic and representative government in South Africa.

These coordinated activities of the U.S. churches are part of an intentional and continuing effort to seek justice for black South Africans. We shall persevere.

CHAPTER 27

The Apartheid Debate on American Campuses

by JOSEPH MURPHY

At first glance, it might seem odd that the issue of apartheid should have emerged as a critical political issue on American campuses in the mid-1980s. So many concerns closer to home have more direct impact on daily life in academia: the Reagan Administration's efforts to reduce aid to students, the impetus for more vocationally oriented programs and less attention to the liberal arts, and the diminished enforcement of affirmative action mandates are just a few. Why in this context have student and faculty activists chosen to focus their attention on the repressive policies of a nation 8,000 miles from our shores?

The answer to that has several elements. First and most important is the fact that the South African government's official policy of racial separatism and enforced discrimination is so blatantly cruel and so morally repugnant as to make it a nondebatable moral issue, one on which Americans covering a broad ideological spectrum can unite. With no significant exception, spokesmen for all of our major national institutions deplore apartheid; even Jerry Falwell admits that it is a bad thing. We can argue vehemently over tactics of opposition (or even whether a foreign regime's policies are within our legitimate sphere of moral or political influence), but that apartheid is abhorrent is a subject on which there is rare consensus.

Second, apartheid is a highly visible sin. We read about it daily in *The New York Times*. We see an average of three graphic reports per week on the nightly news. The policy is easily described and its impacts are clearly depicted. In that sense, South African racial struggles are more immediate to us than are many of our own domestic conflicts over abstract propositions about budgets and priorities. We see how the Botha government's edicts affect people in black villages in a way that we cannot see how the Reagan Administration's budget cuts affect minority or low-income people in the ghettoes of the United States; as we all learned in the 1960s, police confrontations make good news footage and subtle acts of repression do not.

Finally, and perhaps more subtly, we sense that apartheid is one of those issues about which we just might be able to do something — although we are not at all clear or united about what that something is. We deplore repression in Eastern Europe, but we sense that Americans have little leverage to exercise there. In South Africa, whether because of some shared linkage with Anglo-Saxon political and juridical traditions or because of a common set of material interests and lifestyle patterns among our two nations' elites, or simply because of U.S. business involvement, we perceive some possibility that we are in a position to exercise influence for change.

Thus, that rare contemporary phenomenon: an evil at once clearcut, visible, and conceivably amenable to remedy. To those of us who talk about ethics and think about ideas, apartheid offers a compelling opportunity to translate moral conviction into political action. It is in this context not ironic but perfectly logical that the question of what we ought to do about South Africa should assume so great a place of importance on the American higher education community's agenda.

Prior to much of the public debate about divestiture of stock in corporations doing business in South Africa, a number of universities had already begun to take some small, relatively noncontroversial but significant steps to express disdain for the white regime's policies. Several institutions — Harvard notable among them — made a point of bringing nonwhite South Africans to the United States for college training in the hope that these students would return to their native land and form a leadership corps of educated blacks pushing the society toward progressive, nonviolent change. Currently, under the auspices of the National Council of the South African Education Program, over 200 blacks receive scholarship support to study at universities in the United States. Colleges have offered a forum for discussion and dissemination of public information on the nature and effects of apartheid; examination of the South African situation is routinely integrated into coursework in political science, history, and sociology; lectures on campus by such prominent black spokespeople as Desmond Tutu and Denis

Brutus have become routine.

And yet despite all of this, many of us feel that we are under moral obligation to do more — to take all legitimate steps within our power to dissociate our institutions from the practitioners of racial discrimination in South Africa and to make that practice costly to the point that even its advocates accept pragmatic arguments for change. It was out of a desire to fulfill this obligation that leaders of the American academic community began a few years ago to turn their specific attention to the issue of using investment leverage in the battle against apartheid.

IDEAL WORLD

I have always felt personally uncomfortable with the concept of university stock and bond portfolios. An investment, even in a noncontroversial corporation, is in itself a political act; it makes the university a player in the system of private enterprise that it ought to be impartially examining and evaluating from afar. Even if we accept the current wisdom that managers, not shareholders, have the power and responsibility to make business decisions, we are still implicit accomplices in what corporate bodies in which we hold stock do. In my ideal world, no university would play that role.

But we do not live in my ideal world. In the world we do inhabit, universities control large endowments. They seek to use those endowments for worthy purposes, ranging from scholarship aid to the disadvantaged to construction of new facilities. The greater the return on investment of endowment assets, the more worthy purposes may be served. The more profitable the corporations in which endowment monies are placed, the greater the return on investment. Our standard investment policy is to generate more resources to help us fulfill our basic educational mission; it is not to change the realities of the world. My own university's pre-1984 investments in such corporations as Burroughs, Citicorp, Coca-Cola, and General Electric, all of which did business in South Africa and all of which made us and their other shareholders a lot of money, were guided by that policy.

The question that we at the City University of New York and our colleagues across the nation confronted in the early 1980s was whether conditions in South Africa were such as to warrant deviation from that basic and traditional approach to investment practice. As we approached the question of divestiture, we found ourselves grappling with four basic arguments against selling off our stock; only if we could respond cogently to each could we justify taking what we all recognized as a serious and unprecedented action. Essentially the antidivestiture arguments were as follows:

• Divestiture is a wrong-headed approach to resolution of the South African problem. American corporations actually represent progressive, integration-fostering elements in the South African economy. Those opposed to apartheid should encourage American investment, not seek to prevent it.

In support of this proposition, advocates present evidence showing that more than 100 U.S. firms in South Africa follow the Sullivan Principles of nondiscrimination in and around the workplace. Black South Africans employed by U.S. businesses enjoy wage levels, benefits, and opportunities for advancement far in excess of those available to blacks elsewhere in that nation's economy. Presumably, over time, the advocates argue, South African firms will be forced by market pressure and moral example to offer black and coloured workers terms of employment similar to those provided by U.S. corporations.

• Even if American firms are not now acting as progressive influences, their shareholders (including universities and other institutional investors) can use leverage to force implementation of nondiscriminatory practices and adherence to the Sullivan Principles.

Approximately 250 U.S. corporations doing business in South Africa have not accepted the Sullivan Principles, although many claim to act in a nondiscriminatory manner nonetheless. Conceivably, colleges could use proxy votes in shareholder resolutions, moral argument, and threats of disinvestment to force corporations to change their ways—to pull out of South Africa entirely or to adopt rigidly enforced codes of nondiscrimination. Once a university sells its stock in a firm, this leverage is gone.

• Whether or not corporations discriminate is of no legitimate concern to the university. Those charged with investing college funds have one basic responsibility: to maximize return on capital outlay. To take *any* action for political or moral cause is to abandon the university's proper fiduciary role.

In Milton Friedman's memorable phrase, "The social responsibility of the corporation is to make a profit." By implication, the investor's responsibility is to garner a positive return. Social policy is for voters and their representatives in Congress to determine—not for corporate directors or college trustees who are, after all, playing with other people's money.

• Divestiture hurts those in our institutions most dependent on marginal dollars—primarily the economically disadvantaged. To vent moral outrage at policies abroad by hurting those at home least able to sustain the blow is bad policy.

Given the recent pattern of federal aid cutbacks to students and to campuses, American higher education depends increasingly on revenue from investment. Endowment-earnings dollars can provide low-income students with tuition assistance, work-study support, living stipends, and other aid. Selling off profitable but morally unpalatable securities in exchange for holdings more ethically pure but less financially renumerative will force us to spend less than we otherwise would on socially and educationally desirable programs. Divestiture may mean less help to the needy. It will hurt not the trustees who make the decision but those who depend on the aid.

REFUTING CONTENTIONS

Each of these contentions was advanced with sincerity and each had some intellectual merit. Each deserved a detailed response. Fur CUNY in 1984, that response ran along these lines:

• Divestiture is not wrong-headed. Our analysis of the South African situation showed the positive impact exerted by U.S. corporations to be limited at best and far outweighed by the negative effects of corporate participation in the economy of a repressive state. Some 100,000 South African blacks were employed by U.S. firms, in a nation whose population included 27 million nonwhites. Of those 100,000 people, a significant number worked for firms refusing to sign the Sullivan Principles. There has been little evidence of South African firms following an American lead toward progressive workplace policy. While not ignoring the benefits U.S. employment offered some blacks, we could not avoid the conclusion that the U.S. corporate presence in South Africa represented basic recognition of the legitimacy of the white regime. American corporations pay South African taxes and abide by South African laws. In so doing they tacitly accept the right of a minority regime to govern a disfranchised majority.

• American firms' shareholders have found it difficult to use leverage to force implementation of nondiscriminatory practices. Marginal success in this effort (and there has been some) has had no significant impact on the overall situation in South Africa. Moreover, this approach would not work for CUNY. The practical obstacles to such an effort were formidable. In no firm did the City University hold more than a negligible proportion of outstanding stock; our proxy votes might have symbolic significance but they would lack real clout. We did not possess the energy, the manpower, or the expertise necessary to lead the battle on controversial shareholder resolutions, and we were not in a position to allocate staff resources away from educational programs to such an effort. We had no effective precedents to guide us in this approach in any event.

Some individuals argued that we possessed sufficient moral authority to force corporations in which we owned stock to answer for their actions. Harvard, Yale, and other universities have indeed used institutional prestige and media access to force a public accounting of South African activities; where the corporate response to university probing was unsatisfactory, those institutions have fulfilled a public commitment to sell stock. The option to try this approach was open to us as well.

We rejected it on pragmatic grounds. As a public institution dependent on support from all segments of the community, the City University could not easily engage in a protracted public debate with a specific business firm. Our moral authority is not, moreover, universally recognized and accepted; as a competitor with other social service agencies for public funding, we are suspected of political motives in most of what we do. To cut and cut cleanly seemed the more practical course.

• In unusual circumstances, our proper fiduciary role may indeed encompass taking some actions for political or moral cause. We are not discussing here a close question, on which a fiduciary's prescribed political neutrality might make sense and in which trustees bring ideological considerations to bear at the risk of misplaying their part in institutional guidance.

There are some questions — South Africa currently among them — that are not close. Would 1930's investments in firms supplying German armaments have been appropriate had stock analysts predicted a high rate of return from those firms? No, because such investments would have run counter to clearly defined and well-understood definitions of the larger social interest. Would current investment in corporations operating on the borderline of environmental regulations be justifiable if the likely appreciation and dividend rates looked good? No again, because the element of risk to us as a culpable partner in environmental disaster would be uncomfortably great.

So, too, with investments in most South African operations. The long-term risks of involvement in tainted enterprises are unacceptably large. We are not willing to use our endowment dollars in such a way as to make us accomplices in activities that prop up a regime whose activities run counter to the broad interests and ideological goals of our society. We cannot take the chance that the firms in which we invest will escape the consequences of a revolutionary overthrow of apartheid. As fiduciaries, we could in good judgment conclude that divestiture represented a prudent and responsible course of behavior.

• Divestiture might adversely impact on some in our own institution. It can nevertheless be justified on the basis of the greater good it will yield to the university and all those we serve — including the disadvantaged. In this sense the decision to divest is conceptually similar to all other policy decisions we as institutional leaders are called upon to make.

Fortunately for all of us whose colleges opted to divest in the mid-1980s, however, the "lower rate of return" issue has proved to be fairly moot. The rising tide of the post-1982 bull market has lifted virtually all ships; few of us lost money when we sold off our holdings in South Africa-related corporations. We found other firms in which to place our money; our experience with them has been about as good as our record would have been with the corporations whose stock we sold off.

But this pleasant piece of data helps us avoid the difficult question. We might not be as lucky if we have to grapple with a similar issue at some point in the future. Then our choice would boil down to a high profit with bad firms or a lower profit with good ones — and the latter option would mean fewer scholarships, fewer remedial programs, less enrichment activity, and reduction in other desirable campus enterprises. By what right do we forego those things — or, more accurately, force our students to forego them — as we pursue some higher social value?

I would answer that we do so by the same right that we cite as we set institutional priorities in all other areas. We deem that an extra course in ethics is more valuable than extra computer terminals, even though computer training might make our students more marketable and able to command higher salaries; we adopt the course and essentially impose its cost on our students. We spend scarce dollars to bring controversial spokespeople to campus and presumably force some of our enrollees to forego extra tuition support that the funds paid to those spokespeople might have been used to provide. We engage in costly social service activities that benefit the communities that surround our campus, cutting back on intramural enrichment activities in order to do so. We make these choices partly because we believe that they are intrinsically right and socially worthy and partly because they enable us to establish and protect our identity as moral, responsible institutional members of society. That identity is an essential asset in assuring for ourselves a continued, meaningful existence.

SUBJECTIVE CHOICES

Choices between immediate gains and long-run benefits are usually not quantifiable and may not even be evaluable; they are to some extent subjective. Nonetheless, they represent the standard workday agenda items for people who run major institutions. For university leaders to opt to pay the price of a morally correct choice—when the moral debate is in their view a clear-cut one—is to take a legitimate stance in the context of institutional responsibility. We are hired to make trade-offs, and we make them as best we can.

For us at the City University of New York, the decision to divest ourselves of stock in eight South Africa-based corporations was a careful and deliberate one. It was made easier by the general consensus prevailing within our institution: Divestiture had the unanimous support of the presidents of CUNY's colleges, the endorsement of student government, and ultimately total support by our board of trustees. It was made easier still by the fact that we could sell the shares in a way that would do our financial condition little harm.

We did not accept—or even seriously consider—the counsel of those who urged such radical action as boycotts of firms engaged in South African activities. We recognized the limitations of our leverage and the nature of our legal authority to act as a player in the marketplace. Our goals were to dissociate ourselves from tacit support of a repressive regime, to provide some statement of sympathy for that regime's victims, and to help focus attenion on the issues surrounding an evil system of human exploitation. Our goal was not to cover ourselves with glory in a set of costly but futile gestures.

I believe that we accomplished most of what we set out to do. As we and others have divested our stock, public concern with the South African issue has grown. (*The Chronicle of Higher Education* now has a regular "Divestment Watch" column—a sure sign of the academic community's sustained interest in the matter of investment policy.) Virtually every important university that has not as yet chosen to divest has insisted on corporate compliance with the Sullivan Principles as a condition of continued stock ownership. There are ripple effects of all this as well: Few U.S. corporations are opening new South African operations and more major U.S. enterprises than before are proclaiming and implementing nondiscriminatory policies. All of us must concede, however, that it seems likely that apartheid will be dismantled only as the result of a protracted, internally directed South African struggle in which U.S. corporations and U.S. universities will play at most only a marginal role.

For CUNY, the endowment divestiture debate is over. The growing dispute over pension fund investments is in some respects even more important, but it is somewhat different. More money is involved, but pension funds are controlled not by the university but by administrators of central retirement funds where legal constraints on fiduciary latitude are more tightly drawn.

But, of course, the underlying issues are much the same. Those who advocate total divestiture must still demonstrate that that policy is a sensible, productive, appropriate, and ultimately prudent course for all institutional investors to follow. Those who oppose divestiture must refute those claims. In our view, and in the view of a list of divesting institutions, which grows longer each month, the weight of argument is on the side of those who would opt to break all links with a social system whose philosophy and whose deeds shock the conscience of the world.

CHAPTER 28

Divestment Steamroller Seeks To Bury Apartheid

by CHRISTOPHER COONS

Pressures from institutional investors have played a major part in recent changes in the role of U.S. corporations in South Africa. The divestment movement in particular has spurred new activism by U.S. and South African corporations and has changed the political situation within South Africa. More institutions have adopted South Africa-related investment policies and divested their portfolios of South Africa-related holdings — either partially or totally — in 1985 than in all the previous years of divestment activism combined. Among the eleven states, thirty-five cities and counties, and 100 colleges and universities that have so far divested themselves of some holdings, more than $5.96 billion in holdings has been or is committed to be divested. The combined portfolios of these institutions represent more than $95.77 billion in holdings that are now managed under a South Africa-free investment policy. Divestment, understood as the ethically or politically motivated sale of holdings in companies with direct investments in South Africa, has had a powerful impact on many of America's largest institutional investors. Yet, what impact has divestment had on U.S. corporations that do business in South Africa, on the divesting institutions or on South Africa itself?

INSTITUTIONS CONSIDERING DIVESTMENT

A surprising array of institutions have adopted divestment policies, ranging from the New York City Employees' Retirement System and Teachers' Retirement System, with combined holdings of more than

$17.5 billion, to small state colleges, learned societies, and private schools with endowments under $1 million. Institutions as diverse as the Smithsonian Institution, the American Bar Association, and the Episcopal Church have divested. Divestment policies in turn have an equally wide range of standards and effects on portfolios.

The first institutions to exclude certain companies from their investment portfolios were churches, many of which have long-standing policies of refusing to profit from alcohol, tobacco, gambling, or defense-related companies on ethical grounds. South Africa-related divestment, however, has only become a concern since the 1976-1977 cycle of unrest in South Africa that began with the Soweto student riots. The first divestment actions were small and scattered: Divestment policies were adopted by Berkeley, California in 1979, Hartford in 1980, and Smith and Amherst Colleges and the University of Massachusetts in 1977. The first divestment policies adopted by states came in 1982 in Connecticut and Michigan, then in 1983 in Massachusetts. Forty-eight colleges and universities adopted divestment policies in the period 1977-1980, yet the divestment actions that resulted affected a relatively small amount of holdings. The movement has gained momentum. More than half of all institutions that have divested did so in 1985. Since most of the large portfolios that have adopted divestment policies intend to divest over a two-to-three-year period, the majority of funds that are committed to be divested have yet to be sold.

COLLEGES AND UNIVERSITIES

Colleges and universities are the institutions most visibly affected by the debate over divestment; more than 100 campuses witnessed demonstrations, sit-ins, or occupations in the spring and fall of 1985 and roughly 1,500 students have been arrested in divestment protests in 1985. A recent IRRC survey found that sixty-five of the educational institutions with the 100 largest endowments in the United States have adopted South Africa-related investment policies, and that forty-seven of those institutions had divested themselves of some holdings. Altogether, 100 colleges and universities have divested themselves of more than $410 million in holdings. Total divestment policies account for $190 million of those actions and have been adopted by thirty-nine institutions as of March 1986. While divestment by prestigious universities has attracted great attention, the amount of investments affected has actually been quite small in comparison with recent actions by public pension funds.

One university-related action, however, involves the largest pension fund in the nation. A loose coalition of academic officials, African affairs scholars, and political activists launched a nationwide campaign for divestment by TIAA/CREF (Teachers Insurance and Annuity Association/College Retirement Equities Fund), which has a combined portfolio of roughly $39 billion, of which an estimated $7.6 billion is in South Africa-related holdings. TIAA/CREF counts some 525,000 employees on more than 1,900 campuses among its participants. In November 1985, TIAA/CREF announced that it would sponsor twenty shareholder resolutions asking portfolio companies to sign the Sullivan Principles or withdraw from South Africa. TIAA/CREF President James G. MacDonald said the board had voted to file the resolutions as an alternative to divestiture, which "simply amounts to making a political statement and walking away from the issue."

CHURCH ACTIVISM

Although churches have been active in the American antiapartheid movement for many years, particularly in the realm of shareholder activism, none of the major church pension funds has divested so far. According to Diane Bratcher, director of publications for the Interfaith Center for Corporate Responsibility in New York, ten major churches have adopted total divestment policies and at least seven more have partial divestment plans. Nearly all of the affected funds are in endowment and ministry portfolios, rather than in the much larger pension funds; those pension funds with divestment policies have yet to divest themselves of any holdings. The size of funds involved can be impressive; the Board of Pensions of the United Methodist Church controls $1.8 billion in assets and the Episcopal Church has a roughly $900 million pension fund. Knowledgeable sources say that church-related pension and ministry funds control more than $20 billion in investments.

Why have churches been so reluctant to divest? Bratcher told the IRRC: "While churches may be openly against apartheid, their pension boards are wrestling with whether divestment would violate their fiduciary responsibilities to the pensioners. Divesting from multinationals is different from selling stocks in alcohol or gambling firms where churches objected to the nature of the company's entire business. For years churches have hoped to affect corporate policy in South Africa through pressure from within—through letters and shareholder activism—and they are reluctant to give up on this tradition of witnessing from within by divesting." In an important symbolic move, as well as being the largest divestment action by a single parish, the governing vestry of Wall Street's Trinity Church voted in February 1986 to divest totally, leading to the sale of $10 million in South Africa-related holdings out of Trinity's $50 million portfolio. "Because of its traditional links with Wall Street," said Tim Smith, executive director of the Interfaith Center, Trinity Church "sent a serious signal to the business community concerning American involvement in South Africa."

PENSION FUNDS

Whereas most large church funds have at least issued statements on South Africa-related investments, few large union funds have even discussed divestment. In early 1985, the $600 million International Ladies' Garment Workers Union National Retirement Fund adopted a policy of holding no investments in Sullivan nonsignatories. The United Auto Workers successfully negotiated in 1984 with Ford, General Motors, and Chrysler for the right to exclude from those companies' pension plans between seven and nine corporations based on their involvement in South Africa.

Despite these actions, officials at several major union pension funds expressed sympathy for the divestment cause but stated that divestment had never been seriously discussed. The most serious limitation on divestment by union and corporate pension plans is the Employee Retirement Income Security Act of 1974 (ERISA), which requires the fiduciaries responsible for the plans to invest prudently and "solely in the interest of the beneficiaries." Regina Markey of the *Journal of Labor and Investments* commented in an interview with the IRRC that "union fund managers are highly concerned about how the courts will interpret ERISA; they're afraid that divestment will be found imprudent and that they will have broken the law."

The institutions that appear least likely to divest are the thousands of U.S. corporate pension funds. Such funds control investments with a combined worth of nearly $1 trillion. A recent survey of corporate pension fund managers by *Institutional Investor* revealed that only 2.7 percent had felt pressure from shareholders, employees, or other groups to divest. Of the 11.6 percent reporting that their corporations had seriously considered divestment, many were primarily concerned that South Africa-related investment might decrease in value if the divestment movement continues to grow.

To the IRRC's knowledge, only two companies — Levi Strauss & Co. and Lotus Development Corp. — have divested their pension funds. Lotus has had a policy of making no investments in any South Africa-related companies "virtually since the day we were founded," according to treasurer Joe Ahearn. Lotus's policy applies not only to its $3 million pension, profit-sharing and 401(k) plans, but also to the corporate cash balances, worth more than $190 million at the end of 1985.

Levi Strauss & Co. adopted a policy of selective divestment for its pension and retirement-oriented plans in November 1985. Katherine Durgin, director of corporate communications, told the IRRC: "We directed our investment managers to divest all holdings in companies doing business in South Africa that had not signed the Sullivan Principles and we will consider divesting those signatories that consistently receive poor ratings over a period of years." Levi Strauss's aggregate pension and retirement-oriented plans had $370 million in holdings as of March 31, 1986. Durgin explained that "Levi Strauss has taken a clear stand against doing business in South Africa ourselves because of our opposition to the government's apartheid policies. Our position is not to be judgmental towards those companies that do have operations in South Africa. Instead, we want to encourage them to be good corporate citizens through actions such as signing the Sullivan Principles." Levi Strauss is known for its early efforts at integrating plants in the American South and its ongoing commitment to equal employment opportunity in this country. "One of the company's core values is its opposition to racial discrimination," Durgin said, "Our divestment action was made in keeping with that tradition."

PUBLIC FUNDS

Public employee pension funds controlled $352 billion in assets in 1984, according to Census Bureau figures. Of those holdings, roughly $85 billion were restricted by a South Africa-related investment policy in 1985, and $5.55 billion had been or was committed to be divested. Divestment by cities and states has increased rapidly in the last year and has contributed the greatest amount of the funds so far affected by divestment. A small number of cases make up the majority of the total for city and state actions. In California, for example, Governor

Deukmejian issued an executive order in September 1985, requiring the state's four pension systems to divest themselves "over a reasonable period of time" from holdings in companies that are not Sullivan signatories rated in the top two categories. While actions in response have been limited so far, the four funds combined control nearly $40 billion in investments. The state of New Jersey, which adopted a three-year total divestment plan in August 1985, will divest $2 billion of the $10.3 billion managed by the state treasury department. New Jersey's policy prohibits investments in companies doing business in South Africa or in banks that make loans to the South African government. The city councils of Los Angeles, San Francisco, and Baltimore all passed divestment resolutions in 1985 that will lead to the divestment of more than $1.3 billion over the next five years.

INVESTMENT STANDARDS

Partial or selective divestment policies affect a majority of both the institutions that have divested and the funds operating under South Africa-related investment policies. Most partial divestment plans depend on the Sullivan Principles as a measure of corporate responsibility in South Africa. The IRRC estimates that 255 U.S. corporations had operations in South Africa as of March 1986; 75 percent of all U.S. firms with South African operations are Sullivan signatories. Most of the remaining nonsignatories are relatively small companies with few employees in South Africa who view the Sullivan signatory fee and reporting process as a greater burden than is warranted by the size of their operations there. An institution can thus adopt a policy of holding no investments in Sullivan nonsignatories without having to sell a significant amount of its South Africa-related holdings. The Maine State Retirement System, for example, divested itself of all holdings in Sullivan nonsignatories in 1985, resulting in the sale of $11 million in holdings or 1.1 percent of its $845 million portfolio. In several states, investment boards have voluntarily adopted policies of selling Sullivan nonsignatories, partly as a means of forestalling broader and more expensive divestment action by the legislature.

A related policy standard followed by many institutions with divestment policies requires all South Africa-related companies in the portfolio to sign the Sullivan Principles and receive a rating in the top two categories among Sullivan signatories in the annual rating program (Category III rates a company as "needs to become more active" in implementing the Principles). The state of Connecticut, for example, adopted such a policy in a 1982 law and divested itself of $79 million in holdings out of its portfolio of $2.6 billion at the time.

TOTAL DIVESTMENT

Few large institutions have adopted total divestment policies, policies that would require the sale of all holdings in South Africa-related companies. Depending on the definition of "South Africa-related companies," such a standard could require the sale of 30 to 40 percent of an investment portfolio; the University of Wisconsin system, for example, divested itself of approximately $10.2 million in holdings in 1978 under a total divestment policy, equal to 34 percent of its $30 million endowment portfolio. Eliminating the 255 U.S. companies with direct investments in South Africa from a portfolio would remove more than one third of the market value of all equities in the United States and roughly 130 of the Fortune 500, making total divestment a potentially costly process for large, actively managed portfolios. Thus, most total divestment policies have been adopted by smaller institutions such as state universities and colleges.

Several large entities, such as New Jersey, Los Angeles, and New York City, have adopted phased divestment policies that will gradually lead their multi-billion-dollar pension funds toward total divestment over a three-to-five-year period, allowing time for the funds to find suitable alternative investments and for market fluctuations to bring the prices of prohibited stocks to more favorable levels. Phased divestment plans can also serve to combine divestment with other forms of pressure on South Africa-related companies; the New York City Employees' and Teachers' Retirement Systems both adopted five-year divestment plans that require the systems initially to introduce shareholder resolutions calling on companies to change their practices in South Africa before they begin a process of gradual divestment from those companies.

One major factor that may drive divesting institutions toward total divestment policies is the possible end of the Sullivan Principles program. In May 1985, Rev. Sullivan stated that "if apartheid has not, in fact, ended legally and actually as a system within the next twenty-four months, there should be a total U.S. economic embargo against South Africa, including the withdrawal of all U.S. companies." In accordance with this statement, nine leading colleges and universities have adopted policies committing themselves to total divestment if substantial reform has not occurred by May 1987. Roughly $170 million in holdings would be sold as a result. Should Sullivan withdraw his support from the Principles that bear his name, the program might end and pressure might greatly intensify for increased divestment and the withdrawal of U.S. companies from South Africa.

BANK LOANS

The focus of antiapartheid activism in the United States in 1978-1980 was largely on preventing bank loans to the South African government. In a campaign launched and managed by church groups, many institutions put pressure on major U.S. banks to stop financing the South African regime. When in 1980 Citicorp participated in a multi-million-dollar loan to the South African government to finance development in the homelands, the largest divestment actions ever taken against one corporation occurred; Harvard College alone divested itself of roughly $51 million worth of Citicorp debt securities. According to Diane Bratcher of the ICCR, most of the divestment by churches that has taken place came at this point, as "probably more than fifty" churches disposed of investments in or withdrew deposits from Citibank.

During this period of activism, a number of educational institutions and several cities adopted policies of not holding the securities of or making deposits in banks providing loans to the South African government. Such policies began to have a more serious financial impact on banks over the last two years with the adoption of policies by twenty-five municipalities restricting which banks would be used for financial services or bond underwriting. For example, Los Angeles adopted, in August 1985, a policy prohibiting the city from depositing funds with any banks that lend to the South African public sector or South African-based private firms or that maintain branch offices in South Africa. The city places an average of $1.5 billion in short-term deposits in banks every day.

Many South Africa-related investment policies contain provisions for actions other than divestment. The most significant pressure for withdrawal on U.S. corporations in South Africa comes from the possibility of selective boycotts of their products and services. Eleven cities have passed selective purchasing laws so far — including New York, Newark, Oakland, Pittsburgh, and Rochester. By cutting a company off from major municipal contracts, such laws have had a direct economic impact on South Africa-related companies. At least two major multinational corporations have withdrawn from South Africa in the past year rather than lose lucrative sales opportunities in the United States. Whereas selective purchasing laws are undoubtedly more effective than stock divestment actions in pressuring firms to leave South Africa, they are also more costly than divestment for the entity enforcing them. The cost to a city, for example, of being unable to purchase Ford or General Motors trucks, IBM typewriters, or GE lightbulbs could be prohibitive. Nevertheless, selective purchasing laws are pending in more than twenty cities, states, and counties.

EFFECTS OF DIVESTMENT

What has been the effect of divestment so far? Divestment will in all probability never have a direct economic effect on any South Africa-related company. Of the $352 billion held by public employee pension funds, $5.55 billion — only 1.6 percent — has been or will be divested under policies adopted to date. Of the $33 billion held in college and university endowments, $410 million — about 1.2 percent — has been or will be divested. Sizable divestment actions are commonly spread out over two-to-five-year periods to avoid unnecessary financial losses. Thus, when divestment actions do involve the sale of blocks of holdings large enough to affect the price of a particular company's stock, they are staggered so as to avoid any such effect.

The high market capitalizations of many South Africa-related companies and the relatively small size of most divestment actions imply that selling South Africa-related holdings will not affect stock or bond values. However, divestment might depress stock prices slightly as the continued dumping of certain issues by large institutional investors creates a downward pressure on prices and a psychologically dampening effect on the attraction of South Africa-related investments. In any case, divestment's main effect is on corporate public images, spurring managements to reconsider their position on South Africa and to justify their actions to shareholders. While divestment may not affect a company's economic stability, it does attract the attention of business leaders when their alma maters and hometowns refuse to hold investments in the corporations they direct.

Although it is difficult to corroborate a direct linkage between the U.S. divestment movement and either political change in South Africa or the recent increase in U.S. corporate activism, there is nevertheless a strong connection between increasing pressure from institutional investors and changing attitudes among the business community. Investor pressure, expressed through shareholder resolutions, divestment actions, and canceled contracts, has clearly motivated many corporations to sign the Sullivan Principles. Calls for divestment have also affected U.S. national policy, the position of the South African business community, and the South African political climate.

Different political camps have varying perspectives on how significant are the changes brought about by the Sullivan Principles and the efforts of U.S. companies. Nevertheless, much has changed in recent years in the workplace practices, community involvement, and political position of U.S. firms operating in South Africa. Reports by the IRRC and other firms on the implementation of the Sullivan Principles by U.S. companies show that a demonstrable improvement in working conditions for black South African employees of Sullivan signatory firms did take place. Such companies also poured an estimated $100 million into community development and black advancement projects around the nation over the last eight years. Sullivan signatories, it has been argued, have made more advances in breaking down the color barrier in the workplace than any other group of employers in South African history. The divestment movement in the United States played an obvious role in pressuring companies to adopt such policies. American corporate activism has also increased significantly in the past year, with the American Chamber of Commerce in South Africa and the recently formed U.S. Corporate Council on South Africa both making public declarations calling for the end of apartheid. Under an amplification of the Sullivan Principles announced in November 1984, signatory companies must be active in publicly working for the end of apartheid laws to receive a top Sullivan rating. Thus, recent corporate actions are partly the result of increased pressure on U.S. companies to sign and abide by the Sullivan Principles that resulted from the domestic divestment movement.

Some South Africans and Americans question whether such actions by U.S. corporations are positive. Many antiapartheid activists in the United States have attacked the Sullivan Principles as a "corporate smokescreen" that was not designed by, audited by, or run for the benefit of black South Africans. Many black South African leaders argue that moderate reforms in workplace and community conditions such as those brought about by the Sullivan Principles program and the moderate agenda for political change promoted by the business community only paper over the underlying interracial power struggle and thus postpone the inevitable day of confrontation. In this view, divestment has had a positive impact on South Africa only in as much as it encourages many American companies to withdraw from South Africa, which may, in turn, weaken the South African economy and contribute to the instability of the government. Although a few black South African leaders speak out against divestment, the majority—ranging from Desmond Tutu and Allan Boesak to the ANC and Azapo—support the divestment movement as a way to advance the liberation struggle in South Africa.

In fact, of the estimated 290 U.S. firms with direct investment in South Africa as of January 1985, thirty-eight sold or closed their operations in 1985. All such companies cited the weak South African economy as their rationale for leaving, but a few also mentioned political instability in South Africa and the domestic damage to corporate image caused by the divestment campaign. South Africa-related companies in recent years have received literally thousands of letters from colleges and universities, church and labor groups, and public pension funds challenging their position on South Africa. Many have also repeatedly faced management-opposed shareholder resolutions at their annual meetings. For some, the cost of the public relations effort required to defend an operation in South Africa simply was not outweighed by the profits made in the currently sluggish South African economy.

The campaign for divestment has affected the South African political situation in other ways as well. The Executive Order issued by President Reagan in September, 1985, which imposed a variety of restrictions on U.S. business with South Africa, was adopted in response to the threat of stronger action by Congress, which was in turn motivated to act by the broad-based divestment movement at the local, city, and state levels. Pressure from institutional investors to end loans to the South African government probably contributed to the decision by Chase Manhattan and other banks to call in their loans in the summer of 1985. The resulting South African debt crisis, which led to the closing of the Johannesburg Stock Exchange and a default on international loan payments by South Africa in August 1985, spurred the rise of political activism by the South African business community and created an increased sense of the threat of economic isolation for the South African white community. The South African government clearly sees the divestment movement in America as a part of that threat; a representative of the South Africa Foundation in the

United States told the South African *Financial Mail*: "In one respect at least, the divestment forces have already won. . . . They have discouraged new companies, new investors who were looking for foreign opportunities from coming to South Africa."

In recent months, the rhetoric of the South African government has changed dramatically as it attempts to convince the world community of the sincerity of its reform efforts. Black South African activists have increased their calls for U.S. disinvestment and have seen the growing divestment movement in the United States as support for their cause. The result of the divestment campaign has been to increase the pressure both on U.S. companies to either act or withdraw and on the South African government to either reform or face increasing international isolation. In the already pressurized South African situation, these added pressures serve to signal moderate forces that the time for peaceful political change in South Africa is fast running out.

CHAPTER 29

Social Investing: Potent Force for Political Change

by ALICE TEPPER MARLIN

Socially responsible investing has been "discovered" in the last five years or so by a growing cross-section of Americans, particularly those concerned about developments in South Africa. Giant pension funds, religious organizations, retired persons, and "yuppies" are making a conscious decision to invest their money in a socially responsible way. Their individual and concerted efforts have made a tremendous contribution to the average person's awareness of the apartheid system and its devastating effects on millions of people of color in South Africa.

Before I spell out the important role ethical investing can play in this regard, let me give some background on where this kind of investment has come from and how fast it is growing.

In 1968, when controversy about the proper U.S. role in Vietnam was at its peak, many individuals and religious groups seeking avenues of constructive protest decided to clear their investment portfolios of companies profiting from the war. In answer to this desire, several social mutual stock funds were founded in the 1970s, most notably Pax World and the Four Square Fund. Some funds choose to apply other criteria, such as employee relations, nuclear power, and environmental records. Dreyfus Third Century Fund, for example, screens companies primarily according to environmental criteria and, more recently, involvement in South Africa.

The author wishes to thank Steven D. Lydenberg and Ros Will for their assistance in the preparation of this chapter.

The 1980s have witnessed a rebirth of interest. Several new mutual stock funds have emerged, including New Alternative, an environmental fund. There are two new mutual money market funds, Calvert and Working Assets, both of which use military and South Africa along with other social criteria. Two large institutional equity portfolio managers, Alliance Capital Management and Loomis Sayles, now offer South Africa-free index funds designed to match the performance of the S & P 500.

The growth of interest in managing funds by social criteria has been impressive indeed. Over $40 billion is now managed under some sort of social guidelines, according to the Social Investment Forum, a trade association of 130 brokers, money managers, and other professionals concerned with socially responsible investing. The Social Investment Forum offers a free guide to socially responsible funds and a listing of investment managers and research organizations that can help you apply apply social screens to your investments.

Such renewed interest, of course, has made social investing a rapidly growing new field for investment advisers such as Franklin Research and Development and U.S. Trust of Boston (which manages Calvert as well as its own social accounts). Although they do not advocate the use of social criteria, numerous trust managers, including Chemical Bank and J.P. Morgan, do apply social screens as requested by their clients.

The record over the past six to eight years helps to answer definitively the first question usually asked about social investing: Does using social criteria necessarily mean lower returns? Recent figures would seem to indicate otherwise. In 1985, the Lipper average of general equity mutual funds was up just over 27 percent. During that same period, Pax World was up 24 percent and Calvert's stock fund up 27 percent. Calvert's money market fund averaged 7.78 percent, exceeding Donoghue's money fund average. Working Assets was equal to the average.

DIVESTMENT DILEMMA

Just now the divestment debate centers on whether pension funds and endowments that exclude companies operating in South Africa can still achieve competitive investment performance. Robert J. Schwartz, investment adviser with a major New York investment firm, has this to say: "My investment results for the past ten years, together with significant studies and computer analyses of South Africa-free portfolios, have established clearly that performance need not be impaired. With proper selection, it may actually be improved. In the case of South Africa-related investments, the facts are clear. Divestment should not be ruled out on financial grounds."

Three major questions need to be addressed: Can a portfolio be sufficiently diversified if companies operating in South Africa are excluded from it? Can a portfolio manager successfully pursue strategies designed to outperform or at least maintain parity with the stock market or the average investment manager? How significant are the transaction costs arising from divestment and from a continuous policy of exclusion?

Research to date has focused primarily on the exclusion of companies doing business in South Africa. Some of the most interesting come from U.S. Trust of Boston and SEI, which has acquired the highly respected funds evaluation of A.G. Becker. The weight of the evidence supports the position that even complete South African divestment need not impede competitive investment performance to any significant degree. Such a policy excludes nearly half the market value of the S & P 500 and a similar or greater percentage of specific industry groups. A number of studies compare how well the movements of the S & P 500 or a comparable index are tracked by a portfolio excluding South African companies. In some of these studies, the South Africa-free portfolio is rebalanced to match the characteristics of the target stock market indices. All of these studies show that the South Africa-free portfolio tracks the index extremely closely. About 98 percent of the movements on the stock market can be matched.

A policy of complete divestment still leaves ample room for implementing diverse investment strategies. If the set of South Africa-free stocks closely duplicates the performance of all stocks, it follows that almost any investment style or strategy can be implemented after divestment. Reducing the universe is not necessarily detrimental to investment performance. Most meaningful strategies involve being undiversified so as to overweight areas that could provide superior performance. For example, eliminating nuclear utilities reduces the universe but has improved performance. As another example, investors can profit or avoid losses by anticipating changes in the price of oil. But, having done so, it is not necessary to invest in or sell the industry called "international oil." The industry called "domestic oil" contains many large, well-managed companies that are not in southern Africa and which will respond in the same way to oil price developments. It is also possible to benefit from lower oil prices by investing in industries like airlines, which benefit from lower oil prices, or insulation, which benefits from higher energy prices. The real proof of these points is that large managers of divested portfolios, such as Trinity, Wilshire Associates, and U.S. Trust, have achieved the same, superior results for these portfolios as for the others they manage.

TRANSACTION COSTS

The attack on the feasibility of divestment has shifted lately to transaction costs, which are said to grow prohibitive for large portfolios. The most often cited study on transaction costs of divestment, by Wilshire Associates, concludes that these costs will be on the order of several percent of portfolio value divested initially and a considerate fraction annually in the future.

In fact, these cost estimates are much too high, for they are based on weak conceptional and empirical support. In a study that U.S. Trust authored with SEI Funds Evaluation, Inc. for the state of Michigan's $5.2 billion stock portfolio, the estimated initial onetime transaction cost was put at 0.35 percent (sales and repurchases) of the value of the stocks that would not otherwise have been divested. There will also be an addition to transaction costs every year as a result of investing in smaller companies that will be traded more frequently at higher costs. Again, in their Michigan study, U.S. Trust and SEI estimated this as 0.1 percent of the proportion of the portfolio affected, based on SEI's actual monitoring of trading costs as they relate to trade difficulty.

Edward V. Regan, comptroller of the state of New York, complained in a recent *New York Times* op-ed piece that he could not comply with proposed legislation asking him to sell $6 billion worth of securities of companies doing business in South Africa. "I cannot meet the bill's requirement to sell the portfolio without seriously breaching my fiduciary obligation," he said. He asserted that "commissions and management fees incurred in buying replacement stocks and restructuring the original portfolio could run to $840 million over a five-year period."

Robert Schwartz, Joan Bavaria (Franklin Research and Development Corp.), Jack Scheinkman (ACTWU), and I have refuted Regan's arguments on the basis that his estimate is unrealistic and neglects several important factors. First, a large percentage of the state retirement fund is in fixed-income securities. There would be no additional cost or loss of income if, over a period of time, those fixed-income securities held for companies doing business in South Africa were replaced by at least equally high-yielding and quality bonds, amply available. Second, there is no reference to the normal turnover rate of securities in the portfolios due to changing investment factors and market conditions. If divestment were to take place over a reasonable time, such as four years, there would be little additional cost. Before that period was over, the system in South Africa might have changed. Third, the reference to larger management fees is strange, for we know of no investment management company that would charge more for a screened portfolio than it charges for a conventional one. Fourth, it is generally recognized that good performance does not require investing in the large multinational companies. Fifth, commission costs as a portion of total portfolio value are of little significance compared with appreciation or depreciation of securities held.

A January 1986 report prepared by Peter L. Bernstein, Inc. analyzed the impact of the planned first phase of divestiture on New York City Employees' Retirement System's (NYCERS) total portfolio. The study covered thirty-one companies held in the portfolio as of August 1985 and 137 companies outside the portfolio. The report focused on what the divestiture would mean in terms of portfolio risk, diversification, expected return, and transaction costs. The report concluded that the limited liquidation of assets worth $170 million under Phase I would involved an increase in the uncertainty and variability of future rates of return, but it also presented evidence suggesting that available techniques for rebalancing the portfolio can moderate this shift in the risk level.

Transaction costs (revised downward in a March 3 addendum) were estimated to be 1.1 percent of the total dollar value of the positions liquidated under Phase I divestiture. "On the assumption that the distribution of replacements would be evenly spread across large companies, medium-sized companies and small companies, we now estimate the total transaction cost at $1.7 million," states the March 3 addendum to the report.

TWO LARGE FUNDS

Six years ago, the Council on Economic Priorities (CEP) studied the portfolios of the two largest state pension funds in the country, California's Public Employees' Retirement System (PERS) and State Teachers' Retirement System (STRS). This analysis was commissioned by the

California State and Consumer Services Agency, in part to assess the social performance of portfolio companies with special regard to South African involvement and the legal and investment implications of providing companies with incentives to achieve top Sullivan ratings or withdraw from South Africa.

CEP recommended a moderate approach, which stressed the following:

• Query each company about its role in relation to apartheid (is it strategic?) and its adherence to the Sullivan Principles.
• After evaluating the company's answers, take whatever action is deemed necessary ranging from letter writing to voting proxies against management to joining with other shareholders in sponsoring resolutions.
• If these steps do not bring about the desired effect, implement divestment and/or exclusion.
• To curb cost, funds might simply halt new purchases of proscribed securities, rather than purging existing holdings. If holdings are to be sold, they could be phased out slowly. A rebalancing of the portfolio is needed to minimize risk. Roughly, for every equity dollar the funds divest, CEP estimated a onetime transaction cost of about 2 cents. For every bond dollar divested, CEP estimated a onetime transaction cost of approximately .3 cents.

PARAMOUNT ISSUE

The appalling situation in South Africa has done more to compel institutional investors to take social criteria seriously than has any other single issue. Spurred by interest in South Africa, other social issues, such as the nuclear arms race, are now receiving increased attention.

The crucial question in the debate over U.S. corporate involvement in South Africa is not whether the apartheid system should be abolished but when and how. For the most part, U.S. companies operating in South Africa have spoken out against apartheid recently. Almost unanimously they argue that they can be most effective in dismantling apartheid by maintaining their presence in South Africa and applying pressure for orderly change from within.

More radical critics of the U.S. business role advocate immediate withdrawal, arguing that the presence of major U.S. corporations gives moral and economic support to the Pretoria government which has little intention of ever instituting meaningful change. Increasingly, the escalating violence in South Africa has led many members of the business community to regard investment in that country as posing more risk than is prudent.

The highly volatile South African situation and increasing pressure from the international community on the Pretoria government have diminished the significance of the previous benchmark for measuring the progressiveness of individual U.S. corporations in their operations—their rating for compliance with the Sullivan Principles. Reverend Sullivan has now gone on record to declare that if apartheid is not abolished by 1987, all U.S. companies should withdraw from South Africa. Church leaders, arguing for withdrawal in 1984, put it simply: "We do not believe that being a responsible employer or active philanthropist in South Africa offsets the many ways in which U.S. companies give the South African government support and sustenance."

In contrast, those advocating that U.S. companies remain argue that withdrawal would be little more than a symbolic gesture. Its practical effect would be to throw out of work blacks and coloured persons who have well-paid jobs in integrated workplaces. Withdrawal would remove a positive model for employment practices and a constructive force working to support black schools, health care, legal assistance, low-interest loan funds, and other positive initiatives. Advocates of withdrawal respond that U.S. firms employ less than 1 percent of the black and coloured labor force.

As an industry, U.S. oil companies are especially heavily involved in South Africa. According to the Investor Responsibility Research Center (IRRC), over 90 percent of the international oil companies on the Standard & Poor's top 500 list have South African operations. Their presence is considered of particular strategic importance because of the country's dependence on imported oil. Computer firms doing business in South Africa arouse controversy as well because of the role computers play in enforcing the elaborate apartheid regulations throughout the country. By contrast, some other heavily involved industries, such as major U.S. drug companies of which almost 90 percent have operations there, are not generally seen as playing an equivalently vital role in suport of the current Pretoria government and its policies.

AN AID TO THE DEBATE

How might individuals or institutions use social investing as a tool to promote and add to the ongoing debate — and what effects could they reasonably hope to have? The method most usually pursued by individuals, religious groups, and pension funds is not to invest in the stocks of companies in South Africa. That can be accomplished easily through the funds or investment advisers I have mentioned and many others. The Council on Economic Priorities *Newsletter*, the Interfaith Center for Corporate Responsibility's *Corporate Examiner, Good Money*, Franklin's *Insight*, and the Investor Responsibility Research Center all provide relevant information. The Social Investment Forum will provide a long list of money managers and funds. And CEP will screen any investment portfolio upon request.

STOCKHOLDER POWER

A second approach is equally valid: remain (or even become) a stockholder in these companies and raise the issue with them. Here, church groups and some pension funds have been particularly active as have a number of individual stockholders. South Africa has been a key issue, as evidenced by resolutions listed in CEP's February *Newsletter*, which details most of the 132 social issue resolutions filed for 1986. (*Business and Society Review* readers may obtain a complimentary copy by writing CEP, 30 Irving Place, New York, NY, or calling us at (212) 420-1133.)

Thirty-one church groups, for instance, are asking IBM to notify South Africa of its intention to withdraw by the end of 1986 unless key components of apartheid are abolished. Similar resolutions were filed with Burroughs, Chevron, Citicorp, Exxon, General Electric, General Signal, Newmont Mining, Mobil, Schlumberger, Timken, and United Airlines.

Asked not to make new loans to South Africa, eight banks have given different replies, according to Timothy Smith of ICCR. Bankers Trust and Barclays Bank have agreed to make no further loans of any sort to South Africa; Chemical Bank will make no loans to South Africa for one year; Chase Manhattan plans no South African loans "for the forseeable future" because of instability in the region. Citibank, Manufacturers Hanover, J.P. Morgan, Bank of America, and Irving, in contrast, wish to reserve the right to make loans to the private sector in South Africa. Many church groups argue that these are in reality helping the government.

WIDE RANGE OF OPTIONS

After writing to forty-three of its portfolio companies, the Teachers' Insurance and Annuity Association/College Retirement Equities Fund (TIA/CREF), the largest pension fund in the United States, found that many firms had recently signed the Sullivan Principles or withdrawn from South Africa. The fund then filed resolutions with the nineteen companies remaining, asking them to become signators or to withdraw from South Africa. The New York City Employees' Retirement System concentrated on specific requests, such as a ban on selling or giving services to the South African police and military and an end to services to the South African government's electricity supply commission, an oil-from-coal facility.

A socially conscious investor can move from one investment approach to another or combine options in a particular way. One may decide to sell the stock of all companies involved in South Africa or, perhaps, only the stock of those with a poor Sullivan rating or which provide special services to the government. Voting proxies is another way to press for positive change. The Unitarian Church of All Souls in New York City, for example, voted in 1985 to co-sponsor with other church groups a resolution asking IBM to withdraw from South Africa unless substantial changes are instituted to end apartheid by December 1986. They also signed on to a NYCERS resolution requesting General Motors not to sell to South African military or police. In addition, All Souls resolved not to increase holdings in companies with operations or investments in South Africa and to divest holdings in any non-signator or poor performer relative to the Sullivan Principles.

There are several reasons why social investing is an effective means of raising the South African issue. First, it is orderly in its procedures and constructive in its tone, while still allowing for high visibility. Its reasoned and reasonable approach attracts much attention from the media. Second, it provides an opportunity to raise the South African issue within the business community. Third, the social investment approach raises economic as well as ethical issues when it comes to South African matters. As important as ethical matters may be, the high risk of holding an investment in South Africa in 1986 may well outweigh them, purely as a fiduciary matter. Fourth, social investment questions force an ongoing debate because social investment decisions are an ongoing matter. Unlike a onetime demonstration on the street, these questions cause us to reexamine continually the investment decisions that are a part of our daily lives. Fifth, the business community is a very powerful one. When economic or ethical arguments convince business leaders to take a stand on an issue, the message that emerges is truly influential. Who would have predicted five or even three years ago that there would be a decline in U.S. business in South Africa by 1985? But that is what we see today, although few say they are doing it on ethical grounds.

When the commercial banks in August 1985 refused to renew their loans, it had a devastating effect. As of January 1986, over twenty-five U.S. corporations have either closed or curtailed operations in South Africa, according to the Interfaith Center on Corporate Responsibility.

Investing according to one's conscience will not guarantee a higher dollar return, but neither will it significantly handicap a diverse investment portfolio. Social investment alone will not end apartheid. But it is another way of pressuring the government of South Africa and continuing and broadening public awareness about this vitally important issue. Ethical investment is a means particularly well-suited to promoting a constructive and sharply focused debate while at the same time fostering social and personal good.

Part VI

EUROPEAN PRESSURES
FOR SANCTIONS

CHAPTER 30

The Corporate Role in Fighting Apartheid: British Style

by MICHAEL IVENS

South Africa, Israel, the United States, and Chile are those countries exposed to criticism in the British media, plus the Soviet Union when Russia's inhumanity to dissidents becomes newsworthy. The first four countries are well entrenched in the British left's demonology, though at one time Israel ranked as virtuous and Utopian like prewar Viennese worker flats, the Spanish Republican Government, and heroic North Vietnam. All four are open societies and, therefore, well equipped to present visual criticism on television. In contrast, Iran's acts of genocide on the Bahai, the Chinese execution and persecution of political and religious dissidents, and atrocities committed in African states pass relatively unobserved in Britain.

South Africans sometimes put down British criticism as a relic of paternalist, colonialist conscience. "You go on," they say, "feeling responsible for us. You forget that we are no longer tied to Britain's apron-strings." It's an engaging theory, but I doubt its efficacy. No similar British preoccupation applies, for example, to Australia, New Zealand, India, Pakistan, and the West Indies — not unless the issues are those of cricket, the game which above all holds the Commonwealth together and transcends race and color. It is interesting that the main political issue between Britain and Caribbean countries at present concerns the presence of English cricketeers who have played in South Africa and who are facing political demonstrations in the West Indies.

South Africa is very often in the news in Britain for a number of reasons: The British dislike apartheid; London attracts many South Africans who oppose their government's policies; London also attracts

South African intellectuals who can find a wider audience there than in their homeland. Another reason is the highly expansive race relations industry; this splits between those who are genuinely concerned with improving British race relations and those who are interested in exacerbating them. The latter are often funded by the far left councils that run some of Britain's biggest cities: London, Manchester, Liverpool, and Sheffield. For these, the South African card is played regularly in order to attack the Thatcher government, capitalism, racism, and militarism and to associate all these together.

Finally, Britain along with the United States, Western Europe, and other democratic areas has been subjected to a well-organized and orchestrated international campaign to introduce an economic boycott of South Africa. It is being mounted in the same way that the campaign against the neutron bomb and so-called Star Wars have been orchestrated. To recognize the orchestration is not necessarily to reject the boycott, but it is an essential part of political sophistication.

The boycott campaign in Britain has made a good deal of stir in some universities. Many British students are financially sponsored by their local authorities. They only get the money if they belong to the National Union of Students (there have been cases of students who have had to give up universities because they refused to belong to the NUS).

The National Union of Students is very much controlled by the left and by the political lethargy of most students. Let me give one recent example: At Brunel University, 200 students voted that the Student Union should refuse to cash any check from Barclays Bank, because of its investment in South Africa. Those at the meeting agreed that in the future all 3,500 Brunel students should use alternative banks. This was impossible for those students who had overdrafts at Barclays. Not surprisingly, the Brunel student body overthrew this decision. But Barclays has tended to rank high on the hit list of student organizations and so it is worth considering Barclays' record in South Africa.

BARCLAYS BANK

Barclays, one of Britain's leading banks, has expressed its total opposition to apartheid and maintains multiracial policies for staff and customers. Barclays has been in South Africa since 1925. In 1971, its 100 percent-owned bank was incorporated in South Africa as Barclays National Bank and its ownership has been reduced over the years to

50.4 percent in 1984. Last year, Barclays Bank shareholdings in its South African company were reduced to about 40 percent.

It is ironic that Barclays should have been under attack because its policies have been remarkably virtuous. Barclays has been particularly critical of the South African government's failure to give black Africans a proper education and has been involved in loans, with other international banks, to assist projects for African education and housing. Barclays has categorically refused to lend to the South African government unless the loan is going to improve the living standards of the black population and can be monitored. Barclays does not debar itself from financing trade in goods between Britain and South Africa, which totaled £1,931 million in 1984 and provided 150,000 jobs in Britain.

In South Africa, Barclays has been the major employer of black, coloured, and Asian staff. Barclays employs about 43 percent of all nonwhites in the South African banking industry—although it has only about a quarter of the banking business. Wages of African employees in Barclays exceed by at least 50 percent the EEC minimum level in its code of conduct for employment practices in South Africa. Between 1983 and 1988, Barclays will have given £1 million to finance housing and other projects set up by the Urban Foundation. Barclays National also played a leading role in setting up the African Bank with capital and seconding staff.

Faced by a political campaign against its South African interests, Barclays reacted with sensitivity but came back with reasoned replies. Its reduced shareholdings in Barclays National in South Africa may have been a tactical reaction although the company has insisted on its rights to continue its business there.

Its declared policy is worth quoting because it sums up well the policies of most responsible British companies operating today in South Africa: "Barclays is totally opposed to apartheid. The bank differs from its critics only on the question of how change can be brought about. It is Barclays' view that change should be peaceful and should not further disadvantage those already disadvantaged. The bank considers that this decision imposes an obligation to use its presence as a major shareholder in Barclays National Bank to encourage the establishment of a fairer society by peaceful means. The board and management of Barclays National Bank have given repeated evidence of their determination to pursue the policy of peaceful change. In this determination they are second to none among South African businesses."

What is less typical about Barclays has been its hard-hitting statements about the need for change in South Africa. Not all British companies operating there are so forthright.

Sir Timothy Bevan, chairman of Barclays Bank, has called for reforms in apartheid laws and demanded the release of Nelson Mandela as a basic step forward. On a business basis, he regards the 5 percent down payment which has been put forward as part of a deal between South Africa and its main credit banks as probably the best that could be expected at present.

EXTENT OF TRADE

Any serious boycott of South Africa by Britain must be seen against the extensive trade between the two countries. Britain is South Africa's third largest export market after Japan and the United States. U.K. imports from South Africa in 1984 amounted to £726 million. Major commodities imported from South Africa by Britain are metal ores and metal scrap, fruit and vegetables, textile fibres, nonferrous metals, and pulp and wastepaper.

About 30 percent of Britain's economy is dependent on exports and South Africa is the United Kingdom's thirteenth largest market after North American and European nations. U.K. exports to South Africa in 1984 amounted to £1,205 million. The major commodities exported to South Africa by Britain are road vehicles, general industrial machinery and equipment, office machines and data processing equipment, and machinery specialized for particular industries. The book value of U.K. direct investment in South Africa was—at the end of 1981—£2,826 million.

Both those opposed to an economic boycott of South Africa by Britain and those in favor seem to agree on one thing: It will lead to unemployment not only in South Africa but also in Britain. An international boycott policy that seriously damaged South Africa would, in addition, lead to a large-scale white migration from South Africa to Britain which would exacerbate the already large unemployment.

ESSENTIAL MINERALS

Over and above the matter of trade, Britain must be concerned—as must the U.S.—that the West is highly dependent on essential minerals from South Africa. Without them, Britain's factories could be brought to a standstill. There is an awareness and anxiety over the fact that the Soviet Union is not only a major producer of essential minerals but also has been stockpiling from South Africa and from other sources of supply. Here we face the possibility of a resource war. A southern Africa whose supplies of essential minerals were committed to the Soviet Union would provide Russia with overwhelming military, strategic, industrial, and financial advantages. These minerals are essential for the manufacture of Britain's high technology as well as its weaponry. Britain is highly reliant on South Africa for supplies of chromium, vanadium, platinum, manganese, gold, industrial diamonds, uranium, cobalt, bauxite, antimony, nickel, tungsten, and niobium.

The steady shipment of vital resources from the Cape Route remains as vital a need for Britain as for the United States. Steady shipments in the oil trade have looked less secure in recent years. Then there is the vital and strategic importance of Simonstown as a naval base in any future conflict.

RHODESIAN BOYCOTT

Britain's recent history makes it aware of the interdependence of national economies. This is highlighted by the sense of living on a small island, dependent on a thriving import and export trade.

When Britain first imposed sanctions on Rhodesia after the Unilateral Declaration of Independence (UDI), many people thought this would bring Rhodesia's economy to a standstill. At that time Rhodesia's economy was heavily dependent on foreign trade and half of its gross national product was exchanged with the rest of the world.

The impact of Britain's sanctions was sharp in the period immediately following UDI. But after September 1966, when the Security Council of the United Nations followed Britain by imposing mandatory sanctions on Rhodesia, the Rhodesian regime began to weather the storm, despite the fact that all U.N. member countries were directed to stop exporting petroleum, arms, ammunition, military equipment, vehicles, aircraft, and equipment and materials for the manufacture and maintenance of arms and ammunition in Rhodesia and also to abstain from importing Rhodesian tobacco, sugar, meat and meat products, asbestos, copper, pig iron, chrome and iron ore, hides, skins, and leather.

A ban was added in 1968 prohibiting the provision of funds for investment or the provision of any other financial or economic resources to the Rhodesian government and commercial, industrial, or public utility enterprises. Rhodesia retaliated by introducing a system of import licensing. The purchase of foreign securities was prohibited and foreign travel allowances were cut. As a means of retaliation, particularly against Great Britain, interest payments were suspended on loans issued in London or guaranteed by the British government. Despite the sanctions and countersanctions, Rhodesia developed favorably.

BOYCOTT REPERCUSSIONS

The Confederation of British Industries has suggested that a boycott of South Africa would increase Britain's unemployment by about 70,000. If Britain withdrew one half of its South African capital commitments, it would be likely to throw approximately 160,000 men and women out of work. An economic boycott against South Africa would also seriously affect Swaziland, Lesotho, and Botswana; some 90 percent of their imports come from South Africa. Britain is concerned with the well-being of these three small nations.

Some major British companies have withdrawn from South Africa. Their reasons for doing so are far from idealistic. Two major companies that have withdrawn made it clear that they did so not to assist the cause of the blacks but to escape political embarrassment. Some of their shares, for example, had been bought by campaigners against apartheid and they did not enjoy rows at their annual general meetings. Although excellent companies, they were less committed to the political and social cause of an open South Africa than many companies that have stayed there and continue to press for change. In one case, the company sold out and invested the money in Iran—not a productive decision. The other company invested more wisely elsewhere.

By moving out of South Africa they have exercised some political pressure on the South African government. On the other hand, they are no longer playing their part with many British, U.S. and other foreign companies which have been campaigning within South Africa for better education for blacks, the scrapping of apartheid and pass laws, and a movement toward a just political representation for non-whites.

Britain has had a marked influence on the structure of South African parliamentary and legal processes. Although the political power is now in the hands of the Afrikaans population, the impact of English culture is still strong. In South Africa, the 1820 Foundation (previously called the 1820 Settlers' Foundation) has a magnificent establishment at Grahamstown to encourage, on a nonracial basis, the study and practice of British culture and political thinking. The 1820 Foundation has exercised a great deal of pressure on the South African government recently to improve black education, and its efforts are well supported by British firms in South Africa as well as by indigenous companies.

CORPORATE RECORD

The most important way, perhaps, that British companies can help is by their actual practices — as well as by pressure on the South African government. A recent study of fifty British subsidiary or associate companies in South Africa throws an interesting light on the way that British firms are helping with black development.

• Out of the total work force of 30,846, only five workers in the survey were paid below the lower datum level, while 29,107 black African workers were paid above the higher datum level.

• Forty-eight of the fifty companies operate common pay scales for employees of all racial groups, and forty-seven companies have an integrated grade structure through which black employees can advance on an equal basis with whites.

• Forty-eight companies representing 99.9 percent of the work force are willing to recognize a black trade union, and 26,581 blacks work for companies that recognize trade unions, although all of that number may not necessarily belong to a union.

• Forty-eight of the fifty companies operate a pension scheme, forty-three an insurance scheme, forty-seven a medical scheme, and twenty-three of the companies supply free or subsidized meals in addition to emoluments.

• Desegregation at the workplace has been achieved in forty-four of the fifty companies, representing 98.7 percent of the total black work force covered by the survey, while twenty-four out of thirty-five companies that operate canteens have desegregated them.

• Forty-six percent of the companies contribute to the Urban Foundation. British companies have subscribed over £2 million to the Urban Foundation since it was formed. Much of the work of the foundation is in the field of housing, and in addition five of the fifty companies provide family housing.

• Nine companies support small business development projects, and eight of the fifty companies contribute to the Black African

Chambers of Commerce.

These results indicate that British companies are playing a prominent part in assisting black development in South Africa. Some years ago these figures would have been very different. There is now a great awareness by British companies in South Africa that they have important responsibilities in assisting black development and the work and living conditions of black employees.

THE BRITISH GOVERNMENT

The attitude of the British government does not, of course, duplicate that of the public but it, too, has an historical basis. The British government is very much aware of the high investment by British Industry in South Africa and that many white South Africans are of British ancestry and have relatives in Britain. In the last war many South Africans, including Afrikaners, fought for the Allies. On the other hand, there were a number of Afrikaner politicians, some who became prominent, who were positively pro-Hitler.

The attitude of British governments, both Conservative and Labour, has been to drop apartheid and the inhumane racial legislation; also to give effective political representation to nonwhites.

Although the British government wants to see immediate progress, the pace it desires is slower than that required by many Commonwealth countries and it has resisted being pushed into large-scale economic boycotts. It is influenced, too, by the fact that many black countries in Southern Africa which have been started off on Western-style voting patterns have lapsed swiftly into tyrannies. Conservative ministers tend to speak out more openly than present members of the government. Nicholas Fairbairn, the former Solicitor General for Scotland, has been frank:

It is in the interests of no one who lives in the South African Republic, far less anyone who lives in the states which surround South Africa, to destroy, or even to compromise that huge prosperity which the Europeans have created, except of course for those who would personally enrich themselves and their fellow conspirators by powers as contemporary Africans have done, or by those who have such a Hitlerian insanity, that they believe that it matters not if they lay their country in ruins and ashes, so long as the Marxist cause triumphs.

He adds:

Apartheid is the most logical and the most ludicrous and the most loathsome theory for solving the problems of ethnic diversity. Though it had historical origins and foreign inspiration, it is well to ponder that Dr. Verwoerd was a sociologist. We suffer from them too. But President Botha, having reversed the train, must neither fear to be accused of doing so, nor be frightened to drive at full speed. His was an act of unique political courage; it would be a tragedy if he did not now obtain the prizes of his brave decision but suffered the disaster of his indecision.

Fairbairn makes an important point:

There are two separate issues which must not be confused, but will be inextricably interwined by delay—domestic reform and reasoned constitutional rearrangement. The slower the pace of the first the less likely the achievement of the second. . . . To achieve a system of one man, one vote, which does not mean majority rule and therefore one man, one vote, depends on the pace of domestic legislative reform.

Fairbairn echoes the remark made many years ago by one of Britain's colonial administrators who was given the task of implementing self-government for the Sudan and a number of other countries: "The right time is always too late." Similarly, Fairbairn argues that the whole apartheid legislation must be scrapped enthusiastically: "The government must not fear to do right for fear of the Right. If Ian Smith had taken the terms Tiger or Fearless, and gone over the heads of his politicians to his electorate, he would have triumphed, but he so feared the spectre of the Right, that he handed over his country grudgingly but inevitably to the Left."

How, then, can the West help? Fairbairn argues that the West has been negative in its approach and has reinforced the laager reaction. He states that Britain and America and Europe should form a new trading constellation to invest in and develop the whole of southern Africa, which is rich or prospectively rich in minerals and agriculture.

That is probably going further than most members of the present Conservative government would do. If, however, the Conservatives lose the general election next year, a labour government backed by the trade unions is likely to be much less sympathetic to South Africa. So far British policy on that country does not appear prominently in any labour election thinking. The Alliance is likely to be split between the rather hardheaded approach of David Owen and the more left-wing approach of the Liberals under David Steel.

The media in Britain, especially television, tend to be very critical of South Africa, and the Government does respond to that. In the early 1970s a critical article on South Africa in *The Guardian* followed by a television program led to immediate action by the Convervative government in setting up a committee to vet the employment practices of British companies in South Africa.

CODE OF CONDUCT

British companies are still under pressure to fall in line with the European Code of Conduct for companies with interests in South Africa. The latest government statement showed that the continued economic recession in South Africa was characterized by wage rates shown failing to keep pace with consumer price inflation. But against this background, British subsidiaries have continued to increase the provision of fringe benefits to their black employees. The returns also showed evidence "of increasing dealings with South Africa's emerging trade unions and a growing commitment to training, education and community projects."

This latest analysis showed that progress during the life of the European Code of Conduct has been considerable both in terms of the pay and conditions provided by UK companies and of companies' willingness to comply with and submit reports under the Code.[1]

There is a sharp reduction in the number of companies declining to report. The vast majority, some 98 percent of UK companies, with significant interests in South Africa submitted reports. Nearly a third of the companies reported that their black workers were represented by trade unions on the Industry Council in which wages and working conditions are set in industrywide bargaining between employer organizations and unions. "This system has tended to inhibit involvement of direct company-union negotiations," adds the report, "but a growing number of companies covered by industrial council agreements claimed they were ready to negotiate supplementary agreements at the plant level."

The total of migrant labor employed by British subsidiaries remains at about 11,000. About 80 percent of the migrants continue to be employed by one company. Twenty-two companies reported improvements in the accommodations provided for migrant workers, and thirteen stated they regarded migrant workers as entitled to the same benefits as their permanent workforce.

During the reporting period, both the number of black Africans paid below the lower datum level and the number paid below the upper datum level increased (from 1.9 to 2.4 percent and from 5.2 to 7.6 percent, respectively). This should be seen against the background of recession.

THE COMMONWEALTH SECRETARIAT

The Commonwealth Secretariat and its Secretary General, Shridath Ramphal, takes a very much stronger line against the South African government. It is backed by the Declaration of Commonwealth Principles at the Commonwealth summit at Singapore in 1971. At that summit, Commonwealth leaders affirmed, "No member country will afford to regimes which practice racial discrimination assistance which in its own judgement directly contributes to the pursuit or consolidation of this evil policy."

At their next summit in London in June 1977, Commonwealth leaders called on the international community to take urgent action to apply an immediate arms embargo on South Africa and to make such an embargo effective. In November of that year, the U.N. Security Council adopted, unanimously, Resolution 418 imposing a total, mandatory arms embargo on the apartheid regime.

With the Gleneagles Agreement Commonwealth leaders sought to cut the sporting connection. Member governments agreed "To combat the evil of apartheid by withholding any form of support for, and by taking every practical step to discourage, contact or competition by their nationals with sporting organizations, teams or sportsmen from South Africa or from any other country where sports are organized on the basis of race, colour or ethnic origin."

A notable breach of the Agreement occurred in 1981 when the New Zealand Rugby Union, ignoring the New Zealand government's advice, invited the South African National Springbok team to tour. This led to a Code of Conduct adopted by the Commonwealth Games Federation at Brisbane in 1982. It includes provision to suspend from the Games a country which breaches its obligations under the Gleneagles Agreement.

Ramphal has written a number of booklets on South Africa published by the Commonwealth Secretariat, as well as acting as Chairman of the Third World Prize Committee and announcing that the Third World Foundation had awarded its 1985 Medallion and prize of $100,000 jointly to Winnie and Nelson Mandela. Ramphal, addressing the North American Regional Conference for Action Against Apartheid in New York in 1984, made his position clear:

South Africa has fed, and feeds upon, these tensions; has sought systematically to divert North America from an unequivocal stand against apartheid by an invocation of cold-war attitudes which depict South Africa as a country under siege from international communism and an ally of the West and of Western influence in a strategic area threatened with instability. It is an invocation to which some have regrettably succumed to the point of excusing, or at least acquiescing in, Pretoria's excesses, in the wholly mistaken belief that South Africa is an ally of the West.

He has argued that "apartheid is not being dismantled, it is being repackaged." he and the Commonwealth Secretariat have attacked the South African government's argument that blacks have a better economic situation in South Africa than other black African workers.

Mr. Ramphal rejects the arguement "Why a boycott of South Africa and not of other dictatorships?" on the grounds that "apartheid is a system unlike any other in the world whose every function turns on the pernicious factor of racism."

There is no doubt that his position is backed by a number of Commonwealth governments. Although Britain sometimes disagrees with a number of Commonwealth countries in action on South Africa, official communiqués of Commonwealth meetings appear to resolve and paper-over the disagreements.

The 1985 Commonwealth conference led to the establishment of the so-called Group of Eminent Persons who are to encourage political dialogue in South Africa with a view to establishing a nonracial and representative government. This was one of the elements of the Accord on Southern Africa agreed by Commonwealth leaders at their Nassau summit in 1985. The members of the group are

Malcolm Fraser, former Prime Minister of Australia

General Olusegun Obasanjo, former Head of the State of Nigeria

Lord Barber of Wentbridge, Chairman, Standard Chartered Bank, and former Minister of the Government of the United Kingdom

Dame Nita Barrow, a President of the World Council of Churches, former President of the World YWCA, and Chairman of the International NGO Women's Forum in Nairobi

John Malecela, former Minister of the Government of Tanzania

Sardar Swaran Singh, former Minister of the government of India

Archibishop Edward W. Scott, Primate of the Anglican Church of Canada

The announcement of the Group was hardly received with enthusiasm by the South African government. Nevertheless, they have been politely met during their tour of South Africa.

Although the Group of Eminent Persons is unlikely to produce world-shattering impact, it may be some held to State President Botha in his arguments against the members of his party who wish to see no change at all. And a critical or a rebuffed report will give strong opponents of South Africa arguments for some decisive action at the next Commonwealth conference.

There is likely to be impact, too, in the United Nations, where the Commonwealth Committee on Southern Africa has links with the U.N. special committee against apartheid.

NOTES

1. "Code of Conduct for Companies with Interests in South Africa," Department of Trade and Industry, London, 1985.

CHAPTER 31

How the West Gains from Apartheid: The Case of the United Kingdom

by N. CRAIG SMITH

A WORSENING SITUATION?

Apartheid to South Africa has never been under greater threat. The current unrest, which is generally considered to date back to 1984, does not seem to be of the transient nature that many observers predicted. The death toll mounts at an increasing rate[1] and civil war, more than ever before, seems imminent. Against this backdrop, the pressure in the United Kingdom for substantial economic sanctions against South Africa has reached an unprecedented level. Public opinion would appear to be in favor,[2] especially in the light of recent government support for actions against Libya. The UK government is also under pressure from the opposition parties, the United Nations, the Commonwealth (some countries have even spoken of leaving the Commonwealth if further sanctions are not applied)[3] and, to a lesser extent, the European Economic Community (EEC).

Many refer to a worsening situation in South Africa. And an expressed desire by some for the alleviation of this does not always hide an underlying self-interest, especially when such apparently compassionate statements are made alongside criticisms of further sanctions. Others view the situation with optimism. While deeply regretting the seemingly inevitable loss of life, they believe they are witnessing the death throes of apartheid and the heralding of a majority rule South Africa.

It is not appropriate here to speculate on the exact timing of the demise of apartheid; current events may too easily color objective assessment. Nor should it make what is essentially a value judgment on the desirability of an end to apartheid at the cost of many lives. This demands taking a position on ends and means and makes the possibly contentious assumption that peaceful change in South Africa is not possible. However, it will be assumed that the end of apartheid is close at hand, that is, likely within the next five years. And, moreover, that this will be achieved largely through violent coercion of the South African authorities, as it is at least the (reported) perception of many blacks within South Africa that the government's intransigence precludes a peaceful solution.

This chapter examines the prospects for business in South Africa within these parameters. It thereby considers the role of business in apartheid, the arguments for and against economic sanctions on South Africa, including their costs and the constructive engagement argument, and the challenges to be faced by business up to and after the end of apartheid. A UK perspective is adopted.

BUSINESS AND APARTHEID

Apartheid in South Africa is a highly charged issue. It is also a complex issue and one that has remained exceptionally prominent since the Sharperville shootings in 1960. Even before the current unrest, hardly a day would pass without some reference in the UK press to oppression in South Africa. The South African government, in a series of advertisements in the national press in the United Kingdom in 1983, commented: "South Africa arouses more controversy than almost any other country in the world." In motivations in running this campaign and pointing to this controversy aside, the observation is acceptable as accurate. In looking at how the West gains from apartheid and the role of business in this, it is necessary first to examine the nature of apartheid itself. This examination is based on many sources, including an interview with the commercial minister at the South African Embassy in London.[4]

Apartheid is an Afrikaans word meaning separateness or segregation. It has long been used by the South African government to describe its policy of pursuing the separate development of the races in South Africa, though it is arguable that, as "Grand Apartheid," the policy has now been largely abandoned. It was, at least, followed by the National Party after it came to power in 1948 and particularly after it was formally established under Hendrik W. Verwoerd, known as the architect of apartheid, Prime Minister from 1958 till his assassination in 1966. Many, though, would suggest apartheid's origins go back a lot further, to the Land Act of 1913, which established the Native Reserves, and even to British colonist rule prior to the Act of Union in 1910.

Apartheid is also considered to mean institutionalized racism. Oliver Tambo, President of the African National Congress (ANC), has described it as "the sum total of all the policies, strategies and methods, beliefs and attitudes that have been marshalled and are being employed in an attempt to ensure and entrench the political domination and economic exploitation of the African people by the white minority." While Nobel Peace Prize winner Bishop Desmond Tutu, in reference to the oppression of the black population in South Africa, has said: "When the missionaries first came to Africa they had the Bible and we had the land. They said 'let us pray.' We closed our eyes. When we opened them, we had the Bible and they had the land."

This implication of colonialism, however, and any suggestion that the white population has less of a claim to the land in South Africa than the blacks, would be swiftly denied by white South Africans. The South Africa *Yearbook*, produced by the South African government, describes both the whites and blacks in South Africa as being descendants of immigrants, the only indigenous people of South Africa being the Bushmen (San), now "numerically insignificant." It suggests the (Bantu-speaking) blacks of South Africa are the descendants of Iron Age farmers who arrived from central Africa in the eleventh and twelfth centuries. The whites are the descendants of seventeenth- and eighteenth-century European settlers. The Afrikaners largely Dutch and Germany ethnic composition dates back to the Dutch administration of the Cape originating with Jan van Riebeeck in 1652. This perspective is emphasized in history lessons in South Africa's schools.

It is the ethnic diversity of South Africa and the requirement to defend the claims of minority groups (including, of course, the whites) that provides the official rationale for apartheid. Government statistics put the population at just under 24 million in 1980 (excluding Venda, Bophuthatswana and Transkei). Within this there are many different ethnic groups, the *Yearbook* lists nine ethnic divisions to South Africa's black population of just under 16 million. The whites number about 4.5 million, the coloreds, 2.5 million, and the Asians .75 million. This heterogeneity inspires the policy of separate development, apartheid. White South Africa claim the West does not understand South Africa's situation and especially this racial complexity. Accordingly, while Western critics view separate development as racist, particularly given the West's approach of integration to ethnic differences, many white South Africans argue that separate development is necessary for South Africa's situation.

The far greater diversity of South Africa is not the only reason for President Botha saying the West does not understand "the realities of the subcontinent." The West is also criticized for judging South Africa by Western standards when, in fact, it forms part of the Third World. Separate development is defended because of the differences between the various groups in South Africa but most notably the differences in "sophistication." Pointing to Zimbabwe, many white South Africans suggest that majority rule in an integrated South Africa would mean "tribalism would win out." The Zulus, the largest group in South Africa (6 million), are particularly feared.

South Africa's solution to the problem it identifies of ethnic diversity and the potential threat of continual interracial violence under an integrated South Africa, is a confederation of states. This is known as "Grand Apartheid." Separate development involves the blacks living outside white South Africa, ultimately all within ten states. These were formally the Native Reserves, which the government has now designated as "homelands" (or Bantustans). If Grand Apartheid were to be realized, there would be no black South Africans. The homelands would be independent — and Venda, Bophuthatswana, Transkei, and Ciskei are already "independent" (but no country other than South Africa recognizes this).

So apartheid is purportedly a system whereby the many races of South Africa may coexist securely and separately, different but equal. Yet it is in effect a racist ideology advancing separate development to maintain the economic exploitation of the black majority. Ideologies serve to explain the world to their adherents but in a way that justifies their interests. Many whites in South Africa still believe the differences between the races demand their separateness, each in the land which "belongs" to them. In its exteme form, this belief finds its expression in support for the parties of the far right in South Africa — for instance, in the recent rise to prominence of Eugene Terre'Blanche and the Afrikaner Weerstandsbeweging (AWB). Other whites reject this view but are not willing to accept or are frightened of the consequences of an integrated South Africa under majority rule.

Black leaders reject all arguments about ethnic differences among the blacks. They see themselves as black first and foremost and it is noted that the South African authorities make and encourage the divisions, including, through the use of vigilantes, the fighting among blacks that characterizes much of the current unrest. Apartheid cannot be accepted as simply a solution to a problem of ethnic diversity as an alternative to integration. And it is more than overt racial discrimination. It is fundamentally about economic exploitation. This is where business is involved and why corporate involvement in South Africa is widely condemned.

The homeland represent only 13 percent of the country's land mass, incuding some of the poorest land in the country, yet they are (or were) intended to contain 73 percent of South Africa's population. Every black already has a homeland and consequently, in response to the criticism that the blacks are completely without political rights, the government responds that they have political rights in their "independent" homelands. However, only about half (12–13 million) actually live in the homelands; many have not seen their homeland and will probably never do so. Despite a policy of repatriation – the forced removal to these homelands – the government recognizes that a large proportion of blacks will remain in the townships. The size of the black urban population is dictated by economic requirements, for apartheid in its effect if not its design means the creation of a migratory labor system. Under such a system cheap labor is used as and when required without the disadvantages of "having to put up with it" in the community.

Apartheid involves even the urban blacks (and the coloreds and Asians for that matter) living outside white South Africa. The Group Areas Act provides for the different racial groups to live in separate areas. Accordingly, the urban blacks live in townships, many of which are shanty towns, on the edges of the cities. Soweto, for example, is a township of 1.25 million people southwest of Johannesburg. If the

This perspective, however, no longer satisfies many opponents of apartheid. While the average black is materially better off than most of his or her counterparts elsewhere in Africa, this does not compensate for the absence of political rights and the great disparity between blacks and whites, with the latter having probably the highest standard of living in the world. Little real progress is evident, few reforms have been more than cosmetic, despite Botha's "Adapt or die" slogan.

South Africa is extremely prosperous by African standards, its current troubles notwithstanding. This prosperity is built upon an economic dependence on the blacks. It has long been claimed that it is this dependence, which continues to grow and particularly now in its demands for skilled workers (including middle managers), that will bring an end to apartheid. It is estimated that by the year 2000 the black population in South Africa will be 37 million but the white population only 6 million. Already the practice of reserving jobs for whites has ended due to recruitment difficulties. Continued growth will mean greater economic incorporation of the blacks. With this, it is argued, political and social incorporation cannot but follow. In other words, apartheid as a means primarily for economic exploitation, but which also involves social and political exclusion, will be destroyed through economic progress.

This perspective, however, no longer satisfies many opponents of apartheid. While the average black is materially better off than most of his or her counterparts elsewhere in Africa, this does not compensate for the absence of political rights and the great disparity between blacks and whites, with the latter having probably the highest standard of living in the world. Little real progress is evident, few reforms have been more than cosmetic, despite Botha's "Adapt or die" slogan. The current economic problems in South Africa can only exacerbate the situation. The armed seizure of sate political power by the ANC and economic sanctions applied by the outside world to hasten the defeat of the government are viewed by many as the only means of ending apartheid. At the very least, those advocating further sanctions are seeking more rapid change in South Africa than its government seems prepared to concede.

It has been suggested that South Africa's apartheid system has always been a mutually beneficial alliance between a minority government and private business; that there is a convergence of interest between business in South Africa and the upholders of apartheid. The basis for this, as indicated above, is apartheid's role in the provision of cheap labor, particularly in establishing a migratory labor system, and in the grossly unequal apportionment of the country's wealth. The international Labour Organization (ILO) has described apartheid as "a system of forced labour." Efficient use of this labor resource has demanded capital investment, which has come from the West. South Africa's development has consistently involved the combination of cheap labor and Western capital, from the late ninteenth century when British settlers such as Cecil Rhodes first started large-scale mining of diamonds and gold, to more recent times and the creation of South

Africa's now quite substantial manufacturing base. Business, and British business in particular, has long been implicated in apartheid.

Of course, Western businesses operate in other countries characterized by oppression, exploitation, and great differences in wealth. However, none of these countries are as extreme as South Africa and operate as overtly. Nor do they wish to be considered as part of the West, a (white) South African aspiration, but not be judged by Western standards and values. Moreover, corporate activity in other unsavory countries should also be held up to scrutiny and South Africa is symbolic in their respect. Calling attention to the wrongs of South Africa and corporate involvement in them highlights other less noticeable wrongs elsewhere. But if they are not addressed in South Africa, why should they be addressed in other countries?

South Africa is dependent on Western capital. Recognition of this gives support to the calls for economic sanctions against South Africa. However, Western capital is also dependent on South Africa. Both benefit from apartheid. This complexity underlies demands for sanctions and affects the likelihood of their imposition.

SANCTIONS AGAINST SOUTH AFRICA

Arnt Spandau, Professor of Business Economices at Witwatersrand University, Johannesburg, suggests "trade is the most important lifeline" of South Africa.[5] The *Yearbook* also recognizes the importance of trade to the South African economy. It refers to a "great but declining dependence on external trade" (the decline is due to the expansion of domestic consumer markets). Among Western countries, in 1980, South Africa occupied fifteenth position in the value of imports and exports of merchandise, while the total reciprocal flow of goods and services between South Africa and the rest of the world amounted to 63 percent of South Africa's gross domestic product, described by the *Yearbook* as "one of the highest proportions in the Western world." In 1981, 14.4 percent of South Africa's exports were to the United States, 13.6 percent to Japan, 11.8 percent to the United Kingdom, and 22.5 percent to the rest of the EEC. Less than 10 percent were to Africa.[6] Later figures put, in order of size, the United States, Japan, Switzerland, the United Kingdom, and West Germany as South Africa's largest export markets, worth around $5 billion.[7]

Western investment in South Africa is substantial and, until most recently, continued to grow, much of it is British and American. The

Reverend Jesse Jackson has commented, "The US and Britain, which consider themselves to be the crown jewels of democracy, in fact have the heaviest investment in South Africa. South Africa could not exist in its system of apartheid without the propping up from the US and Britain.[8] Britain is by far the largest single foreign investor in South Africa, both directly and indirectly. The United Kingdom South Africa Trade Association (UKSATA) estimates that almost 10 percent of all British overseas direct investment is in South Africa, the market value of which in January 1982 was estimated at about £5,000 million. Indirect (portfolio) investment was estimated at £6,000 million, putting a total of £4 billion investment at stake in South Africa. They suggest British investment accounts for almost 50 percent of total foreign investment in South Africa.[9] More recent sources refer to a figure of around £12 billion invested, though some suggest the direct investment has been reduced by up to half its value three years ago because of the drop in the value of the rand.10 U.S. direct investment is put at $2.5 billion, though this is, in contrast with the United Kingdom, less than 1 percent of American overseas direct investment.[11]

South Africa's reliance on trade and Western investment has led to demands for economic sanctions. however, despite frequently professed abhorrence of apartheid, the only significant economic sanctions imposed by governments up to 1985 were the United Nations Security Council Resolution 418, prohibiting arms sales to South Africa, and the Organization of Petroleum Exporting Countries (OPEC) oil boycott. Subseqently, events in South Africa have prompted other measures, but these have been largely of a token nature or by countries with only minor interests in South Africa. Britain, for example, has placed a ban on Krugerrand sales.

In considering international economic sanctions there is an important distinction between effectiveness and success. The distinction is based on the difference between the achievement of an economic impact and realizing the objectives of the action. Writers on sactions make the distinction to emphasize that effectiveness does not necessarily give rise to success, as in the case of American sanctions against Cuba.[12] While it is generally assumed that effectiveness is necessary for success, some writers on sanctions question this. Galtung, for instance, observes that the goals in their use may involve punishment and the enforcement of international morality as well as changes in the boycotted country. In other words, sanctions have expressive and instrumental functions. So they may be successful without being effective.[13]

It follows then that measures which appear to be of a token nature can be important in a symbolic way. They lend support to declarations of abhorrence of apartheid. Yet while they may say something to the rest of the world they may not say enough to South Africa, the intended target. However, a range of sanctions are available. Token measures suggest the prospect of further, more substantial measures. But will they follow in South Africa's case?

Four principal arguments are advanced against economic sanctions on South Africa: the costs for those imposing them, that they would harm the blacks of South Africa most, doubts as to their effectiveness, and constructive engagement. Each is examined in turn as follows.

THE COSTS FOR THOSE IMPOSING SANCTIONS

The United Kingdom would incur some of the greatest costs in imposing sanctions. Estimates of these costs vary and, of course, their impact would depend upon whether a total boycott was imposed or selective sanctions. Margaret Thatcher has on many occasions spoken out against sanctions, though in June 1986 there was a perceptible change in attitude as pressure for sanctions mounted, and the possibility of further UK sanctions has been admitted.

Trade and investment involves an interdependence. The size of Britain's investment in South Africa has already been shown to be substantial. British trade with South Africa is also important. in 1985, Britain's visible exports to South Africa were worth £1 billion, 1.28 percent of the total. Invisible earnings from South Africa, from shipping, banking interests, and so on was worth £1.9 billion in 1984. This was 2.3 percent of total British invisible credits.[14]

The costs of this loss of trade have been assessed in terms of increased unemployment. UKSATA suggests a figure as high as 250,000 additional unemployed in Britain with a boycott against South Africa.[15] More recently, while the Prime Minister's officer has been quoting 120,000 and the Foreign and Commonwealth office 50,000, Anti-Apartheid estimates that less than 10,000 UK jobs would be lost as a result of sanctions.[16] Clearly some jobs would go with a total boycott of South Africa. GEC (General Electric Company), for example, has a big contract to supply machinery for three South African power stations. Other companies in the power engineering industry, which accounts for a lot of UK trade with South Africa, would also suffer. However, job loss estimates do not seem very reliable, and one recent source comments: "It is Britain's invisible trades with South Africa—banking, shipping, investment, air travel—not UK jobs, which does seem to be the key issue. Forget the impact of losing £1 billion of power stations and chemical and whisky exports, and look to invisible earnings of £1.9 billion last year, most of which were payments of interest, dividends, and profits from British investments in South Africa."[17]

UKSATA has also expressed a concern about questions of principle affecting the British national interest arising from the use of economic sanctions, as well as the practical effects on the British economy. The trade association suggests Britain's role as a leading trading nation would be threatened, that "Companies are not the instruments of government, they have no role to play in judging issues which only governments can resolve." In other words, "Don't mix businss and politics"—social and political issues are the concern of governments, not business. However, the idea of business and politics as two separate and autonomous areas should be recognized as notably suspect. The role of business (or capital) in South Africa means that it is involved in, and some would argue responsible for, the political situation in South Africa. As one source puts it, referring to both business interests and business's political lobbying to protect those interests: "The claim for the separateness of politics and business is never more frivolous or irrelevant than in its application to apartheid."[18]

UKSATA's arguments about South Africa offering Britain one of the best prospects for trade growth, about the high profits from South African operations, and on South African's relatively "liberal" exchange controls (permitting repatriation of profits and dividends without great restrictions), are all but negligible in South Africa's current situation. They were, however, historically of great importance and explained much of Britain's commitment to the stability of South Africa (and, thereby, the maintenance of apartheid).

Britain's trade with South Africa is important for Britain, or, at least, some sectors of British business. However, so is Britain's trade with black Africa, which is greater. So Denis Healey, as British shadow foreign secretary, in demanding economic sanctions against South Africa, has commented: "the British Government will face a choice between losing its trade with black Africa, which is much greater than its trade with South Africa, and its investments in South Africa. They are likely to become dangerous and unprofitable so long as apartheid remains." More recently, some black African states have threatened sanctions against the United Kingdom if action is not taken against

South Africa.[19] UKSATA points to South African trade with black
Africa, though this seems small given the geographic proximity. Black
Africa has also called for sanctions against South Africa, despite the
considerable costs that would be incurred. These costs would not only
involve probable loss of trade with South Africa but also difficulties
for land-locked countries such as Lesotho and Swaziland, which would
probably be denied their supply routes through South Africa. International economic sanctions involve costs for the target of the action,
but also the various participants. As the costs borne by the paticipants
will vary, some suffering more than others, a further problem is agreeing
and effecting compensation for those bearing greater costs. Increased
aid to Africa may be necessary if major sanctions are imposed.

Disinvestment, voluntarily or otherwise, is regarded by UKSATA
and others as impracticable. Should companies be forced to withdraw,
they would have to sell their assets — always assuming they weren't first
expropriated by the South African government and that capital would
be permitted to be repatriated. This could presumably only be done
at a considerable discount. It may be the likelihood of this that has
prompted companies such as Metal Box, Pilkington, and ABF
(Associated British Foods) to reduce their South African involvement,
to "get out while the going's good," as it were. There has at least been
a trend toward smaller shareholdings in South African operations,
though this may also have something to do with a desire for lower
visibility as much as less risk exposure. Moreover, the South African
government has encouraged reduction in foreign shareholdings to
increase local ownership, financed, however, by Western capital. Indirect
investment via Western banks, by the South African private sector and
increasingly the state or semistate sector, initiated by the government,
has been replacing direct investment via companies. This switch to
indirect forms of investment is as susceptible as the direct forms, if
not more so, as South Africa could simply choose not to repay loans
should sanctions be imposed.

This strategy of the South African government is important because,
as one source explains: "Its indirect nature depoliticizes the European
economic link with apartheid by making it more diffuse and hard to
identify."[20] It is also a major reason for the emphasis on banks and
loans to South Africa by antiapartheid protestors.

Restricted access to strategic raw materials is a further consideration in the use of economic sanctions against South Africa and potentially a great cost for those imposing sanctions. UKSATA suggests access

to raw materials from South Africa is as necessary to the industrial West as accecss to Middle Eastern oil, and "without these raw materials vital sectors of British, West European, American and Japanese industry would be crippled and it follows that world trade would be seriously disrupted if South African raw material were denied to the West as a result of a trade embargo." As the South African Commercial Minister remarked, trade is "a two-way process." And the importance of trading for South African raw materials should not be overlooked. The European Community imports something like 80 percent of its platinum, 91 percent of its chromium ore, 90 percent of its manganese and 36 percent of its vanadium from South Africa. An interruption in supplies would certainly push prices up. However, it has been argued that scarcity would encourage recycling, conservation, and substitution and would not be sufficient to hold the West to ransom.[21]

So, in sum, the costs of imposing economic sanctions for the West, and the United Kingdom in particular, could be considerable. There would also be costs for the black African countries. Loss of trade with its consequences for the domestic economies, loss of substantial investments as well as investment income, and the likely restricted access to key minerals are major disincentives in considering such action. This is aside from the country's perceived political and military significance as a bastion against communism in Africa and protector of the Cape of Good Hope sea route. This economic, political, and strategic interdependence has always made the use of effective international economic sanctions by the West unlikely. However, the costs of sanctions could be borne without substantial hardship, even assuming a total boycott. Depending on how involved the West became, the establishment of majority rule need not automatically mean an end to Western influence in South Africa. Certainly sanctions and the likely subsequence changes in South Africa are less easy to contemplate than maintenance of the statusquo. But can this position of inaction be defended, especially given the current level of violence in the country and the corresponding increase in pressure for sanctions?

To trade with or invest in South Africa is viewed as supporting apartheid. Denial of trade and investment in South Africa is considered the most appropriate way in which the West can seek an end to apartheid. Yet such measures, the opponent of sanctions claim, would harm most those that they are intended to help. The second major argument against sanctions is that they would harm the blacks most. Given that it is claimed that the blacks of South Africa are in favor of sanctions, this argument can be usefully considered alongside the costs for those imposing sanctions.

Sir Anthony Kershaw, as chairman of the House of Commons select committee on foreign affairs has commented in opposition to sanctions: "Cutting South Africa off from the rest of the world would not do anything about apartheid and would harm the blacks." To which the reply, as often expressed, was that the blacks are already suffering "beset with hunger and humiliations, as well as mortal danger from the police," according to Shridath Ramphal, the Commonwealth Secretary General.

Some black leaders have declared themselves opposed to sanctions, such as Lucy Mvubelo, General Secretary of the National Union of Clothing Workers and Vice-President of the Trade Union Council of South Africa, and Chief Mangosuthu Buthelezi, Chief Minister of the Zulu homeland, Kwazulu. Such government-appointed black leaders are often viewed with suspicion, however. The ANC and many black union leaders continue to call for sanctions and the Commonwealth Secretary General reports that the information reaching Commonwealth governments in Africa was that the black South Africans still wanted sanctions. These would, of course, be suffering for both South African blacks and those from neighboring countries that work in South Africa, but then it is said they are already suffering. This assumes that sanctions would be substantial and effective. The third argument against sanctions is that they would not work.

THE EFFECTIVENESS OF SANCTIONS

UKSATA claims there is no evidence that trade sanctions have been successful elsewhere. UKSATA and other opponents of sanctions point in particular to the alleged failure of fanctions against Rhodesia following UDI (Rhodesia'a unilateral declaration of independence). However, the limits to the effectiveness of sanctions against Rhodesia were largely as a result of sanction-busting by South Africa. In the case of sanctions against South Africa, there would be less scope for third party sanction-busting. Moreover, Rhodesia has become Zimbabwe, and sanctions played a part in this. one observer writing prior to the transition commented on sanctions against Rhodesia and others: "If agreements are reached, the more probable causes will not be economic but changed political bases for compromise or the imminence of military, rather than strictly economic, warfare."[22] In South Africa sanctions would be likely to achieve majority rule alongside the efforts of the ANC.

South Africa's response to sanctions would include countervailing measures, such as import substitution, rationing, and the use of gold to pay for boycott-busting. The transnational socialist group Agenor has identified oil as South Africa's jugular vein, as "one of the few commodities where South Africa is really vulnerable." But even an (effective) oil boycott is rejected by Spandau as unlikely to be successful.[23] The bulk of South Africa's energy needs is supplied by coal. Cost supplies are estimated to last at least 130 years and less than one-fifth of South Africa's energy demands are met from oil. The transport sector, however, is 80 percent dependent on oil. But already a substantial proportion of this is provided by the Sasol oil from coal process. Investment in the technology continues and as an additional anticipatory measure, South Africa is stockpiling fuel (in 1978 it had at least 2½ years' supply at current rates of consumption). Spandau calculates that South Africa could withstand an oil boycott for at least 11 years through (25 percent) rationing sanctioning by South Africa of its bunker oil sales. Sasol output, and the use of stockpiled crude. In the longer term, further investment would be made in the Sasol process and possibly nonconventional energy sources, fuel alcohols such as ethanol and methanol (Brazil is already using an ethanol-gasoline mixture for its motor fuel, derived from sugar-cane). South Africa continued to obtain oil despite the OPEC boycott, by buying from Iran prior to the revolution and on the spot market subsequently (but it is estimated that the South African oil bill doubled in 1979).

Gold is an alternative commodity which might be more effectively used with a program of selective sanctions. It accounts for around half of South Africa's export earnings of foreign currency. A halving of the gold price would cut foreign earnings by a quarter and this sanction could not be easily avoided. Stockpiles held by the International Monetary Fund or the United States could be used to achieve this.[24]

The United Nations' arms embargo, although mandatory, has proved ineffective, though as with oil, South Africa incurs considerable extra costs. Despite the boycott, South Africa continues to spend half its arms budget overseas (1983), most notably in Israel, and has now become an arms exporter through the development of its own production facilities.[25] Historically then, there is some support for the criticism of the effectiveness of sanctions. But, the critics ask, if sanctions are so ineffective, why oppose their introduction? Further sanctions would, as earlier noted, be of symbolic importance. They can be successful without being effective and they should not be assessed in isolation from other efforts. Of course, if a role is to be acknowledged for the ANC, this presumes this organization and its aim of majority rule are favored by the West.

The most convincing and prominent argument against sanctions was always the idea of bridge-building and change from within. This is known as constructive engagement.

CONSTRUCTIVE ENGAGEMENT

The fourth and final major argument against sanctions is that "constructive engagement" is more likely to be successful. This term has been attributed to Chester Crocker, the U.S. Assistant Secretary of State for Africa, and has only come into use quite recently. However, it describes a long-standing approach to the South African problem: the idea of reform from within and the "change through prosperity" argument; the more business we do the more effectivly we undermine apartheid. In foreign policy it is exemplified by the efforts (and failure) of the United States and the rest of the Contact Group (Britain, France, West Germany, and Canada) to gently persuade rather than coerce South Africa to give up its illegal occupation of Namibia. It is the principal justification given for involvement with South Africa not only at a diplomatic or political level, but also in terms of trade. So Chester Crocker has earlier said: "The point is that among all the objectionable features of apartheid, there may be some that would logically go first if an open-ended process of change is to take root. The true friends of South Africa may be those who are prepared to talk now about short-term and intermediate goals consistent with the ultimate goal of a nonracial society. Our role is to support and applaud progress that does occur while maintaining pressure for continued movement."

Accordingly, business interests describe their involvement in South Africa as a positive force for change. UKSATA observes: "There is no evidence to suggest that either disinvestment, or a trade embargo, would help black South Africans. On the contrary, moderate black leaders want more, not less, foreign investment, in order to achieve the economic and political benefits they and their people desire." They then suggest "British companies are a force for good."

Firms involved in South Africa will almost without exception defend their position on the basis of the constructive engagement argument. Sir Anthony Tuke, as chairman of RTZ (and former Barclays chairman), has commented: "The question both we as investors and the people who will be affected by a new operation must ask is, whether the benefits of a major investment outweigh the disadvantages change may bring. We do believe that the advantages overwhelmingly outweigh the disadvantages as we see the rising standards of living in the areas where we operate. These are evidenced by the high quality of housing, education, health." No doubt, until most recently, the White House preference for constructive engagement lent support to such a position. It is one that companies have consistently advanced. Nearly fifteen years ago First et al. wrote on business involvement in South Africa:

In their reply to the suggestion that this involvement puts a special onus on British firms to help to end apartheid, businessmen generally give one of two answers: the first is that business and politics (like sport and politics) should not be mixed, and the second that apartheid may be objectionable, but that business is "doing its bit behind the scenes" to change it; the alternative to this reform-by-participation would, after all, be to try to bring down South Africa's regime and consequently her economy. So let us opt for reform through business rather than for revolution.[26]

However, they could find little evidence to support the claim that industrialization was breaking down apartheid. More recently, but perhaps with more cause to do so, Spandau found there was evidence to suggest business involvement was improving the position of blacks, if not eroding apartheid. He identifies a closing of the gap between black and white wages and has high hopes for the small but growing black middle class.[27] Similarly, another South African report, by the Centre for Business Studies, writing after the Wiehann and Riekert commissions had advocated union recognition and other labor law changes which were accepted by the government, found further evidence of change for the better.[28] And, indeed, it must be acknowledged that black union recognition is probably the most substantial change of the Botha government to date.[29]

An important feature of the constructive engagement argument is the role of codes of conduct for companies operating in South Africa. UKSATA, for example, in response to the criticism that British companies in South Africa exploit cheap labor with low wages and poor working conditions for blacks, replied: "Of the many Blacks employed by British subsidiaries, 99% are paid above the lower rates set by the European Code of Conduct, and 92% are paid more than the higher rate set by that code."

THE EEC CODE OF CONDUCT

The European Economic Community's Code of Conduct replaced the UK Code of Practice established by the Government in 1974, and was adopted by the governments of the EEC in 1977. The code is voluntary, but as the white paper observes, "It is in the interests of companies themselves that they should maintain the best employment practices in South Africa and be seen to do so."[30]

1. Relations within the undertaking, particularly the recognition and encouragement of trade unions
2. Migrant labor—described as "an instrument of the policy of apartheid—the effects of which employers "should make it their concern to alleviate"
3. Pay, which should exceed the minimum effective level (MEL)
4. Wage structure and black advancement, particularly equal pay for equal work and training programs for blacks
5. Fringe benefits; the improvement of employees living conditions, education, and so on
6. Desegregation at work and equal working conditions
7. Reporting companies should report annually on these provision to their national governments, which should review progress made

Reporting requirements of companies vary according to the amount of equity held by a British company and the number of black employees. The code principally refers to those with more than 50 percent of the equity of a South African company and employing twenty or more black Africans. The 1984 analysis of companies' reports for 1982–1983 is based on 142 reports from companies meeting these specifications, known as Category A. Twelve companies had not submitted reports and were expected to. These companies are listed and include John Brown, Gallaher, and Trusthouse Forte. (It is noted however that some of these companies have stated it is not their policy to submit a report and inclusion in this list does not necessarily mean failure to comply with the standards suggested in the code.) Moreover, just as reporting is voluntary, so is compliance with the code's provisions for those that do choose to report. Current government policy is not to identify firms reporting but failing to conform with the code's provisions. However, as the Secretary of State for Trade and Industry reported in a written reply in the House "the vast majority of British companies already comply, and endeavour to meet the guidelines." Paul Channon then expressed satisfaction with the operation of the code.[31]

Others are less happy with the operation of the code. While some of its provisions are seemingly quite far-reaching, they do not provide for ready implementation because they are too general and, of course, they are entirely voluntary. In other words, the code lacks teeth. Quinton Hazell, for example, reports to the Department of Trade and Industry, but in its submission in 1984 justified its failure to comply with the code by remarking that it is "a labour intensive company operating in a highly competitive market." While Pritchard Services Group, in its 1985 submission, reveals that nearly 80 percent of its 1,926 black employees were paid below the poverty line. Pay, of course, is effectively the only pass or fail criterion in the code. The penalty for failure to comply or report, because the code is not mandatory, is criticism in the press.

The EEC code is largely concerned with employment practices. Most major American firms in South Africa are signatories of the Sullivan code, which is a little wider in scope and has been expanded to include the provision that companies should lobby vigorously within South Africa against apartheid. Both codes have, until most recently, been useful in protecting firms from criticism at home. However, although they have raised black living standards, they have not really challenged apartheid.

A PRICE TO BE PAID?

Critics of constructive engagement see little evidence of it working, and particularly with the recent unrest, it has come to be seen as tactic support for apartheid. With the South African authorities unable to suppress challenges from the black majority within South Africa, the constructive engagement argument loses its credibility. The continued violence in South Africa demonstrates, in a dramatic and forceful way, the failure of constructive engagement to achieve any real change.

Corporate involvement in South Africa is defended by following the government's line. As this has become untenable, and with domestic pressure from shareholders and consumers boycotts and other actions increasing, companies have started withdrawing from South Africa. American companies have been more active in this respect, particularly those companies with only a limited involvement.[32] For many British companies withdrawal is less easy. There is, for example, evidence of a phased withdrawal by the parents of two of the biggest banks in South

Africa, Barclays and Standard Chartered. However, a complete and immediate withdrawal, while apparently still possible, would be at a substantial loss.[33]

As the violence continues and the corresponding pressure for sanctions increases, it seems ever more likely that this is a price that must be paid by those Western businesses still operating in South Africa. If they choose to stay, or no longer have any choice in the matter, they must accept that their assets could be lost under a government established by the ANC. As yet, the ANC has given little indication of likely support for capitalism in its meetings with representatives of South African business. South Africa under socialism may find it needs Western business as much as white South Africa needs it now. But given the role of business in apartheid to date, it is not unlikely that a majority rule South Africa would wish to exact a considerable price in return for renewed Western corporate involvement there.

1. It has been reported that 754 people were killed in the first five months of 1986, compared with a total of 879 for 1985. See the report by the South African Institute of Race Relations, referred to by David Beresford and Patrick Laurence in "Soweto Day violence cost 11 lives," *The Guardian*, June 18, 1986.
2. Evidenced in the pro-sanctions stance of much of the national press and an opinion poll by the Harris Research Centre which found 51 percent in favor and 39 percent against. See Peter Kellner, "South Africa: more want sanctions," *The Observer*, June 15, 1986.
3. Zambia, for example, as reported in Robert Chesshyre, "Anti-apartheid—anti-sanctions," *The Observer*, June 8, 1986
4. Interview conducted February 1984. Other major sources include Foreign and Commonwealth Office, *The South African Homelands* (London: HMSO, 1978); Ronald Segal, (ed.), *Sanctions against South Africa* (Harmondsworth, England: Penguin, 1964); South African Department of Foreign Affairs and Information, *South Africa 1983: Official Yearbook of the Republic of South Africa* (Johannesburg: Chris van Rensburg Publications, 1983); Jan Marais, *The New South Africa: A Unique Opportunity!* (Cape Town: Maskew Miller, 1982); and of the many press articles too numerous to mention, the following were particularly useful: Michael Hornsby, "South Africa's bad neighbour policy," *The Times*, December 13, 1982; Dan van der Vat, "Mr. Botha's key to the final stage of apartheid," *The Guardian*, November 23, 1982; Eric Marsden, "Yes or no, a bleak future looms after South Africa's referendum," *The Sunday Times*, October 30, 1983; Basil Davidson, "Two-way bet on progress," *The Guardian*, December 16, 1983; Dan Jacobson, "Workers of the world apart," *The Guardian*, January 28, 1984; Frank Giles, "The moving staircase," *The Sunday Times*, May 27, 1984; a series of articles in *The Guardian*, December 10–15 1984 by Terry Coleman, including interviews with representatives of the major white South African political parties; and Allister Sparks, "Kennedy to lead crusade in US over apartheid," *The Observer*, January 13, 1985
5. Arnt, Spandau, *Economic Boycott against South African: Normative and Factual Issues* (Kenwyn: Juta, 1979).
6. South Africa Department of Foreign Affairs and Information, *South Africa 1983*.

7. "The pressure for sanctions becomes inescapable," *The Guardian*, June 13, 1986.
8. Victoria Brittain, "Investments by Britain 'Props Up Apartheid'," *The Guardian*, January 7, 1985.
9. United Kingdom South Africa Trade Association, *British Trade with South Africa: A Question of National Interest* (London: UKSATA, 1982).
10. See, for instance, Martin Bailey, "Smaller price to pay for curbs," *The Observer*, June 15, 1986.
11. Jonathan Kapstein, John Hoerr, and Elizabeth Weiner, "Leaving South Africa," *Business Week* (international edition), September 23, 1985.
12. See, for example, Donald L. Losman, "The effects of economic boycotts," *Lloyds Bank Review*, no. 106 (October 1972).
13. Johan Galtung, "On the effects of international economic sanctions: with examples from the case of Rhodesia," *World Politics 19*, no. 3 (1967).
14. Christopher Huhne, "Hurting them may not hurt us," *The Guardian*, June 24, 1986.
15. UKSATA, *British Trade with South Africa*.
16. Andrew Cornelius, "Numbers that don't add up," *The Guardian*, June 26, 1986.
17. Ibid.
18. Ruth First, Jonathan Steele, and Chrisabel Gurney, *The South African Connection: Western Investment in Apartheid* (London: Temple Smith, 1972).
19. Hella Pick, "African threat to impose sanctions against Britain," *The Guardian*, June 26, 1986.
20. Agenor, *EEC Life-Blood of Apartheid* (Brussels: Agenor, 1980).
21. Huhne, "Hurting them may not hurt us."
22. Losman, "The effects of economic boycotts."
23. Spandau, *Economic Boycott against South Africa*.
24. Huhne, "Hurting them may not hurt us," Dan van der Vat and Christopher Huhne, "The West's solid gold opportunity," *The Guardian*, June 25, 1986.
25. David Leigh, Paul Lashman, and Martin Bailey, "South Africa's secret lifeline," *The Observer*, June 3, 1984.
26. First, Steele, and Gurney, *South African Conection*.
27. Spandau, *Economic Boycott against South Africa*.
28. Centre for Business Studies, *A Case against Disinvolvement in the South African Economy* (Johannesburg: University of Witwaterstand, 1980).
29. Less partisan sources, such as Robin Smith of Durham University Business School, also applaud union recognition. He suggested in a paper presented to a conference at York University in March 1984 that incorporation and a more peaceful solution to South Africa's problems was more likely than revolution. See Robin Smith, "South African Black Unions: Revolution or Incorporation?" (unpublished paper available from the author).
30. Her Majesty's Government, *Code of Conduct for Companies with Interests in South Africa*, Command 7233 (London: HMSO, 1978).
31. *Hansard*, January 25, 1984.
32. Kapstein, Hoerr, and Weiner, "Leaving South Africa."
33. Peter Rodgers, "Scoring an own goal is the risk in Standard v. Lloyds," *The Guardian*, June 24, 1986.

Part VII

THE ROLE OF THE SOUTH AFRICAN BUSINESS COMMUNITY

CHAPTER 32

The South African Private Sector: Agent for Change or Government Stooge?

by A.M. ROSHOLT

In the continuous discourse about South Africa, the significant role played by the business sector as a positive force in breaking down apartheid's barriers has been overshadowed by the weight of diatribe and political rhetoric waged against the country itself.

What are the facts? Is South African business guilty of exploitation and complicity with the government in perpetuating the economic subjugation of the country's 20 million black people? Or has it been an effective agent for change? And if so, does it have a continuing role to play?

In putting forward the view that the private sector has been a considerable force in the socioeconomic reform process of recent years, I shall examine the performance of my own group, Barlow Rand, an employer of 234,000 people (79 percent of them non-Caucasian) the multifaceted operations of which in mining, industry, and commerce, reflect the South African economy in microcosm. But in doing so I would emphasize that it is only one company among many others that can claim to have evolved and implemented programs to eradicate discrimination in the workplace and to enhance the quality of life of its disadvantaged employees.

CODE OF EMPLOYMENT PRACTICE

As far back as 1960 the late chairman, Punch Barlow, was advocating higher wages for people of color as "one of the most important contributions that commerce and industry can make toward better race relations." And over the years he continued to enunciate his views on their education, training, welfare, and general advancement.

Flowing from those statements and the appearance in South Africa in 1977 of two important codes of employment practice of overseas origin — as group's chief executive officer, I decided that Barlow Rand should consolidate the most important of the group's personnel policies and philosophies into a code tailored to the group's own circumstances and designed to meet the rapidly changing socioeconomic circumstnaces that were clearly coming.

Published in 1978 as the first indigenous code, it was subsequently revised four times to reflect the changing employment and industrial relations scene. Its underlying strength and value lies in the fact that it is a working document and is not merely a pious statement of intent: and that its principles and objectives are challenging, but at the same time achievable. In essence, it serves as a guideline for operating company managers while at the same time fulfilling the additional purpose of making the group's employment practices known to employees, shareholders, trading partners, bankers, and other interested stakeholders. Of interest to U.S. readers may be the fact that the code has been discussed at various stages with the Reverend Leon Sullivan and that satisfctory comparisons have been made between the two codes.

The code starts with certain basic commitments, and a general pledge to work for changes in any laws or attitudes that involve discrimination or which prevent the achievement of the code's goals. It goes on to state policies and to set objectives in selection and promotion, training and manpower development, communication, negotiating rights, remuneration, retirement benefits, security of employment, integration of facilities, and the quality of life of employees. The underlying principles are equality of service conditions, of opportunities, and of rewards for all employees irrespective of race or gender.

Perhaps one key to any success Barlow Rand has enjoyed in the turbulent industrial relations field lies in the monitoring process. In the course of annual presentations to myself and other members of our board, the CEO of each division is expected to review not only achievements, but also problem areas. This calls for an honest comparison of current practices with the commitments of the code, for the identification of gaps that may exist and finally for programs and timetables to eliminate those gaps.

I would not however for a moment claim that we have achieved complete success in all of our diversified activities. Labor practices in some industries lag far behind those in others; prejudices in some industries are difficult to eradicate; some managements are not nearly as forward looking as others. But there is no doubt that the introduction and implementation of our code has had and will continue to have significant effects both on black advancement and white attitudes. Indeed I go so far as to say that it has been the single most important contributory factor in attitudinal changes within the group and in ensuring all managers are aware of group values.

WAGE GAP

In the early stages wage gaps, identified by means of extensive job evaluation exercises, were perceived to be a crucial problem. Their extent and the cost of closing them was determined and as a consequence significantly large sums of money were allocated, and continue to be allocated, to meet the goal of nondiscriminatory renumeration. It is incidentally said to have to relate that the fixing of unrealistic minimum wages has proved to be a mixed blessing in South Africa. Supported in good times for humanitarian reasons, it has led to retrenchments in the current severe recession, particularly in those companies situated in areas of rural proverty where creation of employment and generation of any cash income in practical terms outweight commitments to an urban living wage.

TRADE UNIONS

Another feature of the code is its insistence on freedom of association, which in the early years before black trade unions could be registered, evoked adverse reactions from sections of both the public and private sectors. Black trade unions were eventually legalized in 1979 and are now accepted by most companies as having an essential if sometimes uncomfortable role in our industrial relations scene. In Barlow Rand's case, by the end of 1985 more than 120 recognition agreements formalizing relationships between group companies and unions had been concluded, and a further 72 were in the process of being negotiated.

TRAINING

A major challenge confronting all South African managements is how to deal with our unique demographic mix, a largely black Third World community living and working side by side with a substantial and growing multiracial First World society. The plethora of differeing values, cultures, languages, and behavioral norms create enormous difficulties in communication, and these problems are compounded by the complete inadequacy of black education to meet modern industrial conditions. As a result most employees enter industry ill equipped to perform unskilled let alone semiskilled or skilled jobs. In an attempt to remedy the situation and in line with similar efforts by many other companies, Barlows has invested considerable sums for many years. The 1985 figure for direct costs, that is excluding wages of trainees and overheads, was R37.8 million and no fewer than 163,000 employees, representing 70 percent of our total workforce, participated in various training courses. Of the apprentices 25 percent were non-Caucasian.

In addition as far back as 1976 Barlow Rand companies began to provide literacy and numeracy education and by 1982 the group had established sixty-five centers at its mines and industrial facilities to address this shortcoming. Employees who took these courses were better able to undergo conventional training aimed at improving their work performance and fitting them for increased responsibilities.

EDUCATION

In South Africa, education at all levels is a State responsibility, although there have always been a number of privately funded schools. Nevertheless, because of serious inadequacies in the educational system, particularly black, the private sector has found itself called upon increasingly to devote resources to education. Our group has been active internally and externally. Internally, thirty-nine preprimary and primary schools mainly for the children of black employees have been established on group properties. These are heavily subsidized to ensure that teachers, teaching aids, and the facilities are of comparable standards to those enjoyed by other ethnic groups.

Externally, we have contributed a technical trades school to the Lebowa government and a technical high school to the Ciskei government. We have provided the equipment and funded a computer-aid arithmetic teaching project in Soweto and a science teaching project in Kwazulu.

The group also has a bursary scheme aimed principally at tertiary education, university, and technikon. In the first six months of the 1986 financial year 707 bursaries have been awarded (of which 178 were to blacks) at a cost of R1.4 million.

BLACK ADVANCEMENT

The group is completely committed to the advancement of blacks into senior positions and eventually into management, but in common with most other companies has found great difficulty in achieving the success rate it would have liked. This is partly due to the educational deficiencies already referred to, partly to the very real cultural problems encountered in entering industry in general and management in particular, and partly, but to a diminishing extent, to white prejudice. However, a group task committee that spent six months analyzing our performance and pinpointing obstacles found that the single greatest barrier was the apartheid system. Nevertheless, it found that our record of promoting blacks into responsible jobs that brought them considerably better standards of living was very good. It found too that in the last eighteen months white attitudes on the acceptance of black managers had changed for the better considerably. It was in the area of management appointments that it found that more and new initiatives were necessary.

SMALL BLACK BUSINESS

The group recognizes that much of the current unrest has economic roots and in particular that unemployment is a critical factor. At the same time it is concerned, as are many major companies, that the capitalist and free enterprise system is looked upon with such considerable skepticism by the great majority of our black population basically because they have never enjoyed its fruits. This has led us to recognize the fact that one of the most effective ways of alleviating both problems lies in the promotion and development of black small businesses. Barlow Rand was a founder member of the Small Business Development Corporation, a joint public/private sector concern aimed at promoting small business, particlarly black. In addition, a number of years ago in conjunction with Norton Company it formed a nonprofit organization, Small Business Advisory Services, to provide advice to black businessmen on how to run and finance their enterprises. It is very encouraging to be able to report that these businessmen have in turn created more than 50,000 new jobs in the past twelve years.

Recently the group together with National African Chambers of Commerce and Industry (NAFCOC), which represents organized black business, has established Job Creation (S.A.). Its objectives are similar to those of Small Business Advisory Services, but it differs in that it seeks to promote and set up small black business concerns which in turn will provide more jobs for blacks. The group has committed R2.5 million to this company with the objective of directly creating 500 jobs over the next three years.

THE REFORM PROCESS

I have dealt so far with the group's direct efforts in the elimination of discrimination and in the improvement of the quality of life of our black population, particularly those employed by the group. But in addition it has played an indirect role in that it has consistently encouraged government to undertake and expedite the reform process and to complete the elimination of apartheid measures. It has done so in public statements and in private discussions with the South Africa's president, individual cabinet ministers, and senior civil servants. It has done so too in its strong support of the Urban Foundation, a body entirely funded by the private sector, which has had considerable success in promoting the reform process.

We are very well aware that the stage has now been reached in South Africa where although socioeconomic reforms must and will continue, political issues are preeminent. And that business which has not up to now entered into political debate to any marked extent must do so. In common with other business leaders we are accordingly committed to a process of encouraging government to start the inevitable negotiations with all credible black leaders on the crucial and unavoidable subject of power-sharing.

CONCLUSION

I hope that I have made a sufficiently credible case to support my strong contention that South African business has been, and will continue to be, an effective agent for change in our country. Barlow Rand has been with the leaders in urging reform and change and in implementing it wherever it has been in a position to do so. Its top management has also been instrumental in pressuring for changes in attitudes within the group with the objective of creating an environment in which steady and continuous change will take place and will be accepted by all employees. This was, I believe, acknowledged in 1980 when the group was awarded the prestigious *Rand Daily Mail* "Business Achievement Award," the citation recording "its diverse and outstanding contribution to the South African economy" and paying particular tribute "to the courageous and far sighted lead Barlows has taken in human and industrial relations."

CHAPTER 33

Business Offers a Bill of Rights for South Africa

by J.C. VAN ZYL

Early in January, 1986 the South African Federated Chamber of Industries reached an important milestone. With full support of its wide membership it adopted a business charter of social, economic, and political rights—in short, a fully fledged bill of rights. In so doing, it threw out a serious challenge to all South Africans regardless of race, color or creed to build their political future around firm adherence to basic human rights and universal democratic values.

The spirit and content of the business charter is well illustrated by its first article which states unequivocally in time-honored tradition that "all human beings are born free and equal in dignity and rights." In fact, the twenty-five articles contained in the charter are based on and openly employ the traditional rhetoric of the best-known bills of rights in the Western world from the Magna Carta to the U.N. International Declaration of Economic, Social and Political Rights and the European Convention of Human Rights. Acceptance and support of this extensive declaration of human rights thus links the South African business community firmly and directly to the great traditions of Western democracy.

An obvious question that arises is how deep business support for these ideals really goes, not to mention the support of all South Africans. And more pertinently, are the goals of the business charter achievable?

It would be naive to assume that the charter by itself will activate the government to implement an urgent program of fundamental reform or to convince blacks and critics abroad that business has a positive role to play in transforming South African society. Clearly, the charter is but a first step in a process. Nevertheless, we believe that it is an important step and an essential one.

A significant factor that emerged from the FCI initiative to seek support for a human rights charter from its membership was the high degree of acceptance and commitment obtained. The FCI is a federal body with a membership of some 10,000 companies drawn from chambers representing all major regions and subsectors of industry in South Africa. Membership is voluntary and consists mainly of industrialists, large and small, regardless of race, color, sex, or creed.

To test grassroots support, the FCI executive council last year referred the business charter back to its many constituent organizations for comment, acceptance, or rejection. This process took some time, but the end result was particularly gratifying—full support from all member bodies all over the country. In fact, the FCI was urged to pay careful attention to effective marketing, especially in the South African government.

Most sister organizations also responded enthusiastically. Dr. Sam Motsuenyane, president of NAFCOC, the black business federation, issued a statement in which he "congratulates the FCI for having come forward with a bold and clear statement of goals and policies toward which the country should be directed in the future. The FCI has now with its courageous statement conclusively dispelled any doubt as to where the future of industry in Southern Africa lies."

The American Chamber of Commerce (AMCHAM) undertook "to ask our entire membership to endorse and support this business charter and to give it our full support" and urged "all business undertakings of whatever affiliation to give their firm commitment to these initiatives by the South African business community."

Although by no means conclusive, this degree of support says something about the extent to which the basic tenets of an extensive bill of rights are already part of the proverbial hearts and minds of many South Africans. Editorial comment in South African newspapers was extensive and also generally positive. Of particular interest, perhaps, was a remark made by the editor of the *Sowetan*, which has the largest black readership in the country: "The value of the document is in its saying the things that, if said by us or others to the left of center, could be perceived as an attempt to subvert the government. What the world of business is saying in a cold, analytical fashion is that they would be unable to operate and deliver if certain basic political tenets are not respected."

Business was further encouraged to note that the principles outlined in the charter apparently had a noticeable effect on the formulation of the State President's address in opening Parliament in January. Nailing the basic tenet of liberty to the walls of the highest institution in the land in the clearest of language, as he did, was an important breakthrough for which the FCI may well claim some credit.

WHAT ROLE FOR BUSINESS?

Business is well aware that overt and concerted involvement by any business community in the national politics of a country, even its own, is a high risk and by international standards a very unusual role to play. Nevertheless, the business sector has a very real interest in the environment within which it operates and a deep commitment to the future of South Africa. Hence, the recent FCI initiatives were very much motivated by the seriousness of the country's political and economic situation and the need to bypass the current stalemate by offering a new rallying point for genuine negotiation.

In strategic terms, business has been developing a two-tier approach to its political role: It has both a basic stance to proclaim and a transformation process itself.

The stance of the business community in terms of fundamental values and goals has now been clearly enunciated in the business charter: It stands for basic human rights, a democratic government, freedom of choice, and a market economy with minimum bureaucratic intervention. In more specific terms, organized industry and commerce representing the great majority of business interests, white and black as well as English- and Afrikaans-speaking, have stated clearly and publicly the reform objectives it regards as essential and urgent for South Africa. These are:

- The removal of statutory racial discrimination from all the affairs of state.
- Negotiation of a dispensation of genuine political power sharing by all South Africans right up to the highest level on the basis of an open-ended agenda and participation by all accepted leaders.
- Effective implementation of the maximum devolution of power to local levels of government with full participation by all local constituents.

- Full and equal citizenship for all South Africans.
- The further development of a strong, free, and independent trade union movement.
- Equality of opportunity in the provision of education to all population groups as a matter of national priority.

Significantly, the South African government has already committed itself publicly to most of these objectives. In turn, business has pledged its full support and practical assistance in effecting rapid implementation. In these crucial areas, discussions with the relevant government departments are being actively pursued.

Interaction with the process of change itself and the ways and means of doing so are set out in an "action program" which accompanies the publication of the business charter. This program indicates that business has been and will continue to act positively and urgently to facilitate negotiation between the government and legitimate black leadership. Against the background of its industrial relations experience, business is playing an intermediating, catalytic role aimed at confidence building and bringing the various parties closer together so as to establish a climate for real negotiations.

A feature of the current political scene is that real dilemmas seem to abound everywhere. Many of these, however, are interrelated and ultimately converge in the great dilemma of visible negotiation. From the government side, major public commitments have been made in terms of political power sharing through negotiation, a politically unified South Africa, full citizenship for all South Africans, and universal suffrage.

Yet, on the urban black side there has been great reluctance to enter into formal negotiations. The reasons for this attitude are complex but include fundamentally the fact that the credibility of black leaders depends on their not accepting the apartheid framework. This means, in turn, that before joining serious negotiations, they have to be assured that the political framework of the country itself will be the true subject of negotiation and not merely the means of making the system of apartheid more acceptable to blacks.

Thus, near stalemate currently prevails against a background of increasing polarization and hardening of political attitudes. Under these strained circumstances, it is very doubtful whether the government as a major negotiating partner itself can generate the necessary breakthroughs to establish a credible process of peaceful negotiation among all the major interests on the South African political scene. Government must be willing to accept assistance, perhaps especially from the business community, which will not be a party at negotiating tables, to get informal and private discussions going with the whole spectrum of important political leaders in South Africa. Business is actively engaged in this vital activity.

At present, a particularly promising area of promoting the negotiation process are the regional and local levels. Resolving the serious problems currently being experienced in black local government features prominently on the priority lists of many black community leaders. Hence, there is a willingness to enter into talks with regional chambers of industry and commerce supported by their national organizations.

Business is involved in a number of such initiatives:

• The Eastern Cape has been hard hit by unrest and upheaval. Discussions with the UDF leadership in the region about alternative structures of local government in Port Elizabeth were well under way when prominent figures Mkhuseli Jack and Henry Fazzie were served with banning orders restricting their freedom of movement. Subsequent meetings with government by the FCI, ASSOCOM, and their respective regional chambers contributed to the rapid unbanning of these individuals. At present, talks are starting up once again.

• In Natal/Kwazulu, local business interests have actively promoted and supported a wide-ranging *indaba* (a Zulu word meaning an important tribal conference) among all population groups and political organizations inside and outside the area to thrash out proposals for the constitutional future of that region. This time around, unlike the case of the 1980-1981 Buthelezi Commission, the South African government is sending an important delegation to attend as observers. This should facilitate the subsequent phase of negotiating with the government whatever consensus is achieved at the *indaba*. Business stands ready to intermediate whenever needed.

• Discussions with prominent leaders from all groupings in the Western Cape are under way to explore the possibilities of a political *indaba* for that important region of the country.

INFLUENCING NATIONAL POLICY

On many important economic and sociopolitical policy issues, organized business is increasingly speaking to government with a coordinated voice rather than individually as in the past. A pertinent example of such project-orientated cooperation is the formation of the Private Sector Urbanization Council. This body is representative of all the major business organizations in industry, commerce, mining, and agriculture and also includes key individuals of all races in these spheres of activity. The council has made its views known to government in no uncertain terms on important apartheid issues such as influx control, the pass laws, forced removals of people, freehold title for all South Africans, an effective low-income housing delivery system, black township upgrading, and the like. In addition, cooperative business initiatives are being actively pursued regarding major policy issues such as education, privatization and deregulation, general economic policy, and alternative political structures.

It cannot, however, be enough to urge government to act. The concern of business must also find expression in active policies at the company level, in contact with organized labor, and in supporting appropriate socioeconomic reforms. Many reactions to the recent FCI initiatives, especially from blacks, indicated support for the spirit and the goals of the business charter but particular concern about their implementation. This is fair comment.

Aware of the importance of producing concrete results, the FCI has been actively pursuing a program of translating the broad principles contained in the charter into practical and operational guidelines for implementation at the company level. This is a large task, but we have been assisted in the process by numerous requests and advice from individual member companies and business consultants. It is clear that the principles embodied in the charter provide an important basis for dialogue between management and labor on which black advancement within companies and sound industrial relations generally should be based. Detailed plans have not been completed but are well under way. We hope to initiate workshops, conferences, and seminars involving various groupings of businessmen all over the country within a short period of time.

These days, business leaders are often asked, despite their best efforts, "Is it not too late?" Presumably this means either too late to avert large-scale revolution or too late for power sharing. However, regardless of what is meant, business tends to react to this line of questioning by arguing that the really important issue lies elsewhere. Are there, in fact, enough South Africans of vision, courage, and initiative to avert the Armageddon scenarios envisaged by those asking such questions? From our own experience we would reply in the affirmative.

Despite the controversy and the public rhetoric, the basic message from South Africa is clear-cut and positive. Fundamental political realities dictate that there is no other alternative for the many diverse interests involved but to negotiate about the constitutional future of their country. Whether the various political groupings may actually wish to share power is ultimately irrelevant. They simply will have to. This basic truth applies as inevitably to black politics on the left as to the South African government on the right, as well as to white extremists on the far right.

Unquestionably, the road to political negotiation, which lies ahead, will be bumpy and difficult. But the outcome is certain. Too many powerful internal processes and developments are moving irreversibly toward fundamental shifts in the contours of power and a new nonapartheid society. International interests would do well to join the South African business community in actively supporting these internal forces to ensure that the process of transition to a shared democracy is as nonviolent and nontraumatic as possible.

CHAPTER 34

Corporations: Catalyst for Change

by SAL G. MARZULLO

The growing escalation of violence and the increasing racial divisiveness taking place in South Africa forces us to address this issue in a most urgent and compelling manner. People of goodwill understand that there are many legitimate strategies for dealing with this issue, but I think one may honestly question the basic thrust of the debate on South Africa as it presently exists in the United States. The fact that this is a highly emotional and complex issue demands more from each of us than the passion that racial oppression and injustice rightly evoke. One cannot argue with passion. Apartheid is an evil and oppressive system that must disappear from South Africa and ultimately *will* disappear from that country. All our energies should be directed toward meeting that objective. The debate and strategy all Americans should be focusing upon now is how best to create those coalitions that will bring structural change and economic equality about quickly, peacefully, and democratically. Violent revolution will only make the chances for the emergence of a nonracial, democratic, just society less likely and economic sanctions could prove to be not only counterproductive but highly dangerous as well in searching for ways to diffuse black rage and white fear and move toward racial accomodation and reconicilia- tion.

Business corporations' philosophy for remaining in South Africa is both a moral and pragmatic one. Corporate presence is better than corporate absence. Such presence allows companies to shape and be participants in those dynamic forces present in the South African en- vironment that can lead to the erosion and final elimination of apar- theid. It is very much in order at this point therefore to stress what companies can and cannot do, since they are accused by some of endorsing actions that are only "comsmetic" and by others of trying to undermine the sovereignty of the South African state. U.S. companies have never claimed to be able to do more than they could deliver. The Sullivan Principles by themselvs were not meant to be a guaranteed and sure method of providing quick and simple solutions to the grave and fundamental injustices that exist in South African society. Companies have been and can continue to be an effective catalyst for change by working with and supporting local institutions in that society that are having an impact on initiating and accelerating the process of change. These groups have, in their own way, begun to perceptibly change attitudes among many white South Africans who understand that fundamental structural reform and absolute equality for South Africans of all races is essential to the long-term survival of that country. What, then, has been done? Since 1977 through June 1985, U.S. subscribing to the Sullivan Principles spent more than $158 million in the areas of health, education, community business development, training, housing, and black entrepreneurship in South Africa. Firms cannot bring about genuine change alone, however, so they also support institutions like the American Friends of Community Development – PACE, the Cape of Good Hope Foundation, Friends of SOS Children's Village, Get Ahead, Institute of International Education, Institute of Natural Resources, Lawyers' Committee for Civil Rights under Law, Medical Education for South African Blacks (MESAB), St. Barnabas, Southern Africa Legal Services and Legal Education Project U.S. Committee for the Friends of Baragwanath, United States South African Leadership Exchange Program, United States Zululand Education Foundation, University of Cape Town Fund, the Urban Foundation, and many others that can work more efficiently than they can in particular areas in securing justice for all of South Africa's racial groups. This support will continue. But beyond the traditional support areas companies have now moved to new challenges. American companies, both in the United States and in South Africa, have unequivocally urged the South African government to take action in the following areas. These movements forward are an expansion of the Sullivan Company Fourth Amplification originally announced by the Reverend Leon H. Sullivan in Washington, D.C. on November 8, 1984. Companies are calling for

• Elimination of Influx Control and the Group Areas Act of South Africa

- Establishment of an equal national educational system
- End of apartheid in the workplace, including the elimination of the pass laws and the last job reservation remaining in the mining industry
- Establishment of freehold rights for all South Africans regardless of race
- Establishment of a unified health delivery system available to all races
- Elimination of residential segregation and forced removals and the promotion of black land ownership in all areas of South Africa
- Maintenance of the existing independence and integrity of the South African judicial system
- Development of the leadership abilities of all black South Africans so they can work for the elimination of apartheid and be prepared to assume their rightful role in the running of that society

The transition from company involvement with the local workplace and community to regional and national issues lasted from 1982 to 1984, when the presence of U.S. companies in South Africa became an increasingly emotional and partisan political issue in the United States. Three separate developments, both in the United States and South Africa, helped to publicize and polarize this complex issue: First was the awarding of the Nobel Peace Prize to Bishop Desmond Tutu, a powerful religious and moral voice of South Africa's oppressed people, who warned of the dangers of mass violence if blacks were not given the rights of free men in the country of their birth.

Second, anger was growing among South Africa's black population at being excluded from the 1984 constitutional dispensation that opened political participation to the country's "coloured" and Asian populations. The exclusion of black South Africans from any political process whatever led to a growing demand for sanctions against South Africa.

The third development leading to increased domestic pressure on the South African issues was the 1984 U.S. presidential campaign. The involvement of American politicians in South African issues was raised to its highest level by the Reverend Jesse Jackson's campaign for the presidential nomination. The creation of a Free South Africa Movement (FSAM) helped provide a way for American politicians to exert political clout on an issue (the removal of apartheid) about which most Americans agree. South Africa and change in South Africa became a full-blown domestic political issue.

American companies in 1985-1986 responding to those pressures became far more public and vocal in their advocacy of change. For example, American companies in South Africa in September of 1985 in newspaper advertisements printed in both South Africa and the United States unequivocally called for

- The abolition of statutory race discrimination wherever it exists
- Negotiation with acknowledged black leaders about power-sharing
- The granting of full South African citizenship to all South Africa's people
- The restoring and entrenching of the rule of law for all of South Africa's people

The companies also have declared that they continued to reject violence as a means of achieving change and would support only the politics of negotiation and reconciliation.

This call for political change and the extension of human rights for all of South Africa's people was renewed by the U.S. Corporate Council for Change in South Africa (formed in September 1985) in October 1985 in newspaper advertisements run in major U.S. newspapers all over the United States. In November 1985, a meeting in London of selected Council members and South African business leaders occurred during which a frank exchange of views took place. South African business leaders conveyed the views of U.S. business calling for the rapid elimination of apartheid directly to State President P.W. Botha. In January 1986, W. Michael Blumenthal of Burroughs Corporation and Roger Smith of General Motors, co-chairmen of the Council, met with Bishop Desmond Tutu for a full discussion of South African issues, including that of the role of U.S. business in South Africa. In March, selected Council members met in England with Rev. Leon Sullivan and business representatives from five other countries to discuss South African problems and possible solutions to those problems.

The International Chamber of Commerce (ICC), representing over 7,000 companies all over the world, in its hearings before the United Nations on September 16, 1985, proclaimed its total opposition to apartheid and its support for the passage of laws leading to its elimination. Let me quote briefly from that declaration:

The ICC condemns racially discriminatory policies and practices anywhere in the world. Consequently, it opposes the South African system of apartheid and believes it should be abolished as quickly as possible. This system is morally indefensible. It is also economically counterproductive and fundamentally irreconcilable with the principles of free enterprise.

The international community as a whole has a responsibility to engage in such positive action as may help to eliminate apartheid in South Africa. The international standards of business behavior set by transnational corporations (TNCs) in South Africa are a force toward this end. Efforts of individual companies operating in South Africa, through compliance with the Sullivan Principles, or the European Economic Community's Code of Conduct, or other instruments of that nature, or through their own guidelines, have contributed to

- Promoting racial equality in employment practices
- Training and developing black managers and skilled and educated black manpower at all levels
- Developing a free trade union movement open to all races
- Generating the fundamental attitudinal changes necessary to bring about racial reconciliation and greater social equality
- Improving the quality of life of people in the region through social actions at the community level, particularly through assistance to education and housing

The South African business community has itself actively begun to challenge rather than to accept government policies. I would call the attention of the nonbusiness world to an *Action Program of South African Business* issued by the Federated Chamber of Industries in South Africa in January of this year. This Charter of Social, Economic, and Political Rights for all South Africans is a truly unique document for South Africa and for many other countries of the world as a matter of fact. It should be read carefully by all those seeking to learn how both South African and American business are pressing for political change in South Africa. It should be noted that U.S. business firms in South Africa are members of these national business groups calling for change in that country. Let me quote from this South African Business Charter of Social, Economic, and Political Rights at some length since the delcaration is far reaching and unequivocal in its language:

CIVIL AND POLITICAL RIGHTS AND PRINCIPLES

- Every human being has the right to recognition as a person before the law.
- Everyone is equal before the law, and is entitled to equal protection of the law without any discrimination on the basis of race, colour, language, sex, religion, eithnic or social origin, age, property, birth, political or other opinion, or economic or other status.

   1. Everyone has the right to life, liberty and security of person.
   2. No one shall be arbitrarily deprived of these rights.
   3. No one shall be deprived of his liberty merely on the grounds of inability to fulfill a contractual obligation.

- No one shall be subjected to arbitary arrest, detention or exile, and everyone shall be entitled to a fair and public hearing by an independent and impartial tribunal in the determination of his rights and of any obligations and of any criminal charges against him.
- No one shall be subjected to torture or to cruel inhuman or degrading treatment or punishment.
- No one shall be held in slavery or servitude, and no one shall be required to perform forced or compulsory labour.

   1. Everyone has the right to freedom of movement and residence within the borders of the State.
   2. Everyone has the freedom to leave the country and, if having the right of permanent residence, to return.
   3. Everyone has the right to freedom of opinion and expression; this right includes freedom to hold opinions without intereference and to seek, receive and impart information and ideas through any media, regardless of frontiers.
   4. Any advocacy of national, racial or religious hatred that constitutes incitement to discrimination, hostility or violence shall be prohibited by law.

- Everyone has the right to freedom of association and freedom of peaceful assembly.

   1. Everyone born in South Africa or the independent or national states, or naturalised in accordance with law has the right to South African citizenship.
   2. Every citizen has the right to take part in public affairs, directly or through freely chosen representatives.
   3. Everyone has the right of equal access to the public service.
   4. Due regard being given to the protection of the rights of minorities, the will of the people is the basis of the authority of the government, and this will shall be expressed by way of periodic and genuine elections which shall be by universal suffrage and shall be held by secret vote or by equivalent free voting procedures.

- The institutions of democratic government, and in particular, the separation of state powers, the independence of the judiciary, and the supremacy of the legal system, the freedom of the press and the free formation of political parties shall be the foundations of South African statehood.
- The State shall not be above the law, but shall be, through decentralisation and devolution of state powers, close to the people and responsive to their needs.
  1. South Africa, as a sovereign state, shall respect the rights and independence of all nations and shall strive to maintain world peace and the settlement of all international disputes by negotiation, not war.
  2. The right of other peoples to independence and self-government shall be recognized and shall be the basis of close cooperation.

I truly believe that the efforts of the U.S. business community in particular and the business community in South Africa generally have borne fruit in changing white attitudes and in legislation recently passed by the South African government to remedy some of the inequities and injustices that unfortunately still exist — though much remains yet to be done and at a faster pace. I believe that this assessment is based on more than hope or wishful thinking. Some of the Sullivan companies' task group chairmen and I recently returned from another three-week trip to South Africa. In meeting after meeting, we all listened to much that was critical, but these same critics also told us privately that they do not seek disinvestment, that what they want is a continuation of corporate efforts leading to jobs, mobility, equality, training, housing, community development. They also urged us to be more outspoken, to deal more directly with challenge to the laws that still keep black South Africans out of the mainstream of both political and economic life. "Do not leave, do more, be more outspoken" — that is the message we received. Of course, many blacks support disinvestment; many, however, also advocate continued and even expanded foreign investment. We in business have a role to play and we accept pressure to do more in South Africa. But we cannot agree with the forced withdrawal of the American business presence or with the imposition of economic sanctions. This is why we oppose legislative proposals seeking to impose these measures. Yes, we share the objective of the proponents of such legislation — peaceful change as quickly as possible — but we seriously doubt, however, that this objective would be the result of American withdrawal or South African isolation.

This is a time of great frustration with the existing conditions in South Africa, but it is also a time of challenge and yes, even hope. Growing numbers of people within South Africa begin to demonstrate a commitment to change. Let us pursue honest and sincere policies of support for the unification of these groups—businesses, labor unions, educators, students, church people, and others—in the peaceful pursuit of change, rather than pursue strategies which will have a strong potential for further polarization.

Ad run by South African businessmen in September 1985

The year ahead in South Africa could be one unfortunately of protracted struggle, violence, and risk. But it can also be one during which steps can yet be taken to bring about genuine power sharing and negotiations leading to full citizenship for all of South Africa's people.

Alan Paton, one of South Africa's great writers, is a man of uncompromising principles. He reflects the torment of his torn land. He writes: "If the nations of the West condemn us, they will only hinder the process of our emancipation from the bondage of our history. But if they stay with us, rebuke us, judge us and encourage us, the chances are that we shall do better."

One must also listen to the many black voices speaking for freedom and power sharing in South Africa including that of Mangosuthu Gatscha Buthelezi, chief minister of Kwazulu and president of Inkatha and the South African Black Alliance. On July 5, 1985, he greeted a group of American black leaders. Among his comments to them were the following:

I am not heard in the United States when I say that apartheid is far more vulnerable to democratic opposition now than it has ever been before, and that apartheid is certainly far more vulnerable to democratic opposition than it has ever been to the politics of violence. I am not heard when I say that the scales are tipping in favour of the politics of negotiation, and that America more than at any other time in history should be strengthening the democratic process. They should be strengthening the circumstances which favour the continued growth of democratic opposition to apartheid, and they should be strengthening those who have made it their task to hold political violence at bay, and to employ the forces of democracy to bring about real change.

The escalation of violence both on the part of the State and by those who oppose the State, can only lead to ever diminishing prospects of salvaging this country from destruction. I am not heard in the United States when I say that we must increase white dependency on blacks; that we must tip the scales even further in favour of the politics of negotiation; that we must increase black bargaining power and that these things must be done by increasing the rate of industrialization in South Africa.

In summary, any effective leverage to induce peaceful change in South Africa requires a business presence. Business withdrawal would neither bring down the South African government nor affect the policies of that government, except perhaps to make it more rigid and truculent as it feels itself more isolated. To the extent that sanctions or isolation or withdrawal seek to govern the actions of South African affiliates of U.S. companies, they place these companies in an impossible situation between two governmental authorities at a time when engagement of a more active character remains one of the last hopes for a peaceful resolution to South Africa's problems. Americans must not be passive actors in this South African drama, but we must be careful that we do not exaggerate our ability to influence the course of events in South Africa by ourselves. Only South Africans themselves can be the key actors—black and white alike. We must work to bring the races together so they can negotiate their future peacefully. Withdrawal would be a disaster for all of South Africa's people and would exacerbate the tensions that sadly already exist. Pretoria must quickly and unequivocally make the ultimate commitment to ending apartheid and to begin a process of negotiation with all of its people for a transition to true democracy in that country. We must certainly help in that process not by isolating South Africa but by pushing and prodding that country and showing that change can come peacefully. In the midst of the pain, anguish, and violence which exist in that anguished country, we may yet all of us who seek peaceful change, see the emergency of a politics of negotiation in South Africa. It must happen. It can yet happen. It is that process we should press for and encourage, not sanctions, not mindless confrontation which will bring about only mass violence and increased racial division. This is what we must avoid at all costs if the struggle for equality is to succeed.

Part VIII

THE ROLE OF THE
U.S. BUSINESS COMMUNITY

CHAPTER 35

Should U.S. Corporations Abandon South Africa?

by LOU H. WILKING

General Motors assembles vehicles at several locations on the conti-
nent of Africa, including Egypt, Kenya, Tunisia, Zaire, and South
Africa. In total, these operations market GM products in thirteen
African countries. However, of the 4,500 people that General Motors
employs throughout Africa, over 90 percent are located at General
Motors' wholly owned subsidiary in South Africa, General Motors
South African. GM South African operates two facilities, one in Port
Elizabeth and a second plant in nearby Aloes. GM South African pro-
duces passenger cars, commercial vehicles, a variety of automotive parts,
and components and locomotives.

GM's original decision to locate in South Africa in 1926 was based
on the excellent economic prospects and low political risks that existed in South Africa at that time, which convinced General Motors
of the long-term profitability of an operation in that country. However, the economic and political environments have changed. South Africa
has suffered through a variety of negative economic developments including double-digit inflation averaging over 16 percent in 1985,
deteriorating gold prices, declining foreign exchange, widespread
unemployment, and extremely high interest rates.

The South African automotive industry has been affected by the
changing economic and political environment. The 1985 industry results
reflected a decrease in vehicle sales of 25 percent from 1984 to an annual sales volume of just over 300,000 units. This means that the South
African automotive industry is attempting to survive on a volume level
that is less than one half of single-shift capacity.

Moreover, the South African government's apartheid policies are a source of social unrest that threatens to undermine the political stability of that country and a financial burden that diverts the government from attending to its economic problems. As such, it has become exceedingly more difficult for General Motors to operate as a profitable, ongoing concern in South Africa. Despite these adverse conditions, GM South African has continued to provide its customers with the products they want, maintaining a substantial supplier and dealer network while at the same time acting as a major force in the reversal and elimination of South Africa's untenable social structure.

Recognizing the interdependence of South Africa's economic and social problems, GM believes that the future growth and profitability of both the South African automobile industry and the economy in general will depend largely on the more effective integration of the black majority into the economy. As a contributing and participating member of the South African free enterprise system, the black majority not only would provide the necessary skills needed to sustain economic growth but also represents an enormous and as-yet-untapped consumer market.

It follows that if the black majority is to represent a major force in the South African economy, continuing efforts will have to be made in education, training, and housing for black South Africans. However, the South African government will face a shortage of available funds over the next few years because of the country's current economic situation and the government's apartheid policies which restrict nonwhite South Africans from fully participating in the economic development of the country. This makes it all the more imperative for U.S. companies to address and try to improve that country's economic and social situation.

GM'S RECORD

One demonstration of GM's opposition to apartheid and commitment to improve the socioeconomic conditions in South Africa was the corporation's adoption of the Sullivan Principles when they were introduced in 1977. Recognition of GM's continued progress in implementing the Principles in 1985 earned GM South African its sixth consecutive Category I, or "Making Good Progress," rating. This is the highest possible rating a company can receive. However, not only by its compliance with the Sullivan Principles, but by going beyond what is required, GM South African has greatly improved the quality of life for blacks in South Africa in the realm of employee facilities and work areas, equal employment opportunity, employee training, and community action programs. For the last six years, all GM South African employee facilities and work areas have been completely desegregated as a result of a $4.5 million project completed in 1980. As part of this project, GM South African constructed a new training center, modern locker facilities, new comfort and rest room facilities, and a modern dining room.

GM South African has also aggressively pursued the objectives of equal employment opportunity for all its employees in that country. Early in 1980, GM South African developed and implemented an affirmative action plan to increase the overall utilization of blacks and coloureds in the total work force in line with local population demographics in Port Elizabeth and to increase the number of blacks and coloureds in positions of responsibility within the hourly skilled and salaried work force.

Total nonwhite employment, 48 percent in 1979, has increased to 59 percent in 1985 with corresponding increases in nonwhite salaried and hourly employment. The increase in nonwhite salaried employment, from 5 percent in 1979 to 12 percent in 1985, was realized in spite of a decline in the total salaried work force. It is interesting to note that since 1979, the proportion of blacks and coloureds in supervisory positions increased by 65 and 213 percent, respectively. Also, the proportion of black and coloured employees supervising whites in 1985 has increased from a 1984 level of 2.6 to 4.1 percent. Additionally, nonwhites accounted for 25.8 percent of all supervisors.

TRAINING PROGRAMS

One of the most critical factors limiting GM South African's ability to more fully implement equal employment policies is the recognized limited education of the nonwhite population brought about by the inadequate educational infrastructure for nonwhites in South Africa. In an attempt to eliminate these deficiencies, GM South African has developed a number of programs aimed at training high-potential black and coloured employees for positions of greater responsibility and, ultimately, supervisory and managerial status.

These training programs are run by a multiracial staff of sixteen instructors who teach courses in toolmaking, fitting, turning, electricity, patternmaking, and auto mechanics. Since 1980, 1,560 nonwhite employees have received formal operator training in welding, metal finishing, and spray painting. To supplement in-plant training programs, GM South African makes use of outside organizations such as the University of Port Elizabeth, New Brighton Technical Institute, and various other technical colleges and facilities offering specialized training. To achieve our objectives in the area of nonwhite advancement, GM South African conducts special training programs that include a College-Graduate-in-Training Program, an Undergraduate Scholarship Program, and a Black Supervisor-in-Training Program.

To improve the nonwhite educational system, GM South African contributes personnel, equipment, and funds to organizations such as the University of Port Elizabeth's Center for Continuing Education, the Teacher Opportunities Program, Project PACE, and the READ Library Project. GM also participates in the Adopt-A-School project which provides managerial, financial, and vocational guidance assistance to local schools. Currently, twenty black schools, with an annual enrollment of more than 15,500 students, have been adopted by GM South African in the Port Elizabeth area. Contributions to the University of Port Elizabeth's Center for Continuing Education were made to fund special training programs for nonwhites in order to upgrade their level of mathematics, science, and English language instruction.

A major effort of General Motors and other companies in the Port Elizabeth area was the establishment of the first black technical training center, New Brighton Technical Institute. Based on its success, the government has decided to sponsor fourteen more such colleges throughout the country. Further, in February 1985, GM South African successfully lobbied the South African government to allow a nonwhite employee to enroll at a previously all-white technical college. Since that time, other nonwhites have been allowed to enroll at the technical college.

HEALTH AND HOUSING

In the area of community health education, General Motors is loaning two vehicles, free of charge, to the Friends of Baragwanath to serve as mobile training units to help disseminate information on personal health care to outlying areas. In total, this organization has assembled a library of over 500 videotapes regarding personal health care which, with the help of the mobile training units, are viewed by an estimated 2.9 million people over the course of a year.

In the area of housing, GM has endorsed a five-year program with the Urban Foundation, a nonprofit institution in South Africa committed to the reform of government urbanization policies, freedom of movement, and improved living conditions for blacks in South Africa. GM's commitment supports the Urban Foundation's urbanization initiatives designed to bring about the abolition of influx control and projects designed to upgrade the housing and infrastructure at Crossroads and other black townships. In addition to this commitment, GM provided the Urban Foundation with a substantial low-interest loan for the development of a nonwhite, self-help housing project in the Port Elizabeth area. This loan will provide for the construction of 272 new homes for coloured and black families. The loan will also be used to provide utilities to forty-four existing homes and to build a day care clinic.

In addition to the Urban Foundation commitment, GM South African also sponsors a Home Improvement Loan Program for its employees, providing interest-free loans for one year. Since the inception of the program in 1973, over 2,700 employees have participated. Our Home Ownership Program, which provides down payment assistance to nonwhites, has also been in existence since 1973 and has enabled 542 coloured and 252 black employees to purchase their homes. GM South African employs a full-time housing programs coordinator who advises employees of the housing alternatives available to them and the responsibilities of home ownership.

Another aspect of GM South African's community action program is its active involvement in the identification, training, and appointment of nonwhite businesses. To date, the company has thirty-two nonwhite suppliers and pursues every opportunity to strengthen its dealer organization through the appointment of nonwhite dealers. There are currently seventeen such dealerships, the majority of which are highly successful business ventures. The black female partner in one of these dealerships was named the 1983 "Black Businesswoman of the Year" in South Africa. To further promote nonwhite entrepreneurship, General Motors South African contributed to the Small Business Development Corporation in mid-1985 to promote the business undertakings of nonwhite entrepreneurs.

OPPOSING APARTHEID

General Motors has consistently taken a lead role in demonstrating its opposition to the South African government's apartheid policies through individual initiatives, as well as through its involvement in various business group activities. In addition to holding very frank private discussions with members of the South African government whenever possible, senior GM South African executives, through their active participation in a number of influential bodies representing organized industry and commerce, have been able to exert positive influences on government policy formulation and to urge legislative changes to provide equality of opportunity for South Africans of all races. Three such organizations in particular are the Associated South African Chamber of Commerce, the Federated Chamber of Industries, and the American Chamber of Commerce. Through GM participation in the Federated Chamber of Industries, it joined with other South African employers in unveiling a charter for reform that calls for the government to:

• Create a climate for negotiations by releasing all political prisoners;
• Abolish discriminatory laws;
• Allow blacks to work and live wherever their skills and wealth allow; and
• Share power in the central government.

And in March 1985, GM South African's public criticism of apartheid received wide media coverage in South Africa when I publicly called on the government to do away with the Mixed Marriage Act, the Immorality Act, the practice of detention without trial, and other acts and practices that form the roots of apartheid. More recently, in February 1986, R.A. White, managing director of GM South African, offered financial and legal assistance to any nonwhite GMSA employee prosecuted for using designated white-only beaches in Port Elizabeth. As a result of White's initiative, the Port Elizabeth Town Council voted to open the city's beaches to all races beginning July 1, 1986.

In the United States, Roger B. Smith, chairman of General Motors, recently stated publicly that the system of apartheid just cannot continue and that U.S. companies should work with South African business leaders to determine how U.S. businesses operating in South Africa can expedite the abolition of that country's apartheid policies. In this regard, the U.S. Corporate Council on South Africa, of which Smith is co-chairman, was formed in September 1985. The council is comprised of the chief executive officers of major U.S. corporations with subsidiaries in South Africa. To date, over 100 companies have joined the council and more are expected. The council has publicly endorsed the call of many South African business leaders for abolition of statutory racial discrimination. It is now actively consulting with influential South African businessmen on the development of a program that combines political and economic initiative which can hasten progress toward meaningful reform.

General Motors actively lobbies the South African government for social change through the U.S. Corporate Council, business group participation, public speeches, and implementation of various programs designed to improve the livelihood of nonwhite South Africans. The evidence shows that U.S. companies in South Africa associate more with the causes for the abolition of apartheid than with the South African government.

PULL OUT OR STAY PUT

There is an increasingly strong movement within the United States calling for economic sanctions, legislated divestment, and/or disinvestment of U.S. operations in South Africa. Some of these proponents are relying on the assumption that the South African economy is dependent on American investment. However, South Africa has a highly developed economy, generating 90 percent of its capital internally. American investments in South Africa amount to less than one fifth of the country's total foreign investments. Therefore, American disinvestment is unlikely to have any material effect except to isolate South Africa from the progressive employment practices of U.S. firms.

Further, consider the fact that every embargo the United States has imposed in the recent past has failed. This includes the grain embargo, the embargo on Iranian oil, and the Russian pipeline embargo. An example of the resiliency of South Africa to economic sanctions is documented historically in connection with the 1978 U.S. Armanents Embargo which restricted the export of U.S. origin commodities and technical data to the South African military and police. Instead of being hurt by the embargo, South Africa developed a vigorous arms industry of its own and has evolved into a net exporter of arms.

If, through legislation, American companies were forced to pull out of South Africa and to terminate their operations, it would undoubtedly have the effect of exacerbating an already severe unemployment problem — estimated at more than 50 percent among blacks in the Port Elizabeth area where GM operates. Due to the dire economic conditions in South Africa, GM South African and presumably a number of other foreign firms are already under severe pressure. Further economic deterioration in South Africa can hardly be expected to lay the foundation for shared prosperity among all racial groups.

The only basis on which constructive reform can go forward is one that contains the promise of economic and social progress for all racial groups in South Africa. Termination of operations by U.S. companies in South Africa could undercut that very foundation. Constructive reform on political and economic fronts would make it attractive to invest more in South Africa, employ more, and reinvest more in the local economy. I would therefore argue that the pressures we are exerting on the South African government for speedier reform and the continued actions General Motors and other companies are taking to better the livelihood of our work force are a more productive course of action.

In intangible terms, some of the proponents of divestment argue that the South African government realizes substantial moral support through the presence of American investments and that Americans should refuse to associate with the instruments of repression. However, the facts simply do not support the contention that General Motors or any Sullivan signatory company is in agreement with or an instrument of the South African government's apartheid policies.

CRITICAL JUNCTURE

We are at a critical juncture in South African history. Many white South Africans now understand that the need for meaningful advancement for the nonwhite population and their own long-term survival are only possible if fundamental structural reforms are made. And on January 31, 1986, in his address to Parliament, State President Botha announced that South Africa has outgrown the outdated concept of apartheid. This statement was supported by the commitment to abolish passbooks and replace them with a uniform identity document for all races by July 1, 1986 and to replace the influx control policy with a new urbanization strategy.

More important, President Botha announced the formation of a National Statutory Council to begin negotiations with black leaders for power sharing. Although President Botha's speech did not address the Population Registration Act or the Group Areas Act, which are the basis of apartheid, it appears that the South African government is moving forward in the reform process. However, the commitments outlined in the President's speech must still be followed by prompt legislative action on the part of the South African government and the commencement of visible negotiations with authentic black leaders.

There are constructive alternatives for conveying our abhorrence of South Africa's apartheid policies. By combining the human and financial resources of the U.S. government, the U.S. educational system, and U.S. private enterprises operating in South Africa, Americans can have a positive impact on the housing and educational facilities for South Africa's nonwhite population. In addition, if assistance were conditional on South Africa's instituting specific reforms such as the abolition of the Group Areas Act, the U.S. effort would act as an economic lever to undermine the laws that form the roots of apartheid.

The job of abolishing South Africa's apartheid policies has just begun. The future of South Africa can only be built upon the willingness of all South Africans to resolve their differences. The single most important factor in the creation of a more promising socio-economic climate in South Africa is the involvement of blacks in negotiations for political power sharing. Recent events indicate that the South African government is prepared to move in the right direction, including giving blacks all-important political rights. This makes it imperative for U.S. companies to remain in South Africa to help create the basis for participation of all peoples in a sound, healthy economy. Disinvestment would only add to the pressures of economic downturn and social chaos.

We intend to press strongly for peaceful change in South Africa and pursue all constructive alternatives that have any reasonable prospect of rectifying that country's racial policies. At the same time, we will try to run our business in a manner that promotes the welfare of our employees, dealers, and suppliers and the interest of our stockholders. This is becoming increasingly difficult as GM faces deteriorating economic and financial conditions in its business. GM or any other organization cannot help provide a better life for all racial groups unless South Africa is able to enjoy a sustained high level of economic growth. Hopefully, through our adherence to sound operating principles, General Motors has the opportunity to continue to be a positive force for change in South Africa.

CHAPTER 36

The Evolution of Sullivan Principle Compliance

by D. REID WEEDON, JR.

American companies with operations in South Africa have proved agents of change in a region that is presently undergoing change. The catalyst that has been in the forefront of the struggle to bring an end to existing inequalities in South Africa is the Sullivan signatories program, subscribed to by about 200 of the approximately 275 American companies presently operating in that country.

The signatories program is based on the Sullivan Principles developed by the Reverend Leon H. Sullivan of the Zion Baptist Church, based in Philadelphia. The operations of these signatory companies in South Africa vary widely in the number of employees (i.e., one to several thousand) and equity ownership (i.e., a few percent to 100 percent ownership). Primary focus is on operations with more than twenty-five employees and 50 percent or more equity controlled by a U.S. parent company.

Of the companies that have more than twenty-five employees and at least 50 percent equity, fewer than thirty are not signatories. Those thirty employ about 5 percent of the employees of all such U.S. signatory and nonsignatory companies in South Africa. All of these companies employ slightly less than one percent of the economic labor force of the country.

The number of signatories has grown from the original twelve who made a voluntary commitment when Rev. Sullivan, a member of the board of directors of General Motors Corporation, announced his Principles in 1978, following an unsuccessful effort to encourage GM to leave South Africa. Several other codes came into being at about the same time, including those of South African organizations and the British Code, adopted by the EEC as the European Code standard.

The South African codes have fallen into disuse except for some individual company efforts. The EEC Code is a government effort, but administered in varying degrees by several countries. The Sullivan code is unique in having the following features:

- Voluntary and nongovernmental, but with required annual reporting;
- Periodic updating as to both requirements and level of expectation;
- Independent evaluation of performance and public grading of individual companies;
- Establishing specific standards that include employee monitoring and required certified public accounting firm verification of specific information;
- Requiring corporate action, not just in the workplace but also in the community and in interaction with the government to press for change; and
- Participation open to all companies no matter what their origin.

No other code of conduct followed by companies operating in South Africa has any of these six important features.

SETTING AN EXAMPLE

From the outset, Rev. Sullivan expressed the view that this program alone could not bring an end to apartheid, but it could make a meaningful contribution to that end. Some people have undertaken to dismiss the Principles as unsuccessful or irrelevant, or both, because apartheid still exists eight years after the Principles were first espoused. It is totally unrealistic to expect that U.S. companies employing less than one percent of the economically active labor force in South Africa will, by themselves, be responsible for ending apartheid. These U.S. companies are expected, as a part of the price for being in the country, to press for the ending of apartheid and to set an example for others.

From the very beginning, Rev. Sullivan laid down the requirement that the signatory companies must report regularly and be graded on their conduct in South Africa. Although both requirements were accepted by the signatories, their managements acknowledged that grading was (fortunately for them) an unachievable dream. This did not deter Rev. Sullivan, however; nor did the fact that there existed no precedent for such an evaluation of corporate social responsibility. The situation was further complicated by the disparate nature of the signatories' businesses — from low-technology manufacturing to white-collar enterprises, a range of sizes from one employee to over 10,000 employees, and locations ranging from the very rural, comparable to the Third World environment, to modern urban, comparable to a modern industrialized setting.

Uninhibited by these variations, Rev. Sullivan hired Arthur D. Little, Inc. to devise a reporting system and a grading procedure. At first there was continual discussion of on-site monitoring. Finally, an extensive reporting document, subject to annual revision, was developed as the vehicle for the collection of data about individual company operations with respect to the Principles.

The use of a data collection system in which only the respondent has responsibility for the information provided immediately raises the specter of accuracy. There is no absolute solution to this problem. However, some of the information gathered by independent certified public accountants can be organized so as to be subject to local employee review and different information. Some information, particularly of a qualitative nature and having to do with corporate activity outside the workplace, is difficult or, at the least, costly and time-consuming to verify. With respect to this last category, on the other hand, regular visits to South Africa to observe what is being done and to talk with a wide range of beneficiaries do provide a degree of insight into the issue of accuracy of reporting and appropriateness of activities.

The evolutionary process is currently in its tenth annual cycle. In the fourth cycle, the concept of "basic requirements" was introduced in order to enable employee monitoring. Questions are asked pertaining to freedom of association, benefits, equal pay for equal work, minimum pay, employee/management communication, review of ratings with employees, and desegregation. Such questions are asked on a yes-and-no basis and employees are told whether the answers are affirmative. All the required actions are readily communicated to employees, making it easy for them to raise questions if a company is not doing what is required. Whether or not a company fulfills all of the basic requirements is crucial. A company meeting these requirements is eligible for further evaluation of its activities with respect to the remaining Principles, and the company that does not meet the basic requirements automatically receives a failing grade.

The involvement of certified public accounting firms enables the verification of quantitative data which is important to the rating process. Information so verified includes employment data, minimum wage compliance, total payroll, and contributions and expenses in support of activities and organizations dedicated to improving South Africa's social conditions. In the early years of the CPA review process, which started with the sixth cycle, some errors were found as a result of over- as well as underreporting. That situation now seems to have been corrected.

As indicated, the rating sequence begins once a signatory passes the basic requirements. The actual scoring is divided into two parts and, in the tenth cycle, will be based on a company's actions in four programmatic areas: social justice, education for nonemployees, training and advancement, and community development. Each of these areas receives equal weighting and is scored both quantitatively and qualitatively.

Quantitative scoring for training and advancement is based on the proportion of blacks, coloureds, and Asians who fill vacancies in management, supervisory, sales, and professional positions. The objective — warranting a top score — is that these races will fill 50 percent or more of the vacancies in a given year. This goal is challenging since, traditionally, positions at these levels all have been filled by whites because others generally did not have the appropriate education.

The other three action areas are measured quantitatively by the ratio of payroll to expenditures. A single, fixed scale is used for the assessment of points for various levels of ratios. Custom dictates using profits as the standard for comparison, but this is not deemed relevant in a situation that calls for sustained financial support that is not subject to the fluctuation of earnings. The level of such corporate expenditure in South Africa by U.S. companies is manyfold the level of giving in the United States itself, which is about 0.4 percent of payroll.

QUALITY EVALUATION

The qualitative evaluation of each of the above four areas is subjective. The evaluation standards are somewhat comparative, but even this is limited given the characteristics of each business and the specific circumstances of the particular company. What is appropriate and possible for one company is not the rule for other businesses. The easiest and perhaps most popular solution for the companies would have been to give up, but Rev. Sullivan's prodding did not permit this escape.

The procedure is for each company report to be read separately by two Arthur D. Little staff members who use an agreed-on scale for the rating of the many individual questions. They subsequently compare their evaluations step by step and resolve differences or involve a third rating person to provide a resolution. Someone uninvolved in the process would be surprised at the extent to which different people doing the rating are in agreement in their respective evaluations.

Based on the sum of the point scores for the quantitative and qualitative analysis in all four areas, a determination is made of the range of total points appropriate to being rated good, passing, or failing. Admittedly, this is an agonizing process and is not based on a predetermined distribution of the number of companies in any one of the three grade levels. Thus, there could be, and hopefully will be, no failing companies. Unfortunately, in each cycle so far some companies have clearly merited a failing grade.

With the experience of nine rating cycles, the rating teams are now quite satisfied that there are meaningful distinctions between the three grade levels. There is an opportunity for informal validation with those signatories that report separately on their multiple subsidiaries in South Africa. While every signatory would like to have all of its subsidiaries in the top rating category, the rating process usually ranks the multiple subsidiaries of a company in the same order that the company would expect.

In any examination of what the signatories have done and what has been achieved, certain caveats must be kept in mind. First, the signatories and their operations are constantly changing from year to year, both as to number and, especially, as to size. Second, changes in a society are rarely the result of a single effort.

The first three Principles apply solely to the workplace and a signatory's performance is assessed in the basic requirements. The first three Principles are:

- Principle 1: Nonsegregation of the Races in All Eating, Comfort, Locker Rooms, and Work Facilities.
- Principle 2: Equal and Fair Employment Practices for All Employees.
- Principle 3: Equal Pay for All Employees Doing Equal or Comparable Work for the Same Period of Time.

In the ninth reporting cycle, each of the 146 reporting signatories met all of the Principles with the exception of one that failed the nonsegregation requirement and three that failed the minimum wage requirement. Compared to the late 1970s, when only a few companies in South Africa complied with the Principles, it is all too easy to underestimate the magnitude and difficulties involved in what the signatories have accomplished.

EARLY COMPLIANCE

In the first years of the Sullivan effort, desegregation was against the law. A few short years ago, when one of the last signatories to remain segregated was trying to effect the change to a desegregated workplace, white employees filed an unfair labor practice charge against the company for having eliminated segregated facilities. However, the situation in the country had progressed to the point that the government informed the company that the charge would never come to a hearing.

In another instance, a signatory with retail stores successfully undertook to press building and shopping center landlords where its stores were located to desegregate the toilet facilities. In yet another instance, signatories in public buildings successfully mobilized the tenants to pressure building managers to eliminate all segregation in the buildings.

The eradication of segregation's symbolism was extremely important. That it was not done just inside a company's own premises is an example of the extended effect achieved. Many other companies in South Africa, not physically adjacent to signatories, have had to follow suit in order to stay competitive and not lose their most essential employees to the more attractive conditions existing at signatory companies.

Another example worth noting is the recognition of black, coloured, and Asian unions. In the late 1970s, at the time (perhaps because) the Principles were announced, the government formed the Weihahn Commission to review labor laws and regulations. As a result, the government recognized unions which were registered regardless of race. Some of the black, coloured, and Asian unions refused to register in the belief (probably correctly) that furnishing the required information for registration would subject them to external pressure. The signatories took the stand that they were willing to recognize representative unions whether or not they were registered. As a practical matter, this distinction has ceased to be relevant in South Africa.

MINIMUM WAGES

Minimum wage deserves special mention because this issue is so different from the minimum wage laws in the United States. There is no national, mandated minimum wage in South Africa. Naturally, with a large surplus of labor and high unemployment, actual wages can be — and are in many instances — very low. The national approach is the separate effort of two South African universities to publish minimum wages which, at their lowest level, represent what people in the United States would describe as a poverty wage. In an example of the escalation of the standards, for the fifth cycle Rev. Sullivan negotiated with the companies to achieve a minimum wage for the signatories at 30 percent above the basic level for a wage earner with five or six dependents. While that number of dependents is typical, published wages are given for different geographic areas and various numbers of dependents. The appropriate wage for a person with five dependents tends to be more than twice that for someone with no dependents. Many people who are paid at a company's entry wage level are young, single, and have no dependents; it is unfair to use this standard and assign a different standard to employees doing the same work but with a greater number of dependents. To do so would defeat the principle of equal pay for equal work. The combination of applying the 30 percent premium and using the dependents-oriented wage scale results in a very wide wage differential at the entry level. There are examples of higher wages being paid by signatories, thus causing an increase in the wage level at neighboring companies.

The fourth and fifth Principles require the training and advancement of blacks, coloureds, and Asians. Given the comparatively poor educational quality and opportunities for these races compared to those for whites, there are widespread challenges facing companies in their efforts to advance black, coloured, and Asians, particularly into professional, supervisory, and managerial positions. Signatories must provide both education and training to qualify such people. Signatories also must institute a variety of remedial, role-model, and mentoring programs to help these employees succeed.

Rev. Sullivan has set the target that 50 percent of the vacancies should be filled by black, coloured, and Asian employees at the supervisory and managerial levels. In the last reporting period, vacancies at these levels were filled by those races at 41 percent and 14 percent respectively. These rates are down from recent periods, and it is likely that they reflect both the economic recession in South Africa and the absorption of the reservoir of candidates from prior years. The future is apt to prove especially challenging.

There is no available basis on which to compare the performance of signatories with that of other companies in South Africa, or to assess the effect of training and advancement outside the individual companies. Many signatories are training people in excess of their own needs.

OUTSIDE THE WORKPLACE

The sixth Principle addresses the improvement of the quality of employees' lives outside the work environment in such areas as housing, transportation, schooling, recreation, and health facilities. Of all the various codes for companies operating in South Africa, this is the only requirement for specific efforts outside the workplace. It is in this area that the signatories have a broad impact on their communities without relying on employees and their families to lead the drive for changing their living environment.

As an example, there is a program (which originated outside the signatory companies) for corporate support to individual primary and secondary schools. The program, known as Adopt-A-School, has companies helping such schools with physical facilities, teacher training, libraries, student activities, formation of parent-teacher associations, and many other activities. The signatories have adopted 332 schools that serve 232,000 students. Unfortunately, very few nonsignatory companies have adopted schools even though this is a program with tremendous leverage and satisfaction for all involved.

One company found that its truck driver had been elected head of the parent-teacher association it had stimulated. The company seized the opportunity to provide this employee with special training and coaching to help him fill his new community leadership role. In other instances, companies have enabled school principals to enroll in internal company management development training programs.

In housing, the signatories have been leaders in explaining the benefits of home ownership and enabling employees to surmount the various hurdles. A few years ago, the government made ninety-nine-year land leases available in urban areas to qualified blacks. These companies have positioned many employees to take advantage of this dispensation.

As a result, although the signatories employ less than one percent of the economically employed labor force, such employees had 15 percent of the ninety-nine-year leases executed in the country at mid-1983, and as of mid-1984, they still held 5 percent of the total.

In the most recent reporting period, which ended in mid-1986, companies are being asked to report on their response to the so-called Fourth Amplification dealing with social and political justice—the newest Sullivan program requirement. It is too early to comment on this new activity, but early efforts raise expectations.

The addition of new signatories to the program provides a standard of comparison with nonsignatories. Experience indicates that new companies joining the Sullivan program must invariably increase their efforts in order to meet the standards of the program. Similarly, a significant sample of informal information about companies of other nationalities indicates that they would receive a failing grade if their performance were to be measured against the Principles.

The South African employers were quoted in *USA Today* on March 5, 1986:

Many South African employers think the Sullivan influence goes far beyond the 63,000 employed by the signatories. 'They have affected the hopes and aspirations of hundreds of thousands of people,' said Tony Bloom, chairman and CEO of the $1.16 billion Premier Group of 600 companies employing 33,000 here.

"The U.S. is the leader in uplifting—the others tend to follow," said Brian Matthew of the Midland Chamber of Industries in Cape Province. 'Sullivan is one of the straws on the camel's back.' "

These external evaluations by South African leaders who are outside the Sullivan program best describe the impact of the signatories. An exodus of U.S. companies will remove the role-model leaders for change in South Africa.

A final example is one signatory company where, after some difficulty, the managing director raised the company's performance from the bottom rating to the top. The day after receiving the good news, he was informed by the U.S. parent corporation that his company had been sold to a South African conglomerate. At his first meeting with the new owners, he was told that he should no longer run the company as a charitable institution and that he should cease the activities he had instituted in line with the Principles. He was able to arrange for the U.S. company to commit some of the proceeds of its sale to funding scholarships for existing recipients to complete their programs. His dilemma was whether his conscience would let him continue with his new employers in a business to which he is very much attached.

CHAPTER 37

The Inadequacy of Sullivan Reporting

by KAREN PAUL

Multinational corporations based in the United States have come under intense public scrutiny in recent years with regard to their dealings in South Africa. They are being called on to withdraw their investments from that country and, at the same time to use their influence there to pressure the South African government to dismantle the system of apartheid. The pressure to withdraw has been mounting steadily, but most companies have resisted it, arguing that they can do more good by remaining in South Africa, acting as model employers, and providing job opportunities for blacks. They maintain that should they withdraw, their potential for influence would be nonexistent, that the black population would suffer economically from lost employment opportunities, that the South African economy would continue to function, and that the government would quite likely become even less accommodating to the interests of blacks than it is today.

These companies can demonstrate the extent of their social responsibility in South Africa through being a signatory of, and in compliance with, the Sullivan Principles. The Sullivan Principles were developed about a decade ago by the Reverend Leon Sullivan, and they specify six dimensions of desirable behavior on which companies can be rated. Nine reports have now been issued that categorize companies as "Making Good Progress," "Making Progress," or "Needs to Become More Active." Approximately 200 companies are now signatories.

Some critics argue that the Sullivan Principles are no longer relevant, that the system of apartheid is so odious that to be an active participant in the South African economy is evil, that believers in the Sullivan Principles are only deluding themselves about the possibility of meaningful change in South Africa, or that the Sullivan Principles are a mere palliative to substitute for a while for the more radical changes needed. Antiapartheid sentiment has become strong enough that a significant number of city and state pension funds, some university endowments, and certain other institutions have been selling their stock in companies that invest in South Africa. In addition, a number of public investment funds and even a few private ones have made their investments contingent on a company's scoring either "Making Good Progress" or "Making Progress" on the Sullivan Principles. For example, Connecticut has legislation that restricts state investments to companies that score in either of these two categories, whereas Nebraska requires companies to be in the highest one.

Performance on the Sullivan Principles has become a litmus test used to judge companies on their social performance in South Africa. According to the Investor Responsibility Research Center, Inc., there are currently 275 U.S. firms in South Africa; twenty-eight left the country in 1985. In the ninth report on the Sullivan Principles, published in 1985, there were 178 U.S. signatories and three non-U.S. signatories. Of these, sixty-six did not report data because they were either new signatories or endorsers which are not required to report because they have few or no employees or have only a minority equity in a South African subsidiary. The ninth report was compiled from data supplied from 112 signatories which reported on a total of 146 reporting units (some signatories have more than one subsidiary).

In the ninth report, thirty-six companies were rated as Category I, "Making Good Progress." There were eighty-nine companies in Category II, "Making Progress." Category III-A, "Needs to Become More Active — Received Low Rating," contained seventeen companies. Category III-B, "Did Not Pass Basic Requirements," had four companies. These ratings have at least the potential for significant impact on the investment community. It is appropriate to examine the way this monitoring system functions, the type of information it provides, and the extent to which it is a useful indicator of the kinds of activities that benefit blacks and help to bring about change in South Africa.

SERIOUSLY FLAWED

In 1978, there were 105 signatories to the Sullivan Principles. This seemed like an adequate number with which to establish an effective reporting system under complex and difficult circumstances. However, as we look over the series of nine reports that have now been compiled, we see that they are seriously flawed. The accuracy and objectivity, the consistency and reliability, and the validity and relevance of these reports are all open to question. Partly, these deficiencies may be due to the inherent difficulties of creating a reporting system in such an emotionally charged and politically explosive setting. But this fact itself should have made those responsible for the reports especially mindful of the need for reports that would be accurate, objective, consistent, reliable, valid, and relevant.

The monitoring system embodied in the Sullivan Principles and the nine reports is time-consuming and expensive. The direct cost of each report is now running to more than $250,000 annually, and the costs incurred by the companies in assembling their data are in excess of that. The resources devoted to this endeavor might be well spent if the results were useful. However, the methodological flaws in the report are serious. Moreover, the external validity of the reports is questionable. The resources currently given to the preparation of these reports might be better used in alternative efforts of research or to support activities beneficial to South African blacks.

The data that comprise the basis for the annual reports are self-reported responses by signatories to a rather lengthy questionnaire prepared and distributed by Arthur D. Little, Inc. A few items are verified by the companies' own auditors: total payroll, total employment, percent by which the lowest paid employee's pay exceeds minimum living standards, and total expenditures made for education, training, and community-development programs. Items not subject to verification include such critical pieces of information as the number of job vacancies in various categories, the total number of people in trainee positions, and the total number of black, coloured, and Asian workers in various occupational categories. These items are particularly significant because they are used in calculating ratios that then determine the rating of signatories in quantitative points for Principles 4, 5, and 6. Principle 4 relates to the development of training programs that will prepare blacks, coloureds, and Asians for supervisory, administrative, clerical, and technical jobs. Principle 5 concerns increasing the number of blacks, coloureds, and Asians in management and supervisory positions. Principle 6 involves improving the quality of employees' lives in such areas as housing, transportation, schooling, recreation, and health facilities. Of the three Principles, the only one based primarily on verified data is Principle 6, and even this verification is extremely broad — total expenditures made for education, training, and community-development programs.

This lack of verification of data may or may not be a serious problem. If we assume that all companies are equally inclined to present distortions of similar magnitude, the result might be a consistent picture. Companies are rated in broad categories at the end of the rating process, so as long as "greater than" and "lesser than" conclusions can be drawn, precision of the ratios may not be so important. But it would be ironic if companies with more rigorous standards for data collection received depressed ratings as a result of their methodological precision whereas companies with less rigorous standards received inflated ratings.

The appropriateness of a company's using its own auditors to verify data is another issue that merits further attention. When all the data on which the reports are based comes from the companies themselves, and when their own auditors have sole responsibility for verifying data, certainly some distortion could creep into the figures, if only inadvertently and through different interpretations of what is being measured. And yet the phrase "verified data" inspires trust in readers. Surely some independent verification of at least a representative sample of signatories is indicated.

EMPLOYEE REVIEW

The verification issue needs to be taken seriously, with more data included in the verification process as it currently stands and mechanisms developed to allow for more and better feedback by workers in the signatory companies in South Africa. One of the basic requirements to be in compliance with the first three Principles is that, in the words of the most recent report, "The company agrees to make its rating category in the ninth report known to all employees and to review the rating with representative groups of employees." What form do these reviews take? Is there a mechanism whereby discrepant information can be transmitted directly from workers to Arthur D. Little? A simple review that allows for no further participation by workers would seem to be an exercise in futility. Another basic requirement is that the company agreee to review the implementation of the Principles with representative groups of employees several times each year. This is a step in the right direction, but again we need to know which representative groups of employees are involved, and on what basis, and whether their active participation is encouraged — especially since these basic requirements are now seen as largely accomplished goals.

Another problem with accuracy and consistency occurs in the assignment of qualitative points to companies on the last three of the Principles, the areas currently denoted as the most problematic in the reports and the areas in which the most action is currently required by the signatories. A team of five readers from Arthur D. Little works on this task, and the process has been described as follows: The first reader reads through each report and evaluates it, assigning a numerical indicator to individual parts of the questionnaire. Then a second reader does the same, independently and without seeing the evaluation of the first. When the readers agree and the joint evaluation is markedly above the mean or below the mean, the process stops and qualitative points are assigned on a scale of 0 to 10 for each of the last three Principles. When the two readers disagree, or when a given company is at the margin of two categories, further discussion ensues. Other readers may become involved, often reading through the whole questionnaire and taking it as the unit of analysis rather than taking the specific answers to particular questions. A total of five readers are involved in the assigning of qualitative points, with at least two readers participating in the assignment for any one signatory.

WHY NO SOUTH AFRICANS?

All of the readers are located in one space of the social universe, the Arthur D. Little organization in Cambridge, Massachusetts. Why no South Africans? Why no religious leaders? Why no academicians? Arthur D. Little consultants carry around a cognitive map, which may or may not coincide with the worldview of other parties interested in and knowledgeable about South Africa. A more diverse and representative group of readers might add vitality to the assignment of qualitative points.

This becomes extremely important when one realizes that the impact of these qualitative points on a company's rating is just as great as the impact of the quantitative data on these last three Principles. A maximum of ten points is given on both the quantitative side and the qualitative side. It would be interesting to know the variability on each component and the correlation between the quantitative and the qualitative scores.

AGGREGATE DATA

The presentation of the reports is heavily weighted toward aggregate data. The reporting system will indicate that a certain company is in Category II, "Making Progress." However, no information is provided on the dimensions in which it might be doing well or doing poorly. Within the three basic categories, companies are listed alphabetically rather than rank ordered. Thus, when comparing the performance of two different companies, we can make only one of these three conclusions: Company A is greater than, equal to, or less than Company B in its overall compliance with the Sullivan Principles. This is not saying much. Company B may, in fact, have an outstanding program in the area of Principle 4, training programs, but it will be obscured in the present reporting system. And Company B may be performing at an abysmal level on another Principle, but this too will be obscured. Presumably the signatories do not want this type of detailed data to be made public, but why not? If they do, indeed, subscribe to the Sullivan Principles, why should data that have been collected be so closely guarded? Why shouldn't those companies that have made outstanding progress on one or another of the Principles be recognized for their efforts and held up as exemplars?

Another way in which the aggregation of data leads to problematic conclusions is that all companies end up being judged equally on the basis of all criteria. A manufacturing company is different from an advertising agency; a rental car agency is different from a food processing company; a pharmaceutical company is different from a company that owns and operates a chain of hotels. Their potential for compliance on the various Principles varies. Certainly the hotel company is in a unique position to take a stand regarding public accommodation of the various races, whereas the advertising agency might have a potential for developing an unusually effective set of public service messages. But this level of detail and example is found only in the very early Sullivan reports and has almost completely dropped out of the more recent reports.

We should recognize that a moderate level of achievement under conditions of high external or internal constraints may be more impressive than a high level of compliance under conditions of few constraints. Indeed, the use of ratio measures is a tacit acknowledgement of this idea in the present reporting system. Companies are judged on their advancement of blacks, coloureds, and Asians on the basis of how many job openings they had in the relevant categories rather than on the basis of absolute numbers. This recognition that all companies do not have the same possibility of achievement in all areas should be extended and emphasized in the reports.

MANAGEMENT POSITIONS

Another source of distortion lies in the aggregation of data on of black, coloured, and Asian workers. The signatories have not done very well on Principle 5, increasing the number of blacks, coloureds, and Asians in management and supervisory positions. But their performance becomes even more unimpressive when one disaggregates the three groups, as the charts presented in recent reports allow us to do.

For example, in the eighth report (1984), a marked increase of non-whites is noted in those occupying managerial openings, a movement from 6 percent in the seventh report to 15 percent in the eighth. But a careful look at the data shows that blacks only increased their representation from 3 to 5 percent, whereas Asians increased from 2 to 6 percent, and coloureds increased from one to 4 percent. These statistics are even more disappointing when one realizes that there are 23 million blacks in South Africa, as compared with 800,000 Asians and 2.6 million coloureds. If we compare the seventh, eighth, and ninth reports, we see a relative decline in the percentage of blacks in supervisory vacancies and an almost level percentage of blacks in managerial vacancies. Asians and coloureds are making greater gains than blacks, especially at the managerial level.

With regard to Principle 5, the report does allow us to disaggregate the data. It is a pity that in many other parts of the report the three categories are combined and cannot be disaggregated. For example, in the ninth report in the area of education for nonemployees, only one table, which relates to bursaries or scholarships, provides a breakdown by particular racial group. Phrases such as "27 teachers" and "14 nurses" appear in the narrative. Why not provide the racial categories into which these individuals fall according to the designation of the South African government? If opportunities are being targeted at the most disadvantaged group, blacks, wouldn't the signatories want us to know? But if, as in the case of those newly advanced to managerial positions, these opportunities are going mainly to Asians, partly to coloureds, and less so to blacks, then shouldn't we know?

This kind of reporting becomes especially significant since the governing party of South Africa has strategized as part of its alleged political reforms to provide increased political representation and more commercial opportunities on the part of these less disadvantaged of the disadvantaged groups. For example, Asians and coloureds were given representation in racially segregated parliaments in the election of November 1984. Certain opportunities to conduct business are available to Asians and to coloureds but not to blacks. It would be unfortunate if the signatories were to engage in programs that give the black population further cause to feel that a political wedge is being driven between themselves and the other nonwhite groups.

The combining of the nonwhite groups in the present reports is regrettable. Asians and coloureds occupy a disadvantaged but strategically vital place in South African society. Blacks, numerically by far the majority, do not necessarily benefit when the other nonwhite groups do. In fact, targeting opportunities to the other nonwhite groups may alleviate some of the combined frustration of their members and actually reduce the momentum for dismantling apartheid. We should be able to separate the companies that are developing programs to help blacks specifically, since blacks are the most disadvantaged and the most numerous group.

FRAGMENTARY DATA

The data presented in the reports as presently published are simply too fragmentary to allow us to identify patterns of social performance, causes and effects of compliance with the Principles, or generalizations we might wish to develop to increase our understanding of the factors that contribute to socially responsible corporate behavior. A more rigorous research approach might enable us to come to a greater understanding of the interpaly between social expectations, economic motivations, and corporate actions. Companies sometimes complain of the extensive paperwork involved in the compliance effort, but perhaps their complaints reflect a sense of futility that comes from reporting extensive data and then seeing only a portion of the data used for very limited purposes.

Why is it that McGraw-Hill has scored well historically, but Reader's Digest has not? Why has General Motors scored well, but International Harvester has not? Why has Borden scored well, but Carnation has not? Why has Eli Lilly scored well, but Squibb has not? What enables one subsidiary of Masonite Company to be rated in Category II and another subsidiary of Masonite to be rated in Category III-B for the year 1984? What kinds of internal and external variables make a difference in the outcome variable, the company's rating? Without this kind of discussion, it is hard to point the way for companies to bring about positive change in the direction embodied in the Sullivan Principles.

A case for simplicity in presentation of data can be made if these reports are intended for an audience that would have difficulty understanding a more rigorous methodology and statistical analysis, but surely the audience for these reports can comprehend conventional research methods. The signatories themselves do highly sophisticated research for product development and marketing. The citizen groups and religious activists who pressure companies about the South African issue generally contain members of a rather high educational level who would be more than competent to understand true research reports. Unless we know why certain companies perform better than others, and how they perform better than others, and why companies improve or deteriorate in their performance, we can say little about the circumstances or conditions that will enable the signatories to become a more potent force for social change in South Africa.

THE ARTHUR D. LITTLE CONNECTION

With about 200 companies now signatories, reports are that their collective contributions to the Industry Support Unit came to more than $500,000 in 1985. This money is paid into a trust fund which then pays certain expenses including the fee charged by Arthur D. Little for preparing the annual report. In past years, this fee was in the range of $180,000, but now, with the increased number of signatories, the billing is more than $250,000. These reports are precisely that, reports—not research projects—within Arthur D. Little. When this firm was brought into the project in 1978, the initial questionnaires had already been designed, distributed, and collected. In more recent years, the activities of Arthur D. Little have been to assemble the questionnaires, to receive the data reported by the signatories, to do a series of rather simple tabulations but no real statistical analysis, and to prepare a report of less than fifty pages nicely printed on heavy stock paper.

When one looks closely, there is less to these reports than meets the eye. There are some serious methodological problems with the reports as they are presently done. The reports are not adequate for us to make informed investment decisions based on the ideals embodied in the Sullivan Principles. They give the impression of being serious research without the substance that would be necessary for readers to have confidence in their findings. The ratings that companies are assigned may not be accurate indicators of the level of social responsibility actually exhibited. The resources currently devoted to the preparation of these reports might be better spent on a more conventional research project.

If the Sullivan Principles and these reports continue to be used as the litmus test of social performance for U.S. companies in South Africa, the process should be improved by the following modifications. Companies should be required to supply fewer data better verified by external observers, and by the people most concerned — South African blacks as well as academic and religious leaders. Companies should be rated on the extent to which they achieve objectives that are tailored to their individual circumstances. Internal and external constraints should be considered as well as opportunities unique to the particular type of company. Surely the monopoly of Arthur D. Little, Inc. should be reexamined. Its analysis of data, and particularly its use of qualitative points, appears not to reflect the degree of research sophistication that one would like to see. And finally, we should probe further to see if South African blacks themselves accept the premises and the findings of the Sullivan Principles reports. In the final analysis, it will be their evaluations that will determine what the future holds for U.S. firms in South Africa.

Bibliography of Publications on South Africa

by ERIC NEUBACHER

Politics and Government

Adam, Herbert. *Modernizing Racial Domination: South Africa's Political Dynamics.* Berkeley: University of California Press, 1971.

Adam, Herbert and Giliomee, Hermann. *Ethnic Power Mobilized: Can South Africa Change?* New Haven, Conn.: Yale University Press, 1979.

The Annual Survey of South African Law. Cape Town: Juta, 1947-.

Barber, James. "South Africa: A Society at War With Itself," *World Today* 41 (July 1985): 129-132.

——. "South Africa: The Regional Setting," *World Today* 42 (January 1986): 8-12.

Benson, Mary. *Nelson Mandela.* New York, W.W. Norton, 1986.

Benyon, John A., ed. *Constitutional Change in South Africa.* Pietermaritzburg: University of Natal Press, 1978.

Berman, John Kane. *Soweto: Black Revolt, White Reaction.* Johannesburg: Ravan Press, 1978.

Biko, Steve. *I Write What I Like.* San Francisco: Harper & Row, 1978.

Boulle, Laurence. *Constitutional Reform and the Apartheid State: Legitimacy, Consociationalism, and Control in South Africa.* New York: St. Martin's Press, 1984.

Brewer, John D. *After Soweto: An Unfinished Journey.* New York: Clarendon Press, 1984.

Breytenbach, Breyten. *End Papers: Essays, Letters, Articles of Faith, Workbook Notes.* New York: Farrar, Straus & Giroux, 1986.

——. *The True Confessions of an Albino Terrorist.* New York: Farrar, Straus & Giroux, 1985.

Brooks, Alan and Brickhill, Jeremy. *Whirlwind Before the Storm: The Origins and the Development of the Uprising in Soweto and the Rest of South Africa, from June to December 1976.* London: International Defence and Aid Fund for Southern Africa, 1980.

Brotz, Howard. *The Politics of South Africa: Democracy and Racial Diversity.* Oxford: Oxford University Press, 1977.

Bunting, Brian. *The Rise of the South African Reich.* Revised Edition. Baltimore: Penguin, 1969.

Bush, Ray and Kibble, Steve. *Destabilisation in Southern Africa: An Overview.* Uppsala, Sweden: Scandinavian Institute of African Studies, 1985.

Carter, Gwendolen M. *Which Way is South Africa Going?* Bloomington: Indiana University Press, 1980.

. *The Politics of Inequality: South Africa Since 1948.* Revised Edition. New York: Praeger, 1959.

Carter, Gwendolen M. and O'Meara, Patrick, eds. *Southern Africa: The Continuing Crisis.* Bloomington: Indiana University Press, 1979.

Cockram, Gail-Maryse. *Constitutional Law in the Republic of South Africa.* Cape Town: Juta, 1975.

Davidson, Basil: Slovo, Joe; and Wilkinson, Anthony, eds. *Southern Africa: The Politics of Revolution.* Harmondsworth: Penguin, 1976.

Davidson, Joshua. "The History of Judicial Oversight of Legislative and Executive Action in South Africa," *Harvard Journal of Law and Public Policy* 8 (Summer 1985): 685-744.

Davies, Robert H.; O'Meara, Dan; and Dlamini, Sipho. *The Struggle for South Africa: A Reference Guide to Movements, Organisations and Institutions.* 2 volumes. London: Zed, 1984.

Davies, R.; Kaplan, D.; Morris, M.; and O'Meara, D. "Class Struggle and the Periodisation of the State in South Africa," *Review of African Political Economy* 7 (1976): 4-30.

De Crespigny, Anthony and Schrire, Robert, eds. *The Government and Politics of South Africa.* Cape Town: Juta, 1978.

De St. Jorre, John et. al. "South Africa and Namibia: Prospects for Change," *Center Magazine* 16 (March/April 1983): 40-48.

De St. Jorre, John et. al. "Inside the Laager: White Power in South Africa," *Foreign Affairs* 55 (October 1976): 169-186.

. "South Africa: is Change Coming?" *Foreign Affairs* 60 (Fall 1981): 106-122.

De Villiers, Richard. "The Pass-Laws: Allocation and Control (1760-1979)," *South African Labor Bulletin* 5 (November 1979): 87-104.

Dean, W.H.B. and Smit, Dirk Van Zyl, eds. *Constitutional Change in South Africa: The Next Five Years.* Cape Town: Juta, 1983.

Dugard, John. *Human Rights and the South African Legal Order.* Princeton: Princeton University Press, 1978.

Duignan, Peter and Gann, L.H. *South Africa: War, Revolution or Peace?* Stanford: Hoover Institution Press, 1978.

Foster, Don and Sandler, Diane. *A Study of Detention and Torture in South Africa: Preliminary Report.* Cape Town: Institute of Criminology, University of Cape Town, 1985.

Frankel, Philip. "The Politics of Passes: Control and Change in South Africa," *Journal of Modern African Studies* 17 (1979): 199-217.

Friedrich Naumann Foundation. *South Africa, a Chance for Liberalism?* Sankt Augustin, [Germany]: Liberal Verlag, 1985.

Gann, Lewis and Duignan, Peter. *Why South Africa Will Survive: A Historical Analysis.* New York: St. Martin's, 1981.

Gerhart, Gail M. *Black Power in South Africa: The Evolution of an Ideology.* Berkeley: University Press, 1978.

Giliomee, Herman. *The Parting of the Ways: South African Politics 1976-82.* Cape Town: David Philip, 1982.

Greenberg. Stanley B. "Economic Growth and Political Change: The South African Case," *Journal of Modern African Studies* 19 (1981): 667-704.

Grundy, Kenneth W. *The Militarization of South African Politics.* Bloomington, Indiana University Press, 1986.

Guelke, Adrian. "Change in South African Politics?" *Political Studies* 31 (September 1983): 479-485.

Hahlo, H.R. and Kahn, Ellison. *The Union of South Africa: The Development of Its Laws and Constitutions.* London: Stevens, 1960.

Hanf, Theo; Weiland, H.; and Viedag, G. *South Africa: The Prospects of Peaceful Change.* Bloomington: Indiana University Press, 1981.

Harris, Richard, ed. *The Political Economy of Africa.* Cambridge, Mass.: Schenkman, 1975.

Harsch, Ernest. *South Africa: White Rule, Black Revolt.* New York: Monad Press, 1980.

Heard, Kenneth. *General Elections in South Africa, 1943-1970.* New York: Oxford University Press, 1974.

Heunis, Jan Christian. "Finding a Formula for Constitutional Reform," *Business and Society Review* No. 57 (Spring 1986): 33-37.

Hirson, Baruch. *Year of Fire, Year of Ash—The Soweto Revolt: Roots of a Revolution?* London: Zed Press, 1979.

Holliday, N. *Federate or Fail: Key to Peaceful, Politically Scientific Change for Southern Africa.* Alice, Ciskei: Lovedale Press, 1985.

Horrell, Muriel. *Laws Affecting Race Relations in South Africa 1948-1976.* Johannesburg: South African Institute of Race Relations, 1978.

Horwitz, Ralph. *The Political Economy of South Africa.* London: Weidnefeld and Nicolson, 1967.

Innes, D. and Plaut, M. "Class Struggle and the State," *Review of African Political Economy* 11 (1978): 51-61.

Isaacs, Henry. *Struggles Within the Struggle: An Inside View of the PAC of South Africa.* London: Zed, 1985.

Johnson, Richard W. *How Long Will South Africa Survive?* London: Macmillan, 1977.

Kane-Berman, John. *Soweto: Black Revolt, White Reaction.* Johannesburg: Ravan, 1978.

Karis, Thomas and Carter, Gwendolen, eds. *From Protest to Challenge: A Documentary History of African Politics in South Africa 1882-1965.* 4 vols. Stanford: Hoover Institution Press, 1972-77.

Karis, Thomas G. "Revolution in the Making, Black Politics in South Africa," *Foreign Affairs* 63 (Winter 1983): 378-406.

Kuper, Leo and Smith, M.G., eds. *Pluralism in Africa.* Berkeley: University of California Press, 1969.

Leach, Graham. *South Africa: No Easy Path to Peace.* Boston: Routledge & Kegan Paul, 1986.

Leatt, James; Kneifel, Theo; and Nurnberger, Klaus, eds. *Contending Ideologies in South Africa.* Grand Rapids, Mich.: W.B. Eerdmans, 1986.

Lijphart, Arend. *Power-Sharing in South Africa.* Berkeley: Institute of International Studies, University of California, 1985.

Lijphart, Arend and Stanton, Diane R. "A Democratic Blueprint for South Africa," *Business and Society Review* No. 57 (Spring 1986):28-32.

Magubane, Bernard. "Imperialism and the Making of the South African Working Class," *Contemporary Marxism* 6 (1983): 19-56.

. "The Mounting Class and National Struggles in South Africa," *Review* 8 (Fall 1984): 197-231.

. *The Political Economy of Race and Class in South Africa.* New York: Monthly Review Press, 1979.

Magubane, Bernard and Nzongola-Ntalaja, eds. *Proletarianization and Class Struggle in South Africa.* San Francisco: Synthesis, 1983.

Mandela, Nelson. *No Easy Walk to Freedom.* New York: Basic Books, 1965.

Mandela, Winnie. *Part of My Soul Went With Him.* New York: Norton, 1985.

Mathews, Anthony S. *Law, Order and Liberty in South Africa.* Berkeley: University of California Press, 1972.

Mayson, Cedric. *A Certain Sound: The Struggle for Liberation in South Africa.* Maryknoll, New York: Orbis, 1985.

Meltzer, Milton. *Winnie Mandela: The Soul of South Africa.* New York: Viking Kestrel, 1986.

Mermelstein, David, ed. *South Africa, The Struggle Against White Racist Rule.* New York: Grove Press, 1986.

Munger, Edwin S., ed. *The Afrikaners.* Cape Town: Tafelberg, 1979.

Nolutshungu, Sam. *South Africa: Political Considerations.* New York: Africana, 1982.

. *Changing South Africa: Political Considerations.* Manchester: Manchester University Press, 1982.

North, James. *Freedom Rising.* New York: North American Library, 1986.

Olivier, Gerrit C. "Is Democracy on the Political Horizon?" *Business and Society Review* No. 57 (Spring 1986): 24-27.

Pakendorf, Harald. "A Frozen Moment," *Leadership* 4, no. 3 (1985): 34-39.

Palmer, Robin and Parsons, Neil, eds. *The Roots of Rural Poverty in Central and Southern Africa.* Berkeley: University of California Press, 1983.

Parker, Frank J. *South Africa: Lost Opportunities.* Lexington, Mass.: Lexington Books, 1983.

Paton, Alan. *Civil Rights and Present Wrongs: Address to the Civil Rights League, Cape Town, 1968.* Johannesburg: South African Institute of Race Relations, 1968.

. *Hofmeyr.* London: Oxford University Press, 1964.

Peele, S. and Morse, S.J. "Ethnic Voting and Political Change in South Africa," *American Political Science Review* 68 (1974): 1520-1541.

Roshalt, A.M. "Can Business Lead the Way to Reform?" *Business and Society Review*, no. 57 (Spring 1986): 38-42.

Rotberg, Robert I. "How Deep the Change," *Foreign Policy* No. 38 (Spring 1980): 126-142.

Rotberg, Robert I. and Barratt, John, eds. *Conflict and Compromise in South Africa.* Lexington, Mass.: Lexington Books, 1980.

Roux, Edward. *Time Longer Than Rope: A History of the Black Man's Struggle for Freedom in South Africa.* Madison: University of Wisconsin Press, 1968.

Rudolph, Harold G. "Two is Company and a Crowd," *South African Law Journal* 93 (1976): 378-383.

Sachs, Albie. *Justice in South Africa.* Berkeley: University of California Press, 1973. "The Instruments of Domination in South Africa," in *Change in Contemporary South Africa,* ed. by Leonard Thompson and Jeffrey Butler. Berkeley: University of California Press, 1975.

Saul, John S. and Gelb, Stephen. *The Crisis in South Africa: Class Defence, Class Revolution.* Revised Edition. New York: Monthly Review Press, 1986.

Schlemmer, Lawrence and Welsh, David. "South Africa's Constitutional and Political Prospects," *Optima* 30 (June 1982): 210-231.

Schrire, Robert A., ed. *South Africa: Public Policy Perspectives.* Cape Town: Juta, 1982.

Steyn, Jan. "Prospects of Peaceful Change," *Disinvestment* (June 1985): 30-35.

South Africa Commission of Inquiry. *Report of the Commission of Inquiry Into the Riots at Soweto and Elsewhere from the 16th of June 1976 to the 28th of February 1977.* Pretoria, Government Printer, 1980.

Spence, J.E. "South Africa: Between Reform and Retrnechment," *World Today* 40 (November 1984): 471-480.

Starcke, Anna. *Survival: Taped Interviews With South Africa's Power Elite.* Cape Town: Tafelberg, 1978.

Suzman, Helen. "South Africa at This Moment," *Freedom at Issue* (March/April 1981): 10-16.

Swan, George Steven. "Comparative Constitutional Law—Communal Self-Determination in the Republic of South Africa's New Constitution," *Whittier Law Review* 7 (Winter 1985): 349-374.

Thompson, Leonard M. and Prior, Andrew. *South African Politics.* New Haven, Yale University Press, 1982.

United States. Congress. House. Committee on Foreign Affairs. Subcommittee on Africa. *Internal Political Situation in South Africa.* Hearings, 98th Congress, 1st Session, 1983. Washington: United States Government Printing Office, 1984.

Van den Berghe, P. *South Africa: A Study in Conflict.* Middletown: Wesleyan University Press, 1965.

Van Der Merwe, Hendrik W. et. al. *African Perspectives on South Africa: A Collection of Speeches, Articles and Documents.* Cape Town: David Philip, 1978.

Van Der Vyver, J.D. "Depriving Westminster of Its Moral Constraints: A Survey of Constitutional Development in South Africa," *Harvard Civil Rights-Civil Liberties Law Review* 20 (1985): 291-337.

Van Vuuren, D.J., ed. *South Africa: A Plural Society in Transition.* Stoneham, Mass.: Butterworth, 1985.

Van Zyl, J.C. "Business Offers a Bill of Rights for South Africa," *Business and Society Review* No. 57 (Spring 1986): 43-45.

Van Zyl Slabbert, Frederik and Opland, J., eds. *South Africa: Dilemmas of Evolutionary Change.* Grahamstown: Institute of Social and Economic Research, Rhodes University, 1980.

Van Zyl Slabbert, Frederik and Welsh, David. *South Africa's Options: Strategies for Sharing Power.* New York: St. Martin's, 1979.

Villa-Vicencio, Charles and DeGruchy, John W., eds. *Resistance and Hope: South*

African Essays in Honour of Beyers Naude. Grand Rapids, Mich.: W.B. Eerdmans, 1985.

Walters, Ronald. *South Africa and the Bomb: Responsibility and Deterrence.* Lexington, Mass.: Lexington Books, 1987.

Wiehahn, N.E. "Trade Unions and Politics in South Africa," *South African Journal of Labour Relations* 6 (June 1982): 36-40.

Wolpe, H. "Political Strategies and the Law in South Africa: Analytical Considerations," *Journal of South African Studies* 12 (1985): 12-24.

. "Towards an Analysis of the South African State," *International Journal of the Sociology of Law* 8 (1980): 399-421.

Wolpe, Harold. "Capitalism and Cheap Labour-Power in South Africa: From Segregation to Apartheid," *Economy and Society* 1 (November 1972): 433-439.

Woods, Donald. *South African Dispatches: Letters to My Countrymen.* New York: H. Holt, 1987.

Worrall, Denis, ed. *South Africa: Government and Politics, Second Edition.* Pretoria: Van Schaik, 1975.

APARTHEID AND RACE RELATIONS

Adam, Heribert and Moodley, Kogila. *South Africa Without Apartheid: Dismantling Racial Domination.* Berkeley: University of California Press, 1986.

Adams, R.C. "The 'Coloureds' of South Africa," in *Ethnicity in Modern Africa,* ed. by Brian M. du Toit. Boulder: Westview, 1978.

African Workers Under Apartheid. Brussels: International Cofederation of Free Trade Unions, 1984.

Bernstein, Hilda. *For Their Triumphs and Their Tears: Women in Apartheid South Africa.* Revised and Enlarged Edition. London: International Defence and Aid Fund for Southern Africa, 1985.

Butheleze, Gatsha. *Power is Ours.* New York: Books in Focus, 1979.

Butler, Jeffrey and Thompson, Leonard, eds. *Change in Contemporary South Africa.* Berkeley, University of California Press, 1975.

Desmond, Cosmas. *The Discarded People: An Account of Resettlement in South Africa.* Harmondsworth: Penguin, 1971.

De St. Jorre, John. *A House Divided: South Africa's Uncertain Future.* New York: Carnegie Endowment for International Peace, 1977.

Dugard, John. "The Legal Framework of Apartheid," in *South African Dialogue: Contrasts in South African Thinking on Basic Race Issues,* ed. by N.J. Rhoodie. Philadelphia: Westminster Press, 1973.

Eglin, Colin W. "The Out-Dated Concept of Apartheid," *Business and Society Review* No. 57 (Spring 1986): 22-23.

Fatton, Robert Jr. *Black Consciousness in South Africa: The Dialectics of Ideological Resistance to White Supremacy.* Albany: State University of New York Press, 1986.

Fleshman, Michael. "In Defense of Apartheid: South Africa and Its Neighbors." *Socialist Review* 16 (January-February 1986): 99-115.

Gordimer, Nadine and Goldblatt, David. *Lifetimes: Under Apartheid.* New York: Knopf, 1986.

Grundy, Kenneth W. *Deending Apartheid: The Rise of South Africa's Security Establishment.* Bloomington: Indiana University Press, 1986.

Hayden, Bill. "Apartheid and South Africa," *Australian Foreign Affairs Record* 56 (September 1985): 826-833.

Hellmann, Ellen and Lever, Henry, eds. *Conflict and Progress: Fifty Years of Race Relations in South Africa.* Johannesburg: Macmillan, 1979.

Holloway, J.E. "Apartheid," *Annals of the American Academy of Political and Social Science* 306 (1956): 26-37.

Horrell, Muriel. *Race Classification in South Africa: Its Effects on Human Beings.* Johannesburg: South African Institute of Race Relations, 1958.

International Labour Office. *Special Report of the Director-General on the Application of the Declaration Concerning the Policy of "Apartheid" of the Republic of South Africa.* Annual. Geneva: International Labour Office, 1965-.

James, Wilmot G., ed. *The State of Apartheid.* Boulder, Colo.: L. Rienner, 1986.

Jordan, Bojana V. *We Will Be Heard: A South African Exile Remembers.* Boston: Quinlan Press, 1986.

Kaplan, David. "The South African State: The Origins of a Racially Exclusive Democracy," *The Insurgent Sociologist* X (Fall 1980): 85-96.

Landis, Elizabeth S. "South African Apartheid Legislation," *Yale Law Journal* 71 (1961) 1-52, 437-500.

Lelyveld, Joseph. *Move Your Shadow: South Africa Black and White.* New York: Time Books, 1985.

Lemon, Anthony. *Apartheid.* Westmead: Saxon House, 1976.

Lewin, Peter. "The Prohibitive Cost of Apartheid," *Intercollegiate Review* 21 (Winter 1985-86): 25-31.

MacArthur, N.M. "Apartheid, the Courts and the Legal Profession," in *Law, Justice and Society,* ed. by Peter Randall. Johannesburg: Study Project on Christianity in Apartheid Society, 1972.

MacCrone, Ian D. *Race Attitudes in South Africa: Historical, Experimental and Psychological Studies.* Johannesburg: Witwatersrand University Press, 1965.

Mare, Gerry. *African Population Relocation in South Africa.* Johannesburg: South African Institute of Race Relations, 1980.

Mayer, P. *Some Aspects of the Sociology of Apartheid.* Johannesburg: Institute on the Study of Man in Africa, 1964.

Meer, F. "An Indian's Views on Apartheid," in *South African Dialogue: Contrasts in South African Thinking on Basic Race Issues,* ed. by N.J. Rhoodie. Philadelphia: Westminster Press, 1973.

Mulder, C.P. "The Rationale of Separate Development," in *South African Dialogue: Contrasts in South African Thinking on Basic Race Issues,* ed. by N.J. Rhoodie. Philadelphia: Westminster Press, 1973.

Murray, Martin J. *South African Capitalism and Black Political Opposition.* Cambridge, Mass.: Schenkman Publishing Company, 1982.

Nkomo, W.F. "An African's View of Apartheid," *South African Dialogue: Contrasts in South African Thinking on Basic Race Issues,* ed. by N.J. Rhoodie. Philadelphia: Westminster Press, 1973.

Nyquist, Thomas E. *Toward a Theory of the African Upper Stratum in South Africa.* Athens: Center for International Studies, Ohio University, 1972.

Paton, Alan. *Towards Racial Justice: Will There be a Change of Heart?* Johannesburg: South African Institute of Race Relations, 1979.

. *Apartheid and the Archbishop: The Life and Times of Geoffrey Clayton, Archbishop of Cape Town.* Cape Town: David Philip, 1973.

. *Case History of Pinky.* Johannesburg: South African Institute of Race Relations, 1972.

. *The Long View,* ed. by Edward Callan. New York: Praeger, 1968.

. *Charlestown Story.* Pietermaritzburg: Liberal Party of South Africa, 1961.

. *Alan Paton on Apartheid* [sound recording]. Berkeley: Pacifica Tape Library, 1960.

. *The Christian Approach to Racial Problems in the Modern World.* Second Edition. London: Christian Action, 1959.

. *South Africa Today.* New York: Public Affairs Committee, 1951.

Peace, Judy B. *The Boy Child is Dying: A South African Experience.* San Francisco: Harper & Row, 1986.

Pehe, Jiri. "South Africa Through East European Eyes," *Freedom at Issue* (May/April 1986): 13-14.

Pomeroy, William J. *Apartheid, Imperialism, and African Freedom.* New York: International Publishers, 1986.

Price, Robert M. and Rosberg, Carl. eds. *The Apartheid Regime: Political Power and Racial Domination.* Berkeley: Institute of International Studies, Univeristy of California, 1980.

Race Relations Survey. Annual. Johannesburg: South African Institute of Race Relations, 1985.

Rhoodie, N.J. and Venter, H.J. *Apartheid: A Socio-Historical Exposition.* Pretoria: Haum, 1959.

Ross, Howard. "South Africa, Apartheid, and Economic Exploitation," *Free Inquiry in Creative Sociology* 9 (November 1981): 206-210.

Savage, M. *The Challenge of Change and Some Arithmetic of Apartheid.* Johannesburg: South African Institute of Race Relations, 1977.

. "Costs of Enforcing Apartheid and Problems of Change," *African Affairs* 76 (July 1977): 287-302.

Scott, Otto J. *The Other End of the Lifeboat.* Chicago: Regnery Books, 1985.

Smith, David M. ed. *Living Under Apartheid: Aspects or Urbanization and Social Change in South Africa.* London: Allen & Unwin, 1982.

Stadler, Alfred W. *South Africa: The Political Economy of Apartheid.* New York: St. Martin's Press, 1987.

Stultz, Newell M. *Transkei's Half Loaf: Race Separatism in South Africa.* New Haven: Yale University Press, 1979.

Suzman, Helen. "Remarks of Helen Suzman." New York: American Jewish Committee, 1985.

Thompson, Leonard M. *The Political Mythology of Apartheid.* New Haven: Yale University Press, 1985.

Timal, Razia and Mazibuko, Tutuzile, eds. *Soweto: A People's Response.* Durban: Institute for Black Research, 1977.

Uhlig, Mark A, ed. *Apartheid in Crisis.* New York: Vintage Books, 1986.

Ume, Kalu E. "The Origin of Apartheid in South Africa: A Review," *Journal of African Studies* 8 (Winter 1981/82): 176-181.

United Nations Centre Against Apartheid. *Local Authority Action Against Apartheid: A Survey.* Sheffield: Sheffield Metropolitan District Council on Behalf of the National Steering Committee on Local Authority Action Against Apartheid, 1985.

———. "The Effects of Apartheid on the Status of Women in South Africa," *Black Scholar* 10 (September 1978): 11-20.

Van Der Horst, Sheila. *Progress and Retrogression in South Africa.* Johannesburg: South Africa Institute of Race Relations, 1971.

Van der Merwe, H.W. et. al. *White South African Elites.* Cape Town: Juta, 1974.

West, Charles C. *Perspective on South Africa.* Princeton: Princeton Theological Seminary, 1985.

Whitney, Robert A. "New Apartheid: International Law and the Transfer of South African Territory to the Kingdom of Swaziland," *Boston University International Law Journal* 2 (Summer 1984): 417-448.

Williams, Michael. *South Africa: The Crisis of World Capitalism and the Apartheid Economy.* London: Winstanley, 1977.

Woods, Donald. *Apartheid: The Propaganda and the Reality.* London: International Affairs Division, Commonwealth Secreteriat, 1985.

LABOR

Belcher, T. "Industrial Decentralization and the Dynamics of Forced Labor in South Africa," *Journal of Modern African Studies* 17 (1979): 677-686.

Bell, R.T. "Issues in South African Unemployment," *South African Journal of Economics* 53 (March 1985): 24-38.

———. *Unemployment in South Africa.* Durban: Institute for Social and Economic Research, University of Durban-Westville, Occasional Paper no. 10, June 1984.

Bell, R.T. and Padayachee, V. "Unemployment in South Africa: Trends, Causes and Cures," *Development Southern Africa* 1 (1984): 426-438.

Bergsman, Joel. "Apartheid, Wages, and Production Costs in South Africa: An Application of the Crowding Hypothesis," *The Journal of Human Resources* XVII (Fall 1982): 633-645.

Bonner, P. "Independent Trade Unions Since Wiehahn," *South African Labor Bulletin* 8 (1983): 16-36.

———. "Black Trade Unions in South Africa Since World War II," in *The Apartheid Regime: Political Power and Racial Domination,* ed. by Robert Price and Carol G. Rosberg. Berkeley: Institute for International Studies, University of California, 1980.

Bozzoli, Belinda, comp. *Labour, Townships and Protest: Studies in the Social History of Witwatersrand.* Johannesburg: Ravan Press, 1979.

Brand, S. "An Employment Strategy for South Africa," *Development Studies Southern Africa* 5 (1983): 186-196.

Breytenbach, Willie, ed. *Job Advancement in South Africa.* Johannesburg: South

Africa Foundation, 1980.

Clarke, Duncan and Simkins, Charles. *Structural Unemployment in South Africa.* Johannesburg: South Africa Foundation, 1980.

Davies, R. and O'Meara, D. "The Workers' Struggle in South Africa. A Comment," *Review of African Political Economy* 30 (1984): 109-116.

Davies, Robert H. "Capital Restructuring and the Modification of the Racial Division of Labour in Southern Africa," *Journal of South African Studies* 5 (April 1979): 181-198.

. *Capital, State and White Labor in South Africa, 1900-1960: An Historical Materialistic Analysis of Class Formation and Class Relations.* Atlantic Highlands, New Jersey: Humanities Press, 1979.

De Clerq, F. "Apartheid and the Organised Labour Movement," *Review of African Political Economy* 14 (1979): 69-77.

Desmond, Cosmas and Simkins, Charles, eds. *South African Unemployment: A Black Picture.* Pietermaritzburg: Development Studies Research Group and Agency for Industrial Mission, 1978.

Du Toit, Darcy. *Capital and Labor in South Africa.* Boston: Kegan Paul International, 1981.

Fine, B.; de Clerq, F.; and Innes, D. "Trade Unions and the State: The Question of Legality," *South African Labour Bulletin* 7 (1981): 39-68.

Geldenhuys, Deon, ed. *The South African Labour Scene in the 1980s: Discussions of the Study Group on Multinational Corporations.* Johannesburg: South African Institute of International Affairs, 1980.

Gerson, J. "The Question of Structural Unemployment in South Africa," *South African Journal of Economics* 49 (March 1981): 10-25.

Gerson, J. and Kantor, B. "An Analysis of Black Unemployment in South Africa," *Studies in Economics and Econometrics* No. 8 (August 1980): 83-87.

Gervasi, Sean. *Industrialization, Foreign Capital and Forced Labour in South Africa.* New York: United Nations, 1970.

Godson, Roy. *Black Labor as a Swing Factor in South Africa's Evolution.* Washington: International Labor Program, Georgetown University, 1979.

Gottschalk, K. "Industrial Decentralization: Jobs and Wages," *South African Labor Bulletin* 3 (1977): 50-58.

Hauck, David. *Black Trade Unions in South Africa.* Washington: Investor Responsibility Research Center, 1982.

Hemson, David. "Trade Unionism and the Struggle for Liberation in South Africa," *Capital and Class* No. 6 (Autumn 1978): 1-41.

Houghton, D. Hobart. "Men of Two Worlds — Some Aspects of Migratory Labour in South Africa," *South Africa Journal of Economics* 28 (September 1960): 177-190.

Imrie, Ruth M. *A Wealth of People: The Story of Trade Union Council of South Africa.* Johannesburg: Trade Union Council of South Africa, 1979.

Jones, Robert A. "The Changing Structure of Industrial Relations in South Africa," *Managerial and Decision Economics* 6 (1985): 217-225.

Knight, J.B. "The Nature of Unemployment in South Africa," *South Africa Journal of Economics* 50 (March 1982): 1-12.

. "Labour Allocation and Unemployment in South Africa," *Oxford Bulletin of Economics and Statistics* 40 (May 1978): 93-129.

Knight, J.B. and Lenta, G. "Has Capitalism Underdeveloped the Labour Reserves of South Africa?" *Oxford Bulletin of Economics and Statistics* 42 (August 1980): 157-201.

Knight, J.B. and McGrath, M.D. "An Analysis of Racial Wage Discrimination in South Africa," *Oxford Bulletin of Economics and Statistics* 39 (November 1977): 245-271.

Lambert, R. and Lambert, L. "State Reform and Working Class Resistance," *The South African Review* 1 (1983): 218-250.

Lawson, Lesley. *Working Women.* Braafontein: Ravan Press, 1985.

Luckhardt, Ken and Wall, Brenda. *Organize or Starve: The History of the South African Congress of Trade Unions.* London: Lawrence & Wishart, 1980.

McShane, D.; Plaut, M.; and Ward, D. *Power! Black Workers, Their Unions and the Struggle for Freedom in South Africa.* Nottingham: Spokesman Books, 1984.

Maree, Johann. "The Dimensions and Causes of Unemployment and Underemployment in South Africa," *South Africa Labour Bulletin* 4 (July 1978): 15-50.

Marsh, P.A. "Labour Reform and Security Repression in South Africa: Botha's Strategy for Stabilizing Racial Domination," *Issue* 12 (1982): 49-55.

Massey, David. "Class Struggle and Migrant Labour in the South African Gold Mines," *Canadian Journal of African Studies* 17 (1983): 429-448.

Nasser, Martin. *Report on Black Employee Attitudes to Capitalism.* Pretoria: UNISA School of Business Leadership, 1984.

Nattrass, Jill. "The Narrowing Wage Differentials in South Africa," *South Africa Journal of Economics* 45 (1977): 408-432.

"Organizing the Struggle," *Africa Report* 31 (March/April 1986): 10-14.

Plaut, M. "Changing Perspectives on South African Trade Unions," *Review of African Political Economy* 30 (1984): 116-123.

Porter, Richard C. "Apartheid, the Job Ladder, and the Evolutionary Hypothesis: Empirical Evidence from South African Manufacturing, 1960-1977," *Economic Development and Cultural Change* 33 (October 1984): 117-141.

Pursell, Donald E. "Bantu Real Wages and Employment Opportunities in South Africa," *South Africa Journal of Economics* 36 (June 1968): 87-103.

Pursell, Donald E. "South African Labor Policy: 'New Deal' for Nonwhites?" *Industrial Relations* 10 (February 1971): 36-48.

Republic of South Africa. *A Strategy for the Creation of Employment Opportunities in the Republic of South Africa.* Pretoria: Government Printer, 1984.

Schlemmer, Lawrence. *Black Worker Attitudes: Political Options, Capitalism, and Investment in South Africa.* Durban: Centre for Applied Social Sciences, University of Natal, 1984.

South Africa. Commission of Inquiry Into Labour Legislation. *Report of the Commission of Inquiry Into Labour Legislation,* Part 1. Pretoria: Department of Labour and of Mines, 1979. Parts 2-6. Pretoria: Department of Manpower Utilisation, 1980.

South Africa. Commission of Inquiry Into Labour Legislation. *Report of the Commission of Inquiry Into Legislation Affecting the Utilisation of Manpower. Report of the Commission of Inquiry into Legislation Affecting the*

Utilization on Manpower. Pretoria: Government Printer 1979.

Structural Unemployment in Southern Africa. Pietermaritzburg: University of Natal Press, 1978.

Simkins, Charles and Desmond, Cosmas, eds. *South African Unemployment: A Black Picture.* Pietermaritzburg: Development Studies Research Group, University of Natal, 1978.

Sutcliffe, M.O. and Wellings, P.A. "Worker Militancy in South Africa: A Sociospatial Analysis of Trade Union Activism in the Manufacturing Sector," *Environment and Planning D: Society and Space* 3 (1985): 357-379.

Trade Unions Against Apartheid. Proceedings of a Symposium to Evaluate the ICFTU Programme of Action in Support of the Independent Black Trade Union Movement in South Africa, Düsseldorf, January 19-20, 1984. Brussels: International Confederation of Free Trade Unions, 1984.

United States. Congress. House. Committee on Foreign Affairs. Subcommittee on Africa. *Labor Situation in South Africa.* Hearings...96th Congress, 2nd Session, 1980. Washington: United States Government Printing Office, 1981.

Van der Merwe, Petrus J. "Unemployment and Employment Creation," *Development Studies Southern Africa* 5 (1983): 146-159.

———. *Black Employment Problems in South Africa.* Pretoria: Bureau for Economic Policy and Analysis, University of Pretoria, 1976.

Vose, W.J. "Wiehahn and Riekert Revisited: A Review of Prevailing Black Labour Conditions in South Africa," *International Labour Review* 124 (July-August 1985): 447-464.

Walker, Ivan and Weinbren, Ben. *2000 Casualties: A History of Trade Unions and the Labour Movement in the Union of South Africa.* Johannesburg: South African Trade Union Council, 1961.

Wiehahn, N.E. "Trade Unions and Politics in South Africa," *South African Journal of Labor Relations* 6 (June 1982): 36-40.

Webster, Eddie, ed. *Essays in Southern African Labour History.* Johannesburg: Ravan Press, 1978.

Wilson, Francis. *Labour in the South African Gold Mines, 1911-1969.* Cambridge: The University Press, 1972.

Wolpe, H. "Capitalism and Cheap Labour Power in South Africa: From Segregation to Apartheid," *Economy and Society* 1 (1972): 425-.

ECONOMY AND INDUSTRY

Abedian, I. "A Quantitative Review of the Economy of Transkei," *South Africa Journal of Economics* 51 (1983): 2525-269.

Ariovich, G. "The Comparative Advantage of South Africa as Revealed by Export Shares," *South Africa Journal of Economics* 47 (June 1979): 188-197.

———. "A Note on Export Shares and Capital Intensity in South African Industry," *South Africa Journal of Economics* 48 (June 1980): 211-213.

Bell, R.T. *Industrial Decentralization in South Africa.* Cape Town: Oxford University Press, 1973.

———. "Some Aspects of Industrial Decentralization in South Africa," *South Africa*

Journal of Economics 41 (1973): 401-431.

Best, A. "South Africa's Border Industries: The Tswana Example," *Annals of the Association of American Geographers* 61 (1971): 329-343.

Bienefeld, M. and Innes, D. "Capital Accumulation and South Africa," *Review of African Political Economy* 7 (1976): 31-55.

Blumenfeld, Jesmond. "South Africa: Economic Responses to International Pressures," *World Today* 41 (1985): 218-221.

Blumenfeld, J.P. "The South African Economy: Potential and Pitfalls," *World Today* 36 (September 1980): 334-342.

Bozzoli, B. "Capital and the State in South Africa," *Review of African Political Economy* 11 (1978): 40-50.

Bruce, Nigel. "The Rand and the Cash Crisis," *Leadership* 4, no. 3 (1985): 42-47.

Collings, John. "African Links," *Disinvestment* (June 1985): 77.

Cox, B.A. and Rogerson, C.M. "The Corporate Power Elite in South Africa: Interlocking Directorships Among Large Enterprises," *Political Geography Quarterly* 4 (July 1985): 219-234.

———. "The Structure and Geography of Interlocking Corporate Directorates in South Africa," *South African Geographer* 12 (1984): 133-148.

Department of Foreign Affairs and Information. *The Promotion of Industrial Development as an Element of a Coordinated Regional Development Strategy for Southern Africa.* Pretoria: Government Printer, 1982.

Du Plesis, P.G. "Concentration of Economic Power in South African Manufacturing Industry," *South Africa Journal of Economics* 46 (1978): 257-269.

Du Toit, P. "South Africa's Regional Industrial Development Plan for the 1980s: Its Possible Role in Regional Development," *Development Studies Southern Africa* 4 (1982): 249-267.

Emdon, E. "The Planning Act and the Transvaal Clothing Industry," *South African Labor Bulletin* 3 (1977): 59-64.

Giliomee, H. and Schlemmer, L., eds. *Up Against the Fences: Passes, Privilege in South Africa.* Cape Town: David Philip, 1985.

Green, P. and Hirsch, A. "The Ciskei — Political Economy of Control," *South African Labor Bulletin* 7 (1982): 65-85.

Hirsch, A. "The Study of Industrial Decentralization Policy in South Africa: Some Comments," in *Southern African Studies: Retrospect and Prospect.* Edinburgh: Centre for African Studies, University of Edinburgh, 1983.

Hyslop, J. and Tomlinson, R. "Industrial Decentralization and the 'New Dispensation'," *South African Labor Bulletin* 10 (1984): 114-122.

Innes, Duncan. "Capitalism and Gold," *Capital and Class* No. 6 (Summer 1981): 5-35.

———. "Monopoly Capitalism in South Africa," in *South African Review,* edited by the South African Research Service. Johannesburg: Ravan Press, 1983.

Johnstone, Frederick. *Class, Race and Gold.* London: Routledge & Kegan Paul, 1976.

———. "White Prosperity and White Supremacy in South Africa," *African Affairs* 69 (1970): 124-140.

Legassick, M. and Innes, D. "Capital Restructuring and Apartheid: A Critique of Constructive Engagement," *African Affairs* 76 (1977): 437-482.

Liff, David M. *The Computer and Electronics Industry in South Africa.* Washington: Investor Responsibility Research Center, 1979.

. *The Oil Industry in South Africa.* Washington: Investor Responsibility Research Center, 1979.

Main, T.R.N. "Gold Production in South Africa: A Look at the 1980s," *Mining Survey*, no. 94 (1979): 2-8.

Martin, V.M. and Rogerson, C.M. "Women and Industrial Chagne," *South African Geographical Journal* 66 (1984): 32-46.

McCarthy, C.L. "Industrial Decentralization — Reflections on the New Initiatives," *South Africa Journal of Economics* 50 (1982): 238-252.

Mohr, P.J. "Some Thoughts on Regional Economic Development in South Africa, with Special Reference to the New Industrial Development Policy," *Development Studies Southern Africa* 5 (1983): 67-75.

Murray, F. "The Decentralization of Production — The Decline of the Mass-Collective Worker?" *Capital and Class*, No. 19 (1983): 74-99.

Myers, Desaix III and Liff, David. "The Press of Business," *Foreign Policy*, no. 38 (Spring 1980): 143-163.

Propp, Kenneth and Myers, Desaix III. *The Motor Industry in South Africa.* Washington: Investor Responsibility Research Center, 1979.

Ratcliffe, A. "Industrial Development Policy: Changes During the 1970's," *South Africa Journal of Economics* 47 (1979): 397-421.

Relly, Gavin. "Gavin Relly: In Conversation with Hugh Murray," *Leadership* 4, no. 3 (1985): 10-20.

Rogerson, Christian M. "Growth Point Problems — The Case of Babelegi, Bophuthatswana," *Journal of Modern African Studies* 12 (1974): 126-130.

. "Industrial Movement in an Industrializing Economy," *South African Geographical Journal* 57 (1975): 88-103.

. "The Spatial Concentration of Corporate Control in South Africa, 1965-1980," *South African Geographical Journal* 66 (1984): 97-100.

Schlemmer, Lawrence. *Black Attitudes and Business in South Africa.* Durban: Centre for Applied Social Sciences, University of Natal, 1983.

Trapido, Stanley. "South Africa in a Comparative Study of Industrialization," *Journal of Development Studies* 7 (April 1971): 309-320.

Van Zyl, J.C. "South Africa in World Trade," *South Africa Journal of Economics* 52 (1984): 42-62.

Viljoen, S.P. "The Industrial Achievement of South Africa," *South Africa Journal of Economics* 51 (1983): 29-57.

Wellings, Paul and Black, Anthony. "Industrial Decentralization under Apartheid: The Relocation of Industry to the South African Periphery," *World Development* 14 (1986): 1-38.

Wilson, Francis. *South Africa: The Cordoned Heart.* New York: Norton, 1986.

ECONOMY— BACKGROUND

"The Banks Abandon South Africa," *Euromoney* (December 1985): 64-77.

Bloch, G. "Room at the Top? The Development of South Africa's Manufacturing Industry 1939-1969," *Social Dynamics* 7 (1981): 47-57.

Clarke, S. "Capital, Fractions of Capital and the State: Neo-Marxist Analysis of South Africa," *Capital and Class* 5 (1978): 32-77.

Cobbett, W.; Glaser, D.; Hindson, D.; and Swilling, M. "Regionalization, Federalism, and the Reconstruction of the South African State," *South African Labor Bulletin* 10 (1985): 87-116.

Du Plessis, J.C. *Economic Fluctuations in South Africa, 1910-1949.* Stellenbosch: Bureau of Economic Research, University of Stellenbosch, 1950.

Franzsen, D.G. "Monetary Policy in South Africa 1932-1982," *South Africa Journal of Economics* 51 (1983): 88-131.

Harris, Richard. *The Political Economy of Africa.* Cambridge: Schenkman Press, 1975.

Houghton, D. Hobart. *The South African Economy,* 4th ed. Cape Town: Oxford University Press, 1976.

Houghton, H. Hobart and Dagut, Jenifer. *Source Material on the South African Economy 1860-1970.* 3 vols. Cape Town: Oxford University Press, 1972-73.

Leftwich, Adrian, ed. *South Africa: Economic Growth and Political Change.* London: Allison and Busby, 1974.

Legassick, M. "Legislation, Ideology and Economy in Post 1948 South Africa," *Journal of Southern African Studies* 1 (1974): 5-35.

———. "South Africa: Capital Accumulation and Violence," *Economy & Society* III (August 1974): 253-291.

Lipton, Merle. *Capitalism and Apartheid.* Totowa, New Jersey: Rowman & Allanheld, 1985.

Lombard, Jan A., ed. *Economic Policy in South Africa: Selected Essays.* Cape Town: H.A.U.M., 1973.

Lombard, Jan A. *Freedom, Welfae and Order: Thoughts on the Political Cooperation in the Economy of Southern Africa.* Pretoria: Benbo, 1978.

Lundahl, Mats. "The Rationale of Apartheid," *American Economic Review* 72 (December 1972): 1169-1179.

Matthews, Jacqueline. *South Africa in the World Economy.* Johannesburg: McGraw Hill, 1983.

Mouton, D.J. and Lambrechts, J.A. "Official Competition Policy in the Republic of South Africa," *Finance and Trade Review* 15 (June 1982): 1-23.

Nattrass, J. *The South African Economy: Its Growth and Change.* Cape Town: Oxford University Press, 1981.

Porter, Richard C. "A Model of the Southern-African-Type Economy," *American Economic Review* 68 (December 1978): 743-755.

Republic of South Africa. *Report of the Commission of Inquiry Into the Regulation of Monopolistic Conditions Act, 1955. RP 64/1977.* Pretoria: Government Printer, 1977.

Robertson, Hector M. "150 Years of Economic Contact Between Black and White, Parts I and II," *South Africa Journal of Economics* 2 (December 1934): 403-425; 3 (March 1935): 3-25.

Scheepers, C.F. "The International Trade Strategy of South Africa," *South Africa Journal of Economics* 50 (1982): 13-25.

Schlemmer, Lawrence; Geerdts, P.; and Van Schalkwyk, L. "Industrial Relations in South Africa: Some Evidence for a Future Scenario," *South African Industrial Relations Journal* 4 (1984): 40-49.

Schlemmer, Lawrence and Webster, Eddie, eds. *Change Reform, and Economic Growth in South Africa.* Johannesburg: Ravan Press, 1978.

Smit, D.J. and Van Der Walt, B.E. "Growth Trends and Business Cycles in the South African Economy," *South African Reserve Bank Quarterly Bulletin* (June 1982).

INTERNATIONAL BUSINESS RELATIONS

Barber, James. "The EEC Code for South Africa: Capitalism as a Foreign Policy Instrument," *World Today* 36 (March 1980): 79-87.

Bates, Timothy. "The Impact of Multinational Corporations on Power Relations in South Africa," *Review of Black Political Economy* 12 (Winter 1983): 133-143.

Blumenfeld, Jesmond. "South Africa: Economic Responses to International Pressures," *World Today* 41 (December 1985): 218-221.

Campbell, Duncan C. "U.S. Firms and Black Labor in South Africa: Creating a Structure for Change," *Journal of Labor Research* 7 (Winter 1986): 1-18.

Communications Task Group of the Sullivan Signatory Companies. *Meeting the Mandate for Change: A Progress Report on the Application of the Sullivan Principles by U.S. Companies in South Africa.* New York: Industry Support Unit, 1984.

Corporate Data Exchange, Inc. *Bank Loans to South Africa, 1972-1978.* New York: Centre Against Apartheid, 1979.

Corporate Information Center, National Council of Churches. *Church Investments, Corporations and Southern Africa.* New York: Friendship Press, 1973.

Du Plessis, J.C. "Foreign Investment in South Africa," in *Foreign Investment: The Experience of Host Countries* ed. by Isaiah A. Litvak and Christopher J. Maule. New York: Praeger, 1970.

Fields, Lorraine. "United States Investment in South Africa," *International Property Investment Journal* 2 (September 1985): 451-469.

Frankel, S. Herbert. *Capital Investment in Africa: Its Course and Effects.* London: Oxford University Press, 1958.

Hauck, David. *Can Pretoria Be Moved? The Emergence of Business Activism in South Africa.* Washington: Investor Responsibility Research Center, 1986.

Holland, Martin. "The EEC Code for South Africa: A Reassessment," *World Today* 41 (January 1985): 12-14.

Jankowitsch, Odette and Seidensticker, Ellen. "Transnational Corporations in South Africa," *Dissent* 26 (Fall 1979): 473-477.

Kaplan, D. "The Internationalisation of South African Capital: South African Direct Foreign Investment in the Contemporary Period," *African Affairs* 82 (1983): 465-494.

Leape, Jonathan; Baskin, Bo; and Underhill, Stefan. *Business in the Shadow of Apartheid: U.S. Firms in South Africa.* Lexington, Mass.: Lexington Books, 1985.

Arthur D. Little, Inc. *Eighth Report on the Signatory Companies to the Sullivan Principles.* Philadelphia: International Council for Equality of Opportunity Principles, 1984.

Litvak, Lawrence; DeGrasse, Robert; and McTigue, Kathleen. *South Africa: Foreign Investment and Apartheid.* Washington: Institute for Policy Studies, 1978.

Mackler, Ian. *Pattern for Profit in Southern Africa.* New York: Atheneum, 1975.

Marzullo, Sal G. "Corporations: Catalysts for Change?" *Business and Society Review* No. 57 (Spring 1986): 51-55.

——. "South Africa: The Hard Questions, IV," *America* 153 (August 10, 1985): 53-56.

Myers, Desaix, III. *Labor Practices of U.S. Corporations in South Africa.* New York: Praeger, 1977.

——. *U.S. Business in South Africa: The Economic, Political, and Moral Issues.* Bloomington: Indiana University Press, 1980.

Ndaba, Benjamin Alan. *Political Change in South Africa: The Contribution of Foreign Investment and Western Countries.* Geneva: Institut Universitaire de Hautes Etudes Internationales, 1986.

Nickel, Herman. "The Case for Doing Business in South Africa," *Fortune* 97 (June 19, 1978): 60-74.

Nyangoni, Wellington Winter. *The OCED and Western Mining Multinational Corporations in the Republic of South Africa.* Washington: University Press of America, 1982.

Paul, Karen. "The Inadequacy of Sullivan Reporting," *Business and Society Review* No. 57 (Spring 1986): 61-65.

Razis, Vincent Victor. *The American Connection: The Influence of U.S .Business on South Africa.* New York: St. Martin's Press, 1986.

Rogers, Barbara. *White Wealth and Black Poverty: American Investments in Southern Africa.* Westport Conn.: Greenwood Press, 1976.

Rogerson, C. "Spatial Perspectives on United Kingdom Investment in South Africa," *South African Geographical Journal* 63 (1981): 85-106.

——. "Multinational Corporations in South Africa: A Spatial Perspective," in *The Geography of Multinationals,* ed. by M.J. Taylor and N. Thrift. London: Croom Helm, 1982.

——. "Patterns of Indigenous and Foreign Control of South African Manufacturing," *South African Geographer* 10 (1982): 123-134.

Schmidt, Elizabeth. *One Step in the Wrong Direction: An Analysis of the Sullivan Principles as a Strategy for Opposing Apartheid.* Revised Edition. New York: Episcopal Churchpeople for a Free South Africa, 1985.

Seidman, Ann Wilcox. *The Roots of Crisis in Southern Africa.* Trenton: Africa World Press, 1985.

Seidman, Ann and Neva. *South Africa and U.S. Multinational Corporations.* Westport, Conn.: Lawrence Hill & Co., 1978.

Setai, Bethuel. "The Role of International Companies in the Economy of South Africa," *Review of Black Political Economy* 8 (Summer 1978): 346-359.

Sincere, Richard E. *The Politics of Sentiment: Churches and Foreign Investment in South Africa.* Washington: Ethics and Public Policy Center, 1984.

Sullivan, Leon Howard. *The Role of Multinational Corporations in South Africa.* Johannesburg: South African Institute of Race Relations, 1980.

Thomas, W.H. "The Structure of the South African Economy and the Nature of Its Ties with the International Economy," in *The Conditions of the Black Worker.* London: Africa Publications Trust, 1975.

Taylor, Michael J. and Thrift, Nigel, eds. *The Geography of Multinationals.* New York: St. Martin's, 1982.

Tomlinson, Blaine. *The Role of Private Foreign Investment and Multinational Corporations in the Economic Development in South Africa.* Cape Town: The Graduate School of Business, University of Cape Town, 1975.

United Nations Centre on Transnational Corporations. *Activities of Transnational Corporations in South Africa and Nambia and the Responsibilities of Home Countries With Respect to Their Operations in This Area.* New York: United Nations, 1986.

———. *Policies and Practices of Transnational Corporations Regarding Their Activities in South Africa and Nambia.* New York: United Nations, 1984.

United Nations Department of Public Information. Division for Economic and Social Information. *International Focus on Transnational Corporations in South Africa and Nambia.* New York: United Nations, 1985.

U.S. Congress. House. Committee on International Relations. Subcommittee on Africa and on International Economic Policy and Trade. *United States Private Investment in South Africa.* Washington: United States Government Printing Office, 1978.

Weedon, D. Reid Jr. "The Evolution of Sullivan Principle Compliance," *Business and Society Review* No. 57 (Spring 1986): 56-60.

Wilking, Lou H. "Can U.S. Corporations Play a Positive Role?" *Business and Society Review* No. 57 (Spring 1986): 46-50.

Williams, Oliver F. *The Apartheid Crisis: How We Can Do Justice in a Land of Violence.* San Francisco: Harper & Row, 1986.

SANCTIONS – DIVESTMENT

"Across the Board: Six Leaders Take a Brief Look at the Disinvestment Question," *Disinvestment* (June 1985): 86-88.

Adam, Heribert. "Outside Influence on South Africa: Afrikanerdom in Disarray," *Journal of Modern African Studies* 21 (1983): 233-251.

Baade, Robert A. and Galloway, Jonathan C. "Economic Sanctions Against the Union of South Africa: Policy Options," *Alternatives* IV (1978-1979): 487-505.

Baigrie, James. "South African Trust Director Opposes Sanctions as Policy to Speed Reform," *Trusts & Estates* 124 (October 1985): 18-23.

Bailey, Martin and Rivers, Bernard. *Oil Sanctions Against South Africa.* New York: United Nations Centre Against Apartheid, no. 15/80, April 1980.

Barber, James and Spicer, Michael. "Sanctions Against South Africa: Options for the West," *International Affairs* 55 (July 1979): 385-401.

Billings, David M. "Economic Sanctions: United States Sanctions Against South Africa," *Harvard International Law Journal* 27 (Winter 1986): 235-242.

Bloom, Tony. "The Great Paradox," *Disinvestment* (June 1985): 60-65.

Brand, Simon S. "How Economic Sanctions Could Cripple A Reform," *Busines and Society Review* No. 57 (Spring 1986): 75-78.

Buthelezi, Mangosutho G. "Discerning the Divestment Debate," *Business and Society Review* No. 57 (Spring 1986): 79-81.

———. "Inkatha Says No," *Disinvestment* (June 1985): 72-76.

Coons, Christopher. "Divestment Steamroller Seeks to Bury Apartheid," *Business and Society Review* No. 57 (Spring 1986): 90-95.

D'Agostino, Robert J. "Politics, Sentiment, Disinvestment and South Africa," *Delaware Lawyer* 4 (Fall 1985): 52-54.

Davis, Jennifer. *Economic Disengagement and South Africa: The Effectiveness and Feasibility of Implementing Sanctions and Divestment.* New York: Africa Fund, 1983.

De Villiers, Marq. "The Case for Staying Put," *Canadian Business* 59 (March 1986): 38-40.

Dobris, Joel C. "Arguments in Favor of Fiduciary Divestment of South African Securities," *Nebraska Law Review* 65 (Spring 1986): 209-241.

"Economic Sanctions Against South Africa: Problems and Prospects for Enforcement of Human Rights Norms," *Virginia Journal of International Law* 22 (Winter 1982): 345-380.

Hasselkus, Walter. "The German Connection," *Disinvestment* (June 1985): 69-71.

Ivens, Michael. "The Corporate Role in Fighting Apartheid: British Style," *Business and Society Review* No. 58 (Summer 1986): 49-52.

"European Community: Actions and Statements of Foreign Ministers [Sanctions Against South Africa]," *International Legal Materials* 24 (September 1985): 1474-1482.

Jubinsky, Grace A. "State and Municipal Governments React Against South African Apartheid: An Assessment of the Constitutionality of the Divestment Campaign," *University of Cincinnati Law Review* 54 (Spring 1985): 543-578.

Kassebaum, Nancy Landon. "Caution Signs on the Road to Reform," *Business and Society Review* No. 57 (Spring 1986): 9-11.

Koenderman, Tony. "Sanctions," *South Africa International* 9 (January 1979): 150-158.

Langbein, John H.; Schotland, Roy A.; and Blaustein, Albert P. *Disinvestment; Is It Legal?; Is It Moral?; Is It Productive?; An Analysis of Politicizing Investment Decisions.* Washington: National Legal Center for the Public Interest, 1985.

Litvak, Lawrence; Estrella, Julia; and McTique, Kathleen. *Divesting From South Africa: A Prudent Approach for Pension Funds.* Washington: Conference on Alternative State and Local Policies, 1981.

Lundahl, Mats. "Economic Effects of a Trade and Investment Boycott Against South Africa," *Scandinavian Journal of Economics* 86 (1984): 68-83.

McCarroll, Patricia. "Socially Responsible Investment of Public Pension Funds: The South Africa Issue and State Law," *New York University Review of Law and Social Change* 10 (1980-1981): 407-434.

Magyar, Karl and Konar, Len. "Disinvestment: The Myths Examined," *Leadership* 4, no. 3 (1985): 70-79.

Marlin, Alice Tepper. "Social Investing: Potent Force for Political Change," *Business and Society Review* No. 57 (Spring 1986): 86-100.

Murphy, Joseph. "The Apartheid Debate on American Campuses," *Business and Society Review* No. 57 (Spring 1986): 113-117.

Nickel, Herman. "Will Sanctions Harm the Oppressed or the Oppressor?" *Business and Society Review* No. 57 (Spring 1986): 82-86.

——. "American Realities," *Disinvestment* (June 1985): 22-26.

Olson, Martha J. "University Investments with a South African Connection: Is Prudent Divestiture Possible?" *New York University Journal of International Law and Politics* 11 (Winter 1979): 543-580.

Oppenheimer, Harry. "Disinvestment: Will it Conduce to Peace and Justice in South Africa?" *Disinvestment* (June 1985): 8-14.

Paton, Alan. "An Act of Immorality," *Disinvestment* (June 1985): 27-29.

Porter, Richard C. "International Trade and Investment Sanctions: Potential Impact on the South African Economy," *Journal of Conflict Resolution* 23 (December 1979): 579-612.

Proxmire, William. "The Proxmire Factor," *Disinvestment* (June 1985): 36-38.

Robinson, Randall. "Investments in Tokenism," *Foreign Policy* No. 38 (Spring 1980): 164-167.

"Sanctions and South Africa," *Harvard International Law Journal* 19 (Fall 1978): 887-930.

Schatz, Willie. "S. Africa: Pulling the Plug," *Datamation* 31 (October 1, 1985): 22-28.

Schlemmer, Lawrence. "The Dynamics of Sanctions," *Disinvestment* (June 1985): 39-43.

Seidman, Ann W. *Economic Sanctions as a Basic Choice in Southern Africa.* London: Africa Bureau, 1981.

Solarz, Stephen. "Solarz Speaks," *Disinvestment* (June 1985): 48-50.

South Africa and Sanctions — Genesis and Prospects: Papers and Comments Delivered at a Symposium Jointly Organised by the South African Institute of Race Relations and the South African Institute of International Affairs, on February 24, 1979. Johannesburg: South Africa Institute of Race Relations-South Africa Institute of International Affairs, 1979.

Spandau, Arnt. *Economic Boycott Against South Africa: Normative and Factual Issues.* Kenwyn: Juta, 1979.

Stevens, Catherine. "The Impact of Divestment," *Financial World* 154 (October 16-29, 1985): 92-97.

Sutcliffe, Michael O. "Plenty of Propaganda to Prop Up Pretoria," *Business and Society Review* No. 58 (Summer 1986): 53-56.

Suzman, Helen. "The Folly of Economic Sanctions," *Business and Society Review* No. 57 (Spring 1986): 87-89.

Tillet, Rebecca. "Pretoria's U.S. Lawyers Succumb to Student Pressure," *Business and Society Review* No. 58 (Summer 1986): 22-24.

Train, John. "Staying Power: A Wall Street Analyst Asks Black and Union Leaders What They Think About the Disinvestment Issue," *Across the Board* 22 (November 1985): 51-58.

Troyer, Thomas A.; Slocombe, Walter B.; and Boisture, Robert A. "Divestment of South Africa Investments: The Legal Implications for Foundations, Other Charitable Institutions, and Pension Funds," *Georgetown Law Journal* 74 (October 1985): 127-161.

Tutu, Desmond. "A Plea for International Sanctions," *Business and Society Review* no. 57 (Spring 1986): 66-67.

——. "Tutu," *Disinvestment* (June 1985): 15-17.

U.S. Congress. House. Committee on Banking, Finance, and Urban Affairs. Subcommittee on Domestic Monetary Policy. *Impact of Withdrawal and Disinvestment From South Africa on the U.S. Economy.* Hearings...99th Congress, 1st Session, 1985. Washington: United States Government Printing

Office, 1985.

. House. Committee on Banking, Finance, and Urban Affairs. Subcommittee on Financial Institutions Supervision, Regulation and Insurance. *South African Restrictions.* Hearings...98th Congress, 1st Session, 1983. Washington: United States Government Printing Office, 1983.

. House. Committee on Foreign Affairs. Subcommittee on Africa. *Economic Sanctions and Their Potential Impact on U.S. Corporate Involvement in South Africa.* Hearings...99th Congress, 1st Session, 1985. Washington: United States Government Printing Office, 1985.

. House. Committee on Foreign Affairs. Subcommittee on Africa. *Enforcement of the United States Arms Embargo Against South Africa.* Hearings...97th Congress, 2nd Session, 1982. Washington: United States Government Printing Office, 1982.

. House. Committee on the District of Columbia. Subcommittee on Fiscal Affairs and Health. *South Africa Divestment* . Hearings...98th Congress, 2nd Session, 1984. Washington, United States Government Printing Office, 1984.

Wassermann, U. "Apartheid and Economic Sanctions," *Journal of World Trade Law* 15 (1981): 366-369.

Williams, Grayling M. "In Support of Azania: Divestiture of Public Pension Funds as One Answer to United States Private Investment in South Africa," *Black Law Journal* 9 (Winter 1985): 167-188.

Wright, Sanford. "Struggling Against Apartheid: The Use of Economic Sanctions on South Africa," *Review of Black Political Economy* 13 (Winter 1984-85): 37-47.

FOREIGN RELATIONS

Barber, James P.; Blumenfeld, Jesmond; and Hill, Christopher R. *The West and South Africa.* London: Routledge & Kegan Paul, 1982.

Barber, James P. *The Uneasy Relationship: Britain and South Africa.* London: Heinemann, 1983.

Barratt, C. John A. "Can External Leverage Pressure South Africa?" *Business and Society Review* No. 57 (Spring 1986): 68-74.

Barratt, John. *The Namibian Dilemma: Factors Preventing a Settlement.* Braamfontein: South African Institute of International Affairs, 1982.

. *The Soviet and Southern Africa.* Braamfontein: South African Institute of International Affairs, 1981.

. "Southern Africa: A South African View," *Foreign Affairs* 55 (October 1976): 147-168.

Bowman, Larry W. "South Africa's Southern Strategy and Its Implications for the United States," *International Affairs* 47 (January 1971): 19-30.

Belfiglio, Valentine J. "South Africa's Relations with Botswana, Lesotho, and Swaziland," *Journal of Asian and African Studies* (July, October 1980): 217-228.

Butts, Kent Hughes and Thomas, Paul R. *Geopolitical Power in Southern Africa.* Boulder: Westview Press, 1986.

Coker, Christopher. "South Africa and the Western Alliance 1949-81," *Journal of the Royal United Services Institute for Defense Studies* 127 (June 1982).

. *The United States and South Africa, 1968-1985: Constructive Engagement and Its Critics.* Durham: Duke University Press, 1986.

Conway, Robert. "South Africa: Can U.S. Policies Influence Change?" *Worldview* 27 (January 1984): 12-14.

Crocker, Chester A. "South Africa: The Hard Questions; II," *America* 153 (August 10, 1985): 48-50.

. "South Africa: Strategy for Change," *Foreign Affairs* 59 (1981): 323-351.

Dale, Richard. "South Africa and the International Community," *World Politics* 18 (1965-1966): 297-313.

Danaher, Kevin. *The Political Economy of U.S. Policy Toward South Africa.* Boulder: Westview Press, 1985.

. "U.S. Policy Options Toward South Africa: A Bibliographic Essay," *Current Bibliography on African Affairs* 13 (1980-81): 2-25.

External Pressure and the Dynamics of Change in South Africa. Berkeley: Institute of International Studies, University of California, 1985.

Ferguson, Clyde and Cotter, William R. "South Africa: The Hard Questions; I," *America* 153 (August 10, 1985): 45-48.

. *Elite Opinion on United States Policy Toward Africa.* New York: Council on Foreign Relations, 1979.

. "United States Policy Toward Southern Africa: Economic and Strategic Constraints," *Political Science Quarterly* 92 (Spring 1977): 47-64.

Geldenhuys, D.J. "South Africa and the West," in *South Africa: Public Policy Perspective,* ed. by Robert Schrire. Cape Town: Juta, 1980.

Geldenhuys, Deon. *What Do We Think?: A Survey of White Opinion on Foreign Policy.* Braamfontein: South African Institute of International Affairs, 1982.

Giliomee, Hermann Buhr. *South Africa's Relationship With the West.* Stellenbosch: Unit for Futures Research, University of Stellenbosch, 1980.

Hero, Alfred Jr. and Barratt, John, eds. *The American People and South Africa: Publics, Elites, and Policymaking Processs.* Lexington, Mass.: Lexington Books, 1981.

Holladay, J. Douglas. "The Limits of American Influence," *Business and Society Review* No. 57 (Spring 1986): 17-21.

Hopkins, Sheila M. "An Analysis of U.S.-South African Relations in the 1980s: Has Engagement Been Constructive?" *Journal of Comparative Business and Capital Market Law* 7 (1985): 89-115.

Kalley, Jacqueline A. *South Africa's Foreign Relations, 1980-1984.* Braamfontein: South African Institute of International Affaiars, 1984.

Kennedy, Edward M. "South Africa: The Hard Questions; III," *America* 153 (August 10, 1985): 51-53.

Kitchen, Helen A., ed. *Options for U.S. Policy Toward Africa.* Washington: American Enterprise Institute, 1979.

Kitchen, Helen A. and Clough, Michael. *The United States and South Africa: Realities and Red Herrings.* Washington: Center for Strategic and International Studies, Georgetown University, 1984.

Legum, Colin. "The Soviet Union, China, and the West in Southern Africa," *Foreign*

Affairs 54 (July 1976): 745-762.

Leistner, G.M.E. "Economic Interdependence in Southern Africa," *Africa Institute of South Africa Bulletin* 16 (October 1978).

Lemarchand, Rene, ed. *American Policy in Southern Africa: The Stakes and the Stance.* Washington: University Press of America, 1978.

Libby, Ronalt T. *Toward an Africanized U.S. Policy for Southern Africa: A Strategy for Increasing Political Leverage.* Berkeley: University of California Press, 1980.

Love, Janice. *The U.S. Anti-Apartheid Movement: Local Activism in Global Politics.* New York: Praeger, 1985.

Lugar, Richard G. "Promoting True Democracy in South Africa," *Business and Society Review* No. 57 (Spring 1985): 7-8.

Manganyi, N. Chabani. "The Washington-Pretoria Connection: Is There a Black Perspective?" in *The United States and South Africa: Continuity or Change?* Johannesburg: South African Institute of International Affairs, 1981.

Martin, David and Johnson, Phyllis. "Africa: The Old and the Unexpected," *Foreign Affairs* 63 (1985): 602-630.

Mayall, James. "The Commonwealth and South Africa," *World Today* 41 (December 1985): 211-212.

Mehlman, Maxwell J.; Milch, Thomas H.; and Toumanoff, Michael V. "United States Restrictions on Exports to South Africa," *American Journal of International Law* 73 (October 1979): 581-603.

Parker, Frank J. "South Africa: The Hard Questions; VII," *America* 153 (August 10, 1985): 62-63.

Pratt, C. "Canadian Policies Toward South Africa," *Canadian Journal of African Studies* 17 (1983): 497-525.

Price, Robert M. "Southern African Regional Security: Pax or Pox Pretoria?" *World Policy Journal* 2 (Summer 1985): 533-554.

Quboza, Percy; Barratt, John; and Vosloo, Ton. *The United States and South Africa.* Braamfontein: South African Institute of International Affairs, 1977.

Sethi, S. Prakash. "How the United States Can Fight Apartheid," *Business and Society Review* No. 58 (Summer 1986): 58-61.

South Africa, the West and the Frontline States. Uppsala: Scandinavian Institue of African Studies, 1981.

Stevens, Richard and Elmessiri, Abdelwahab. *Israel and South Africa: The Progression of a Relationship.* New York: New World Press, 1976.

Study Commission on U.S. Policy Toward Southern Africa. *South Africa. Time Running Out.* Berkeley: University of California Press, 1981.

———. *Study Commission on U.S. Policy Toward Southern Africa: History, Summary of Fundings and Recommendations.* New York: Study Commission, 1981.

Ungar, Sanford J. and Vale, Peter. "South Africa: Why Constructive Engagement Failed," *Foreign Affairs* 64 (1986): 234-258.

U.S. Congress. House, Committee on Foreign Affairs. Subcommittee on Africa. *Namibia: Internal Repression and United States Diplomacy.* Hearings . . .99th Congress, 1st Session, 1985. Washington: United States Government Printing Office, 1985.

fice, 1985.

. House. Committee on Foreign Affairs. Subcommittee on Africa. *The Current Crisis in South Africa.* Hearings...98th Congress, 2nd Session, 1984. Washington: United States Government Printing Office, 1985.

. House. Committee on Foreign Affairs. Subcommittee on International Economic Policy and Trade on African and International Organizations. *U.S. Policy Toward South Africa.* Hearings...96th Congress, 2nd Session, 1980. Washington: United States Government Printing Office, 1980.

U.S. Congress. Senate. Committee on Banking, Housing and Urban Affairs. Subcommittee on International Finance and Monetary Policy. *The Anti-Apartheid Act of 1985.* Hearings...99th Congress, 1st Session, 1985. Washington: United States Government Printing Office, 1985.

. Senate. Committee on Foreign Relations. *U.S. Policy Toward South Africa.* Hearings...99th Congress, 1st Session, 1985. Washington: United States Government Printing Office, 1985.

. Senate. Committee on Foreign Relations. Subcommittee on African Affairs. *U.S. Policy on South Africa.* Hearings...98th Congress, 2nd Session, 1984. Washington: United States Government Printing Office, 1985.

U.S. Department of State. *The United States and South Africa: U.S. Public Statements and Related Documents, 1977-85.* Washington: United States Government Printing Office, 1985.

Van Wyk, J.J. *Elite Opinions on South African Foreign Policy.* Johannesburg: Research Project on South Africa's Foreign Relations, 1984.

Weissman, Stephen. "Dateline South Africa: The Opposition Speaks," *Foreign Policy* No. 58 (Spring 1985): 151-170.

Whitaker, Jennifer, ed. *Africa and the United States: Vital Interests.* New York: New York University Press, 1978.

Winston, Henry. "South Africa and the Reagan Factor" *Political Affairs* 65 (February 1986): 7-11.

Wolpe, Howard. "The Double Standard of American Foreign Policy," *Business and Society Review* No. 57 (Spring 1986): 12-16.

Woods, Donald. "South Africa's Face to the World," *Foreign Affairs* 56 (April 1978): 521-528.

Wright, Sanford. "The Political Economy of South Africa: An Analysis of Selected Economic Factors on U.S. Leverages," in *Human Rights and Third World Development,* ed. by George W. Shepherd, Jr. and Ved P. Nanda. Westport, Conn.: Greenwood, 1985.

HISTORY

Ballinger, Margaret. *From Union to Apartheid.* Cape Town: Juta, 1969.

Beinart, William and Bundy, Colin. *Hidden Struggles in Rural South Africa: Politics and Popular Movements in the Transkei and Eastern Cape, 1890-1930.* Berkeley: University of California Press, 1986.

Bekker, S.B. and Humphries, Richard. *From Control to Confusion: The Changing Role of Administration Boards in South Africa, 1971-1983.* Pietermaritzburg: Shuter & Shooter, 1985.

Brookes, Edgar H. *White Rule in South Africa 1830-1910.* Pietermaritzburg: University of Natal Press, 1974.

The Cambridge History of the British Empire Vol. 8: South Africa Rhodesia and the High Commission Territories, Second Edition. Cambridge: Cambridge University Press, 1963.

Comaroff, Jean. *Body of Power, Spirit of Resistance: The Culture and History of a South African People.* Chicago: University of Chicago Press, 1985.

Davenport, T.R.H. *South Africa: A Modern History.* Second Edition. London: Macmillan, 1978.

Elphick, Richard and Giliomee, Hermann, eds. *The Shaping of South African Society 1652-1980.* London: Longman, 1979.

Eybers, G.W., ed. *Select Constitutional Documents Illustrating South African History, 1795-1910.* New York: E.P. Dutton, 1918.

Fredrickson, George M. *White Supremacy: A Comparative Study in American and South African History.* New York: Oxford University Press, 1981.

Guest, Bill and Sellers, John M., eds. *Enterprise and Exploitation in a Victorian Colony: Aspects of the Economic and Social History of Colonial Natal.* Pietermaritzburg: University of Natal Press, 1985.

Hattersley, A.F. *An Illustrated Social History of South Africa.* Cape Town: Balkema, 1969.

Ingham, Kenneth. *Jan Christian Smuts, the Conscience of a South African.* New York: St. Martin's Press, 1986.

Innes, D. *Anglo-American and the Rise of Modern South Africa.* London: Heinemann Educational Books, 1983.

Keto, C. Tsehloane. *America-South African Relations, 1784-1980.* Athens, Ohio: Ohio University, Center for International Studies, 1985.

Lacour-Gayet, Robert. *A History of South Africa.* New York: Hastings House, 1978.

Marks, Shula A. *The Ambiguities of Dependence in South Africa: Class, Nationalism and the State in Twentieth-Century Nata.* Baltimore: Johns Hopkins University Press, 1986.

Marks, Shula A. and Atmore, Anthony, eds. *Economy and Society in Pre-Industrial South Africa.* London: Longman, 1980.

Marguard, Leo. *The Peoples and Politics of South Africa.* London: Oxford University Press, 1969.

Moodie, T.D. *The Rise of Afrikanerdom: Power, Apartheid, and the Afrikaner Civil Religion.* Berkeley: University of California Press, 1975.

Muller A.L. "Slavery and the Development of South Africa," *South Africa Journal of Economics* 49 (1981): 153-165.

Muller, C.F.J., ed. *Five Hundred Years: A History of South Africa.* Pretoria: Academica, 1969.

Paton, Alan. *The Land and the People of South Africa.* Revised Edition. Philadelphia: Lippincott, 1972.

. *Hope for South Africa.* New York: Praeger, 1969.

. *The People Wept, Being a Brief Account of the Origin, Contents, and Application of That Unjust Law of the Union of South Africa Known as the Group Areas Act of 1950, Since Consolidated as Act No. 77 of 1957.* [n.p., 1957.]

. *South Africa and Her People.* London: Lutterwoth Press, 1957.

Robertson, Janet. *Liberalism in South Africa: 1948-1963.* Oxford: Clarendon Press, 1971.

Simons, Harold J. and Simons, R.E. *Class and Colour in South Africa, 1850-1950.* Harmondsworth: Penguin, 1969.

Spilhaus, M.W. *South Africa in the Making, 1652-1806.* Cape Town: Juta, 1966.

Spilhaus, Whiting. *The First South Africans and the Laws Which Governed Them.* Cape Town: Juta, 1949.

Swan, Maureen. *Gandhi: The South African Experience.* Johannesburg: Ravan Press, 1985.

Theal, George M. *History of South Africa.* 11 Volumes. Cape Town: C. Shruik, 1964.
. *History of South Africa From 1795-1872.* 3 Volumes. London: George Allen & Unwin, 1915.

Wiley, David and Isaacman, Allen F., eds. *Southern Africa: Society, Economy and Liberation.* East Lansing, Michigan: Michigan State University Press, 1981.

Willen, Richard S. "Normative Structure of South African Inequality," *Free Inquiry in Creative Sociology* 10 May (1982): 80-84.

Wilson, Monica and Thompson, Leonard, eds. *The Oxford History of South Africa.* 2 Volumes. New York: Oxford University Press, 1969-1971.

Wright, Harrison M. *The Burden of the Present: Liberal-Radical Controversy Over Southern African History.* Cape Town: David Philip, 1977.

Yudelman, David. *The Emergence of Modern South Africa: State Capital and the Incorporation of Organized Labor on the South African Gold Fields, 1902-1939.* Westport, Conn.: Greenwood, 1983.

BLACK HOMELANDS

Blausten, Richard. "Foreign Investment in the Black Homelands of South Africa," *African Affairs* 75 (1976): 208-223.

Blondel, Alain and Lamb, Shena. *The Parrot's Egg.* Johannesburg: Ravan Press, 1985.

Boulle, Laurence J. and Baxter, Lawrence G., eds. *Natal and KwaZulu: Constitutional and Political Options.* Cape Town: Juta, 1981.

Buthelezi Commission. *The Requirements for Stability and Development in KwaZulu and Natal.* 2 Volumes. Durban: H and H Publications, 1982.

Buthelezi, Gatsha. *White and Black Nationalism Ethnicity and the Future of the Homelands.* Johannesburg: South African Institute of Race Relations, 1974.

Butler, Jeffrey; Rotberg, Robert; and Adams, Joh. *The Black Homelands of South Africa: The Political and Economic Development of Bophuthatswana and KwaZulu.* Berkeley: University of California Press, 1967.

Charton, Nancy, ed. *Ciskei: Economics and Politics of Dependence in a South African Homeland.* London: Croom Helm, 1980.

Coker, Christopher. "Boputhatswana and the South African Homelands," *World Today* 39 (1983): 231-241.

Collings, John. "Dimbaza: A Response to Constructive Pressure," *Disinvestment* (June 1985): 52-59.

Cukwurah, A. Oye. *The Consolidation of the Black Homelands of South Africa.* Victoria Island, Lagos: Nigerian Institute of International Affairs, [1976].

Dugard, John R. *Independent Homelands, Failure of a Fiction.* Johannesburg: South African Institute of Race Relations, 1979.

Geldenhuys, Deon. *South Africa's Black Homeland: Past Objectives, Present Realities and Future Developments.* Braamfontein: South African Institute of International Affairs, 1981.

Hammond-Tooke, W.D. *Command or Consensus: The Development of Transkeian Local Government.* Cape Town: David Philip, 1975.

Hattingh, P.S. "Bophuthatswana at a Glance," *South African Journal of African Affairs* 7 (1977): 213-219.

———. "Boundaries, Surface Areas and Territorial Units: Aspects of Homeland Consolidation in the RSA," *Africa Institute Bulletin* Nos. 9 & 10 (1977): 262-269.

Haysom, N. "Homeland Labor Legislation—A Separate Development?" *Indicator South Africa* 2 (1985): 4-6.

Hemson, Crispin, ed. *Natal/Kwazulu, the Political & Social Environment of the Future.* Durban: University of Natal, 1985

Homelands: The Role of the Corporations in the Republic of South Africa. Johannesburg: Chris van Rensburg, n.d.

Laurence, Patrick. *The Transkei: South Africa's Politics of Partition.* Johannesburg: Ravan Press, 1976.

Lawyer, A. "Homeland Labour Laws," *South African Labour Bulletin* 8 (1983): 65-78.

Lombard, J. and Van der Merve, P.J. "Central Problems of the Economic Development of Bantu Homelands," *Finance and Trade Review* 10 (June 1972): 1-46.

Maasdorp, G. "Industrial Decentralization and the Economic Development of the Homelands," in *South Africa: Public Policy Perspectives,* ed. by Robert A. Schrire. Cape Town: Juta, 1982.

Malan, T. and Hattingh, P.S. *Black Homelands in South Africa.* Pretoria: Africa Institute of South Africa, 1976.

Potgieter, J.J. *The Task and Role of the Black Entrepreneur in the Industrialization of the Homelands.* Kwa-Dlangezwa: University of Zululand, 1975.

Rogerson, C.M. "Industrialization in the Bantu Homelands," *Geography* 59 (1974): 260-261.

Simkins, C.M. "What Has Been Happening to Income Distribution and Poverty in the Homelands?" *Development Southern Africa* 1, no. 2 (1984).

Smit, Philippus. *Urbanisation in the Homelands.* Pretoria: Institute for Plural Societies, University of Pretoria, 1977.

The South African Homelands. Foreign Policy Document No. 1. London: Research Department, Foreign and Commonwealth Office, Great Britain, 1978.

Southall, Roger J. "The Beneficiaries of Transkeian 'Independence,' " *Journal of Modern African Studies* 15 (March 1977): 1-23.

———. *South Africa's Transkei: The Political Economy of an "Independent" Bantustan.* New York: Monthly Review Press, 1983.

The Surplus Peoples Project. *Forced Removals in South Africa.* Pietermaritzburg: The Project, 1983.

Tapscott, C.P.G. *Universities in the Black Homelands.* Umtata, Transkei: Institute for

Management and Development Studies, University of Transkei, 1982.

Thomas, W. "Financing Socio-Economic Development in the Black Homelands of South Africa," *Contemporary African Studies* 1 (1981): 141-166.

Tomlinson, R. "Industrial Decentralization and the Relief of Poverty in the Homelands," *South Africa Journal of Economics* 51 (1983): 544-563.

Ward, M. " 'Homeland' Development? Planning in the Ciskei," *IDS Bulletin* 11 (1980): 15-18.

Wellings, Paul and Black, Anthony. "Industrial Decentralization Under Apartheid: The Relocation of Industry to the South African Periphery," *World Development* 14 (January 1986): 1-38.

Whiteside, A. "Labor on the Industrial Periphery: The Homelands and South Africa," *Indicator South Africa* 3 (1985): 14-17.

MEDIA

Breytenbach, Breyten. "The South African Wasteland: Totalitarianism, Apartheid, and the Responsibility of the Writer," *New Republic* 193 (November 4, 1985): 32-38.

Chimutengwende, Chenhamo C. *South Africa: The Press and the Politics of Liberation.* London: Barbican Books, 1978.

Foisie, John. "South Africa: The Hard Questions; VI," *America* 153 (August 10, 1985): 60-61.

Ginwala, F. "The Press in South Africa," *Index on Censorship* 2 (Autumn 1973): 27-43.

Hachten, William A. "Black Journalists Under Apartheid," *Index on Censorship* 8 (May-June 1979): 43-48.

———. "Policies and Performance of South African Television," *Journal of Communication* 29 (Summer 1979): 62-72.

Heard, Anthony H. and Pakendorf, Harold. "The Press in South Africa: Free to a Degree," *Business and Society Review* No. 57 (Spring 1986): 118-124.

Lacob, Miriam. "South Africa: Battling the Ban," *Columbia Journalism Review* 24 (March/April 1986): 13-15.

Potter, Elaine. *The Press as Opposition: The Political Role of South African Newspapers.* Totowa, New Jersey: Rowan & Littlefield, 1975.

South African Conference on the Survival of the Press and Education for Journalism. *South African Conference on the Survival of the Press and Education for Journalism, October 4-6, 1979.* Grahamstown: Department of Journalism, Rhodes University, 1979.

Switzer, Les. *Media and Dependence in South Africa: A Case Study of the Press and the Ciskei "Homeland."* Athens, Ohio: Africa Studies Program, Ohio University Center for International Studies, 1985.

Tomaselli, K. and Tomaselli, R. "Ideology/Culture/Hegemony and Mass Media in South Africa: A Literature Survey," *Critical Arts: A Journal for Media Studies* 2 (1981): 1-25.

———. "The South African Mass Media and the Dissemination of Apartheid Ideology," in *Journalism I Reader: The Sociology of News.* Grahamstown: Department of Journalism and Media Studies, Rhodes University, 1981-82.

Woods, D. *Asking for Trouble: The Autobiography of a Banned Journalist.* New York: Atheneum, 1981.

CHURCH AND RELIGION

Allmen, Daniel von. *Theology: Advocate or Critic of Apartheid?* Berne: Swiss Federation of Protestant Churches, 1977.

"Apartheid and the Church in South Africa," *Worldview* 16 (1973): 21-28.

Barkat, A.M. "Churches Combatting Racism in South Africa," *Journal of International Affairs* 36 (1983): 297-305.

Boesak, Allan and Villa-Vicencio, Charles, eds. *When Prayer Makes News.* Philadelphia: Westminster Press, 1986.

Boesak, Allan. "Coming In Out of the Wilderness," in *The Emergent Gospel: Theology From the Underside of History,* ed. by Sergio Torres and Virginia Fabella. Maryknoll, New York: Orbis, 1978.

. *Farewell to Innocence: A Socio-Ethical Study on Black Theology and Black Power.* Maryknoll, New York: Orbis, 1977.

. "The Heresy of Apartheid," in *Apartheid Change and the NG Kerk,* ed. by H.J.P. Serfontein. Emmarentia: Taurus, 1982.

Brink Andre P. *Writing in a State of Seige: Essays on Politics and Religion.* New York: Simon and Schuster, 1986.

Brouwer, Arie R. and Castro, Emilio. "Church Groups Lead the Battle Against Apartheid," *Business and Society Review* No. 57 (Spring 1986): 106-112.

Brown, William Eric. *The Catholic Church in South Africa.* New York: P.J. Kennedy, 1960.

Buthelezi, Manas. "Toward Indigenous Theology in South Africa," in *The Emergent Gospel: Theology From the Underside of History,* ed. by Sergio Maryknoll, New York: Orbis, 1978.

Cawood, Lesley. *The Churches and Race Relations in South Africa.* Johannesburg: South African Institute of Race Relations, 1964.

Comaroff, Jean and John. "Christianity and Colonialism in South Africa," *American Ethnologist* 13 (1986): 1-22.

Corke, Michael. "The Church, Social Justice, and Corporate Responsibility," *Disinvestment* (June 1985): 78-85.

De Gruchy, John W. and Villa-Vicencio, Charles, eds. *Apartheid Is a Heresy.* Grand Rapids: W.B. Eerdmans, 1983.

De Gruch, John W. *The Church Struggle in South Africa.* Grand Rapids: W.B. Eerdmans, 1979.

. "The Relationship Between the State and Some Churches in South Africa, 1968-1975," *Journal of Church and State* 19, no. 3 (Autumn 1977).

Edwards, Jan. *Church and State Relationships in South Africa.* Johannesburg: South African Institute of Race Relations, 1974.

Hindchliff, Peter Bingham. *The Anglican Church in South Africa.* London: Darton, Longman & Todd, 1963.

Johanson, Brian. *Church and State in South Africa.* Braamfontein: South African Council of Churches, 1975.

. *The Church in South Africa: Today and Tomorrow.* Johannesburg: South African Council of Churches, 1975.

Jubber, Ken. "The Prodigal Church: South Africa's Dutch Reformed Church and the Apartheid Policy," *Social Compass* 32 (1985): 273-285.

Kairos Group. *Challenge to the Church: A Theological Comment on the Political Crisis in South Africa*. Braamfontein: Kairos Theologians, 1985.

Kellerma, A.P. "Religious Affiliation in South Africa," *Social Compass* 19 (1972): 7-20.

Kierna, James, "The New Zion." *Leadership* 4, no. 3 (1985): 90-98.

Loubser, J.J. "Calvinism, Equality and Inclusion: The Case of Afrikaner Calvinism," in *The Protestant Ethic and Modernization*, ed. by Shmuel N. Eisenstadt. New York: Basic Books, 1968.

Meyer, Paul Michael. *The Roman Catholic Church in South Africa*. Cape Town: University of Cape Town Libraries, 1979.

Moodie, T. Dunbar. *The Rise of Afrikanerdom: Power, Apartheid, and the Afrikaner Civil Religion*. Berkeley: University of California Press, 1975.

Moore, Basil, comp. *The Challenge of Black Theology in South Africa*. Atlanta: John Knox Press, 1974.

Nash, M. and Charton, N., eds. *An Empty Table? Churches and the Ciskei Future*. Johannesburg: South African Council of Churches, 1981.

Neuhaus, Richard John. *Dispensations: The Future of South Africa as South Africans See It*. Grand Rapids: W.B. Eerdmans, 1986.

Paton, Alan. *Creative Suffering: The Ripple of Hope*. Boston: Pilgrim Press, 1970.

——. *Christian Unity: A South African View*. Grahamstown: Rhodes University, 1951.

Randall, Peter, ed. *Apartheid and the Church*. Johannesburg: Study Project on Christianity in Apartheid Society, 1972.

Ritner, R. "The Dutch Reformed Church and Apartheid," *Journal of Contemporary History* 2 (1967): 17-37.

Sjollema, Baldwin. *Isolating Apartheid*. Geneva: World Council of Churches, 1982.

Tutu, Desmond. *Desmond Tutu: Crying in the Wilderness the Struggle for Justice in South Africa*. Second Edition. Oxford: Mowbray, 1986.

——. *Hope and Suffering: Sermons and Speeches*. Grand Rapids, Mich.: W.B. Eerdmans, 1984.

——. "White Salt, Black Wounds," *New Society* 69 (1984): 102-103.

——. *The Divine Intention*. Braamfontein: South African Council of Churches, 1982.

——. *On Trial*. Leeds: John Paul the Preacher's Press, 1982.

——. *Address Delivered to the Assembly of the British Council of Churches, March 31, 1981*. Geneva: Programme to Combat Racism, World Council of Churches, 1981.

University of South Africa. Institute for Theological Research, 7th Symposium, 1983. *Church and Industry*. Pretoria: University of South Africa, 1983.

Walshe, Peter. *Church Versus State in South Africa*. London: C. Hurst, 1983.

Williams, Oliver. "The Religious Rationale for Racism," *Business and Society Review* No. 57 (Spring 1986): 101-105.

Whisson, Michael G. and West, Martin, eds. *Religion and Social Change in Southern Africa*. Cape Town: David Philip, 1975.

Zwane, Mandlenkhosi. *Black Christians and the Church in South Africa*. London: Catholic Institute for International Relations, 1980.

SPORTS

Archer, Robert and Bouillon, Antoine. *The South African Game: Sport and Racism.* London: Zed Press, 1982.

Dommisse, John. "The Psychology of Apartheid Sport," *Journal of Sport and Social Issues* 1 (1977): 32-53.

Hain, Peter. "The Politics of Sport in South Africa," *New Society* 50 (1979): 183-185.

Jarvie, Grant. *Class, Race, and Sport in South Africa's Political Economy.* Boston: Routledge & Kegan Paul, 1985.

Krotee, March L. and Schwick, Luther C. "The Impact of Sporting Forces on South African Apartheid," *Journal of Sport and Social Issues* 3 (1979): 33-42.

Lapchick, Richard. *The Politics of Race and International Sport: The Case of South Africa.* Westport, Conn.: Greenwood Press, 1975.

——. "South Africa: Sport and Apartheid Politics," *Annals of the American Academy of Political and Social Science* 445 (September 1979): 155-165.

Martin, Paul. "South African Sport: Apartheid's Achilles Heel?" *World Today* 40 (June 1984): 234-243.

Van der Walt, J.C. "Autonomy in Sport and South African Statutory Law: A Critical Evaluation," *South African Journal for Research in Sport, Physical Education and Recreation* 5 (1982): 91-103.

GENERAL SOCIAL CONDITIONS

Brink, Andre P. *Writing in a State of Siege: Essays on Politics and Literature.* New York, Summit Books, 1986.

Burman, S. and Huvers, M. "Church Versus State: Divorce Legislation and Divided South Africa," *Journal of South African Studies* 12 (1985): 116-135.

Cilliers, S.P. and Groenewald, C.J. *Urban Growth in South Africa, 1936-2000.* Stellenbosch: Research Unit for Sociology Development, Department of Sociology, University of Stellenbosch, 1982.

Coplan, David B. *In Township Tonight! South Africa's Black City Music and Theatre.* New York: Longman, 1985.

Crapanzano, Vincent. *Waiting: The Whites of South Africa.* New York: Random House, 1985.

De Ridder, Jacobus C. *The Personality of the Urban African in South Africa.* London: Routhledge, 1961.

Hare, A.P. and Savage, M. "Sociology of South Africa," *Annual Review of Sociology* 5 (1979): 329-350.

Heaven, P.L. "Ethnocentrism and Prejudice in a South African Student Group," *South African Journal of Science* 72 (1976): 344-345.

Kuzwayo, Ellen. *Call Me Woman.* London: Women's Press, 1985.

Larlham, Peter. *Black Theater, Dance, and Ritual in South Africa.* Ann Arbor, Mich.: UMI Research Press, 1985.

Lever, H. *South African Society.* Johannesburg: Jonathan Ball, 1978.

Lotter, J.M., ed. *Social Problems in South Africa.* Pretoria: Human Science Research Council, 1979.

Marais, M.A. "The Allocation of Resources to Education in South Africa," *South Africa Journal of Economics* 52 (1984): 75-89.

Mason, David. "Industrialization, Race and Class Conflict in South Africa: Towards a Sociological Resolution of a Reopened Debate," *Ethnic and Racial Studies* 3 (April 1980): 140-155.

Mathabane, Mark. *Kaffir Boy: The True Story of a Black Youth's Coming of Age in Apartheid South Africa.* New York: Macmillan, 1986.

Meyer, Carolyn, *Voices of South Africa: Growing Up in a Troubled Land.* San Diego: Harcourt Brace Jovanovich, 1986.

Morse, Stanley J. and Orpen, Christopher, eds. *Contemporary South Africa: Social Psychological Perspectives.* Cape Town: Juta, 1975.

Naidoo, Beverley. *Journey to Jo'burg: A South African Story.* New York: J.B. Lippincott, 1985.

Orkin, Mark. "A Divided Struggle: Alienation, Ideology, and Social Control Among Black Students in South Africa," *Journal of Intercultural Studies* 4 (1983): 69-98.

Paton, Alan. *Ah, But Your Land is Beautiful.* New York: Scribner, 1981.
. *Towards the Mountain: An Autobiography.* New York: Scribner, 1980.
. *Knocking on the Door,* ed. by Colin Gardner. Cape Town: David Philip, 1975.
. *For You Departed.* New York: Scribner, 1969.
. *Tales From a Troubled Land.* New York: Scribner, 1961.
. *Meditation for a Young Boy Confirmed.* London: S.P.C.K., 1959.
. *South Africa in Transition.* New York: Scribner 1956.
. *Too Late the Phalarope.* New York: Scribner, 1953.
. *Cry, the Beloved Country; a Story of Comfort in Desolation.* New York: Scribner, 1948.

Rex, John. "The Sociology of South Africa: A Review Article," *Journal of South African Studies* 1 (1975): 247-252.

Schlemmer, Lawrence. "Political Adaption and Reaction Among Urban Africans in South Africa," *Social Dynamics* 2 (June 1976): 3-18.

Schurink, W.J. *Class-Based Sociological Theories of Deviancy and Relevant Ecological Patterns in Pretoria.* Pretoria: Human Science Research Council, 1975.

Smedley, L.N. and Groenewald, D.C. *Attitudes of the White Population in South Africa Toward Immigrants.* Pretoria: Human Science Research Council, 1977.

South African Professors World Peace Academy. *The Role of Academics and Human Relationships.* Johannesburg: Professors World Peace Academy, 1985.

Timberlake, Lloyd. *Africa in Crisis: The Causes, the Cures of Environmental Bankruptcy.* Washington: International Institute for Environment and Development, 1985.

Troup, Freda. *Forbidden Pastures: Education Under Apartheid.* London: International Defence and Aid Fund, 1976.

Vukani Makhosikazi Collective. *South African Women on the Move.* London: Zed, 1985.

West, M. "Therapy and Social Change in Urban Churches of South Africa," *Social Compass* 19 (1972): 49-62.

Index

training programs of, 385-386
General Workers Union, 274
Gillette Company, 68
Gleneagles Agreement, 329
Gold, 346
Gray, William, 187
Great Britain, 333-352
  African nations and, 342-343
  early settlers in South Africa and,
  151
  economic sanctions support in, 69,
  333
  strategic raw materials and, 343-344
  trade between South Africa and,
  14, 339, 341
  see also British corporations
Group Areas Act of 1950, 87, 107,
  192
  amendments to, 132
  economic segregation under, 137
  educational segregation under,
  138-139
  legal basis of apartheid and, 132,
  337
  local authorities under, 134
  reform proposals for, 6, 372
Group of Eminent Persons (GEP), 7,
  116, 121, 214-215, 330-331
  members of, 330
Guerrilla activity, 118-119

Harere Declaration, 277-278, 283
Harvard College, 286, 302
Healy, Denis, 342
Heard, Anthony H., 253-262
Herstigte Nasionale Party (HNP), 111,
  113
Hertzog, James, 152-153, 254
Heunis, Jan Christian, 73-83
Higher education, *see* Universities and
  colleges *headings*
Holladay, J. Douglas, 12, 63-71
Homelands, 272
  basis for policy of, 107-108, 336
  black South African view of, 54
  citizenship for residents of, 4
  constitutional reform and, 75,
  77, 80-81, 93, 101, 117-118
  constructive engagement policy
  and, 57
  denationalization of blacks as

  South Africans and placement
  in, 133-134, 337
  legal basis for, 133-134, 145
  partition and, 117-118
  relocation to, 140
  social surveys of, 177
  Verwoerd policy of separate
  development and, 75
House of Representatives, and
  economic sanctions, 58-59, 187
Housing
  black South African protests over,
  86
  freehold rights in, 6, 143
  interracial marriage and, 144
  U.S. corporations and, 25, 386-387,
  400-401
Human rights funds, 66-67
Human rights violations, 36, 207
  264, 283
Human Sciences Research Council,
  142, 172, 239
Huntington, 103-104

IBM, 14, 314, 315
ICCR, *see* Interfaith Center on Corporate
  Responsibility (ICCR)
Identification documents, 139, 145;
  see also Pass laws
Immorality Act, 86, 138, 141, 144,
  153, 388
Imports
  African nations and South African
  economy and, 70
  economic sanctions and ban on, 59,
  212, 339
  oil, 14-15
  strategic raw materials and, 343-344
  trade patterns and, 14-15, 191
Indaba, 367
Indian Education Act of 1956, 138
Indian South Africans
  constitutional reform and, 78
  council limited to, 133
  council participation across racial
  lines by, 143-144
  education for, 138, 139, 142, 231,
  239-240
  group area definition and, 132
  local authorities and, 134, 135
  "own affairs" provisions and, 135

ABOUT THE EDITOR

S. Prakash Sethi is a Professor of Management at Baruch College, The City University of New York, where he also serves as the Associate Director of the Center for Management Development and Organization Research. He has authored, co-authored, and edited eighteen books and written over 100 articles. He has contributed to virtually all of the major journals in the fields of management, international business, strategic planning, and public affairs and public policy. In addition, his writings have appeared in many organs of national and international news media, including the *New York Times,* the *Wall Street Journal*, *Business Week*, and *Advertising Age*, to name a few. He is a consultant to several leading U.S. corporations, industry associations, and international corporations. He has also worked as a consultant to various federal government agencies, congressional committees, and public interest groups in the United States and abroad. Previously, Dr. Sethi taught at the University of California, Berkeley, and the University of Texas at Dallas where he was also the Founder and Director of the Center for Research in Business and Social Policy.

C. John A. Barratt is currently the Director General of the South African Institute of International Affairs in Johannesburg. Previously he served for many years in the South African Foreign Service, in Pretoria, Cape Town, and New York, where he attended United Nations sessions as a member of the South African Delegation. Dr. Barratt is also an Executive Member of the United States-South Africa Leader Exchange Program Inc., a Council Member of the Africa Institute of South Africa, and member of the Ediotrial Advisory Board of "Leadership S.A." He received his B.A. degree from the University of the Witwatersrand and his M.A. in modern history at Exeter College, Oxford, and he was awarded an honorary professorship in International Relations by the University of Witwatersrand. Dr. Barratt is the author of many papers, articles, and chapters in books on South African foreign policy and external relations, other Southern Africa questions, and the United Nations. He is also the co-editor of several volumes, including *Conflict and Compromise in South Africa* and *The American People and South Africa.*

Laurence J. Boulle is Professor of Law, Head of the Department of Public Law, and Dean of the Law School at Natal University. Born in Johannesburg, he studied at the Universities of Natal, Stellenbosch, and London, and received his Ph.D. in constitutional law. Dr. Boulle has published extensively in the fields of constitutional law, administrative law, and constitutional politics. Among his recent publications is *Constitutional Reform and the Apartheid State.*

Simon S. Brand has been Chief Executive and Chairman of the Board of the Development Bank of Southern Africa since its inception in 1983. Previously he held various lectureships and professorships in economics in South African universities and was also Chief of Financial Policy, and Chief Director of Economic Planning in the South African Department of Finance, and Chairman of the State President's Economic Advisory Council. He has served on many commissions and planning councils, including the National Manpower Commission, Energy Policy Committee, the Boards of the First National Development Corporation of South West Africa, and the Small Business Development Corporation, and was elected as one of the Sunday *Times*

(South Africa) top five businessmen for 1984. Dr. Brand holds three degrees in agriculture, a bachelor's from the University of Pretoria, a master's from Stanford University, and a doctorate from the University of Pretoria. He has written more than fifty articles for professional and scholarly publications.

Arie R. Brouwer is the General Secretary of the National Council of the Churches of Christ in the United States. Previously he served as Deputy General Secretary for the World Council of Churches and was on several committees. He has also been active in the Reformed Church in America, serving as General Secretary, Secretary for Program, and member of the Board of World Mission. He has actively challenged apartheid in South Africa, being among the church leaders who responded to the invitation of Bishop Desmond Tutu to testify in defense of the SACC before the Eloff Commission. Dr. Brouwer received his bachelor of arts degree from Hope College, his bachelor of divinity at Western Theological Seminary, and honorary doctor of divinity degrees from both Central College and Hope College. He has published numerous articles and is the author of *Reformed Church Roots*, a popular history of the Reformed Church in America.

Mangosuthu G. Buthelezi, a direct descendant of the founder of the Zulu Nation, is Chief Minister of KwaZulu. As such, he is the traditional and elected political leader of South Africa's largest ethnic group and the senior traditional advisor to His Majesty the King of the Zulus. Chief Buthelezi is also President of Inkatha, South Africa's largest membership-based black political movement, and Chairman of the South African Black Alliance. He holds a B.A. from the University of Fort Hare and honorary degrees of law from the University of Zuzuland, the University of Cape Town, and the University of Tampa, Florida. Buthelezi is the recipient of numerous national and international honors. He was awarded the French National Order of Merit, the Knight Commander of the Star of Africa for Outstanding Leadership, and the George Meany Human Rights Award.

Emilio Castro is the General Secretary of the World Council of Churches. Previously he was Director fo the World Council of Churches Commission on World Mission and Evangelism Coordinator of UNELAM (Commission for Evangelical Unity in Latin America), Executive Secretary of ASIT (South American Association of Theological Schools), and a pastor serving churches in Uruguay and Bolivia. Professor Castro also taught contemporary theological thought at the Mennonite Seminary in Montevideo and is currently rector of Union Theological Seminary (Isedet), Buenos Aires. He received his theological licentiate from Union Theological Seminary, Buenos Aires, did postgraduate work in Basel, and is a doctoral candidate at the University of Lausanne; he received and honorary Doctor of Humane Letters degree from Westmar College. Castro is the author, co-author, or contributor to several books, and author of more than 140 articles.

Christopher Coons is a research analyst with the Investor Responsibility Research Center, a nonpartisan, not-for-profit research group based in Washington, D.C., that investigates issues of concern to institutional investors, focusing primarily on social issues, shareholder resolutions, and specifically on issues related to South Africa, energy, defense, and corporate governance. Coons received a B.A. with honors in chemistry and political science from Amherst College. He has recently completed a combined survey of the South Africa-related investment policies of 175 American colleges and universities and an analysis of the U.S. divestment movement.

Colin W. Eglin, M.P., is leader of the official Opposition in the South African House of Assembly. A founding member of the Progressive Federal Party in 1959, he assumed leadership of the ailing Party in 1971—at that time its only Member of Parliament was Helen Suzman— and built it up to become the Official Opposition in the South African Parliament in 1977. In 1979 he stepped down from the Party leadership but was reinstated in 1986. He is the Party's spokesman on foreign affairs and an authority on constitutional development.

Johan G. Garbers is President of the Human Sciences Research Council, South Africa. Prior to joining HSRC he was Professor and Dean of Education at the University of the North, the University of Port Elizabeth, and the Rand Afrikaans University. The author of thirteen books and some sixty articles, Dr. Garbers' research includes investigation into child development, environmental deprivation, human emotions, and research management and methodology. He holds a B.SC. from the University of Pretoria, an M.SC. from the University of South

Africa, a D. Litt. et Phil. from the State University of Utrecht, a D.ED. from the University of Pretoria, and a D.ED. (honoris causa) from the Rand Afrikaans University.

Anthony H. Heard is the longest-serving editor of a major South African newspaper, having been Editor of the *Cape Times* for fifteen years. Previously, he was Cape Editor of the *Financial Mail*. Heard was arrested in his office at the *Cape Times* in November 1985 and charged in court after publishing a lengthy interview with Oliver Tambo, leader in exile of the guerilla movement, the African National Congress, in alleged defiance of the government's ban on quoting banned or listed persons. A native of Johannesburg, Heard received his B.A. and B.A. (honors) (first class) degrees from the University of Cape Town, where he majored in political philosophy, logic and metaphysics, African government, and constitutional history.

Jan Christian Heunis is South Africa's Minister of Constitutional Development. He has been involved in politics for nearly thirty years, serving as Member of the Provincial Council, George; Member of Parliament for the electoral division of False Bay; Member of Parliament for the electoral division of Helderberg; Deputy Minister of Finance and of Economic Affairs; Minister of Indian Affairs and of Tourism; Minister of Economic Affairs; Minister of Transport Affairs; Minister of Internal Affairs; Minister of Constitutional Development; and Chairman and Member of the Select Committee into the Constitution. Heunis holds B.A. and LL.B. degrees. He received an honorary doctorate in philosophy from the University of Stellenbosch.

J. Douglas Holladay is the Director of the South Africa Working Group, in the U.S. Department of State. He is also an adjunct professor at the University of Virginia. He has been associated with the Reagan Administration for several years, as Associate Director of Public Liaison and as Associate Deputy Under Secretary at the Department of Education. Previously he worked with Oxford Analytica Ltd., a research consulting firm based in England that does political and economic risk assessment for several nonprofit foundations, and was on the staff of Senator Mark Hatfield (Oregon). Holladay holds an A.B. degree in political theory from the University of North Carolina, Chapel Hill, and two master's degrees, from Princeton and Oxford Universities; his doctoral work in the field of ethics and public policy is pending at Boston University. He has published numerous articles on public policy concerns.

Michael Ivens is Director of Aims of Industry, a British organization that campaigns for free enterprise, and Director of the Foundation for Business Responsibilities. He is also a writer and poet.

Jacky Julyan lectures on private law, tort, and succession at the University of Natal. She received a B.A. cum laude and B.L. cum laude from the University of Stellenbosch, and was awarded a Cambridge Livingstone Trust Scholarship to study law at Cambridge University.

Senator Nancy Landon Kassebaum (Republican, Kansas) is Chairman of the Subcommittee on African Affairs of the Senate Foreign Relations Committee. She has played a key role in the Senate's oversight of U.S. policy toward South Africa since 1981, and was involved in shaping the 1985 legislation on South Africa, which formed the basis for President Reagan's executive order.

Arend Lijphart is Professor of Political Science at the University of California, San Diego. He has written extensively about the problems of deeply divided societies and the prospects of democratic solutions in these societies. His most recent book is *Power Sharing in South Africa*.

Richard Green Lugar is the senior Republican Senator from Indiana and Chairman of the Senate Foreign Relations Committee, as well as a member of the Senate Agriculture, Nutrition and Forestry Committee. He was first elected to the Senate in 1976 and reelected in 1982. Originally from Indianapolis, he served as mayor of that city for two terms. He graduated from Denison University; holds a master's degree in politics, economics, and philosophy from Pembroke College; has received many awards, including honorary college and university degrees; and is a Rhodes Scholar. Senator Lugar is also actively involved in agriculture. He owns a 605-acre farm in Indiana and a food machinery company.

Alice Tepper Marlin is the Executive Direcor of the Council on Economic Priorities, one of the leading not-for-profit research groups in the United States that specializes in in-depth study of such areas as the defense procurement industry, environmental issues, ethical investing, and corporate political involvement, to name a few. Previously she worked as Schedule and Advance Planner for the McCarthy for President Campaign and as a securities analyst and labor economist at Drexel Burnham. She holds a B.A. from Wellesley College and has received several academic and professional honors. Editor of more than thirty books and numerous articles, she is also Editor in Chief of the monthly *CEP Newsletter*.

Sal G. Marzullo is Manager of the Marketing and Refining Division, International Government Relations, Mobil Oil Corporation. He has held several positions during his tenure at Mobil and has also been a member or director of many organizations, including the Academic and Institutional Relations division of the Council of the Americas, the Public Relations Society of America, the Advisory Council of the African-American Institute, the Overseas Education Fund, the Industry Support Unit of Sullivan Companies, Rev. Sullivan's Advisory Board, the United States-South Africa Leader Exchagne Program, and the Advisory Board of the African Development Foundation.

Joseph Murphy has served as Chancellor of The City University of New York since 1982. Prior to his appointment, he was President of Bennington College, President of Queens College, Vice Chancellor of Higher Education for New Jersey, Director of the Peace Corps in Ethiopia and the Virgin Islands, and Associate Director of the Office of Economic Opportunity. He received his baccalaureate with honors in philosophy from Olivet College and M.A. and Ph.D. in philosophy and political theory from Brandeis University. He is a Woodrow Wilson Fellow and a Graham Kenan Fellow. Chancellor Murphy is also Chairman of the National Pell Grant Coalition and the Coalition for Aid to Part-time Students. He is the author of *Political Theory: A Conceptual Analysis* and has published numerous articles on philosophy, political theory, and education.

Eric Neubacher is Head of Access Services of Baruch College Library, The City University of New York. He received an M.L.S. from Rutgers University and an M.P.A. from Baruch College.

Herman Nickel served as the U.S. Ambassador to South Africa in 1986. Formerly, he was with Time, Inc. for some thirty years, first as a correspondent in Washington, London, and Johannesburg, then as Bonn Bureau Chief. He has also served as Bureau Chief in Tokyo and London. Nickel attended Union College and Syracuse University College of Law, from which he received an LL.B. degree.

Gerrit C. Olivier is Professor of Political Science at the Rand Afrikaans University, Johannesburg. He previously taught at the University of Zululand and at Pretoria University. Olivier has authored and co-authored twelve books and numerous articles on various aspects of South Africa's domestic and foreign policies. During 1985 he was a Visiting Scholar at the Center for International Affairs at Harvard University researching the impact of international moral issues on South Africa's domestic policies.

Patrick O'Meara is Director of the African Studies Program at Indiana University, one of the national centers designated for the study of Africa by the Department of Education under Title VI of the Higher Education Act. He is also a member of the faculty of the Department of Political Science and the School of Public and Environmental Affairs. An internationally known specialist on the political problems in Southern Africa, and in particular those concerning South Africa and Zimbabwe, he has been a consultant to numerous government agencies and the Ford Foundation, and has testified before Congress. Dr. O'Meara was born in South Africa and has studied in South Africa, Europe, and the United States. In 1981-82 he was the producer of a film project funded by the National Endowment for the Humanities in cooperation with the Agency for International Development and the Club du Sahel, Paris.

Harold Pakendorf is Editor of *Die Vaterland*, an afternoon Afrikaans daily published in Johannesburg. A Nieman Fellow, he was previously Editor of the Harare *Financial Gazette*, a financial and political weekly, and Editor of *Oggenblad*, an Afrikaans morning daily published in Pretoria.

Karen Paul is Associate Professor of Management at Rochester Institute of Technology. She received her B.A. summa cum laude, M.A., and Ph.D. from Emory University. Dr. Paul has published widely on the social control of multinationals and the impact of multinationals on economic development.

A.M. Rosholt is Chairman of Barlow Rand Limited, South Africa's largest industrial group. He is also Chancellor of the University of the Witwatersrand and Chairman of the Residential Development and Construction Division of the Urban Foundation. Rosholt is the recipient of the Harvard Business School Club's Business Statesman's Award and a Paul Harris Rotary Fellowship.

N. Craig Smith is Lecturer in Marketing at Cranfield School of Management, England. His research interests are in business and society and consumer behavior. His Ph.D. examined ethical purchase behavior and social responsibility in business, particularly in the form of consumer boycotts. He has published a number of papers in this area and his book, *Consumer Pressure for Corporate Accountability*, will be published in the United Kingdom in early 1987.

Diane R. Stanton is a Legal Assistant in the San Diego office of the law firm Latham and Watkins. She received a master's degree in political science from the University of California, San Diego. The title of her master's thesis is "Consociational Democracy and Its Alternatives in South Africa: Constitutional Reforms 1948-1983."

Michael O. Sutcliffe is Senior Lecturer in the Department of Town and Regional Planning, University of Natal, and a member of the Built Environment Support Group. His present research is in development planning in South Africa and alternatives to upgrading policy. He has published in international journals on the subjects of worker action in South Africa, the role of Inkatha in black politics, the informal sector in South Africa and the reformist response, the crisis in South Africa, upgrading of Langa, Uitenhage, disinvestment and black worker attitudes, and economic planning alternatives in South Africa. Sutcliffe holds an M.Sc. degree from the University of Natal and a Ph.D. from Ohio State University.

Helen Suzman has been a Member of the South African parliament since 1953 and for thirteen years was the sole Member of the Opposition Progressive Party in Parliament. Previously she taught economic history at the University of the Witwatersrand and has received ten honorary doctorate degrees from institutions including Oxford, Harvard, Columbia, Brandeis, and Witwatersrand.

Alexander Jabulan Thembela is Vice Rector for Academic Affairs and Research at The University of Zululand. He is President of the Natal Africa Teachers Union, Vice President of the African Teachers Association of South Africa, and a member of the South African Pedagogical Society. Prior to assuming his current post, he served as head of the Department of Educational Planning and Administration at The University of Zululand. Professor Thembela is the author or co-author of numerous textbooks, articles, and papers.

Desmond Tutu, the recipient of the Nobel Peace Prize in 1984, is Archbishop of Cape Town, and Metropolitan of the Anglican Church of the Province of South Africa. He is a past Secretary-General of the South African Council of Churches and Bishop of Lesotho. Bishop Tutu received his B.A. and M.A. degrees in theology while studying in Great Britain; he returned to South Africa in 1966 to begin a university career as a lecturer in theology. Among his many honors are the following: Fellow of King's College, London; Prix d'Athene Prize, Onassis Foundation; Honorary Doctorate of Divinity, Aberdeen University, Scotland; Honorary Doctorate of Sacred Theology, Columbia University; and Honorary Doctorate of Theology, Ruhr University, West Germany.

Gerrit Van Niekerk Viljoen is Minister of Education and Development Aid. Previously he served as Minister for Co-operation, Development, and Education, Mininster of National Education, Administrator General of South-West Africa, and a member o Parliament for Vanderbijlpark. During his academic career he was Senior Lecturer and Professor of Classical Languages at the University of South Africa as well as Rector of Rand Afrikaans University. He was also Chairman of the National Education Council, member of the councils of the Universities of Fort Hare and Bophuthatswana, a founder trustee of the Study Trust, member of the Scientific Advisory Council of the Prime Minister, and a member of the Human Sciences Research Council. Dr. Viljoen holds a bachelor's degree of laws and a master's degree in classical languages from the University of Pretoria, an M.A. from the University of Cambridge, and a doctorate in literature and philosophy from the University of Leyden.

D. Reid Weedon, Jr., Senior Vice President of Arthur D. Little, Inc., heads the company's work for Rev. Sullivan. His experience in developing countries has been extensive, beginning with his work for the government of Puerto Rico in 1946. He has made many trips to South Africa in order to increase his understanding of the problems and opportunities for change in that country.

Lou H. Wilking is the Executive Assistant to the Group Executive of the Overseas Group at General Motors. From 1977 until recently he was the Managing Director of General Motors South African, and before that he served as the Treasurer of General Motors South African and as the Managing Director at the GM facility in Iran.

Oliver F. Williams, C.S.C., is on the faculty of the Department of Management at the University of Notre Dame, where he teaches and researches in the fields of business, society, and ethics. He holds a Ph.D. in theology from Vanderbilt University and spent a year doing research at the graduate School of Business Administration of Stanford University. He is co-editor or author of five books, including the forthcoming *The Apartheid Crisis*.

N. Brian Winchester is Associate Director of the African Studies Program at Indiana University. He has written about South Africa for various publications, including *Political Handbook of the World*, *World Encyclopedia of Political Systems and Parties*, and several editions of the annual *Yearbook of the Encyclopedia Americana*. He is currently co-editing a book on *Violence in Contemporary Africa* and co-authoring a chapter on the prospects for revolution in South Africa for a book on *Contemporary Revolutions*.

Howard Wolpe has been a member of Congress since 1979. He is Chairman of the House Foreign Affairs Subcommittee on Africa, Co-chair of the Northeast-Midwest Congressional Coalition, member of the House Budget Committee, and Representative of Michigan's Third District. Before his election to Congress, he was a professor at Western Michigan University, a member of the Kalamazoo City Council, and a member of the Michigan House of Representatives. Wolpe holds a B.A. from Reed College and a Ph.D. from the Massachusetts Institute of Technology.

Johannes Christiaan Van Zyl is Chief Executive of the South African Federated Chamber of Industries. Previously he was an Associate Professor of Economics at the University of Pretoria. He holds a bachelor's degree (with honors) in communication from the University of Stellenbosch, a master's in economics from the University of Cape Town, and a doctorate in philosophy from the University of Pretoria. Dr. Van Zyl has advised and served in many organizations, including the Commission of Enquiry into the Export Trade of the Republic of South Africa (RSA), the Council of the Bureau for Economic Policy and Analysis, the Working Group on Industrial Strategy in South Africa, the Technical Committee on Export Incentives in the RSA, the Prime Minister's Economic Advisory Council, the National Regional Development Advisory Council, the Industries Advisory Committee, the Human Sciences Research Council's Fourth National Research Programme, the Board of Directors of the Small Business Development Corporation, and the Private Sector Urbanisation Council. He has published extensively on a wide range of issues.